Open Architecture

Esra Akcan

Open Architecture

Migration, Citizenship, and the Urban Renewal of Berlin-Kreuzberg
by IBA-1984/87

Birkhäuser
Basel

Preface

Writing this book, I often felt like a weaver, interlacing stories of distinct individuals from different countries, cities, and schools; with dissimilar ideas, life experiences, political positions, and economic conditions; practicing isolated professions; and feeling part of diverse, sometimes opposing affinity groups. At one point in history, the paths of these individuals merged in the same city borough, and this book is a story of this convergence. Through the weaving of these stories and the design of the book's structure, it becomes apparent that these seemingly different experiences of architects and residents, professionals and immigrants, policy makers and refugees, social workers and guest workers were indeed connected, even though the quality and intensity, and sometimes the hierarchical structure of this interaction varied for each example. The book asks what would have happened if the architectural discipline and profession were shaped by a new ethics of hospitality toward the immigrant, and calls this open architecture. It brings together historical projects and thought experiments toward open architecture (or the lack thereof), and conceptualizes open architecture's various types with terms such as flexibility and adaptability of form, unfinished and unfinalizabile design, collectivity and collaboration, participation and democracy, and multiplicity of meaning.

The book explores particularly the urban renewal of Berlin's immigrant neighborhood Kreuzberg to bring this concept and its contradictions to life. This extensive building and renovation practice was carried out by IBA-1984/87, an international building exhibition which was justifiably one of the most important events of its time and a microcosm of international architectural debates from the mid-1960s till the early 1990s. An astonishing number of now-celebrated architectural offices participated in IBA-1984/87, including those of Peter Eisenman, Vittorio Gregotti, Zaha Hadid, John Hejduk, Hans Kollhoff, Rem Koolhaas, Rob Krier, Aldo Rossi, Álvaro Siza, James Stirling, Oswald Mathias Ungers, and many other, rather understudied architects and urbanists whose due acknowledgment will hopefully be given with this book. IBA-1984/87 was also a telling example about the relation between city and statelessness, because the then run-down Kreuzberg has been home to migrants, predominantly from Turkey. My overarching theme is international immigration and the ongoing human rights regime that impaired guest workers' and refugees' right to have rights, and therefore exposed the very limits of these past forms of open architecture. Unlike conventional architectural histories, this topic requires giving voice not only to architects and policy makers but also to noncitizen residents. For every chapter, the immigrant resident is therefore as much a center of the narrative as the architect. In other words, the book extends its theme to its method and explores an open form of writing through a genre inspired by oral history and storytelling. The status of oral history is a supplement in this book when discussing architects and policy makers, whose drawings, photographs, articles and letters can be retrieved in archives and publications. However, I employed it as a crucial method in raising the residents' and the tenant advisors' voices, given the lack of historical documentation. I sought to bridge the fallibility of oral history, which is due to its reliance on individual memories, by cross-checking archival documents if available, bringing different opinions into conversation, and, needless to say, by architecturally analyzing the buildings and spaces under consideration.

The migrations between Germany and Turkey during the first half of the twentieth century, of not only people but also images, ideas, objects, technologies, and information, was the topic of my book *Architecture in Translation: Germany, Turkey and the Modern House.*[1] There, I also commented on the insufficiencies of the dominant ethics of hospitality, by discussing the unresolved points in Kantian cosmopolitanism. While some might argue that Kant's notion of hospitality falls outside the realm of individual moral judgments, because it is concerned strictly with laws and regulations between states, I instead followed the thinkers who discuss this concept of hospitality within the general framework of the philosopher's ethics. Commenting on, first, the potential Eurocentrism and second, the paradoxes of conditional hospitality in Kantian ethics, where unconditional good will is the highest order, I argued that this hospitality does not annihilate the perception of the "guest" as a possible threat. A conditional hospitality that comes with an "if" clause, one that gives migrant individuals cosmopolitan rights only if they comply with the predefined norms of the "host", and therefore one that still construes them as the "other" and constructs a hierarchy, is not true hospitality. I think this is still the dominant mode of hospitality today, and hence constitutes the ethical backdrop of the ongoing human rights regime, even though the current international laws are, strictly speaking, products of more recent times. This book picks up these two debates in *Architecture in Translation,* namely, both the history of migrations between Europe and West Asia, and the discussion on the unresolved nature of the dominant notion of hospitality, by making a plea for a new ethics of welcoming that would inform open architecture to come.

The migration route between Germany and Turkey has been busy in both directions for a long time. After the assumption of power of National Socialism in Germany in 1933, Turkey hosted a large number of exiles, who held significant posts in universities and the country's building programs. Many refugees sought asylum in Germany after the 1980 coup d'état in Turkey and the subsequent violence, thereby joining the guest workers who had been arriving since 1961—the history that is recorded in the following pages. As I was finishing the book, a new phase in the history of migrations between Germany and Turkey came about, which impacted my own professional home much more directly. Due to the violations of academic freedom in Turkey, countless opposition journalists, intellectuals, and academics who signed a peace petition have been seeking to pursue their critical work abroad, including many in Germany, in forced or self-chosen exiles. As I was preparing the final production stages of this book, I was simultaneously reading a myriad of memoirs and articles, and going through applications from threatened scholars, some of whom were even located in asylum sites.

Additionally, during the final years of writing this manuscript, we witnessed the world's biggest refugee crisis since the Second World War due to the war in Syria. Ever since, the conditions of and the conceptual distinctions between refugees, migrants, and asylum seekers have infiltrated daily newspapers and conversations. I observed in passing how some of these refugees who arrived in Germany were treated with varying degrees of hostility and hospitality, also by immigrants from Turkey, who, a generation ago, were subject to similar experiences as guest workers and refugees. I often could not stop comparing the welcoming culture (*Willkommenskultur*) in Germany today and back in the period that concerns this book. Architecture as a discipline has been relatively more attentive to the status of the refugee today, producing some internationally visible exhibitions and publications, which however, in the face of the structural challenges recorded in this book, have only concentrated on immediate solutions. Perhaps deceptively, I observed more generosity than in earlier periods while volunteering in the old Nazi Airport Tempelhof that had been turned into a refugee arrival space, but I also heard alarming signs in the news about the unsanitary conditions in other detention centers including sports halls, about the turning of the temporary community lodgings into permanent spaces, and about pushing refugees to the city's peripheries and sometimes into neighborhoods prone to racism.

Moreover, in the United States, my own country of residence, individuals from certain countries have been subject to travel bans, and immigrants have been stripped of their long established lives and families. Due to these recent global developments and the steep decline of civil liberties around the world, I have confronted numerous times the fact that some of the phenomena that shaped the experience of this book's characters are continuing to pose problems today with little or no improvement, including rightlessness of the stateless, crises of citizenship categories in national and international laws, state brutality, lack of decent housing, quandaries of public housing, and hostility toward immigrants. Such threatening new developments have also propelled scholars to define and create "safe spaces" that protect the stateless—a development which practices a welcoming culture toward the migrant, but at the same time sadly exposes how far the world actually is from the ethos of open architecture that is endorsed in this book.

Given that some of my colleagues and I were also affected by the violations of academic freedom in Turkey, I sometimes wondered if I was turning into a character in my own book, with an eerie feeling that must happen to many writers. But in that case, this book is also a chronicle of hope. It reports inspiring stories against all odds of immigrants who rightfully take credit for making Berlin's Kreuzberg one of the most exciting places to live in the world. In cases of the lack of hospitality reflected in architecture, it records examples where individual residents triumphed over these non-open spaces. It also brings out solidarities between ex-migrants and citizens, despite the overwhelming discriminations. Additionally, it records one of the most successful chapters of public housing in world history, a program that has since then almost disappeared from the purview of architectural publications and discussions.

The contribution of IBA-1984/87 to the history of public housing cannot be overstated. We are living in a world where developers are even hesitant to build middle-income dwellings, let alone low-income housing, and where most architects are designing only for the wealthy one percent in a neoliberal system which produces drastic income gaps. Despite the confusing immigration policies that are recorded in this book, the IBA team achieved a miraculous and rare accomplishment in repairing a working-class neighborhood and supporting subsidized housing designed by an astonishingly large number of established and cutting-edge architects. The gentrification of Kreuzberg's several sections and the ongoing threat of gentrification in its remaining ones are recorded in this book, and constitute yet another example of neoliberalism that puts pressure both on this borough and the idea of public housing. It is not only history but also historiography that seems to be pushing public housing out of the discipline of architecture. Many of the architects who contributed to Kreuzberg's urban renewal in the 1980s continued to have shining careers and came to be identified as stars in multiple venues, but this episode when they designed public housing including units for migrants and disabled individuals has been curiously absent in their tributes.

Before starting, let me say a few words about the structure of this book, which may offer an easier orientation for reading it. Throughout the following pages, I analyze different types of latent open architecture by taking strolls in Kreuzberg through the IBA buildings and stopping at seven locations for a closer look that includes a longer history shaped by different locations around the world. The insert at the end of the book is also its table of contents, represented on a map. These seven stops and six strolls are diagrammed onto IBA's Kreuzberg map on this insert page that also contains my photographs of the buildings on the stroll paths. The other illustrations are spread among the text, including the architectural drawings of the buildings on the stroll paths, and images pertaining to the stops. While the Introduction defines open architecture and discusses some projects and thought experiments toward it in world history, Stops I–III, IV–V and VI–VII discuss open architecture as collectivity, as democracy, and as multiplicity, respectively. The stroll chapters in between carry the reader from one stop to the next. The book's structure therefore reflects the nature of Kreuzberg as not only a city borough that reveals the potentials and contradictions of open architectures, but also a collection of fine public housing designed by hundreds of architectural offices and located in walking distance of each other.

---

1 Esra Akcan, *Architecture in Translation: Germany, Turkey and the Modern House* (Durham: Duke University Press, 2012).

Introduction

Toward an Open Architecture

The word "open" has justifiably become a common metaphor today, as people, artifacts, capital, images, and information travel from one place to another in our age of global connections. The reason that open platforms excite or threaten today's audiences to such a degree, or raise them to such a level of euphoria, may be because they arouse a feeling that is too common, too familiar, so that we respond too easily without checking the causes of this feeling. And the theoretical implications, historical background, and contradictions of this foundational concept remain unexplored.

This book defines "openness" as a foundational modern value that has nonetheless been subject to contradictions, and "open architecture" as the translation of a new ethics of hospitality into architecture. Open architecture is predicated on the welcoming of a distinctly other mind or group of minds into the process of architectural design. It is associated with, for example, flexibility and adaptability of form, collectivity and collaboration, multiplicity of meaning, democracy and plurality, open-sourceable design, the expansion of human rights and social citizenship, and transnational solidarity. Open architecture goes against the grain of the neoliberal ethos of the open market that closes boundaries for the majority, and it is not synonymous with network architectures. This book discusses the inclinations toward open architecture (or the lack thereof) in the context of the urban renewal of Berlin's immigrant neighborhood Kreuzberg, a development known as IBA-1984/87 (International Building Exhibition of 1984/87).

IBA-1984/87 was justifiably one of the most important architectural events of the 1980s. An astonishingly large number of cutting-edge architects from Europe and the United States were invited to contribute to a project that combined urban renewal and public housing. IBA's major area was the Kreuzberg borough along the Berlin Wall that had been heavily bombed during World War II and left to decay afterward. Almost half of the population of the run-down Kreuzberg, sometimes referred to as "the German Harlem," were noncitizens, predominantly from Turkey, and many residents were squatters who had moved illegally into the abandoned buildings. Most of the migrants from Turkey had arrived as part of the guest worker program, since 1961, but some were refugees who fled after the Turkish coup d'état of 1980 and subsequent violence. Building almost entirely on land that belonged to the city government, by 1989 IBA had provided 4,500 new apartments in its Neubau (New Building) section under the directorship of Josef Paul Kleihues and had renovated 5,000 existing apartments and supported 700 self-help projects in its Altbau (Existing Buildings) section under Hardt-Waltherr Hämer. While the eleven-person Neubau team appointed around 200 international architectural firms, the thirty-nine-person Altbau team appointed around 140 mostly local architectural offices, and many historians and artists.

This book discusses IBA-1984/87 as the last episode in the history of the twentieth-century public housing, when housing was part of architects' disciplinary concerns;

as a microcosm of the participatory, postmodernist, and poststructuralist debates in architecture from the mid-1960s till the early 1990s; and as a significant moment that exposes the contradictory relationships between international immigration laws and housing when seen from the perspective of immigrant residents. I analyze these topics in relationship to noncitizen rights to the city and translate the relevant concept of hospitality into design to define different forms and terms of open architecture. The book is composed of seven stops in Kreuzberg, each of which concentrates on a single urban block and a distinct idea of open architecture, and six strolls in between these stops, which are composed of shorter passages and copious images. This structure reflects the character of IBA-1984/87 as both a typical subject of the broad international debates of its time and a collection of projects in the same neighborhood that are in walking distance of each other.

This introduction presents a selection from the architectural practices and thought experiments related to open architecture throughout the twentieth century and the early part of the twenty-first, in order to expand on the examples of latent open architecture that were influential in the discourse from the mid-1960s till the early 1990s and are discussed in the following chapters. The word "open" seems to have two common associations today, which may limit the discussion of other possibilities. First, in the context of late capitalism, it is common to associate the word with the economic practices and the resulting ethical and political values of the open market. However, there are many contradictions involved in thinking about the open market as a metonym of openness, given the evidence about how late capitalism creates uneven economic development and hence closed boundaries for the majority of people. Instead, in this book the concept of openness is related more to open borders than the open market, collectivity more than individuality, the openness of society more than the free circulation of consumer products, user participation in architecture more than author-architect, and the collaborative more than the single-handed designer. The other frequent association with the word "open" in today's networked society is the ever-expanding information highways. While the social impacts, potentials, and contradictions of this relatively new technological development are also discussed in this book, I hope to illustrate that there is a lot more to open architecture in history than its recent association with open-source.

Modernism and New Ground Plan Conceptions (1918–45)

Its genealogy may go back further, but the open plan commonly associated with Ludwig Mies van der Rohe would be an appropriate beginning for a history of latent (in the sense of unpronounced or incomplete) open architecture in the twentieth century. However, not only would it be misleading to think of the open plan as synonymous with open architecture, but it would also be incorrect to limit the history of transformative modern ground plans to the open plan. Mies was far from the only architect to suggest innovative ground plans during the period between the world wars, and the new ideas included the open plan, the free plan, the flexible plan, the *Raumplan* (spatial plan), and the types of plans associated with different nations. There were numerous reasons behind this flood of ideas, including the possibilities created by the new construction materials, reinforced concrete and steel; new conceptions of space;

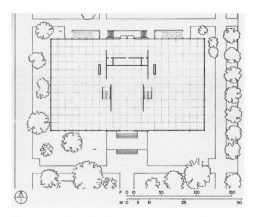

Figure Intro 1 Ludwig Mies van der Rohe, S. R. Crown
Hall, Illinois Institute of Technology, Chicago, 1950–56.

the possibility of, and necessity for, mass production; the women's liberation movement; and the national and postcolonial cultural consciousness. The new ground plans increasingly featured the free design of space, flexibility and adaptability, time-saving household methods and discordant realities.

S. R. Crown Hall (1950–56) at the Illinois Institute of Technology in Chicago and the New National Gallery (1962–68) in Berlin constitute the culmination of Mies's open plan conception, but the architect had been freeing the plan from its structural and dividing walls since the very early stages of his career (Figure Intro 1). The Brick Country House (1924) was composed of walls as independent surfaces rather than boundaries to make closed rooms, and the Barcelona Pavilion (1928–29) was conceived of as a floating platform with just eight cross-shape columns and free-standing vertical planes that functioned as space dividers to determine directions but never enclosed rooms in space.[1] Mies carried the themes of the Barcelona Pavilion to residential buildings in the Tugendhat House in Brno (also 1928–29) and in the Farnsworth House in Plano (1945–51), after he emigrated to the United States.[2] The Crown Hall and the New National Gallery extended the idea of the open plan to its conclusion in public buildings. The elimination of dividing walls and frequent columns in a large building was not only groundbreaking from a programmatic viewpoint, but also challenging from a structural engineering one. In both cases, the piers were taken out to reserve the interior merely for an empty space that was left uninterrupted for both maximum flexibility over time and suitability to a number of functions. Naming the New National Gallery a "universal space," Mies seems to have extended the grid of the floor plan from the boundaries of the building to its platform and then to the city, as if to indicate that the structure provided only a template onto which the whole universe could be potentially brought in. The museum initially was criticized for being too empty and for lacking enough walls on which to hang artwork. Like a stage waiting for scripts or a frame for images, the gallery suggested no predefined exhibition structure, but one that could therefore accommodate numerous options and change over time. The effectiveness of the open plan has been confirmed after decades of exhibitions that experimented with different display strategies.[3]

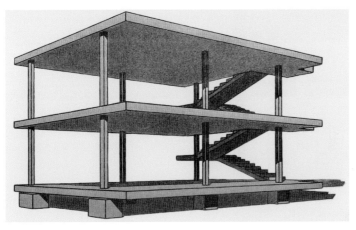

Figure Intro 2 Le Corbusier, Domino system, 1915.

Le Corbusier's free plan was quite different from Mies's open plan. At first sight, Le Corbusier's canonic drawing of the Domino system (1915), which distilled architecture's necessary elements into a mere system of columns, slabs, and stairs, looks like a perfect manifestation of the open plan (Figure Intro 2). Le Corbusier himself identified the free plan as one of the five principles of his modernism, and he celebrated the freedom that was made possible with the use of new construction materials and the elimination of load-bearing walls. However, nothing could be as scripted or as removed from flexibility as Le Corbusier's houses that practiced the five principles. For example, Villa Savoye in Poissy (1928–31) was designed by choreographing the movement of the car and the human body, and Le Corbusier defined a rich promenade carrying the visitor from the ground floor up by way of the ramp or the stairs through the living room to the double-level roof terrace. The variety of spaces along the promenade and the different ground plans at each level were made possible because of the elimination of load-bearing walls. However, Le Corbusier exhausted the openness of the Domino system and the free plan to be able to use his own choreography, leaving less room for freedom of choice or change after the design left the hands of the architect.

Nonetheless, Le Corbusier was a participant in another movement that gave some agency to users and hence opened architecture to residents. With his collaborator Charlotte Perriand, he designed light modern furniture made of tubular steel that was easy to move and allowed for the flexible use of space. Moreover, designers associated with Les Artistes Modernes in France and the Bauhaus in Germany during the interwar period concentrated on making movable and adjustable furniture that could be changed in accordance with user's will. Nowhere was the idea of flexible furniture taken to its highest architectural potential than in the Maison de Verre (1928–32) in Paris, where the designers and craftsmen Pierre Chareau, Bernard Bijvoet, and Louis Dalbet collaborated with each other (Figure Intro 3). As Kenneth Frampton wrote, the entire house was like a big piece of furniture, blurring the definitions of both architecture and object-design.[4] With built-in but movable and adjustable furniture in every corner and surfaces with modifiable levels of transparency, the building offered its residents endless opportunities for change. Accommodating a gynecologist's office on

Introduction

13

Figure Intro 3 Pierre Chareau, Bernard Bijvoet, and Louis Dalbet, Maison de Verre, Paris, 1928–32.

the ground floor, a semipublic salon on the second, and a private residence on the third, Maison de Verre had sliding solid walls in the doctor's examining room, rotating glass walls in the assistant's office, a curved translucent surface that rolled on wheels to close off or open access to the main stair leading up to the second floor, solid sliding walls that separated the doctor's private office from the main living room, a custom-made device that automated the movement of tableware between the dining room and kitchen, moving and revolving cupboards, a foldable stair that enabled or disabled access from the woman resident's private living room on the second floor to the master bedroom on the third floor, bookshelves that served as balustrades along the galleries, a gazing point from where the wife could see the doctor's patients without being seen, toilets enclosed by translucent panels that revolved open or shut, and bathtubs with bookshelves that slid like shower curtains. The whole façade was made out of experimental glass brick that changed its translucency level based on natural and artificial light. With countless movable architectural elements, adjustable transparent and translucent surfaces, and custom-made details for maximum flexibility, the building was like a participatory theater that could accommodate numerous plays that revolved around seeing and hiding, gazing at and making eye contact, and choices between opening and closing.

Another icon with an innovative ground plan was the Rietveld-Schröder House in Utrecht (1924–25), the result of a collaboration between the designer Gerrit Rietveld and the resident Truus Schröder, which could morph into two completely different homes based on the occupants' choices (Figure Intro 4). The interior could be a single

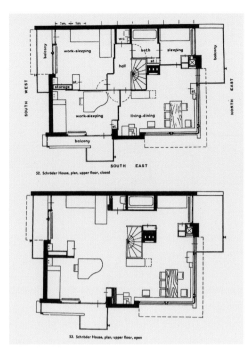

Figure Intro 4 Gerrit Rietveld and Truus Schröder,
Rietveld-Schröder House, Utrecht, 1924–25.

loft-like space when the sliding walls disappeared or an apartment separated into six different spaces—two working or sleeping rooms, a living or dining room, a bedroom, a hall, and a bathroom. The sliding vertical planes slid along the floor that was painted in different primary colors to mark the different possible configurations. Based on its façade and color composition, its freestanding planes, and Rietveld's career in furniture and space design, the house is usually perceived as the architectural manifesto of the De Stijl movement, whose members were interested in the new possibilities of a fluid, open space.[5] The Rietveld-Schröder House did not blur the boundaries between the inside and the outside, but it embodied another definition of openness, one that opened the space to the residents' voices and one that was originally formulated by Schröder herself, so that she could both enjoy time with her children in open space and have privacy when the sliding walls stayed shut.[6]

Among the architects of the interwar period who were inspired by flexible and multi-purpose spaces was Sedad Eldem in Turkey. Undeniably curious about and at many times imitative of the modernist architects in France, Germany, and the United States, Eldem insisted on organizing his residential projects around a space called *sofa*, rather than following the new ground plans that were being used in places he turned for inspiration. Eldem made it his lifetime project to research and categorize the typology of what he called the "old Turkish houses," which he defined as dwellings that shared the conception of the *sofa-oda* duality, despite their differences in style, material, size, climatic environment, or social setting. According to Eldem, the *oda* was the multi-purpose, flexible room used by a small family unit that could morph into a living,

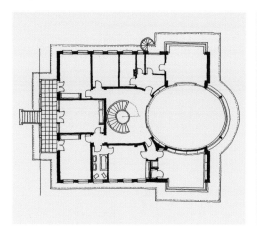

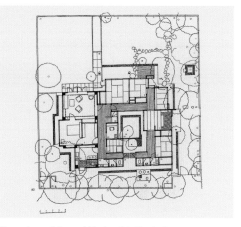

Figure Intro 5 Sedad Eldem, Ağaoğlu House, Istanbul, 1936.

Figure Intro 6 Sutemi Horiguchi, Okada House, Tokyo, 1933.

sleeping, or dining space by virtue of adjustable built-in fixtures, and the *sofa* was the semiprivate gathering space of the extended family that lived together in the house. The "old Turkish house" as an overarching and unifying national typology was a convenient myth that Eldem participated in fabricating, but it served him as a muse for many of his finest designs throughout his career (Figure Intro 5).[7] The architect did not design his own *sofas* and *odas* as multipurpose rooms with flexible fixtures, but as rooms with specific modernized functions and furniture. Neither did he conceptualize resident appropriation as part of his own architectural design process. Nonetheless, like many architects practicing outside the centers of Europe and North America, Eldem was preoccupied with reconciling what he perceived as the modern and the national, the foreign and the local—in his case, the Western and the Turkish. This preoccupation was motivated by what might be called a postcolonial consciousness (even in countries that had not been colonized), in the sense of an anxiety about Western cultural imperialism accompanied by an openness to these foreign influences.

To give another example, Sutemi Horiguchi's work in Japan also resulted from the tension and dialogue between what he perceived as the Japanese and the Western identities. The Okada House in Tokyo (1933), for instance, materialized this duality by literally juxtaposing a "Japanese wood-frame wing" with tatami mats and a "Western concrete frame wing" (Figure Intro 6). The two distinctly different parts of the house were connected with a detailed Edo-inspired garden design, an inner courtyard, and a reflecting pool with stepping-stones.[8] For both Eldem and Horiguchi, modernism involved confronting what they perceived as two worldviews, the Western and the national, which needed to be synthesized, juxtaposed, or brought into conversation through a new plan conception. Their projects were based on their conviction that the two worldviews, materialized in distinct spatial organizations and construction materials, needed to be translated into each other in some way. Being modern involved the welcoming of a distinctly other type of plan conception into one that was more familiar in their immediate surroundings at the time.

Figure Intro 7 Adolf Loos, Villa Müller, Prague, 1928–30.

Even though he faced different dilemmas than Eldem and Horiguchi and practiced in one of the centers of Europe, the Austrian architect Adolf Loos also conceived of modernity as the accommodation of discordant realities, for which the *Raumplan* (a term coined in 1931 by Heinrich Kulka, one of Loos's students) prepared an appropriate stage. Practiced most prominently in the Moller House in Vienna (1928) and the Villa Müller in Prague (1928–30), the *Raumplan* signified a building where volumes flow into each other in three-dimensional ways and spaces connect with one another either physically or visually (Figure Intro 7).[9] Loos's houses are composed of semi-closed spaces of different heights and on multiple levels that pour into each other through steps, of fluid living rooms that can be perceived as both a unitary space and a collection of smaller alcoves, and of rooms adorned with conflicting finishing materials and furniture and interconnected through physical access or visual openings. A *Raumplan* creates the ambiguous feeling of being simultaneously enclosed and under the gaze of someone else, of living on the stage of a theater and watching others through constant framing of spaces in other spaces. Loos defined his intention as "setting free a ground plan in space," rather than stacking floors on top of each other—which, according to Werner Oechslin, was nothing short of a revolution in modern space conception.[10] Hilde Heynen discusses the intellectual implications of the *Raumplan* in terms of a "counterpastoral" conception of modernity, one that does not deny its contradictions and tensions in favor of an illusion of unity, and one that does not use a single programmatic definition of "modernity" as if history were moving toward a predefined ideal or progressing toward a technocratic telos.[11] In the *Raumplan* these contradictory elements are juxtaposed, discordances are brought together, and harmony in domesticity is disrupted.

Eldem's, Horiguchi's, and Loos's modern plans moved toward an open architecture in their own distinct ways, because their goal was to synthesize, accommodate, or juxtapose what they manifested as different or discordant realities. Even when the architects seek to establish unity and harmony, as was the case with Eldem, their suggestions are premised on a perceived alterity. Appreciating Loos's work requires admitting the irreducible differences, contradictions, and incompatibilities of modern life, rather than covering them with a single, overarching framework. This latent open architecture is quite different from that of the New National Gallery, Maison de Verre, and Rietveld-Schröder House, whose flexibility anticipates future actors' agency, even when users are expected to appropriate the space by adapting into the grid structure or by choosing from a number of predefined options. Instead, in Eldem's, Horiguchi's, and Loos's houses the move toward an open architecture—in the sense of welcoming alterity and accommodating discordant realities—takes place on the level of designed metaphor, while the assumption of the architect's authorial status remains intact.

Flexibility and Adaptability of Form (1945–72)

During the 1950s and 1960s, freedom of choice; anticipation of change; and mobility, transformability, and adaptability of form became the common mottos of a new generation of architects. The terms "open society," "open system," and "open form" were also used relatively frequently to designate a world without traditional hierarchies and centralized systems. Alison Smithson associated "open society" with the ability to move freely, viewing communication media and the highway as its symbols: "An open society needs an open city. Freedom to move,—good communication, motorways, and urban motorways, somewhere to go."[12] Her work as part of the Independent Group, especially their *This Is Tomorrow* exhibit (1956), became a turning point in architectural discourse, as it celebrated pop culture and called architects to communicate more directly with the inhabitants of their buildings. Kenzo Tange contrasted the closed and open systems as cities with the possibility of centripetal organizations and linear development, respectively. Oskar Hansen and Zofia Hansen published a manifesto on open form in 1961 to respond to the urgent need for housing large numbers of people, particularly in Poland, by registering the individual in the collective and paying attention to the everyday needs of tenants.[13]

During these decades, few architects moved as far toward open architecture as the Japanese Metabolists. Identifying the sea and the sky as zones of new habitation in response to the limited land in Japan and the country's rapid population increase, and building on the biological metaphors of organic growth and change, the Metabolists conceptualized architecture as process and the architect's role as designing an infrastructure that will accommodate transformation. In an array of paper projects at the turn of the decade in the 1960s, Metabolists such as Arata Isozaki (see stroll 1 for his IBA-1984/84 building), Kiyonori Kikutake, and Kisho Kurokawa (see stop II for his IBA-1984/84 competition project) imagined urban clusters in the air that eliminated land speculation, cities floating on oceans that were renewed by sinking their cells into the water when they became obsolete as residences, and helix cities that were meant to reproduce their DNA like breeding organisms.[14] Large-scale housing, traffic, and mobility had already become the foci of attention for many architects in international

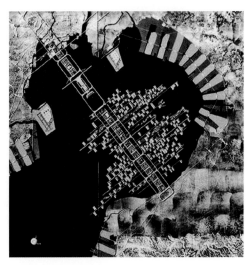

Figure Intro 8 Kenzo Tange, Tokyo Bay project, 1960.

circles during the period immediately after World War II, but the Metabolists were also "trying to revolt against Eurocentrism," as Kurokawa put it years later.[15] Yona Friedman had presented the groundbreaking "Mobile Architecture" project in the Congrès Internationaux d'Architecture Moderne (CIAM) meeting in 1956, which responded to the mass housing crisis by suggesting a permanent overarching structure where everything else was movable and changeable.

Tange's Tokyo Bay project (1960), where Isozaki and Kurokawa also worked, represents the culmination of most of these ideas (Figure Intro 8). Already an established architect in Japan, Tange was not a Metabolist, but he influenced the group. Responding to the need for Tokyo's growth despite its limited land, Tange's team proposed creating large elevated freeways on water that would connect the two shores of Tokyo Bay and extend to Chiba, and gigantic artificial islands on which residents would build their own houses as needed. This was a city of the automobile, bringing together city structure, transportation, and architecture in a single framework and accommodating adaptability and future growth based on society's need. The main points of the Metabolist advocacy of open architecture were the separation of the permanent and the temporary components of urban life, the needs of the collective and individual citizens, and the planned and provisional aspects of cities. The Tokyo Bay project was a settlement with transportation networks conceived of as permanent infrastructure, and housing in the form of flexible structures that were open to constant change based on individual choice. However, as Zhongjie Lin notes, the overbearing formal presence of the fixed freeways or other overdesigned structures created a paradox in relation to the Metabolists' emphasis on individual agency, freedom, and democracy.[16] Peter Smithson, for one, found the Tokyo Bay project authoritarian, rather than democratic. Besides, it was not clear how future citizens would build their houses by plugging into the tent-like structures specified in Tange's renderings and models. The Metabolists contributed the ideals of openness, citizen agency, and future adaptability to architecture, which remained metaphoric and unrealizable in their own projects. A division took place among the Metabolists as a result of a similar self-critique. Fumihiko Maki, a member of the group, formulated a theory of the "group-form" as a bottom-up, more democratic, spontaneous, and less formal accommodation of future growth. Developing additively from small to bigger patterns, "group form evolve[d] from the people of a society rather than from their powerful leadership."[17]

Metabolism is usually associated with the idea of megastructure, a term coined by Maki to mean a "large frame in which all functions of a city or part of a city are housed."[18] In his influential book *Megastructure*, Reyner Banham asserted that the megastructure projects around the world, including those by the Metabolists, Cedric Price, Archigram, and in Montreal Expo 67, and several university campuses were not isolated but connected endeavors, and that there was a lineage between the avant-garde utopian movements of the early twentieth century and the contemporary proponents of megastructure.[19] However, from the perspective of open architecture, the megastructures that accommodated their inhabitants' agency and anticipated changes need to be distinguished from those that used a large-scale structure to impose a controlling order on the whole environment.[20] The fact that Le Corbusier's Plan Obus for Algiers was a frequent reference for megastructures raises questions about the political association of these projects with democracy or egalitarian and free society. The quintessential symbol of the French colonial dominance on the colonized population in North Africa is not an inspiration for open architecture in the sense explored in this book. For a theory of open architecture, megastructures for social agency and as social engineering need to be differentiated. Moreover, Banham's equating of megastructural openness with utopian thinking is also misleading, especially in the context of Karl Popper's 1945 *The Open Society and Its Enemies*, in which historical utopias were questioned from the perspective of what the author called the open society.[21] If utopias' major fallibility was their inability to come to terms with their own fallibility, because they fixed the future from the perspective of the present and because they had full confidence in the single vision of their creator, then the welcoming of change and the inclusion of citizens' voices can hardly be considered "utopian."

Among the megastructures of the 1960s, the Fun Palace (1961–65) embodies the idea of open architecture by virtue of conceptualizing architecture as performance (Figure Intro 9). A project with a ground platform accessible from all directions as its only stable element, the Fun Palace would have been composed of structural steel towers filled with stairs and topped with cranes so that all of its other elements—including floors, walls, galleries and bridges in the air, mechanical equipment, and other types of planes—could be adjusted by the users to fit their shifting needs. Recent developments in cybernetics and game theory would have been employed to collect data on prior use and determine behavioral patterns as well as the probability of new programs. The artists, architects, cyberneticists, game theorists, scientists, and others involved in the Fun Palace each had his and her own intellectual convictions and political position, and as a result the project cannot be covered here in its full complexity. Nonetheless, for the theory of open architecture discussed in this book, the Brechtian intentions of the project come to the fore. Joan Littlewood, one of the masterminds behind the idea of the Fun Palace and a collaborator with its architect, Cedric Price, was a revolution-

Figure Intro 9 Cedric Price, Fun Palace, 1961–65.

ary theater actor and director with decades of experience in agitprop street theater, immediate and agitational plays about class struggle or other political matters, and makeshift theaters trying different formats in provincial towns and working-class districts. Her work is relevant for open architecture in the Fun Palace by virtue of her ties to the Brechtian performance theory that advocated the potential of the theater to mobilize masses and foster critical alertness in the audience through alienation effects, with the unambiguous intention of achieving a classless society.[22] The Brechtian theater closed the traditional distance between the actor and the audience, changed their roles, and invited the audience to act critically, rather than watch passively. The intention was that it would not be the author of the space or the play that dictated the performance. Rather, the theatric experience would be opened to its audience, and space to its users. As Stanley Mathews points out, this signaled nothing short of the death of the architect in his conventional role: "He [Cedric Price] refined the role of the architect from that of master form-giver to that of designer of a field of human potential, a 'free space' in which programmatic objectives are free to develop and evolve."[23] The relation between performance studies and open architecture is discussed in stop VII.

The Italian architecture group Superstudio took the idea of free platforms for free lifestyles to its extreme.[24] In numerous ambiguously ironic drawings, storyboards, collages, and films, Superstudio covered existing cities, landscape, the ocean, the earth's surface as a whole, and even outer space with gridded platforms. The Continuous Monument (1969) that extended the white grid globally was meant to create no interior and hence no exterior, but endless possibilities (Figure Intro 10). In Superstudio's fictional world, which could be interpreted as either an endorsement of utopian thinking or a cautionary tale, the architects offered infrastructural resources on a grid so that humans could plug into them with any lifestyle and any individual choice. Another group that fetishized "open-ended" design during these years as a way to embrace

Figure Intro 10 Superstudio, Continuous Monument, 1969.

individualism, freedom of choice, and constant change was Archigram, whose members celebrated British pop culture by populating their imagery with copious advertisements and everyday objects; endorsed the metropolis as a site of ultimate liberation, adventure, and consumption; and envisioned using advanced technologies to maximize mobility. To those ends, they designed futuristic traffic intersections; plug-in and walking cities containing intelligent robots, nomadic houses, and transitory buildings; interchangeable architectural parts for the user to configure; and self-expanding structures that applied recent advances in cybernetics and systems design. Nonetheless, there was a contradiction in Archigram's openness to the citizens of the metropolis. As Simon Sadler observed, the *Living City* exhibit was declared to be about "the people themselves." However, the objects chosen for the exhibited "survival kit" implied that young, affluent, heterosexual bachelors were the designated "people of the city."[25] Moreover, despite the radical imagery that the group produced, we might as well be living today in the Archigram paradise: a world of endless individualist choices, abundant consumer products and advertisement images, data collection technologies that can predict what we will buy even before we start shopping, time-saving robots, ever-expanding lifestyle possibilities. Freedom according to the individualist ethos and the neoliberal logic today might indeed be seen as the realization of some mid-century utopias. Regardless of the groups' critical or celebratory stance, most of their ideas seem to have been co-opted by the open market and data highway enthusiasm of the world we live in today.

Collectivity and Collaboration (1966–Present)

While freedom of choice and the endless proliferation of new lifestyle possibilities became catchphrases of midcentury modernism, this book picks up the history of open architecture in the mid-1960s, when a number of architects started questioning the idealization of the individualist ethos. Open ground plan conceptions and the flexibility and adaptability of form persisted during the times and in some of the projects covered in this book, but other types of open architecture also emerged. Part 1, "Open Architecture as Collectivity," discusses collectivity and collaboration as latent open architecture by looking at the practices of IBA-1984/87 architects from Western

Europe—particularly those from Italy and Germany who were associated with other architects in Austria, Belgium, Spain, and the United States.

Stop I, "Critical Reconstruction: Open Architecture as Collaboration?" introduces the beginnings of West Berlin's IBA-1984/87 and the organization's goals in the context of the history of public housing. IBA-1984/87 differed from its predecessors by conceptualizing public housing as a form of urban renewal. The organization criticized postwar urban planning models for reducing the city to a collection of traffic systems. During the mid-1970s, the West Berlin Senate was considering a proposal for a mega auto-bahn project in Kreuzberg, which would have created a massive junction over Oranien-platz (Oranien square). IBA directors not only aborted this project but also significantly distanced themselves from the postwar, large-scale urban interventions in which ex-isting buildings were demolished, and from standardized massive housing blocks that were constructed at the peripheries of the city. Instead of demolishing Berlin's nine-teenth-century urban fabric, composed of perimeter blocks, IBA proposed to "carefully repair" and "critically reconstruct" it. Rather than top-down master plans or mega-structures with a single vision for the entire city, IBA-1984/87 suggested that the zone of urban operations should be limited to city districts that a designer could zoom in on an architectural scale.

To explore IBA's urban renewal vision and its beginnings more concretely, Stop I discusses the history of building exhibitions, social housing, and Neubau's beginnings and then concentrates on Rob Krier's urban design for Block 28, where twenty different architectural firms were brought in to design rows of buildings along the new pedestrian streets and an urban plaza at the center, where four proposed interlocking perimeter blocks met. This stop explores collaboration as a form of open architecture, as long as urban design can be achieved as a partnership between nonhierarchically positioned architects and can mobilize groups that work hospitably together. To discuss Krier's ideas about immigration that identified an essential connection between nation and form, the stop presents the story of Hatice Uzun, who lived in several units of this project. Stroll 1, "From Schinkelplatz to Checkpoint Charlie," takes a walk in the neighborhood from Stop I to Stop II, passing through buildings designed by Herman Hertzberger, Arata Isozaki, Daniel Libeskind, and Hans Kollhoff and Arthur Ovaska, among others.

Stop II, "Buildings That Die More Than Once: Open Architecture as Collectivity," traces IBA's intellectual sources back to Aldo Rossi's theories and typological design method in the 1960s and discusses the translation of these ideas into practice in IBA's most prestigious architectural competition and two adjacent blocks at Checkpoint Charlie. To explore the relationship between open architecture and collective ideals, the stop presents the stories of the Italian architect Rossi; the Spanish architect collective Bohigas, Mackay, and Martorell; Günsel Çetiner, the spouse of a Turkish guest worker; and N.Y., a Kurdish refugee. Analyzing Aldo Rossi's 1966 *L'architettura della Città* (*Architecture of the City*) in the context of the Italian journal *Casabella*'s circle, this stop argues that a unique definition of open architecture as collectivity comes out of this book, whose reception generally (mis)treated it as a theory of autonomous architecture.[26] Like the Metabolists, Rossi differentiates between the permanent and transient aspects of urban life, but in reverse order—identifying housing and monuments as permanent, and traffic as temporary, urban elements. The paired concepts type and event, memory and will, death and life, permanence and adaptability, and convention and political motivation construct a theory of open architecture, which views the architect as a participant in both the collective memory emerging from the past and the collective will making the future, rather than a genius creator, a tabula rasa mind, or an all-determining author. What makes Rossi's theory a unique definition of open architecture is his emphasis on design as a product of the collective mind on the one hand, and his acknowledgment of future transformations through the physical signs of continuously unfolding events on the other hand. This stop also identifies the limits of this openness, by exposing Rossi's expectation that a unified architecture will emerge from the collective memory and the collective will, as if a society has no alterity or no class-based, ethnic, or geopolitical dominance that prioritizes one memory and will over others, and as if citizens and noncitizens always reach consensus in the collective making of the city.

Stop III, "Opened after Habitation," discusses Oswald Mathias Ungers's multifaceted career and alternative Berlin projects from the 1960s till the late 1980s, and zooms in on his IBA design for Block 1 to show how architecture is by definition open as residents appropriate spaces whether the architect anticipated or prohibited that appropriation. This stop portrays the transformation of Ungers's ideas about the open city from a collection of multiple heterogeneous entities to autonomous architecture with increasingly exclusivist tones. The de facto openness of architecture is exemplified in Block 1, especially with Fatma Barış's touches in her dwelling, despite Ungers's claims to closed architecture that did not welcome changes by the occupants. Strolls 2 and 3 after Stops II and III, respectively, take walks in IBA-Neubau areas from Checkpoint Charlie to Potsdamer Platz and then to Tiergarten, to show the theme and variations of the urban renewal, visiting the buildings of established architects such as Mario Botta, Peter Cook, Pietro Derossi, Zaha Hadid, Hans Hollein, Vittorio Gregotti, Werner Goehner, Frei Otto, and James Stirling.

As part 1 of this book shows, during these years, the ethos of collectivity was endorsed by architects in Western Europe on both the political left and right. Kleihues commented on the irrelevance of shying away from collective ideals due to their alleged alliance with Eastern Europe. In the early part of the Cold War, the housing models of West and East Berlin had been based on an ideological rivalry. In the mid-1980s, however, Kleihues thought that the Cold War polarity should no longer prevent the conservation of the city's nineteenth-century urban fabric.[27]

Today, the importance of collaboration is taken for granted, given the complex building requirements that can be handled only by professionals of different expertise, but collaboration is seldom endorsed except because of pragmatic necessity. The role played by data collection and digital technologies is celebrated for making collaboration possible, but concerns about surveillance in the cybernetic utopia remain unresolved. For example, Kas Oosterhuis defines the collaborative possibilities emerging from the new technologies as follows: "In the collaborative design process there must be an open channel for incoming raw data from the world around the group design room. ... Citizens become real-time participants in the design game." However, he admits that the question of who has authority over the placement of filters and channels results remains unresolved, which prevents the replacement of the traditional designer who has top-down control.[28] While new online open-source technologies increasingly foster the interaction and exchange of digital information, few architects are willing to give up the notion of individual authorship or "envisage [the development of] open-source-able architectural design—i.e., design notations that others could use and modify at will," as Mario Carpo observed, noting the paradox of parametricism and other aspects of the digital turn in architecture.[29] Collectivity in the sense discussed in this part of the book is also dormant, partially due to the triumph of neoliberalism after the collapse of communism, and partially because of the association of these decades with unwanted revivalism and eclecticism in architectural history. This book examines these practices to excavate theories of collectivity and collaboration as latent forms of open architecture, rather than to investigate their contribution, if any, to the making of the postmodern architectural style. I also argue that the intention to reach unity and harmony in an immigrant neighborhood through collaborative and collective urban design based merely on European models foreclosed architecture's connective and dialogical power.

Participation and Democratizing Democracy (1968–Present)

Few ideas contributed as much to open architecture and its dialogical potential during the social upheavals of the 1960s as the call for participation in public housing. When one reads Giancarlo de Carlo's 1969 "Architecture's Public," one can measure the opposition to the architectural establishment during the student movements in Europe (Figure Intro 11). Questioning architects' submission to power and compliance with the interests of wealthy clients, de Carlo called for a fundamental change in the discipline's self-definition and audience. Who really was architecture's public: the clients, architects themselves, or the people? "Architecture took an elite position on the side of the client rather than on the side of the user" at the expense of its own trustworthiness.[30] "Why should architecture be credible today," de Carlo asked, when architects served only landowners and authorities, when they restricted themselves to the technical questions of the "how" rather than addressing the social and political questions of the "why," and when the question of public housing remained unresolved while architectural education was in crisis and architectural publications were characterized by arrogance? To improve architecture's credibility, de Carlo suggested participatory design, which meant that the architect would design with users rather than for them, and process planning, which meant that participation would be initiated as an open-ended procedure in such a way that users would continue shaping their environments even after the work of the architect ended. In making a distinction between the client and the user, de Carlo was suggesting that architecture ought to work for the common good rather than the particular interests of the wealthy or powerful authorities. While the expectation of change and unfinalizability of design were ideas similar to those endorsed by the Metabolists during the same period, the participatory design procedure that invited a direct connection with future users was another distinct form of open architecture.

Figure Intro 11 Occupation of the Milan Triennale, 1968.

Part 2 of this book, "Open Architecture as Democracy" takes the reader to Altbau areas in East Kreuzberg and analyzes a parallel beginning of IBA with another critique of the idealized architect as author. In contrast to conventional city planning implemented from above, the IBA Altbau team directed by Hämer promoted a participatory model without displacement and insisted that the people living in the buildings and directly affected by the renovation should become the decision makers in a democratic process. Tracing the participatory discourse in architecture from the 1960s onward, Stop IV looks at the city blocks directed by Heide Moldenhauer and Cihan Arın (one of the few women and one of the four Turkish citizens on the IBA team, respectively), bringing the participatory design process to life on a unit-by-unit basis through oral histories with architects, tenant consultants, and other residents, especially the Tuğrul, Nişancı, and Çelik families. Strolls 4 and 5 take walks in Altbau areas via the Kottbusser Tor and Görlitzer Park areas, respectively, giving voice to the subdirectors, tenant advisors, and the architects Uwe Böhm and Bahri Düleç, as well as the residents living in the blocks under their responsibility.

The Neubau and Altbau projects differed because the former involved the design of new buildings in West Kreuzberg and the latter the restoration of existing ones in East Kreuzberg. Another key difference between them was their approaches to residents' contribution to designs. While most of the Altbau team saw user participation as a synonym of democracy in architecture, many architects on the Neubau team diagnosed it as a disabling of architectural expertise and an invitation to mediocrity. In my interviews with them, the Neubau coordinators Hildebrand Machleidt and Günter Schlusche emphasized that they tried to encourage participation as well, and the latter spoke about a 1981 crisis, after which Kleihues was forced to be more responsive to the requests of the local social advocacy groups. There were some participatory meetings and self-help projects undertaken under the auspices of the Neubau team as well—discussed in strolls 1–3—but the key decision makers on the team usually invited architects who advocated the autonomy of architecture in the name of the discipline's integrity and what they saw as a better mode of engagement with cities.

The debate about the relationship between democracy and architecture acquires particular relevance in the context of the mid-1980s, when Western Marxists in other disciplines were revisiting the concept of democracy. For example, Ernesto Laclau and Chantal Mouffe advocated that the Left reclaim democracy in its "radical" form, by acknowledging the proliferation of new subjects and struggles other than those of the working class, such as feminism, minority movements, and noninstitutionalized ecology movements. Only acknowledging the plurality of social struggles and the open-ended possibilities for the emergence of new subjects of history would bring about the transformation of the classical Marxist models and the theorization of radical democracy necessary for a free and egalitarian society in the late twentieth century. Part 2 of this book discusses the complex relation between the client and the state and between the architect and the resident in public housing, linking it to Laclau and Mouffe's contemporary theory of plural and radical democracy. According to this theory, democratization is conceived of as a necessarily perpetually open, "never-ending process,"[31] since the multiple actors who struggle against inequality in the present and the future cannot be foreclosed or predicted. Furthermore, "it is only when the open, unsutured character of the social is fully accepted, when the essentialism of the totality and of the elements is rejected, that this potential becomes clearly visible."[32]

Stop IV also outlines why the relationship between democracy and architectural participation, and especially between plural or radical democracy and noncitizen participation, was not necessarily resolved during the Altbau urban renewal process, despite IBA's earnest attempts. It was unclear who the democratically legitimate participants of an urban renewal process would be. Moreover, it became clear on a few occasions that the Altbau's participatory model welcomed participants only as long as their requests were compatible with IBA's values. All of the abovementioned facts drew a limit beyond which the noncitizens could not speak.

In the context of the perceived opposition between Neubau's autonomy and Altbau's participation, Álvaro Siza's building block, which was a new design but under the purview of the Altbau, offered a significant alternative. Stop V, "A Building with Many Speakers: Open Architecture as Critical Participation," looks at Siza's participatory design practice by tracing it from his early career in Portugal. Siza was not at all romantic about participation. He criticized the "authoritarian politicians" who perceived participation as the subordination of architectural expertise under the demands of what they claimed people wanted, and who reduced the role of the architect to a "tool for people."[33] Nonetheless, he was equally critical of the disengaged architectural practice at the end of the twentieth century that seemed to consider participation as "something shameful and provincial, which is of no interest to anybody."[34] Despite his frustration, Siza continued to find ways to encourage critical participation, and Stop V discusses the open character of his IBA project that included void spaces in anticipation of user appropriation, whose potential was actualized, for instance, with Yüksel Karaçizmeli's designs in her own dwelling.

As Siza predicted, participatory architecture remained at the margins of the profession, embraced occasionally by a few architects such as Charles Correa, when he commented on the role of the architect in developing countries such as India; Hassan Fathy, whose New Gourna village built to address rural poverty in Egypt was constructed by the villagers themselves; the Rural Studio, whose members engaged in a similar co-building practice with residents and students in Alabama; the designers of the Previ housing in Peru that was open to expansion and adaptation over time in relation to changing family needs; and more recently Alejandro Aravena, whose affordable housing projects offer an "open typology" by building only part of the unit so that residents can finish it according to their needs and with available resources.[35]

This disinterest in participatory architecture at the end of the twentieth century is an indication of broader global transformations whose adverse effects have become visible only recently. Many contemporary political philosophers are warning about the de-democratization taking place throughout the world today. The widespread acceptance of Samuel Huntington's rereading of multiculturalism as a "clash of civilizations" and a threat to Western values is a sign of the new intolerance around the world and of reactivated Orientalist stereotypes.[36] The authoritarian turn in many countries that see themselves as liberal democracies has sparked protests and acts of civil disobedience. According to thinkers such as Wendy Brown, it is the new global capital that is "undoing democracy" and turning democratic institutions into something else: "Neoliberal reason, ubiquitous today in statecraft and the workplace, in jurisprudence, education, culture and a vast range of quotidian activity, is converting the distinctly *political* character, meaning, and operation of democracy's constituent elements into *economic* ones."[37] Despite the elusive meaning of democracy and the number of its variants—including liberal, radical, republican, direct, and participatory democracy—, Brown argues that the shift from classical economic liberalism to neoliberalism means the complete economization and hence the emptying out of democracy in all its variants. Neoliberal reason, a geographically dissimilar and shifting signifier most commonly understood as an alliance with the free market, the reduction of welfare state services, and the privatization and conversion of all human activities into profitable businesses, nullifies the distinction between politics and economics. According to Michel Foucault's crisp explanation, this logic formulates competition rather than (economic) exchange, and hence inequality rather than equality as normative.[38] Étienne Balibar has added that the very principle of representation in democracies is disqualified, because "neo-liberal governance is not interested in 'conflict resolution' as such. ... Rather than reducing conflict, neo-liberalism tends to instrumentalize it."[39] In sum, the Enlightenment concept of individuals as free and equal citizens with rights and responsibilities for the public good, as ends in themselves, and as capable of self-governance is at risk. A world where there is only *homo oeconomicus* "leaves behind not only *homo politicus* but humanism itself."[40]

The contemporary processes of de-democratization make the discussion of open architecture as democracy and state-subsidized public housing even timelier.[41] Building on a conversation with authors who see contemporary de-democratization merely as apocalyptic, Balibar continues to suggest the alternative of "democratizing democracy" as a process always in the making, always to come. This could be achieved through affirmative means rather than resistance alone, including democratic inventions that advance and articulate new human rights and the revitalization of the acts of citizenship such as insurrection and civil disobedience.[42] IBA's earnest attempts and methods to democratize architecture in the Altbau, albeit inconsistent with respect to noncitizens, gain further relevance in this context.

Multiplicity of Meaning (1983–Present)

As a microcosm of architectural discourse in the 1970s and 1980s, IBA-1984/87 was also a stage for a new generation of architects who came on the scene criticizing the proliferation of postmodern style, the overemphasis on memory, and the abundant use of historical forms in designing new buildings. Four of the seven architects in the *Deconstructivist Architecture* exhibit at New York's Museum of Modern Art (MoMA) in 1988—an exhibit that owed its title to the philosophy of Jacques Derrida—had been invited to participate in IBA early in their careers: Peter Eisenman and Rem Koolhaas were invited to participate in the competition at Checkpoint Charlie, and both of them were eventually commissioned to design a building in the area (Stop VI); Zaha Hadid built one of her first buildings on a nearby site (stroll 2); and Daniel Libeskind's Jewish Museum was originally commissioned after he had participated in the IBA competition for the museum.

In Part 3, the book returns to Checkpoint Charlie. Stop VI, "Open History in the Past Subjunctive Tense" discusses OMA's (Rem Koolhaas and Elia Zenghelis) and Eisenman and Robertson Architects' unrealized yet renowned competition projects for this area, which offered alternative models of urbanism to the one favored by IBA. These projects are discussed along with a theory of open architectural history as history of possibility. OMA's competition project for Neubau was a manifestation of Koolhaas's ideas on metropolitan diversity as discussed in his 1978 book, *Delirious New York*.[43] It integrated many themes that Koolhaas had used in "The City of the Captive Globe" (1972) and "New Welfare Island" (1975–76), paper projects that were metaphors of his book's argument. Both tributes to Manhattan, the former envisioned an urban grid packed with buildings devoted to different theories and ideologies that rose to the sky or collapsed as an indication of the growth or decline of their conceptual lives; the latter filled Roosevelt Island with projects that had been rejected for Manhattan. Similarly, for the IBA competition site and later, OMA suggested a combination of different urban visions and unbuilt projects from Berlin's history, instead of fulfilling Neubau's requirements such as critically reconstructing the perimeter blocks, restoring the continuity of the street, and establishing the unity of the environment. A place for the manifestation of plurality, the welcoming of all pursuits, the revenge of the hitherto excluded, and the alter ego of the dominant, the cities in OMA's projects for New York and Berlin were meant to be products of an open society. They amounted to a visual history of possibility. The ideally open and democratic society had already become a common topic in architectural circles in the United States and had given rise to such books as Colin Rowe's *Collage City* (with Fred Koetter).[44] Despite their formal differences, Rowe's and Koolhaas's urban theories that promoted open society were reincarnations of the liberal visions of midcentury modernism.

For the same IBA competition site at Checkpoint Charlie, Eisenman and Robertson Architects offered a memorial rather than public housing. The architects also refused to reconstruct Berlin's urban fabric by simply ignoring its historical traumas or designing an illusion of continuity. Stop VI interprets this project as an *avant la lettre* memorial to the Holocaust but also problematizes the writing of Berlin's disrupted, traumatic past without looking beyond 1961—the year when the wall was constructed and guest workers started moving into the area. The final stroll, "History of a Possible Kreuzberg," is a walk in an imaginary Kreuzberg, anticipating the possibilities had the unchosen IBA competition projects by Kollhoff and Ovaska, Raimund Abraham, Giorgio Grassi, Rafael Moneo, Richard Meier, Alison and Peter Smithson, Aldo van Eyck, and others been built.

The relationship between language and architecture was at the forefront of architectural theory in the 1970s. The poststructuralist turn in literary theory, visual arts, and architecture happened against the background of structural analysis and admitted the necessarily uncertain and unfixable meaning of any text, image, or space. In acknowledging the multiplicity of meaning and disrupting the author's authority over a text, no articles were as influential as Umberto Eco's 1962 "The Poetics of the Open Work" and Roland Barthes's 1968 "The Death of the Author."[45] Unlike Derrida's ideas, the theoretical relevance of these texts and their possible reflections on architecture has been largely overlooked. This book's last chapter explores precisely the relevance of open work both in architectural history and for present discussions. Stop VII, "Exit Implies Entries' Lament: Open Architecture in John Hejduk's IBA-1984/87 Immigrant Housing," examines John Hejduk's unbuilt and built projects for IBA, which also constituted an alternative mode of engaging with the city that was quite different from IBA's intention to critically reconstruct Berlin's nineteenth-century urban fabric. This chapter identifies Hejduk's practice as an adventure game, a form of open architecture conceived of as an intersubjective play, or a participatory performance with emancipated spectators. This open architecture is like a happening that both evolves over time and connects individuals by inspiring them to open themselves to a stranger. The story of this openness is retold through the oral history of Yeliz Erçakmak, a second-generation immigrant. This stop also discusses the relevance of open work in contemporary performance studies and interactive and participatory art by adding the voice of Jacques Rancière—who, I argue, politicizes Eco's and Barthes's texts to construct a critical strategy to resist the society of spectacle in late capitalism.[46] This last stop thereby closes the book's circle by bringing the discussion of open architecture as multiplicity together with collectivity and democracy.

Hardly anything but their opposition to the proliferation of postmodern style connected the architects associated with deconstruction at the MoMA exhibit. Bernard Tschumi and Eisenman were the only architects in that exhibit who directly referred to deconstruction in Derrida's sense. In architectural discourse, Derrida's ideas have commonly been integrated into either a theory of autonomous architecture with a closed system of reference, or a set of formal preferences that helped gather different architects under a curatorial narrative. However, the translation of deconstruction into architecture could have inspired other possibilities. In one of his rare texts written

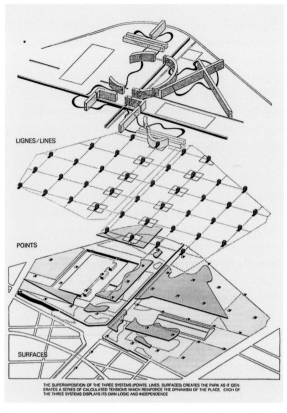

LIGNES/LINES

POINTS

SURFACES

THE SUPERIMPOSITION OF THE THREE SYSTEMS (POINTS, LINES, SURFACES) CREATES THE PARK AS IT GEN-
ERATES A SERIES OF CALCULATED TENSIONS WHICH REINFORCE THE DYNAMISM OF THE PLACE. EACH OF
THE THREE SYSTEMS DISPLAYS ITS OWN LOGIC AND INDEPENDENCE

Figure Intro 12 Bernard Tschumi, Parc de la Villette, Paris, 1983.

directly about architecture, in which he discussed Tschumi's Parc de la Villette in Paris (1983), Derrida identified conventional architecture as the "fortress of Western metaphysics," the figure of an essentialist system of representation and the very target of deconstruction (Figure Intro 12).[47] The aim of deconstruction was therefore to question the architecture of philosophy—what Immanuel Kant called its architectonics—while questioning the very same essentialized values in architecture. Deconstruction was meant to pry open the foundational and constructed value of representation that was taken for granted and naturalized, those principles and fundamental beliefs whose historicity was so forgotten that they were seen as natural laws. After all, Derrida defined deconstruction's intention as thinking about architecture. Rather than asking what deconstruction would look like if it were translated into architectural form, an equally pertinent question would have been to ask what architecture would be like after a deconstructive thinking process, and how it would be practiced after deconstruction had been translated into thinking about architecture. This question is still valid. Hospitality toward the noncitizen, the democratization of democracy, and the citizenship to come—which are basic questions of open architecture as discussed below—may owe much more to the poststructuralist turn in the humanities than the deconstructivist architects do.

The parts of this book analyze latent forms of open architecture from the mid-1960s till the early 1990s as collectivity, democracy, and multiplicity, with the overarching theme of international immigration that exposes the limits of these past forms. In contrast, open architecture, as endorsed in this book, is the translation of a new ethics of hospitality toward the noncitizen into architectural design. The concepts of hospitality and citizenship that are of crucial value for open architecture have recently been at the forefront of discussions on human rights and globalization. Nothing exposes the unresolved contradictions in the current human rights regime as effectively as the concept of the noncitizen.

Giorgio Agamben revisited Hannah Arendt's text "We Refugees," written in response to the biggest refugee crisis during World War II, precisely because statelessness continues to be prolific, and simultaneously exposes the limits of modern institutions in handling citizenship.[48] The stateless puts into question the limits of the human rights that presume the condition of being a citizen of a state. Ever since the first declaration of rights during the global network of people's revolutions, which included the French, American, and Haitian revolutions, the link between natural and civil rights, "man" and "citizen," and birth and nationhood has continued to define human rights, making it impossible to have rights without citizenship. A refugee who loses citizenship status in a country would immediately recognize that the inalienable rights of being a human—the rights that a human being should have by virtue of being born—are actually unprotected unless one belongs to a nation-state. "The paradox here," wrote Agamben, "is that the very figure who should have embodied the rights of man par excellence—the refugee—signals instead the concept's radical crisis."[49] When citizenship rights disappear, so do the human rights. Agamben exposes the paradox in this human rights regime to make the biopolitical argument about the evaporation of bare life, when life enters into the structure of the state. Moreover, the existence of the refugee questions the global nation-state system itself: "The refugee must be considered for what he is: nothing less than a limit concept that radically calls into question the fundamental categories of the nation-state, from the birth-nation to the man-citizen link, and that thereby makes it possible to clear the way for a long overdue renewal of categories."[50]

This book exposes the historical consequences of this human rights paradox as it reflects on housing and urbanism. In another of her texts about the loss of human rights, Arendt specified housing as the first major right lost to the refugee: "The first loss which the rightless suffered was the loss of their homes, and this meant the loss of the entire social texture into which they were born and in which they established for themselves a distinct place in the world."[51] The legal distinctions between different types of noncitizens lose some of their relevance when it comes to housing rights. The refugee is stateless, and the guest worker is in between states—but as one who can hardly claim citizenship in either state, the guest worker is also in some condition of statelessness. The particular case study in this book concerns guest workers and refugees in Germany who had come from Turkey. In 1973, migrants from Turkey already formed the biggest portion of the noncitizen population in Germany (23 percent), followed by those from

Yugoslavia (17 percent) and Italy (16 percent). Just before the wall fell, 12.5 percent of West Berlin's population of two million was composed of what the Germans referred to as *Ausländer* (foreigner), half of whom were reportedly Turkish. Kreuzberg borough had the highest percentage (23 percent), but in some areas of Kreuzberg, including Kottbusser Tor, half the residents were foreigners from Turkey.[52]

By the time of IBA-1984/87, many of the workers from Turkey had decided to stay in Germany more permanently than they had originally anticipated, but according to German law until 2000, citizenship was a right granted by blood and not by birth. Thus, earning citizenship required living and working permanently for at least fifteen years in Germany, and giving up any other citizenship. In other words, it was technically impossible for guest workers to have become German citizens at the time that the housing regulations that affected IBA were put in place.[53]

Before IBA took shape, the Berlin Senate and landlords had used immigrants' lack of rights in quite opportunistic ways. Even though never pronounced as such, there is a general consensus that ghetto making had been an efficient way to start a large architectural development from scratch, since destroying the run-down neighborhood would be relatively easy. There had been a proposal to do precisely that in Kreuzberg before IBA aborted it, and noncitizens without rights would have been much easier to displace than citizens. Civil society groups at the time reported that landlords and housing bureaus consistently turned down foreign families' applications to rent apartments, which pushed them into the run-down buildings in Kreuzberg. "The apartment will not be rented to foreigners" was a common phrase in newspaper advertisements in Berlin.[54] Taking advantage of noncitizens' lack of rights, landlords failed to perform legally required maintenance or repairs, given that foreign families could not make official complaints about the decaying state of their apartments.

IBA's innovative formal ideals were contradicted by its ambivalent immigration politics that responded to the housing regulations of the Berlin Senate. Between 1975 and 1978, the Senate passed a series of housing laws and regulations that were meant to address the so-called foreigner problem. Two of these had serious consequences for guest workers: the *Zuzugssperre* (ban on entry and settlement, which Turkish immigrants called *taşınma yasağı*), which took effect in 1975 and prohibited additional foreign families from moving into three of the city's twelve boroughs (Kreuzberg, Wedding, and Tiergarten); and the desegregation regulations of 1978, which required that no more than 10 percent of the residential units in West Berlin be rented to noncitizens. Justified as a supposed integration of foreign workers into German society by their forced dispersal evenly throughout the city, the restrictions were meant to prevent Turkish families from inhabiting dwellings close to their relatives or other members of their affinity group, and hence to check the construction of social and cultural networks.[55] This program would either reduce noncitizen families' chances to move into IBA's buildings in Neubau or welcome them only after they had changed their lives to fit the German standards for family size. To be precise, the Berlin Senate, IBA's employer, had determined that there were too many migrants from Turkey living in IBA's areas, and the new urban renewal project was a form of social control to regulate what the Senate believed to be desegregation—which would be forced on people from above. Halfway into IBA's realization, the Christian Democrats gained control of the Senate and promulgated anti-immigration policies. In a 1982 speech to the Bundestag, Chancellor Helmut Kohl unambiguously declared that his political party would "first: ... avoid an unbridled and uncontrolled immigration. Second: ... restrict the number of new family members coming to West Germany ... to avoid another immigration wave. Third: assist the foreigners who would like to go back to their homeland."[56] The Christian-Democrat Senator Horst Franke, who was responsible for building construction and IBA, declared: "We want to integrate [the foreigners], if they want. ... Whoever comes to Germany must feel like a German. ... But of course, within the framework of our general foreigner policy, we would like the foreigners, especially the Turks, to go back to their home country. We will help everyone who would like a new orientation in their lives to get out of Kreuzberg."[57]

I argue that these housing laws were translated into IBA's Neubau buildings in several ways. For example, the big apartments that would be appropriate for the stereotypical big Turkish family were in short supply. Even though the share of Turkish immigrants reached 50 percent in many areas of East Kreuzberg, the Senate mandated that only 5 %, sometimes maximum 10 %, of new units would be big (four or more bedroom) apartments,[58] and that foreigners could make up no more than 10 percent of the residents of any building. Coupled with the "ban on entry and settlement," the Senate's restrictions were meant to reduce noncitizen families' chances to move into IBA's Neubau buildings and to change the percentage of the foreign population in the area. Unlike many cases of urban renewal that caused gentrification, IBA remained a public housing project, but one through which the Senate employed discriminatory policies between citizens and noncitizens in the city. The following parts of the book discuss how architects responded with varying degrees of submission or subversion to these housing regulations.

This book tells the stories of guest workers and refugees from Turkey as noncitizens in Berlin in the strictly legal sense of the term, but the concept of the noncitizen is theorized here as the epitome of the excluded and hence made relevant for a much broader set of individuals and conditions. It is important to remember that people have been excluded from citizenship throughout the history of citizenship. Slaves, women, colonial subjects, guest workers, legal aliens, undocumented immigrants, and refugees have all been identified as noncitizens at some point in the past, and some of them continue to be identified in this way today. Moreover, when applied to the notion of social citizenship, as first identified by T. H. Marshall, noncitizens also include people excluded from citizenship because of socially constructed notions of class, race, gender, ethnicity, or religion.[59] People who were once noncitizens often continue to be denied social citizenship, as the exclusion of former slaves, colonial subjects, or guest workers is projected onto the present in the form of class difference and white supremacy. Balibar also theorizes about the relation between internal and external exclusions from citizenship, to understand the mechanism that denies legal citizens the right to have rights. "An 'external' border is mirrored by an 'internal' border,"[60] Balibar writes, to such an extent that citizenship becomes a club to which one is admitted or not regardless of one's legal rights. "It is always citizens 'knowing' and 'imagining' themselves as such, who exclude from citizenship and who, thus, 'produce' noncitizens in such way as to make it possible for them to represent their own citizenship to themselves as a 'common' belonging."[61]

Public housing and housing as a human right continue to be at the forefront of discussions about social citizenship, as the decline of the welfare system around the world today with the advance of neoliberalism puts public housing—and with it, the idea of social citizenship—at even greater risk.[62] This is why IBA's public housing in an immigrant neighborhood at the dawn of the contemporary world order provides an excellent example to theorize open architecture. Some IBA architects inclined toward open architecture to subvert the discriminatory housing regulations, but they still worked with the Kantian notion of hospitality, just as this notion of hospitality within the general framework of Kantian ethics continues to inform the human rights regime. Welcoming the guest only on the condition that he or she behaves according to the host's norms preserves the authority of the host. The guest's norms must either be assumed to be the same as the host's, or they must be considered a possible threat from which the host needs to be protected. In either case, such hospitality conceals the differences between guest and host, and bestows on the guest the right to inclusion only on the condition that she or he is assimilated. According to the Kantian conception, individuals welcome the foreign because they consider it their duty. It was the enlightened person's duty to tolerate the foreign. In this view, the foreign person must be a stranger who is different in a quite uncharming way, a stranger to be tolerated for the sake of reason and peace, but not someone to open oneself to, not someone to translate from, and hence nobody one could expect to be enriched by. This limited hospitality does not necessarily eliminate the perception of the guest as a possible threat, and it draws a border that closes architecture.[63]

What, then, would be another notion of hospitality, one that can inform open architecture to come? This new hospitality toward the noncitizen is continuously left open and in the making, always to come, because unconditional hospitality would mean the end of the authority of the host, and thus the new hospitality continues to expose the contradiction in the existing Kantian notion of conditional hospitality. This new hospitality also coincides with the democratization of democracy, as the latter constitutes democracy as something always to come, in contrast to the present notion of liberal democracy that has either presumably finalized itself at the "end of history" (according to Francis Fukuyama),[64] or been corrupted into imperialistic ambitions (spreading democracy to the whole world through violence). This is "a democracy that can never 'reach itself', catch up with itself, because it involves an infinite openness to that which comes—which also means, an infinite openness to the Other or the newcomer."[65] As Balibar also suggests, democratization of democracy "also means that democracy, insofar as it is identified with its own continuous democratization, requires the deconstruction of the discriminations and exclusions that have been institutionalized in its name (here again, the example of women and foreigners is of particular importance.)"[66] The concept of citizenship has historically been in constant evolution precisely by virtue of the hospitality toward the noncitizen, as women and former slaves and colonial subjects gained rights. It ought to continue to change as refugees and global migrants still remain rightless. The question for the present is how the architects of a connected world whose inhabitants we may call the citizens to come will find new forms and ways of practicing open architecture.

Notes on Method

The stops in this book provide a closer look at a specific type of open architecture and trace a longer history of ideas that culminated in a particular urban block in Berlin. The strolls were inspired by guidebooks and travel literature, but they adapt this genre given travelers' experience in the age of GPS navigation. This is a sort of "remediation in reverse"—a term that Andreas Huyssen coined to explain the emergence of what he calls "urban miniatures," a literary genre developed by authors such as Charles Baudelaire, Franz Kafka, Walter Benjamin, Siegfried Kracauer, and Robert Musil that updated writing in response to the proliferation of visual media such as photography and film.[67] The strolls in this book walk the readers through the streets of Kreuzberg, assuming they will have a clear cognition of the city map because they can locate themselves in the city by using digital navigation devices.

This is not a book on IBA-1984/87 per se, as it does not examine the smaller sites of the exhibition in Tegel and Prager Platz or many important projects in Kreuzberg in detail. The book does not claim to provide a comprehensive picture of the residents of Kreuzberg or of the guest workers and refugees from Turkey in Germany, as it does not contain the stories of German squatters or migrants from other countries in Kreuzberg, or people from Turkey in any part of Germany except Kreuzberg. My main intention is to theorize open architecture in the sense of a new ethics of hospitality that problematizes nation-state formations and comes to terms with the paradoxes of current human rights regime. Nonetheless, I trust that readers interested in the migrant experience in Germany or elsewhere, as well as those interested in IBA or Kreuzberg in general, will find information in this book useful in leading to a more comprehensive understanding of these issues.

The book problematizes not only the history but also the historiography of the noncitizen voice in urban space. Methodologically, I therefore extend the book's theme to its format and explore an open form of writing, by giving voice not only to architects and policy makers but also to noncitizen residents through a genre inspired by oral history and storytelling rather than sociology and ethnography. This creates an alternative both to established architectural history, which stops the narrative at the moment the building's design leaves the architect's hand, and to established forms of environmental science research. In architectural research, the resident—often called the user, an abstract and universal term—is analyzed either scientifically (through sociological methods such as collecting sufficiently large samples and turning results into quantifiable data) or ethnographically (which originally started as a reflection of the concern with what the West deemed to be primitive, other, or non-Western). One can think of Gottfried Semper, Alois Riegl, Heinrich Wölfflin, and many others here.[68] The first approach limits the possibility of open-ended questions in exploring an individual's voice, while the second maintains the authorship of the ethnographer and, more importantly, views an individual as a member of an ethnic group from the start. I propose an alternative by presenting individual noncitizens' voices as an oral historian who does not have claims to representability, but may rely on a single witness, and as a storyteller who alternates between the role of author and resident and who acknowledges that the fabric of everyday life unfolding in an individual's experience of a space is also part of the history of that space. Oral history is not without its problems, as it is always distorted by individual memories, but it is one of the few ways to write participatory architectural history in the absence of official documents that could have given access to the voice of the stateless.[69] In translating these oral histories into my own writing, I entertain the idea of storytelling as a format for participatory architectural history. As opposed to the isolated novel or the ever-speedy information highway, Benjamin characterized storytelling as the experience that is passed from mouth to mouth, and the storyteller as the mediator who conveys "counsel woven into the fabric of real life."[70] Traditional architectural history usually stops at the point when the building is constructed and the design leaves the hand of the architect. In contrast, open architectural history as storytelling extends the narrative by combining the time of its design with the time of a specific occupation. The contingency and partiality of storytelling that results from this specific amalgam of the two time periods acknowledges the necessarily open, unfinished nature of architectural history.

The noncitizen residents whose stories are included in this book were chosen in an almost self-selective way. Between 2009 and 2014, I rang the bell of almost every door in Kreuzberg that I could identify as belonging to an immigrant's apartment due to the name inscribed on the bell, and I asked to interview those who had participated in the urban renewal process in the mid-1980s or who had been living in the IBA buildings since then. The people who agreed to tell their stories at length to me (sometimes over the years) and who happened to live in the buildings that I eventually called latent open architecture are the characters in this book (their names or acronyms appear in the form they wanted). My own interior photographs used in this book have always been taken with residents' permission, and when including photographs of street scenes with city habitants, I tried to make sure to avoid voyeuristic vision (and sometimes preferred empty scenes for this reason). A significant majority of my interviewees, whom I call resident architects, were female immigrants from Turkey (former guest workers and refugees), probably at least in part because of my own gender, language skills, and familiarity with cultural codes.[71] Even though I did not decide initially to interview mostly women, the group of people I interviewed fits well with the book's feminist aspiration to write more women architects into architectural history. Remembering Linda Nochlin's groundbreaking essay "Why Have There Been No Great Women Artists?"[72] I think that historians have filled architectural history books almost exclusively with male characters because they defined Architecture as an occupation historically practiced by men. Yet if we define architecture as design open to residents' appropriation, there would be at least as many women architects as men in history, even though of course there is no biological or essential reason why women should be the makers of a house's interior after the architect leaves the stage. By telling the history of residents as specific individuals who are as influential as specific architects in designing spaces, I try to contribute to the writing of this feminist history. My interviewees came from different ethnic groups in Turkey, including Turkish, Kurdish, and Alevi individuals. The national, ethnic, and religious categories are used in the book as long as they were important for my interviewees. I tried not to perpetuate such identity markers in my own explanatory concepts that aim to move toward transnational categories in defining open architecture as the welcoming of the perceived other.

Having been trained as an architect, I frequently did not agree with the residents' assessments of their living spaces—especially when (not surprisingly) they disliked architectural decisions that I appreciated or criticized as nonfunctional or uncomfortable what I thought was an innovative idea. I tried to report their viewpoints comprehensively without necessarily taking too much time to formulate my own alternative opinions, unless they pertained to the theory of open architecture endorsed in this book. After all, architectural debate is at its best when it is ongoing; when it suppresses the speech of neither the architects, nor the inhabitants or the scholars; and when it is kept open.

Critical reconstruction and careful urban renewal as the urban design themes that developed during IBA-1984/87 have had a long-lasting impact and guided the planning of Berlin's reunification when the Berlin Wall unexpectedly came down just two years after IBA's final opening. Due to the public housing status given to the IBA buildings for twenty-five years, until a few years ago Kreuzberg avoided gentrification, unlike the adjacent neighborhoods of Mitte and Prenzlauer Berg. As I was writing this book, Kreuzberg began to be gentrified, and the IBA buildings lost their public housing status one after another. During the final couple years of my on-site research and writing, I often found myself returning to buildings where I no longer knew anyone and ringing doorbells of empty apartments waiting for their upgrades and new renters. The more I witnessed the IBA buildings being completely abandoned in a week due to sudden and drastic rent increases that forced residents out of their apartments, the more I understood that I was catching the final years of the history of a migrant neighborhood.

As I look back at my on-site research and as my colleagues ask how it was possible for me to have been invited to so many apartments, courtyards, social clubs, and even secret passageways, I can't help thinking that it was a Kreuzbergian mindset (which of course can be found in other parts of the world, and which certainly not everyone in Kreuzberg has) that made this book on open architecture possible. It was this open mindset—a hospitality that at least in theory has the strength of overcoming authority and chauvinism, regardless of the contemporary political forces and legal regulations—that this book records and to which it owes its existence. As I finish writing the book in a world where platforms for free speech, academic freedom, and civil rights are fast diminishing, and where new borders are being built both physically and conceptually to exclude others, I am once more convinced of the importance and urgency of open architecture as the translation of a new ethics of hospitality into design.

1 As if they could slide across the floor, these planes demonstrated the independence of space from vertical boundaries, while the totally transparent glass walls separating the inside and outside theoretically allowed the eye to see to infinity. By placing a column just next to a wall, rather than hiding it inside, Mies was making a statement about the irrelevance of walls for structural purposes and his departure from Renaissance-based plan conceptions. The vertical and horizontal surfaces that were made out of different materials with varied levels of reflexivity and translucency—including the pools, colored glass, chrome-clad columns, onyx dore wall, and three types and colors of marble partitions—contributed to the feeling of a fluid space sandwiched between two horizontal planes. If you turn the historical photographs of the Barcelona Pavilion upside down, the building would still look plausible as a space in this universe, which signaled a departure from not only the classical anthropocentric metaphors of the universe, but also the pragmatic necessities of daily life such as space dividers, doors, and pieces of furniture. For more on the pavilion, see Sonit Bafna, "Symbolic Content in the Emergence of the Miesian Free Plan," *Journal of Architecture* 10, no. 2 (2005): 181–200; Jean-Louis Cohen, *Mies van der Rohe*, 2nd ed., trans. Maggie Rosengarten (London: Springer, 2007); Gevork Hartoonian, "Mies van der Rohe: The Genealogy of Column and Wall," *Journal of Architectural Education* 42, no. 2 (1989): 43–50; Fritz Neumeyer, *The Artless Word,* trans. Mark Jarzombek (Cambridge, MA: MIT Press, 1991). For the significant role of the Barcelona Pavilion and its visual effects in the story of modernism, see Detlef Mertins, "Architectures of Becoming," *Mies in Berlin,* ed. Terence Riley and Barry Bergdoll (New York: Museum of Modern Art, 2001); Josep Quetglas, "Fear of Glass: The Barcelona Pavilion," *Architectureproduction,* ed. Joan Ockman (New York: Princeton Architectural Press, 1988), 122–51; Claire Zimmerman, *Photographic Architecture in the Twentieth Century* (Minneapolis: University of Minnesota Press, 2014). **2** The main living space in the Tugendhat House was composed as an open and fluid space made possible by eight slender columns, while the freestanding walls defined the sitting and dining areas without separating them in enclosed rooms. The idea of an open residential space, an unprivate house without walls and doors, and a space sandwiched between the two horizontal planes of the slab and the podium was nowhere as extremely expressed as it was in the Farnsworth House. For more discussion from the viewpoint of various authors, see: Adolph Stiller (ed.), *Das Haus Tugendhat* (Vienna: Verlag Anton Pustet, 1999). **3** As Detlef Mertins has shown ("Mies's Event Space," *Grey Room,* no. 20 (2005): 60–73), many exhibitions during the life of the museum followed the original Piet Mondrian show in 1968 by hanging panels from the ceiling that floated in space, while others built walls from the ground up. However, the most memorable were the site-specific installations that had a dialogue with the building, which lent "itself especially well to those who enter into its logic and respond—affirmatively or critically—to [Mies's] desire to manifest the deep structure immanent to creation" (ibid., 69). Mertins emphasizes the installations by artists such as Ulrich Rückriem (1983), in which stones on the ground reflected the roof's grid, and Jenny Holzer (2001), in which lit scripts flowed over the beams. I would add the one by David Chipperfield (2014), who turned the space into a forest of columns, with each one marking the intersections in the grid of beams. **4** Kenneth Frampton, "Maison de Verre," *Perspecta* 12 (1969): 77–109. There have been numerous subsequent publications about the house. **5** As Theo van Doesburg stated in his 1924 manifesto, "The new architecture has opened the walls and so done away with the separation of the inside and outside. The walls themselves no longer support [the structural load]. The result is a new, open ground-plan entirely different from the classical one, since inside and outside now pass over into one another" ("Towards a Plastic Architecture," in *Programs and Manifestoes on 20th Century Architecture,* ed. Ulrich Conrads, trans. Michael Bullock [Cambridge, MA: MIT Press, 1970]: 78–80.) **6** Alice Friedman, "Not a Muse: The Client's Role at the Rietveld Schröder House," in *The Sex of Architecture,* ed. Diana Agrest, Patricia Conway, Leslie Kanes Weisman (New York: Harry Adams, 1996), 217–32. **7** For example, his designs for the Ağaoğlu House (1936) integrated many elements that had inspired him during his study trip to Europe, including horizontal windows, linear massing, and whitewashed stucco walls devoid of ornament, but he organized the plan around a central space that he called *sofa*—a type of plan that can be observed in many of his other buildings. See Esra Akcan, *Architecture in Translation: Germany, Turkey and the Modern House* (Durham, NC: Duke University Press, 2012). **8** Ken T. Oshima, *International Architecture in Interwar Japan* (Seattle: University of Washington Press, 2009). **9** For Loos's work, see Benedetto Gravagnuolo, *Adolf Loos: Theory and Works* (New York: Rizzoli, 1982). **10** Werner Oechslin, "Raumplan Versus Plan Libre," *Daidalos* 42 (December 15, 1991): 76–83. **11** In Hilde Heynen's words, "Rather than deceiving people with an illusory harmony, Loos chose a ruthless design that does not gloss over any discontinuities and moments of fissure, but highlights them" (*Architecture and Modernity* [Cambridge, MA: MIT Press, 1999], 93). For more on Loos's style, see ibid., 75–95. **12** Alison Smithson, ed. *Team 10 Primer* (Cambridge, MA: MIT Press, 1968), 61. **13** Oskar Hansen and Zofia Hansen, "The Open Form in Architecture: The Art of the Great Number," in *Opening Modernism* (Warsaw: Museum of Modern Art in Warsaw, 2014, or.1961), 7–9. **14** I owe much of my discussion of Metabolism and Kenzo Tange to Zhongjie Lin, *Kenzo Tange and the Metabolist Movement* (London: Routledge, 2010). See also Rem Koolhaas et al., *Project Japan: Metabolism Talks* (London: Taschen, 2011); Tomoko Tamari, "Metabolism: Utopian Urbanism and the Japanese Modern Architecture Movement," *Theory, Culture and Society* 31, nos. 7–8 (2014): 201–25. **15** Michael Blackwood, dir., *Kisho Kurokawa: From Metabolism to Symbiosis* (Michael Blackwood Productions, 1993). **16** Lin wrote that "from the Metabolist point of view, people would paradoxically achieve freedom through comprehensive planning" (*Kenzo Tange and the Metabolist Movement,* 95). **17** Fumihiko Maki, *Investigations in Collective Form* (St. Louis, MO: Washington University Press, 1964), 19. **18** Ibid., 8. **19** Reyner Banham, *Megastructure: Urban Futures of the Recent*

Past (London: Thames and Hudson, 1976). **20** As Sarah Deyong points out, the megastructure movement had institutionalized beginnings in the period immediately after World War II, when most CIAM members were trying to become official consultants to the United Nations and receive corporate backing to regulate the colonial architecture in Africa and developing nations—projects that did not mesh with the avant-gardist anti-establishment sensibility ("Planetary Habitat: The Origins of a Phantom Movement," *Journal of Architecture* 6, no. 2 [2001]: 113–28). **21** Karl Popper, *The Open Society and Its Enemies* (Princeton, NJ: Princeton University Press, 2013, or. 1945). **22** See Stanley Mathews, *From Agit-Prop to Free Space: The Architecture of Cedric Price* (London: Black Dog, 2007). It is useful to note that leisure was a basic zone of action for the Labour Party in Britain at the time, and fun in the Brechtian sense signaled the role of theater as a place for bemused criticality, rather than elite seriousness. For Cedric Price's relation to left-wing struggles in Britain, see Pier Vittorio Aureli, "Labor and Architecture: Revisiting Cedric Price's Potteries Thinkbelt," *Log*, no. 23 (2011): 97–118. **23** Mathews, *From Agit-Prop to Free Space*, 244. **24** Peter Lang and William Menking, *Superstudio: Life without Objects* (New York: Skira, 2003). **25** Peter Cook, a member of Archigram, had explained that "the image of the city may well be the image of people themselves … and we have devoted much of the exhibition to the life-cycle and survival kit of the people within cities" (quoted in Simon Sadler, *Archigram: Architecture without Architecture* [Cambridge, MA: MIT Press, 2005], 72.) **26** Aldo Rossi, *Architecture of the City*, trans. Diane Ghirardo and Joan Ockman (Cambridge, MA: MIT Press, 1982). **27** Josef Paul Kleihues, "Die Architektur, das wollte ich sagen, bedarf unser aller Pflege," in *Erste Projekte: Internationale Bauausstellung Berlin 1984/87: Die Neubaugebiete – Dokumente, Projekte*, vol. 2 (Berlin: Quadriga Verlag, 1981), 58–71. **28** Kas Oosterhuis, *Hyperbodies: Towards an E-motive Architecture* (Basel, Switzerland: Birkhäuser, 2003), 83–87. **29** Mario Carpo, introduction to *AD Reader: The Digital Turn in Architecture, 1992–2002*, ed. Mario Carpo (London: John Wiley and Sons, 2013), 13. **30** Giancarlo de Carlo, "Architecture's Public," in *Architecture and Participation*, ed. Peter Blundell Jones and Doina Petrescu (New York: Spon Press, 2005), 3–19. Quotation: p. 5. **31** Chantal Mouffe wrote that "a project of radical and plural democracy recognizes the impossibility of the complete realization of democracy and the final achievement of the political community. Its aim is to use the symbolic resources of the liberal democratic tradition to struggle for the deepening of the democratic revolution, knowing that it is a never-ending process" ("Democratic Citizenship and the Political Community," in *Dimensions of Radical Democracy: Pluralism, Citizenship, Community*, ed. Chantal Mouffe [London: Verso, 1992]), 225–239. Quotation: p. 238. **32** Ernesto Laclau and Chantal Mouffe, *Hegemony and Socialist Strategy: Towards a Radical Democratic Politics* (London: Verso, 1985), 176. **33** Álvaro Siza, "Evora Malagueira," in *Álvaro Siza: Complete Works*, ed. Kenneth Frampton (London: Phaidon, 2000), 160–62. **34** Álvaro Siza, "Fragments of an Experience: Conversations with Pedro de Llano, Carlos Castanheira, Francisco Rei, Santiago Seara," in *Álvaro Siza: Works and Projects*, ed. Pedro de Llano and Carlos Castanheira (Madrid: Electa, 1995), 27–55. Quotation: p. 34. **35** Charles Correa, "Urban Housing in the Third World: The Role of the Architect," in *Architecture and Community: Building in the Islamic World Today* (New York: Aga Khan Press for Architecture, 1983); Hassan Fathy, *Architecture for the Poor: An Experiment in Rural Egypt* (Chicago: University of Chicago Press, 1973); Andrea Dean and Timothy Hursley, *Rural Studio: Samuel Mockbee and an Architecture of Decency* (New York: Princeton Architectural Press, 2002); Alejandro Aravena, "Elemental: Santiago, Chile. Democratic Interaction Produces More Benefit by Same Investment," in *Sustainable Design: Towards a New Ethic in Architecture and Town Planning* (Basel, Switzerland: Birkhäuser, 2009); Alejandro Aravena, *Elemental: Incremental Housing and Participatory Design Manual* (Ostfildern, Germany: Hatje Cantz, 2012). **36** Samuel Huntington, *The Clash of Civilizations and the Remaking of World Order* (New York: Simon and Schuster, 1996). **37** Wendy Brown, *Undoing the Demos: Neoliberalism's Stealth Revolution* (New York: Zone Books, 2015), 17. **38** Michel Foucault, *The Birth of Biopolitics: Lectures at the Collège de France, 1978–79*, trans. Graham Burchell (New York: Palgrave, 2008). **39** Étienne Balibar, *Citizenship*, trans. Thomas Scott-Railton (Cambridge: Polity Press, 2015), 118. **40** Brown writes that "when there is only *homo oeconomicus*, and when the domain of the political itself is rendered in economic terms, the foundation vanishes for citizenship concerned with public things and the common good. … The replacement of citizenship defined as concern with the public good by citizenship reduced to the citizen as *homo oeconomicus* also eliminates the very idea of people, a demos asserting its collective political sovereignty" (*Undoing the Demos*, 39 and 42). **41** The fact that in 1979 Foucault had already realized that one of the birthplaces of this neoliberalism was postwar Germany makes the story of immigration and participation in IBA-1984/87 even more exhilarating. Foucault formulated the "first objective of neoliberalism" in the context of postwar Germany immediately after World War II and Nazism as follows: "How can economic freedom be the state's foundation and limitation at the same time, its guarantee and security?" (*The Birth of Biopolitics*, 102). For him, this neoliberalism was different from traditional liberal projects since the eighteenth century: "What is at issue is whether a market economy can in fact serve as the principle, form and model for a state which, because of its defects, is mistrusted by everyone on both the right and the left, for one reason or another. Everyone is in agreement in criticizing the state and identifying its destructive and harmful effects. … Can the market really have the power of formalization for both the state and the society? … It is not just a question of freeing the economy. It is a question of knowing how far the market economy's powers of political and social information extend" (ibid., 117–18). **42** Balibar, *Citizenship*, 119–31. **43** Rem Koolhaas, *Delirious New York: A Retroactive Manifesto for Manhattan* (New York: Monacelli Press, 1994, or.1978). **44** Colin Rowe and Fred Koetter, *Collage City* (Cambridge, MA: MIT Press, 1978). **45** Umberto Eco, "The Poetics of the Open Work," in Umberto Eco, *Open Work*, trans. Anna Cancogni (Cambridge, MA: Harvard University Press, 1989, or. 1962), 1–24; Roland Barthes, "The Death of the Author," in Roland Barthes, *Image Music Text*, trans. Stephan Heath (New York: Hill and Wang, 1977), 142–48. **46** Jacques Rancière, *The Emancipated Spectator*, trans. Gregory Elliott (London: Verso, 2009). **47** Jacques Derrida, "Point de Folie: Maintenant Architecture," in *Architecture Theory since 1968*, ed. Michael Hays (Cambridge, MA: MIT Press, 1998), 566–81. **48** Hannah Arendt, "We Refugees," *Menorah Journal*, no. 1 (1943): 77; Giorgio Agamben, "We Refugees," trans. Michael Rocke, *Symposium* 49, no. 2 (1995): 114–19. For a revised version, see Giorgio Agamben, "Biopolitics and the Rights of Man," in Giorgio Agamben, *Homo Sacer: Sovereign Power and Bare Life*, ed. Werner Hamacher and David E. Wellbery, trans. Daniel Heller-Roazen (Stanford, CA: Stanford University Press, 1998), 126–35. **49** Ibid., 126. **50** Ibid., 134. **51** Hannah Arendt, "The Perplexities of the Rights of Man," in Hannah Arendt, *Origins of Totalitarianism* (New York: Harcourt Brace and Co., 1973), 293. **52** Jürgen Hoffmeyer-Zlotnick, *Gastarbeiter im Sanierungsgebiet: Das Beispiel Berlin-Kreuzberg* (Hamburg: Christians, 1977). **53** Many studies of the legal, sociological, and cultural aspects of immigration were undertaken in Germany during the cold-war years, which will be discussed in the following chapters. For recent scholarly books, see especially: Tomas Hammar, *European Immigration Policy: A Comparative Study* (Cambridge: Cambridge University Press, 1985); Ayhan Kaya, *Sicher in Kreuzberg: Constructing Diasporas: Turkish Hip Hop Youth in Berlin* (Bielefeld, Germany: Transcript Verlag, 2001); Leslie Adelson, *The Turkish Turn in Contemporary German Literature: Toward a New Critical Grammar of Migration* (New York: Palgrave Macmillan, 2005); Timothy Hatton and Jeffrey Williamson, *Global Migration and the World Economy: Two Centuries of Policy and Performance* (Cambridge, MA: MIT Press, 2005); Deniz Göktürk, David Gramling, and Anton Kaes, eds., *Germany in Transit: Nation and Migration, 1955–2005* (Berkeley: University of California Press, 2007); Rita Chin, *The Guest Worker Question in Postwar Germany* (Cambridge: Cambridge University Press, 2007); Ruth Mandel, *Cosmopolitan Anxieties: Turkish Challenges to Citizenship and Belonging in Germany* (Durham, NC: Duke University Press, 2008); Gökçe Yurdakul, *From Guest Workers into Muslims: The Transformation of Turkish Immigrant Associations in Germany* (Newcastle: Cambridge University Press, 2009); Annika Marlen Hinze, *Turkish Berlin: Integration Policy and Urban Space* (Minneapolis: University of Minnesota Press, 2013). **54** Cihan Arın, Safter Çınar, Necati Gürbaca, Hakkı Keskin, M. Yaşar Öncü, and M. Niyazi Turgay, "Yabancıların Yabancılar Politikasına İlişkin Görüşleri/Stellungnahme der Ausländer zur Ausländerpolitik," (Berlin: IGI [Initiativkreis Gleichberechtigung Integration], May 1981), 24. **55** For more discussion of these laws and regulations, see Cihan Arın, "Analyse der Wohnverhältnisse ausländischer Arbeiter in der Bundesrepublik Deutschland – Mit einer Fallstudie über türkische Arbeiterhaushalte in Berlin-Kreuzberg," PhD diss., Technische Universität Berlin, 1979; Cihan Arın, "The Housing Market and the Housing Policies for the Migrant Labor Population in West Berlin," in *Urban Housing Segregation of Minorities in Western Europe and the United States*, ed. E. Huttman (Durham, NC: Duke University Press, 1991). **56** Helmut Kohl, "Coalition of the Center: For a Politics of Renewal," trans. David Gramling, in *Germany in Transit: Nation and Migration, 1955–2005*, ed. Deniz Göktürk, David Gramling, and Anton Kaes (Berkeley: University of California Press, 2007), 46. **57** "Interview mit dem Berliner Bausenator Franke," *Der Architekt*, no. 10, October 1984, 445–447. Quotation: p. 447. **58** See Manfred Schonlau, "Die Berliner Wohnungsbauförderung," special issue, "Internationale Bauausstellung Berlin 1987. Wohnungsgrundrisse," *Baumeister* 84, no. 5 (1987): 20–23. **59** Much has been said about Marshall's tripartite definition of citizenship as civil, political, and social citizenship, and others have challenged him on numerous fronts, especially for his account of the concept's historical evolution and his assumption of a unitary process tied to the British context. Nonetheless, his insight into the three types of rights continues to have an explanatory power. According to this framework, social citizenship rights are those tied to economic welfare and security, such as insurance against unemployment and rights to health care, education, and a pension. See T. H. Marshall, *Social Policy in the Twentieth Century* (London: Hutchinson, 1965). See also Richard Bellamy, *Citizenship* (Oxford: Oxford University Press, 2008); Bryan Turner, "Outline of a Theory of Citizenship," in *Dimensions of Radical Democracy: Pluralism, Citizenship, Community*, ed. Chantal Mouffe (London: Verso, 1992), 33–62. **60** Balibar, *Citizenship*, 69–70. **61** Ibid., 76. **62** Turner has stated that "the problem with Marshall's theory is that it is no longer relevant to a period of disorganized capitalism. … Marshall's theory assumed some form of nation-state autonomy in which governments were relatively immune from pressures within the world-system of capitalist nations" ("Outline of a Theory of Citizenship," 40). **63** Derrida made the same objection to the Kantian definition of hospitality, which he contrasted to that of Emmanuel Levinas. Derrida reads Levinas as referring to a person who desires to open him- or herself to the other, rather than assimilating the other into his or her framework. In Kant, hospitality is a forced way to peace; in Levinas, everything begins with hospitality, as a natural desire to open oneself to the other. See Jacques Derrida, *Adieu to Emmanuel Levinas*, trans. Pascale-Anne Brault and Michael Naas (Stanford, CA: Stanford University Press, 1999). Gayatri Spivak exposes the Kantian conception of hospitality based on duty as one of the shortcomings of the current human rights regime. This conception continues to be used as a justification for imperialism, as long as it is assumed that it is the West's duty and responsibility to carry human rights to its others. See Gayatri Spivak, "Righting Wrongs," *South Atlantic Quarterly* 103, nos. 2–3 (2004): 523–81. For my own interpretation of Kantian hospitality, reading Kant's "Perpetual Peace" and *Prolegomena* together, see: Esra Akcan, *Architecture in Translation: Germany, Turkey & the Modern House* (Durham: Duke University Press, 2012), 21–26, 277–281. **64** For Derrida's rebuttal of Fukuyama's argument, see Jacques Derrida, *Specters of Marx*, trans. Peggy Kamuf (London: Routledge,

1994), 61–95. **65** Jacques Rancière, *Dissensus: On Politics and Aesthetics*, ed. and trans. Steven Corcoran (London: Bloomsbury, 2010), 59. Here Rancière is describing Derrida's project. **66** Balibar, *Citizenship*, 124–25. **67** Andreas Huyssen, *Miniature Metropolis: Literature in an Age of Photography and Film* (Cambridge, MA: Harvard University Press, 2015). **68** For a discussion of the influence of ethnography on the core texts of art and architecture history, see Matthew Rampley, "Anthropology at the Origins of Art History," in *Site-Specificity: The Ethnographic Turn*, ed. Alex Coles (London: Black Dog Publishers, 2000), 138–59. **69** Robert Perks and Alistair Thomson, *The Oral History Reader*, 2nd ed. (London: Routledge, 2006). **70** Walter Benjamin, "The Storyteller: Reflections on the Works of Nikolai Leskov," in *Illuminations*, ed. Hannah Arendt, trans. Harry Zohn (New York: Schocken Books, 1968), 83–109. Quotation: 86. Also see Okwui Enwezor, "What Is It? The Image, between Documentary and Near Documentary," in *The Storyteller* (New York: ICI and JRP/Ringier, 2010). **71** Not having been formally trained as an oral historian (in fact, many oral historians admit that there are no prescribed norms or predefined methods in the field), I can hardly claim to have done oral history successfully for any topic but this one. Nonetheless, I believe my own formation as an architect helped me in this case. I followed the basic interviewing techniques of oral historians, such as "not appearing too obsessed by the equipment, [remembering] the importance of establishing rapport and intimacy, of listening and of asking open-ended questions, not interrupting, allowing for pauses and silences, informality, probing, and above all remembering that 'people aren't boring'" (Robert Perks and Alistair Thomson, "Interviewing," in *The Oral History Reader*, ed. Robert Perks and Alistair Thomson, 2nd ed. [New York: Routledge: 2006], 116). **72** Linda Nochlin, "Why Have There Been No Great Women Artists?" in Linda Nochlin, *Women, Art and Power and Other Essays* (Boulder: Westview Press, 1988), 147–158.

Part 1
Open Architecture as Collectivity

STOP I

Critical Reconstruction:
Open Architecture as Collaboration?

I like the term guest worker. I always think of two people: one just sits there like a guest, the other one works.
Emine Sevgi Özdamar[1]

In 1973, an article in *Der Spiegel* referred to Berlin's Kreuzberg as the Harlem of Germany (Figure I.1, I.2). Mentioning the federal housing minister Hans-Jochen Vogel, who had called the area "a small Harlem," and politicians who often warned about the "Turkish ghetto," the article mourned the replacement of the Kottbusser Tor pub with a restaurant called Hisar (which means fortress in Turkish) where a certain "lamb spit rotating on a vertical axis" stood at the counter (producing a dish called *döner*), a kind of "Oriental sing-song" filled the air, and a group of men "crouch[ed] around, playing a game called Jokey" (Figure I.3). The article warned about the new wave of immigrants who would arrive from Turkey as a result of Germany's upcoming labor law, and whose arrival would undoubtedly increase the number of Turkish-sounding names on mailboxes and "men in pedal pants strolling like flaneurs." Summarizing the general sentiment of the politicians and the commentators, *Der Spiegel* reported: "Ghettos are developing, and sociologists are prophesying the downfall of the cities, increased criminality, and social misery like those found in Harlem. ... The first Harlem symptoms are already visible. In the eroding sectors of German cities, 'a new subproletariat is growing in which the seed of social diseases is sown.'"[2]

Such racialization of noncitizens from Turkey was not an isolated incident in Germany. *Der Spiegel* seemed to take it for granted that readers would see the connection between a neighborhood in New York City whose African American residents were known to be subject to racism and a neighborhood in Berlin renowned for its Turkish guest workers. Even though Germans were careful not to refer to race as a category, due to its association with the anti-Semitic ideology of their country's recent past, many scholars have noted the explanatory power of racism in historicizing the discrimination against people who came to Germany through the guest worker program. The socially constructed category of race implies a hierarchy and stark segregation, in contrast to other markers of difference such as ethnicity and religion—which have been used more often in Germany when referring to immigrants of this period, but whose conceptual boundaries with race are nonetheless fluid and unstable.[3] As Ruth Mandel put it, "'ethnic' is deployed to equalize and relativize peoples, groups and statuses. Instead, such deployment backfires, as 'ethnic' becomes the euphemism for what a generation ago would have been called 'race.'"[4] In the words of Rita Chin, whose work discusses the social and cultural effects of foreigner laws (Ausländergesetz), "if we are to understand German conceptions of difference through apparently neutral terms such as guest worker,

TOP: Figure I.1 View from Naunynplatz in Kreuzberg, photographed by Heide Moldenhauer, Berlin, c. 1981.
LEFT: Figure I.2 View from Oranienstrasse in Kreuzberg, photographed by Heide Moldenhauer, Berlin, c. 1981.
RIGHT: Figure I.3 Hasır Restaurant in Kreuzberg at Adalbert- and Oranienstrasse, photographed by Esra Akcan, Berlin, 2014.

foreigner and migrant, it is important to absorb the crucial lessons that have come out of critical race theory. … Such work helps us see that these categories—like their more obvious 'racial' counterparts—operate as ideological constructs with very particular implications for how social hierarchy is developed and regulated."[5] Urban discourse often referred to city areas whose populations had a high percentage of noncitizens as ghettos, meaning sources of trouble, crime, and chaos.[6] Kreuzberg provides a good example of how legally constructed citizenship status coupled with socially constructed racial or ethnic hierarchies affect urban space and architecture.

Six of the nine sites that were declared as focal points in the Berlin Senate's bill to authorize the hosting of an international building exhibition were in Kreuzberg (Figure I.4).[7] Thereafter to be known as IBA-1984/87, these sites would soon be extended and combined to cover the whole Kreuzberg. A report on "Berlin: IBA" by the Senate introduced them as "threatened areas" and "a challenge to this generation" because of the "urban decay syndrome—substandard apartments, dark courtyards, empty buildings, closed shops, unsafe streets, the departure of long-time residents and the well-to-do, the arrival of foreign and socially underprivileged" (Figure I.5).[8] This 1978 report about the intentions of the bill that was passed in 1979 mentioned the "coexistence" of "natives and foreigners," "forms of integration," and town planning that explores "possibilities of citizen involvement" as important topics of discussion, along with other ecological and economic considerations.[9] However, the same report presented six goals, none of which mentioned the issue of immigration. Reading between the lines of these goals suggests that IBA was organized to bring together architects who had already been brainstorming about these areas in particular and urban design in historical cities in general, but not necessarily about international immigration. These goals were to: address the inequality in "Berlin's polycentric urban structure," acknowledge the "cities within the city," design "a future for our past" by establishing continuity with the city's underlying historical structure, recognize "the city as constant and the building as variable," rediscover the "attractiveness and quality of residential areas" in the central city, and strike a "productive balance of forces between social needs and the individual artistic responsibility" by aiming for an "architectural art with the participation of those affected."[10] These goals bring to mind their unmentioned authors such as Aldo Rossi, Rob Krier, and the collaboration between Oswald Mathias Ungers and Rem Koolhaas, as well as the disagreements between the IBA Neubau and Altbau directors Josef Paul Kleihues and Hardt-Waltherr Hämer. The seven stops in this book trace the history of the ideas and eventual contributions to Kreuzberg's urban renewal of these and subsequently invited architects as stories that overlapped in this neighborhood in the early 1980s. Our first stop is the intersection of Linden- and Ritterstrasse, where IBA Neubau's earliest buildings were constructed and which provides a context to introduce the actors and the process of the building exhibition, as well as the concept of open architecture as collaboration.

The History of Building Exhibitions, Social Housing, and the Historical City

IBA-1984/87 differentiated itself from its predecessors as a building exhibition of social housing in the form of an urban renewal in historical city districts (Figure I.6). In its abundant reports, publications, and press releases designed to produce funding and public support, IBA therefore considered it as important to rewrite the history of building exhibitions, social housing, and Berlin's urban development as it was to introduce the designs of buildings. Unlike temporary buildings constructed for display in large world expositions (which since the nineteenth century have created increasingly more construction waste), architectural exhibitions in a museum or gallery space (where architecture is presented through media such as drawings, models, photographs, and videos, which are made possible with increasingly overblown budgets), and the relatively more recent architectural *biennales* (whose ever growing size and place in the publicity and managerial machine seem to defeat the original purpose), building

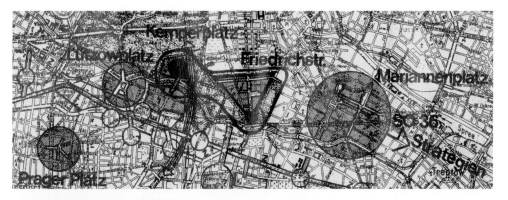

TOP: Figure I.4 Initial proposal for the urban renewal sites of Internationale Bauausstellung Berlin 1984, Berlin, 1978. LEFT: Figure I.5 Aerial view of Kreuzberg, photographed by Cihan Arın, Berlin, 11.2.1980. RIGHT: Figure I.8 Cover of *Idee Prozeß Ergebnis* (idea process result). Catalog of the IBA-1984/87 exhibition at the Martin Gropius Bau in 1984.

exhibitions produce permanent buildings for actual users and functions. Building exhibitions therefore use the idea of exhibiting as a way to raise funds for subsidized public housing and public buildings, rather than spending funds to display architectural representations.

While many authors mentioned that IBA-1984/87 continued the Berlin tradition of building exhibitions, including those in 1911, 1931, and 1957, it was Vittorio Magnago Lampugnani's articles in several venues that contextualized this endeavor in the history of architectural exhibitions. Lampugnani expanded the idea of the architectural exhibition to include different types far beyond venues with drawings and models, such as full-scale structures built for display; buildings in world expositions; building exhibitions as large city segments such as Weissenhof housing and the IBAs; and even entire cities that have now become destinations of architectural tourism, such as Chandigarh and Brasilia.[11] In addition to being a building exhibition that covered an entire city borough, an urban square, and a suburban development, IBA organized many other types of architectural exhibitions every year, launching its big exposition *Erste Projekte* (First projects) on the 200th anniversary of the birth of the architect Karl Friedrich Schinkel in 1981, and making its grand finale with *750 Jahre Architektur und Städtebau in Berlin* (750 years of architecture and urban planning in Berlin) in 1987, to

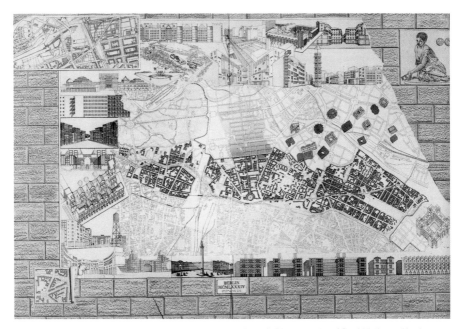

Figure I.6 IBA-1984/87 (Internationale Bauausstellung Berlin). Directors: Josef Paul Kleihues, Hardt-Waltherr Hämer. Site plan and drawings of buildings on the plate presented at the 17th Triennial of Milan. Drawing by Giovannella Bianchi, Ebe Gianotti, Werner Oechslin, Luca Ortelli.

celebrate the 750th anniversary of the city's founding. That finale was accompanied by a number of festive music, literature, and visual art events.[12] Thirty venues were listed in 1984 alone.[13] These included such influential expositions as IBA's central exhibition *Idee Prozeß Ergebnis* (idea process result) in the newly renovated Martin Gropius Bau (Figures I.7 and I.8); *Das Abenteuer der Ideen* (The adventure of ideas) at the New National Gallery, curated by Lampugnani; *Kreuzberger Mischung* (Kreuzberg mixture) at the BEWAG Halle, curated by Hämer (see Figure IV.6); and on important products of Berlin architects such as *Friedrich Gilly* at the Berlin-Museum and *Vier Berliner Großsiedlungen der Weimarer Republik* (originally intended title, Four housing estates of the Weimar period in Berlin) at the Bauhaus Archiv.[14] Newspapers reported that 150,000 visitors and 103 groups from fifteen countries were interested in visiting IBA's building and related exhibitions in the inaugural year of 1987.[15]

Itself a curated production, IBA Neubau invites a discussion of open architecture as collaboration, because Kleihues, its director, hoped to stimulate many different architects to work together in synergic dialogue under the auspices of an urban renewal. The Neubau coordinators Hildebrand Machleidt and Günter Schlusche have indicated that Kleihues was more interested in works of architecture than in a comprehensive approach to the area, while it was the task of the coordinators to produce the collective plan (*Gesamtplan*) that projected on an integral district plan that took into account traffic patterns, green areas, and the layout of streets. Schlusche has also singled out what he referred to as the "1981 crisis," after which Kleihues was pushed to be more attentive to planning, which he had previously regarded as only a technical issue.[16] Rather than open architecture as the collaboration of nonhierarchically positioned partners,

Figure I.7 IBA-1984/87, *Idee Prozeß Ergebnis* (idea process result). Exhibition in Martin Gropius Bau, showing John Hejduk's Studio for a Painter and Studio for a Musician, Berlin, 1984.

however, IBA Neubau evolved as an alliance under the hand of a strong curator. Much like an exhibition with a curator as author, this collaboration was meant to result in a unified environment with a sufficient number of variations. Given the presence of a determined director with diplomatic skills useful in relations with the government, some architects who were in agreement with the main concept found this collaboration enabling, but others found the director to be quite domineering.

Collaboration was also an idea that differentiated IBA-1984/87 from the preceding public housing projects. While situating itself in the long and proud history of public housing in Berlin, IBA was eager to write the history of housing so that it would produce a significant change in established values. IBA proponents sought to align themselves with the public housing tradition in Germany in its heyday. The world-famous *Siedlungen* (housing estates) of the Weimar period in Berlin, especially those designed by Bruno Taut and Martin Wagner that provided state-sponsored housing to thousands of lower- and middle-income families, were justifiably used as historical precedents. However, according to IBA proponents, no other period in the world history of housing was as devastating, as destructive of cities, and as inhumane as the years between the mid-1950s and the mid-1970s.[17] This included IBA-1957 in Hansaviertel, where existing buildings were torn down and replaced with freestanding prismatic blocks (Figure I.9). Kleihues situated the rise of the previous housing model in the context of Cold War rivalry. IBA-1957, in his view, was designed to contrast with the Stalinallee housing in East Berlin, comparing the alleged sensitivity and humanism of Western values to the domineering weight of the Eastern prefabricated high-rise blocks. The "architects in the western half of the divided city attempted to make good what had been declared unacceptable in the eastern half."[18] However, Hansaviertel had demolished existing buildings to create a new city, tearing apart the historical urban fabric even more violently than the bombs of World War II had done. In the 1980s, however, still according to Kleihues, it was no longer the Cold War rivalry that was involved; instead, the very future of the city was at risk. "An international building exhibition in Berlin in 1984 does not need to be justified by single urban planning developments in the other part of the city," Kleihues said,[19] trying to remove the stigma of Stalinallee (Aldo Rossi had also identified it as Europe's last significant street). What Berlin needed was not another wave of demolition as in Hansaviertel. Nor did it need another Gropiusstadt and Märkisches Viertel type of social housing, whose construction had been overseen by Werner Düttmann when he was the building director at the Senate during the 1960s, and which had been built from scratch at the city's periphery with massive, high, and freestanding prefabricated blocks that were detached from the street. Kleihues characterized the Märkisches Viertel as "a prime example of the failings of modern urban design"[20] (Figure I.10).

If one were to collaborate with dead architects, one had to know history. It is therefore not surprising that a significant portion of IBA's financial and intellectual resources was spent on rewriting the history of architecture and urbanism (the two were inseparable from each other), as well as communicating this history to the exhibition's participants and audience (Figure I.11). In the inaugural exhibition catalog *Erste Projekte*, published in 1981, Kleihues introduced the long history of Berlin, moving from its status as a twin city in the second half of the twelfth century to its present and noting its character as an ideal Gothic town in the fourteenth and fifteenth centuries, settled around the now controversially reconstructed Schloss; the influential Peter Joseph Lenné plan of 1840 (revised in 1845) that proposed a ring road to structure the city's traffic and a network of waterways, recreation areas, and railways; James Hobrecht's plan of 1862 that accounted for the western suburbs; the "Great Berlin Competition" of 1910 that extended the planners' attention to the greater city area, including the suburbs, and that aimed to resolve the inner-city problems; the world-famous social housing estates of the Weimar period, designed by Taut and Wagner; the National Socialist seizure of power in 1933 and Albert Speer's proposed interventions; the city's extensive demolition during World War II (Figure I.12); and the reconstruction programs after 1945, including Hans Scharoun's Collective Plan that assumed Berlin would not be divided, as well as the "raze and build" policies of West Berlin, to which IBA-1984/87 was determined to put an end.[24] Needless to say, Kleihues thought the interest in architecture and urbanism's historical development was mandatory for starting a new design.

IBA's grand finale exhibition, *750 Jahre Architektur und Städtebau in Berlin,* displayed in Mies van der Rohe's National Gallery six years later, and the catalog of the same name expanded on the historical narrative of Kleihues's article. The historians who participated in the catalog—including Fritz Neumeyer, Julius Posener, and Wolfgang Schäche—together wrote a comprehensive history of Berlin from 1237 to IBA's achievements, using a historical periodization that added value to the late nineteenth-century urban fabric while disparaging the postwar developments. The explanation briefs of all architectural competitions of IBA included a long and detailed section on the

TOP LEFT: Figure I.9 Model of IBA-1957, Hansaviertel, Berlin, 1957. TOP RIGHT: Figure I.10 Werner Düttmann, Georg Heinrichs, Hans Christian Müller, Märkisches Viertel, Berlin, 1964–74. Image circulated in IBA publication *Modelle für eine Stadt*. BOTTOM LEFT: Figure I.11 Ideal image of Belle-Alliance-Platz (today's Mehringplatz in Kreuzberg), 18th century, reproduced in IBA publication *Modelle für eine Stadt* (creator unknown). BOTTOM RIGHT: Figure I.12 View of Kreuzberg (Mehringplatz and Friedrichstadt) in 1946 after the destruction of World War II, reproduced in IBA publication *Modelle für eine Stadt*.

historical development of the larger site. These reports stressed the intense residential and industrial development in the Kaiser era (1871–1918) "as the most decisive period" that determined the "physiognomy" of the area, and then guided the competitors to "respect the historical ground plan" and take the remaining historical buildings to "serve as orientation for the scale."**25**

These accounts constructed the image of Berlin as a city with a broken history, with wounds and scars, traces of demolished buildings and absences. The continuity of the historical urban fabric was deemed to have been interrupted by World War II because of the rise of Nazism, and by the postwar demolitions in the name of reconstruction. *AD*, one of the most influential professional magazines of the period, published a special issue on Berlin, in which Doug Clelland introduced it as a city with a "broken history"; David Leatherbarrow wrote about the history of Friedrichstadt as a tolerant

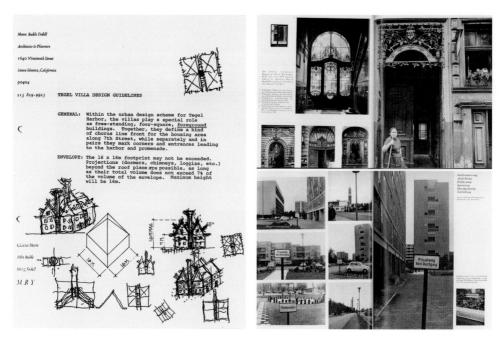

LEFT: Figure I.13 Charles Moore, John Ruble, and Buzz Yudell, Tegel Villa Design Guidelines, IBA-1984/87, Berlin.
RIGHT: Figure I.14 Pages from *Die gemordete Stadt* (1964), written by Wolf Jobst Siedler and Elisabeth Niggemeyer.

city, and Goerd Peschken informed practicing architects about the nineteenth-century rental apartment buildings.[26]

IBA's contribution to architectural scholarship went beyond the history of Berlin. In one of the many exhibitions of 1984, Lampugnani undertook the colossal task of exhibiting the architecture and philosophy of the Industrial Revolution. In IBA's progress report, this exhibition was justified because it presented "architecture as a complex phenomenon which can only be understood in its totality if consideration is also given to that which lies behind the constructed form."[27] Also displayed in Mies's building, the exhibition titled *Das Abenteuer der Ideen* was divided into the following sections: historicism, romanticism, classicism, organicism, technology, expressionism, realism, rationalism, and traditionalism.[28] These categories were the same as the movements that structured Lampugnani's survey book that had already been published in 1980.[29] Despite these rather stylistic categories, the exhibition catalog (translated into Italian the following year[30]) sought to discuss the influence of philosophy on architecture and the philosophical significance of architecture, bringing together essays by the most active architectural historians of the time (such as Alan Colquhoun, Kenneth Frampton, Heinrich Klotz, Seyyed Hossein Nasr, Winfried Nerdinger, Colin Rowe, Joseph Rykwert, Manfredo Tafuri, and Iain Boyd Whyte) and by equally distinguished philosophers (including Jacques Derrida, Agnes Heller, and Jean-François Lyotard).[31]

Lampugnani explained his historiographical motivation for both his survey book and the exhibition as his desire to write a multiple rather than a single history of modern architecture, by tracing its different trajectories as "movements" that are "connected at various levels, overlap in terms of duration, run parallel to each other or even follow divergent courses."[32] Frampton also characterized the exhibition as a daunting task involving new archival materials that culminated in a "kaleidoscopic retrospective of 'modern' architectural endeavor, running back 350 years."[33] At a time when the established histories of modern architecture relied on monophonic, linear, and causal narratives from the late nineteenth century onward, suggested by Nikolaus Pevsner and Sigfried Giedion, Lampugnani's survey contributed to the contemporary historiographical discussions about rewriting a more pluralistic version of the European and the North American canon. It also placed architecture in an intellectual trajectory, tracing the driving forces of modern architecture back to the mental leaps of the Enlightenment. This diversity did not take into account any region except Europe and North America, however. While explaining his work to a Japanese audience, Lampugnani asserted that the exhibition displayed not one but many histories, extending his gesture to the non-West. With the Enlightenment, he said that "the one history (namely of Western Christianity) lost its unique status and was allotted a place alongside a multitude of other histories."[34] For a catalog that was produced as part of a building exhibition in a noncitizen neighborhood but made no mention of immigration and provided hardly any account of architecture outside of Europe, Lampugnani's declaration came as a confession of a significant absence in an otherwise labor-intensive leap toward a more diverse version of architectural history.

The interest in the past as a guide for new design in the present had already become the leading architectural trend at the time. That trend was known as postmodernism, although both its promoters and critics used various meanings for the term. In professional magazines, IBA was sometimes seen as a promoter of postmodern style, due to the initially commissioned projects that attracted public attention—such as James Stirling and Michael Wilford's Science Center in Tiergarten (stroll 3); the housing in Tegel, based on Charles Moore, John Ruble, and Buzz Yudell's winning urban design competition entry (Figure I.13); and Krier's urban design for Prager Platz. However, the IBA Neubau team was determined to differentiate its position from postmodernist historicism, usually associated with making mimetic references to historical buildings with a sense of humor and a desire to appeal to the broader public. Kleihues stated on multiple occasions that IBA invited architects with a variety of stylistic preferences and architectural ideas to participate. Moreover, IBA proponents sought to differentiate their approach as a historical consciousness and an awareness of architectural typology, rather than anything that could be associated with nostalgia, instrumental history, or commercialization of the past. Lampugnani identified this as a "Janus faced" activity with rather commonsensical criteria, such as looking both to the past and future, staying away from "stale historic imagination on the one hand and on the other the over-enthusiastic search for the new for its own sake," and "a willingness to engage in a process of critical reflection."[35] It was time to demand continuity of the historical city, but without freezing it in its past form: "If we like everything to stay the same as it is, everything must change."[36]

The Neubau team settled on the term "critical reconstruction" (kritische Rekonstruktion) to signify this approach. Kleihues often cited as his most important intellectual

MASZSTAB 1:4000   SCALE 1:4000

Figure I.15 IBA-1984/87, Comparison of the existing buildings in the war-torn Kreuzberg and new additions of "critical reconstruction," Berlin, 1979–1987.

sources Siedler's *Die gemordete Stadt* (The murdered city, coauthored with Elisabeth Niggemeyer, 1964) and Rossi's *L'architettura della Città* (Architecture of the city, 1966).[37] In a 1986 interview, he added Jane Jacobs's *The Death and Life of Great American Cities* to this list.[38] These books had raised architects' consciousness about the merits of what Kleihues referred to as the "historical city" as opposed to the modernist values such as functional zoning and detached blocks on a tabula rasa. Siedler and Niggemeyer had criticized the impact of postwar modernist housing on Berlin's existing urban fabric by contrasting the photographs of lively and elegant streets, building entrances, doors, windows, stairs, shop windows, and urban squares in the Altbau areas with those of deserted modern spaces (Figure I.14).[39] Rossi inspired a sharp break in architectural design by calling architects to pay more attention to the historical typology and

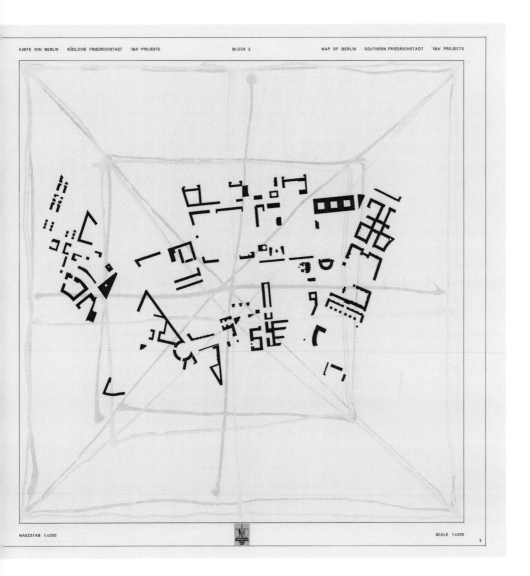

MASZSTAB 1:4000

SCALE 1:4000

morphology of the city (stop 2).[40] Kleihues advocated that an urban rejuvenation without razing the old would be possible by preserving the "ground plan" that he defined as the "gene structure of the city." "It is the *ground plan* in particular that testifies to the spiritual and cultural idea behind the founding of a city," he wrote.[41] It soon became clear that the perimeter block—a group of buildings that encircle a block's borders to concretize street edges in the front and courtyards or gardens at the back—was the "gene" of Berlin, in the eyes of IBA proponents. The new buildings under Kleihues's directorship would thus be conceived as infill projects "critically reconstructing" the existing urban blocks that had been half destroyed during the war and its aftermath. Established architects would offer variations on the theme (Figure I.15).

In Kleihues's eyes, his assignment as the IBA Neubau director was to enable gifted architects to receive public commissions. Born in 1933, Kleihues had studied architecture at the Technische Hochschule in Stuttgart, Technische Universität in Berlin, and Ecole des Beaux-Arts in Paris (1955–1960), and he had established an architectural office in Berlin in 1962. Before he became the IBA director, he had been a professor of architectural design, theory, and urbanism at Dortmund University (1973–94), where he had also edited the *Dortmunder Architekturhefte*, and he had been recognized for his Block 270 housing in Berlin-Wedding (1971–77), which he often referred to as a precedent for the critical reconstruction of the perimeter block.[42] Kleihues explained this "reconstruction of the block on its old site" as "the first consistent attempt at block street edging in Berlin since the War, in its aim to retain the old city ground plan and layouts as far as possible while taking modern residential requirements into account" (Figure I.16).[43]

In his most widely circulated article about IBA, Kleihues wrote: "Unlike other artists the architect is dependent on the support of the world around him. ... Intellectual superiority of any kind is a quality which brings great isolation. ... This reveals a great gap in our cultural and social order: society has lost and is continually losing works of art often of the highest rank, works which could give life meaning, significance and new impulses; these are being replaced by works of fashionable routine—and only because true, intellectually qualified patrons for public buildings are lacking!"[44] Kleihues's tone shows his perception of the architect as the sensitive, intellectually superior but isolated artist above the society and was consistent with the discourse on architectural autonomy as it will be discussed in stops III and V. In any event, his role as mediator between the architects and the policy makers cannot be overstated. Receiving 75 percent of its funding from the city of Berlin and the rest from the federal government, IBA was not the designer, producer, client, or builder. It was a mediating organization that used its resources (including its staff) for historical research; public relations, such as extensive exhibitions, symposia, and publications; and the selection of designers through architectural competitions whom it then suggested to the Berlin Senate. If nothing else, the IBA directors accomplished something very rare: they convinced the authorities to repair a working-class neighborhood and provide subsidized housing designed by a large number of established and emerging architects.

In raising public and political support for the IBA Neubau, Kleihues often mentioned the successful impact of the *Modelle für eine Stadt* (Models for a city) series that he and Siedler edited for the *Berliner Morgenpost*.[45] Through the discussions in this newspaper series that ran between January 16 and September 30 in 1977, at least two significant projects under consideration by the Berlin Senate were abandoned, to be eventually replaced with IBA-1984/87. First, at the time, the Kreuzberg area was threatened by a large *Autobahn* project called the Turbine, which would have reserved much of the northern area of Hallesches Tor for fast-moving cars in the IBA Neubau area, and whose north-south and east-west axes would have crossed at a massive junction over Oranienplatz in the IBA Altbau area (Figure I.17). The IBA team criticized the postwar planning values for reducing the city to a site of vehicular transportation, and the Turbine was one of the most dramatic examples that supported this argument. Second,

LEFT: Figure I.16 Josef Paul Kleihues, Block 270, Wedding-Vinetaplatz, Berlin, 1971–76. RIGHT: Figure I.17 Berlin Senate, The Turbine, Berlin, 1957.

after becoming building director at the Senate in 1967, Hans Christian Müller had proposed an IBA-1981 in the Tiergarten area. Kleihues started a campaign against this proposal, which he found as "an exhibition of 'attractive' housing in an 'attractive' district, totally unconnected with the urban planning issues of any kind." The *Berliner Morgenpost* series "roused a degree of attention that not even the politicians could ignore."[46]

Anna Teut wrote the first opinion piece in this series, where she pointed out that repairing the city was as important as constructing new buildings.[47] The next day, the newspaper launched a campaign, devoting four full pages to contributions from such powerful figures as Kleihues, Siedler, Pehnt, and Klotz, criticizing the projects being considered at the Senate and endorsing a design by James Stirling for Meinekestrasse (a site that was eventually left outside the IBA areas) for re-creating the "beautiful streets" of Berlin.[48] From the handwritten notes that are now in Stirling's archive, it is clear that all this was a well planned and orchestrated campaign that had actually started in August 1976. A core group of architects including Kleihues, Siedler, Stirling, and Rossi met for meetings and site visits in Berlin on August 26–30, and Kleihues explained a "venture" for which the architects initially considered were Stirling, Rossi, Carlo Aymonino, John Hejduk, Mario Botta, Ignazio Gardella, and Hans Hollein.[49] Stirling designed the Meinekestrasse project that would be endorsed in the *Berliner Morgenpost* as a result of this trip and, it seems, as part of the Kleihues-Siedler campaign for a new IBA.[50] The project was an L-shape building that filled in an empty corner with its short wing and extended along the street in front of an existing parking garage from the postwar period (Figure I.18, I.19). As a rather explicit way of joining the broken parts, the corner was monumentalized with a tower that looked like a nail piercing both wings. The hinge metaphor was unambiguously presented in Stirling's concept sketches as well (Figure I.20). Judging from the fact that the proposal was squeezed into the long and narrow site between the existing garage and the street edge, which was denounced as leftover space, the project was designed to mask the postwar façade. While imagining the options for this screen or facade, Stirling seems to have

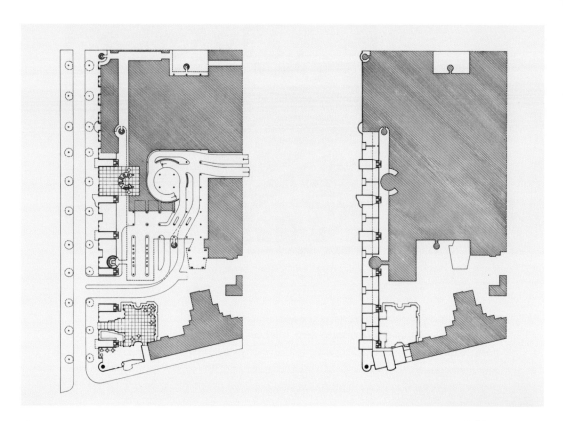

TOP: Figure I.18 James Stirling, Proposal for Meinekestrasse, Berlin, 1976. Ground plans. BOTTOM: Figure I.19 James Stirling, Proposal for Meinekestrasse, Berlin, 1976. View from the street.

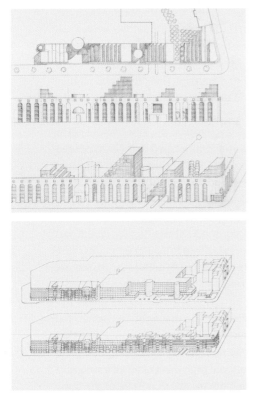

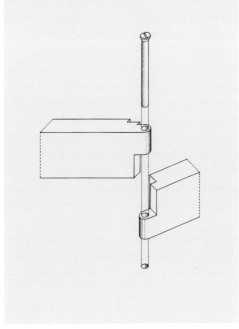

TOP: Figure I.20 James Stirling, Proposal for Meineke-strasse, Berlin, 1976. Concept sketch. LEFT: Figure I.21 James Stirling, Proposal for Meinekestrasse, Berlin, 1976. Façade alternatives.

become almost delirious, sketching choices with horizontal windows (a feature that was selected for the final project), monumental columns, pedestals, entablatures, big arcades, and ziggurats—in a way that was common during the heyday of postmodernist style (Figure I.21).[51] In his report (a German translation of which was published in the *Berliner Morgenpost*), Stirling explained his design using criteria that were very consistent with IBA Neubau ideals:

> To repair the street from the postwar damage done to it by modern architecture and commercialism (i.e. the multilevel parking garage). To restore the street to a pleasant mixed residential character. ...

> To allow the garage to function properly but to conceal its gross overscale appearance. To repair the corner. ...

> To use the established language of the street (i.e. types of windows, entrance doors, gables, balconies, etc.) and the traditional materials of the old buildings (i.e. masonry, rendering, etc.).[52]

Two days after the launch of Stirling's project, the Building Senator Harry Rostock from the Social Democratic Party (SPD), who would be influential in getting the IBA-1984 bill passed, wrote a piece in the *Berliner Morgenpost* series, praising Kleihues's and Siedler's critical writings on the postwar planning and housing policies in Berlin. He confessed that people had always celebrated the new traffic roads and bridges built between 1955 and 1970, but it was important to ask if traffic is everything: "Since 1949, we have built 500,000 new dwellings, but we have not built streets, [and] we have left the inner city to decay."[53] Given its peripheral position in a divided Germany, Berlin had to fight to regain its position as the world center of architecture, theater, opera, philharmonic orchestras, museums, and universities. A "city like Berlin will and must continue to build, or it will die."[54] Seizing the opportunity to answer his call about putting Berlin in the center of international architectural discussions, the newspaper continued its series until the end of September. Ulrich Conrads confirmed that Berlin needed to take action and implement new city planning policies, rather than just talking about "anger and mourning"; a special issue of the newspaper was published on March 22 to praise the Prager Platz projects, in which Aymonino and Krier explained their proposals; another special issue on September 23 about the projects along Berlin's canals, to which Moore, Rossi, and Peter Smithson contributed; and Kleihues, Siedler, Pehnt, and Klotz continued to contribute consistently, each eventually publishing four or five articles.[55] It took a collaborative and calculated effort on the part of architects, historians, and senators to replace the existing projects considered at the Senate with IBA-1984.

In the *Morgenpost* series, it was only Gottfried Wurche, the mayor of Tiergarten and a member of SPD, who mentioned the noncitizen issue, but he did so in a way that aimed to justify the Senate's discriminatory housing regulations for the foreigners (see the introduction). The mayor complained about the high percentage of immigrant population in the areas under his control, and he pointed out that most of the housing stock in this area consisted of small apartments and hence was not suitable for families, especially not for large noncitizen families. He also warned about the lack of "infrastructure" (the term Berlin architects used for public amenities, such as parks, playgrounds, and sports fields) and kindergartens for the high number of immigrant children. He found the ban on entry and settlement (*Zuzugsprerre*) in Kreuzberg, Tiergarten, and Wedding insufficient, and he advocated additional prohibitory measures for the "reduction of the concentration of foreigners."[56] Given that this article was published in a series edited by Kleihues, it is impossible that he or his team were unaware of these discriminatory housing regulations. However, most of the architects usually kept silent about the Senate's use of the building exhibition as a method for the social control of noncitizens.

The IBA-1984 bill was registered in the Senate on February 14, 1979, but the report written in June 1978 was already being discussed, and the Konzepta project at the intersection of Linden- and Ritterstrasse by collaborating architects under the guidance of Rob Krier's urban design had already started.

Rob Krier and the Essentialist Ethnicity of Urban Design

When *Time* magazine published an article on the recent building activity in Berlin in 1987, after Kleihues it mentioned Krier as the most influential architect, given the fact that he had designed the master plans for three blocks of IBA-1984/87.[57] Even before IBA started, the Senate had commissioned Krier to prepare the urban design for Konzepta-Ritterstrasse, an extension of which became the buildings on Schinkel-

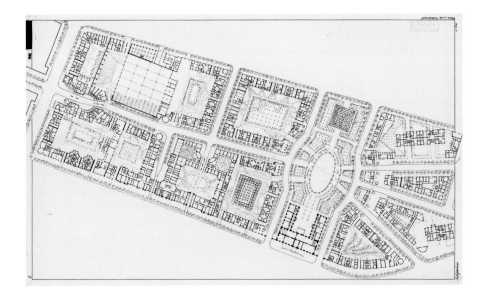

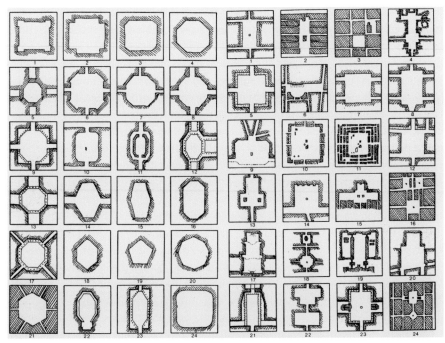

TOP: Figure I.22 Rob Krier, Entry for "Living in Friedrichstadt Competition," IBA-1984/87, Berlin, 1980.
BOTTOM: Figure I.23 Rob Krier, Matrix of urban spaces, 1979.

platz/Block 28 and became IBA Neubau's earliest initiative in Kreuzberg. Krier also undertook the urban designs for the Prager Platz and the housing ensemble with eight freestanding "urban-villas" in Southern Tiergarten (stroll 3). In addition, Krier worked on the unrealized "Ideal Plan" (1977) for Kreuzberg and entered IBA's "Living in Friedrichstadt Competition," (1980, Figure I.22) for which the jury eventually selected Hans Kollhoff's scheme out of 101 entries (stroll 1).[58] Krier's ideas on collaborative urban design and the relationship between architectural form and race or ethnicity are visible in the Konzepta and Schinkelplatz/Block 28 projects, which highlight the contradictions in open architecture during these years.

Before IBA started, Krier had probably already attracted the attention of German policy makers with his ideas on the reconstruction of the war-torn European cities—particularly his extensive project for the reconstruction of Stuttgart, presented at the XIIth Milan Triennale in 1973, San Sebastian in 1974, and London's Art Net Gallery and Stuttgart's Kunstverein in 1975. Having studied architecture in Munich, worked in Ungers's and Frei Otto's offices, and taken an assistantship position at the University of Stuttgart, Krier was best known for his 1975 book *Stadtraum*, published in 1979 in English with a foreword by Rowe.[59] *Urban Space* was a history book and a manifesto, illustrated by the architect's proposal for Stuttgart. Krier had a precise definition of urban space: "This space is geometrically bounded by a variety of elevations. It is only the clear legibility of its geometrical characteristics and aesthetic qualities which allows us consciously to perceive external space as urban space."[60] From this perspective, the lack of urban space was one of the main reasons for criticizing postwar housing and that differentiated it from IBA's approach. The square and the street were by far Krier's two favorite types of urban spaces, and throughout the book he wrote about their possible functions, how the sections and elevations of buildings around them affected their qualities—and, most important, the typology of their ground plans. The book diagrammed possible permutations of the intersections of squares and streets, such as centered, off-center, lateral, and oblique intersections of one or more streets with a square. Krier asserted that the three main groups of urban spaces derived from the basic shapes of the square, circle, and triangle: "A clear, geometric urban spatial form calls for architecture of extreme delicacy and high quality," he wrote, and he drew diagrams illustrating the geometries of famous historical urban spaces in European cities such as Florence, London, Paris, Stuttgart, Turin, and Vienna.[61] He expanded his matrix based on successful historical examples, such as rectangular, circular, or triangular urban squares with central buildings; urban squares with isolated buildings introduced from the side, obliquely or laterally; urban spaces that were angled, divided, added to, or superimposed on each other; composite urban spaces with more complex geometries and larger scales; and so on (Figure I.23). The subsequent chapters made a case against the erasure of this tradition of urban space that had resulted from the town planning practice in the twentieth century. Krier advocated for the reconstruction of this historical heritage.

Krier's insistence on urban design as the collaboration of different architects designing small components of a larger whole must have stemmed from his belief that much of the success of historical urban spaces depended on their scale—another shortcut for criticizing the megastructural tendencies of the 1960s: "Streets and squares on a small scale have for thousands of years proved that they work ideally as zones of communication. By 'small scale' I mean distances easily covered on foot, or (where height is concerned) the number of levels accessible by stair. ... With their superior view over town and country side, many [modernist tower blocks] have become physically comfortable islands of loneliness."[62] When I interviewed him years later, Krier's major critique of some of his colleagues—including Rossi, Hans Kollhoff and Arthur Ovaska, and Klei-

Figure I.24 Rob Krier, Ideal Plan for South Friedrichstadt, Berlin, 1977.

hues himself—was directed at their decision to design single large buildings for their IBA projects. These "worked against the city much as a typical modernist" building would have done, in Krier's eyes, because they intervened in the city fabric "with one solution."[63] Instead, the design of any urban initiative with the collaboration of multiple designers seems to be the most characteristic definition of urban design as a discipline, according to Krier. "Kleihues is an architectural designer, not an urban designer," he said, and Rossi's "urban designs are not urban, they are buildings."[64]

Putting the idea of urban design as collaboration to the test, four architecture teams collaborated under the artistic direction of Krier for Konzepta-Ritterstrasse: Hielscher/ Mügge, Gruppe 67, Krier's own office, and Planungskollektiv Nr. 1. The initiative was proposed in 1974, but the project did not materialize until 1977, after which it was endorsed by important architectural historians and critics of the time, including Klotz, Dieter Hoffmann-Axthelm, and Peter Rumpf, who wrote about it in daily newspapers and professional journals. In the booklet, Konzepta-Ritterstrasse was presented with testimonies of the residents, probably edited for self-serving purposes, but nonetheless driven by an ethos that slowly disappeared from IBA Neubau, while it remained central for Altbau.[65] For example, a member of an immigrant family with four children living in one of the units designed by Krier explained how happy they were with the garden, the terrace, and the fact that the children could play in the Hof for hours.[66] Despite their small size, their bedrooms were functional. The residents wanted to collect money to buy a grill and organize a festival in their common areas.[67] Other families mentioned the pleasures of living in this neighborhood, after moving out of the unrenovated Altbau buildings in Kreuzberg's SO 36 area and Neukölln or postwar housing blocks in Märkisches Viertel.

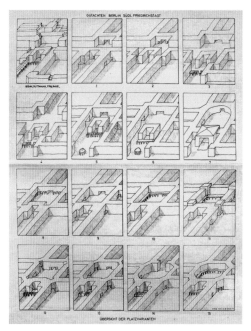

Figure I.25 Rob Krier, Variations of Schinkelplatz, Konzepta, Berlin, 1977.

After being approached by Müller in December 1977, Krier submitted a large album to the Senate that contained his "Ideal Plan" and proposals for Ritterstrasse.[68] The project also involved the reconstruction of Schinkel's Feilnerhaus (1828) and its integration into the overall urban design. In his "Ideal Plan," Krier envisioned the future of Berlin without the wall and reconstructed the city's nineteenth-century layout (Figure I.24).[69] Krier admits that during the IBA years nobody imagined that the wall would come down any time soon. He remembers an emotional moment at a conference in Poland in 1989, when he showed his "Ideal Plan" on the same day that the wall came down: somebody wept, and there was a roar of approval from the audience.[70]

The album contained various urban designs for Block 28 that combined the Konzepta and Schinkel's building in different configurations. Feilnerhaus was treated as a detached building in a rectangular urban square, an attached one that formed the edge of a square plaza, and one that was integrated into an octagonal or an elliptical plaza (Figure I.25). The Senate opened an architectural competition for Block 28, clearly stating that Krier would coordinate the winning entries as the creator of the initial concept and that they would be compatible with the Konzepta project.[71] Krier's urban design complemented the only remaining building on the site by adding four perimeter blocks that created not only large common gardens inside, but also additional pedestrian streets and a small urban plaza at the intersection of the four blocks (Figure I.26). The square plaza was thirty meters on each side and the buildings around it were three stories high, to be integrated with Schinkel's Feilnerhaus without overwhelming it and to allow sufficient daylight to reach the plaza and surrounding interior spaces. Krier suggested naming it Schinkelplatz (Figure I.27).[72]

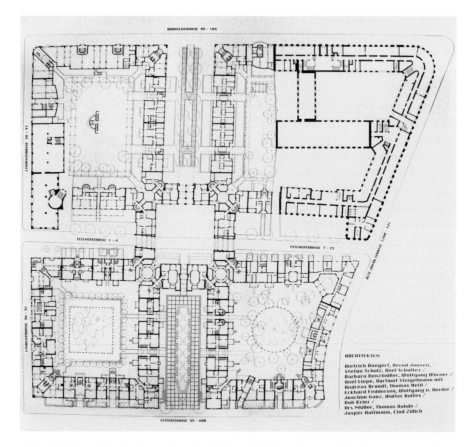

TOP: Figure I.26 Rob Krier, Block 28 (Schinkelplatz), Berlin, IBA-1984/87, 1977–84. BOTTOM: Figure I.27 Rob Krier, Schinkelplatz in Block 28, IBA-1984/87, Berlin, 1977–84.

The row buildings along the new streets were assigned to twenty different architects, including some who would become influential in the future of Berlin, such as Axel Schultes. Krier credits Müller for inviting young German architects to design different units and "initiating this kind of working together in a team."[73] The collaborating architects created different unit plans and façade variations within the framework of Krier's urban design.[74] In his proposal to the Senate, Krier had already defended a multi-authored process to avoid "monotony."[75] He further defended the collaborative process on the grounds that more jobless architects would find commissions and that a diversity of designers would create results that would allow each occupant to easily identify his or her own home from the street: "Multiplicity of differently shaped houses will once again—as in the past—constitute the image of the street."[76] The collaborating architects met every week during the design process to make sure nothing was overlooked, after realizing the admittedly incoherent results of the Konzepta project across the street. Representatives of the different architectural offices brought in their models and drawings, and a team of two or three architects montaged the drawings together. Even though Krier admitted that he could not force architects to change their designs, he wanted to make sure that he was working with those who agreed with his urban design, and the only thing he insisted on was when he "forbid" the use of the horizontal window à la Le Corbusier.[77]

If collective urban design can be achieved as a collaboration of nonhierarchically positioned architects in a given urban setting, it is one form of open architecture. In

Figure I.28 View of Schinkelplatz in Rob Krier's Block 28 for IBA-1984/87, photographed by Esra Akcan, Berlin, 2016.

68

Figure I.29 Views of new streets in Rob Krier's Block 28 for IBA-1984/87, photographed by Esra Akcan, Berlin, 2012, 2016.

inviting architects who were willing to work within the typological design method, IBA must have hoped that this model would enable collaboration and mobilize groups working hospitably together and using collective ideals. When the aesthetic unity of the façades was concerned in a building compound with multiple designers, critics were divided as to whether it was postmodern historicism or something else that combined the parts into the whole (Figure I.28). In a special issue of *AD* on "Free-Style Classicism," Charles Jencks, the editor of the issue and one of the most vocal proponents of the postmodern style, identified Krier's housing as postmodern classicism, "a hybrid of modernism and classicism," given the architect's choices in favor of palazzo orders, classical plans, symmetry, arches, and herms. However, in the same issue Gerald Blomeyer noted that many commentators were surprised when the scaffolding came down to see how "modernist" Krier's "white house" was.[78] The square that included Schinkel's Feilnerhaus was often seen as a clear reference to the baroque city, and the three façades surrounding the urban space were praised for making use of the principal classical elements in Schinkel's building.[79] In its theme issue "Abitare in città—Living in the City," the influential Italian periodical *Lotus* associated the unity achieved through collaboration with urban concerns rather than stylistic harmony: "The unity of the whole thus emerges more from references to the same themes and from having to resolve the same problems than from the use of the same language. On the façades, as on those of the compact city, the quotations range from Schinkel, cited by Krier, to the most recent episodes of European architecture" (Figure I.29).[80]

In addition to collaboration, Krier's ideas on immigration also invite a discussion of open architecture. While explaining the historical origins of urban spaces, Krier relied more on deduction than research: "In all probability the square was the first way man discovered of using urban space. ... The street is a product of the spread of a settlement once houses have been built on all available space around its central square."[81] Krier seemed convinced that these urban design principles are apparent to a designer without or before historical research: they are a priori findings of timeless and universal values, or logical conclusions. He called them "rational." Only three years after the English translation of *Urban Space* was published, Krier distilled these ideas into "Ten Theses on Architecture," which he illustrated with his Berlin projects. "These

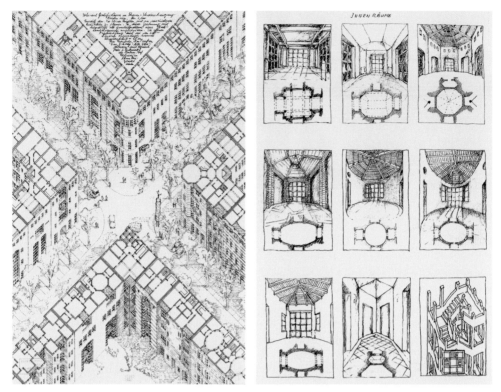

LEFT: Figure I.30 Rob Krier, Block 28, Berlin, IBA-1984/87, 1977–84. Study of apartments with central *sofa* ("Turkish house"). RIGHT: Figure I.31 Rob Krier, Block 28, Berlin, IBA-1984/87, 1977–84. Interior perspectives of apartments with central *sofa*.

principles," he wrote, "have applied since man began to plan his buildings rationally."[82] These books demonstrated Krier's hostility toward what he flattened out as modern architecture and his conviction that historical cities could teach the contemporary architects what he perceived to be timeless design principles:

> The caprices of modern architecture have become an incestuous problem for specialists. Architecture has lost its cultural role. ... The 1960s revealed the need for a more coherent theoretical approach in the social sector. It is now time for architecture to consolidate the theoretical foundation of its long-established craft, the art of building, to re-discover the basic elements of architecture and the art of composing with them. We do not need new inventions for this. In the course of history it has all been played out over and over again in countless variations across the continents.[83]

Krier's ideas on immigration revealed similar essentialist convictions, but his stance on the perceived universality or ethnicity of architectural form was quite ambiguous. Where the design of individual apartments for IBA was concerned, he took the issue of immigration seriously, but in ways that perpetuated an essentialist link between architectural form and ethnic or racial identity. He declared that he had designed the big units in his housing block at Konzepta-Ritterstrasse specifically for Turkish families:

"maisonette flats with a T-shaped layout and a glazed veranda on all sides … are reminiscent of the traditional type of Turkish dwelling. Since 80 percent of the inhabitants of Kreuzberg are Turks I hope these flats will be assigned to them."[84] Many of the unit plans in Block 28 were organized around a central *sofa* used as a living room—a recognizable element of what would be named the Turkish house in Turkey, during the early republican period and afterward (Figure I.30). In my interview with him years later, Krier credited two Turkish employees in his office and a doctoral student who wrote a dissertation on Ottoman houses as the sources of his knowledge about the ground plan typology of "Turkish houses."[85] He drew typological matrices showing variations of ground plans organized around central *sofas* and perspectives demonstrating the quality of space they promised (Figure I.31). For him, a central *sofa* in a plan was like a miniature urban space in a socially bonded city: "Every time I hear the comment that my plans have to be inhabited by a happy family. A living room is where everyone had to meet, like a piazza. People have to live together with a certain generosity."[86] In this same interview, Krier criticized Kleihues for not exhibiting the interiors of apartments, probably because he was not concerned about who would live in them: "Nobody discussed the immigration issue seriously. … Kleihues was not interested in producing good flats."[87]

Krier made use of a perceived essentialist link between nation and form to defend his urban design decisions. Praising what he termed the "European city" for the quality of its pedestrian scale and urban morphology, he said: "The intimate and 'introverted' quality of the square and the adjacent block structure will undoubtedly facilitate the initial process of adaption by its first habitants. Moreover, many Turks live in Kreuzberg and I am convinced that this ethnic group still remembers, having learnt the lesson in their homeland, how to feel at home in a square and a street."[88] Krier offered to provide the urban spaces of a "European city" to defend the rights of those who were deemed non-European and to facilitate their "adaption" to their newly inhabited spaces. However, he also claimed that the European city had a universal significance: "The term 'European city' means the traditional city. … Nobody invented the European city, it could be found in different parts of the world."[89] These statements demonstrate Krier's ambiguity about whether Turkish immigrants were bearers of ethnically different or universal values about urban and architectural spaces. In any case, it seems that there was hardly any opportunity to discuss these sorts of questions among the IBA Neubau circles. In this book, I argue that open architecture can be actualized when a new ethics of hospitality includes the refugee or stateless person, who embodies the limit that in turn exposes the insufficiencies of the ongoing human rights regime. Krier raised the issue of noncitizenship during Kruezberg's urban renewal, but the lack of interest in it among architectural circles at this time seems to have foreclosed a discussion. Additionally, Krier's own essentialist convictions left many questions about the relation between form and ethnicity unanswered.

The Critical Reception of IBA-1984/87

Once the first competitions were announced, celebratory articles about IBA-1984/87 poured out in the national and international press. In addition to the German journals *Bauwelt*, *Arch Plus*, and *Deutsche Bauzeitung*, periodicals in English, Italian, French, and Japanese—including *Architectural Design*, *Review*, *Record*, *A + U*, *Architecture*, AIA

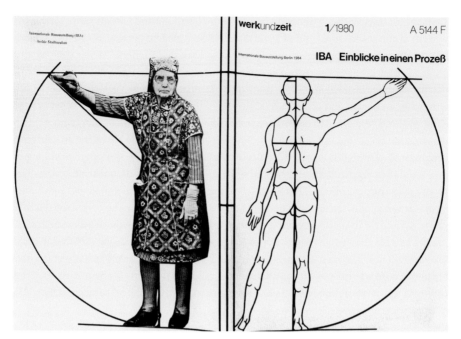

Figure I.32 Cover of *Werk und Zeit*, 1980.

Journal, *Lotus*, *Casabella*, and *Architecture d'aujourd'hui* all had at least one issue on IBA. Promoting IBA-1984/87 as a commitment to public housing, the international architectural community was astonishingly neglectful of IBA Neubau's impact on the noncitizen population, viewing the worker as only an abstract economic category and failing to come to terms with the new forces of multinational capital and international immigration. One exception was the journal *Werk und Zeit*, whose front cover for the first 1980 issue reproduced half of IBA's official logo with the ideal man who showed off his fine, sculpted muscles, while the back cover greeted the readers with the skeptical eyes of an ethnically ambiguous woman who wore working gloves (Figure I.32).

The few criticisms in architectural press were usually directed toward IBA Neubau's urban design approach and its perceived revivalism. In the spring of 1979, the Association of Architects and Engineers of Berlin requested three meetings with the Senate to deliberate on IBA and criticized the lack of a truly democratic process as a result of the shortcutting of the discussion time and the lack of transparency in architectural competitions with invited participants.[90] In the first of his several short pieces about IBA that Conrads published in *Bauwelt*, he raised a similar concern about the lack of public discussion on the overarching approach to urban renewal for the whole area before the launching of the architectural competitions for individual sites. Many questions remained unanswered: Was it appropriate to rebuild the nineteenth-century city using what Conrads called a brutalist and neorationalist aesthetic? Was the Berlin block still an adequate residential form for the lifestyles and needs of the people currently living in Berlin, or were there alternatives?[91] German architects who would become established names also had concerns: Meinhard von Gerkan complained that IBA had invited "international exponents of Postmodernism, who have their names down elsewhere on the hit-lists of Anti-Functionalism." He was also concerned that German architects, with the exception of Ungers, had been pushed to take only "sub-ordinate roles" if they were to build for IBA at all.[92] And looking back at the process in 1989, Matthias Sauerbruch criticized the reduction of the idea of urban renewal into the practice of redrawing the city's map.[93]

Substantial points were raised by critics outside of Germany as well. Marco de Michelis started an article with a quote from Walter Benjamin—"Baudelaire spoke the cruel words: A city is transformed more quickly than a human heart"—and went on to raise doubts about IBA's tendency to follow the sterile reconstruction policies that were be-ing practiced in other German cities at the expense of Berlin's experimental traditions. Reconstructing the nineteenth-century ground plan by stitching the wounds of war with infill buildings was a safe but "defeatist" strategy that disavowed sudden change as the identifying attribute of the modern metropolis and prioritized "reasonableness" over new opportunities: "The danger of the IBA's design strategy lies in a temptation to try and pacify a complex and destroyed city. … The pacific reduction of Berlin's ur-ban form to limpid rules … means sacrificing too wide a range of experiences."[94] De Michelis seemed so concerned about the thin border between critical reconstruction and nostalgic denial of modernity that he glorified destructive creation: "Isn't precise-ly this history of destruction and transformation the very essence of the history of the contemporary metropolis? Isn't it precisely the instability, the changeability, the aggressiveness of the strategy of domination that marks out the metropolis from the ancient city, that makes it a 'city without borders'?"[95]

Not unexpectedly, Bruno Zevi voiced another of the most substantive criticisms. The Italian historian criticized IBA for misrepresenting the achievements of the modern movement in architecture, for being nostalgic about the historical city, and most strikingly for "betraying the lessons of Scharoun."[96] Zevi probably had in mind Hans Scharoun's collective plan for Berlin and his postwar practice that embraced what the historian must have perceived as organicist buildings with angular geometries, decen-tralized spaces, and fragmented masses as opposed to the monumental Nazi edifices with their totalizing compositions, aggrandizing scale, and glorified classicism. As a matter of fact, in debates that were carried into daily newspapers, the Scharoun So-ciety publicly criticized IBA Neubau for selecting a "specific group of architects who dominate … Berlin," Kleihues for "importing postmodernism" with "merely ornamen-tal, aestheticizing and fashionable" buildings, and Krier for the unfunctionality of his IBA buildings.[97] Kleihues responded to Zevi's criticism, pointing out the paradox in the historian's endorsement of an uncritical reception of the past—in this case, modern-ism—while accusing IBA of doing the same thing. Instead, IBA was open to the criti-cal interpretation of both historical and modern architectures, Kleihues argued: "The scope of people we invite to competitions will prove that we are very pluralistic and open minded, but we cannot please everyone."[98] Thomas Maldonado raised doubts about IBA's claims to have developed models applicable to the reconstruction of cities in general, because such claims ignored Berlin's special status as a divided city during the Cold War. With two ideologies and citizens of two different countries, "Berlin lacks the minimal cohesive features underlying the idea of a city."[99]

Figure I.33 Views from street and Hof-garden in Rob Krier's Block 28 for IBA-1984/87, photographed by Esra Akcan, Berlin, 2012.

Moreover, Rowe wrote an open letter that was included in IBA's *Modelle für eine Stadt*, arguing that public housing was a trivial program for the reconstruction of the city. "No city can be made out of *Sozialwohnungsbauten* alone. The great city requires something in excess of *that*," Rowe said, criticizing IBA for falling short on constructing public realms in Hannah Arendt's sense.[100] Rowe also raised questions about IBA's overemphasis on large and generous courtyards inside blocks, at the expanse of a more organized attention to the design of the street life, where Arendtian political action could take place. Paradoxically, he was also concerned about the public accessibility of the large gardens inside blocks. The "potential problems of security terrify me," he wrote, suggesting the privatization of these shared green spaces with fences.[101] Clelland raised similar questions. IBA's collective plan, which provided the framework for the collaborating architects of housing, narrowed the possibility of political actions in a polis, because it provided spaces for "residing" (*wohnen*) rather than "living" (*leben*). This turned the city into a conglomeration of private lives, not a place of public action.[102]

Private Is Political: Hatice Uzun on Rob Krier

The Arendtian public sphere that Rowe and Clelland referred to would not have been unknown to their readers. Frampton had published an essay titled "The Status of Man and the Status of His Objects" in 1979, in which he brought Arendt's distinction between the political and the private to architects' attention.[103] As opposed to its everyday use today as a synonym of governing, the word "political" in its Aristotelian and Arendtian sense referred to actions for the betterment of humanity undertaken through civic engagement. Truly political actions, according to this view, are neither labor nor work; they are not instruments for gaining power or wealth; they are free

Figure I.34 View from Hof-garden in Rob Krier's Block 28 for IBA-1984/87, photographed by Esra Akcan, Berlin, 2012.

from concerns about ruling or being ruled. Frampton had repeated Arendt's opinion that the political had declined into the social in the modern world, and her call for a new public sphere—which would be achieved, in his view, with the reconstruction of urban spaces for public appearance.

However, there is something seriously misleading in treating public housing as something that is not political because it is connected to the private, in the Arendtian sense. That approach disavows the possibility of creating the public sphere through social housing—something that was relevant especially in the case of Kreuzberg, given the contested citizenship of residents in the area. When Arendt suggested that the social had replaced the political in the modern world with the rise of individualism at the expense of the public sphere, she was identifying the rise of the social as the blurring of the conceptual distinction between the private and the political, between the household and the polis. This meant the contamination of the public realm (the political in its ideal sense, but the social in its modern sense) by the values of the household, creating a community whose members lived together and defined its rules but who also formed boundaries based on identity, status, kinship, or favoritism. The household as the private realm in this sense does not translate literally into modern housing. Therefore, it does not follow that the functional program of public housing conceives of the city as a private realm devoid of political action. On the contrary, in this book I suggest that there is hardly anything more political than discussing the effect of public housing on the private lives of its noncitizen and mostly female residents.

Discussing the private politically also plays a role in feminist architectural history with the writing of more women into architecture as resident architects who analyze

Figure I.35 Views of an apartment with a central *sofa* in Block 28 for IBA-1984/87, photographed by Esra Akcan, Berlin, 2012.

and appropriate their living spaces, and as individuals who confirm the openness of architecture by participating in its mutation. While there is no inherent reason for women to be associated with the house interior, and while I want, as do many feminist historians, to undo such essentialist characterizations, the fact that women have historically been seen and constructed as agents of domesticity makes them central subjects of open architectural history. Whether a famous design succeeds or fails according to a noncitizen woman might be a matter of indifference to its architect. However, it is a central topic for open architectural history, which is by definition unfinished because other residents will write their own necessarily partial and contingent stories.

I found Hatice Uzun through two other women whom I met the day I sneaked into one of the four Hof-gardens of Block 28 (Figure I.33). After spending a long enough time

Figure I.36 View of an apartment with a central *sofa* in Block 28 for IBA-1984/87, photographed by Esra Akcan, Berlin, 2012.

wandering in the garden, writing notes, taking photographs, and trying to talk to the two sisters-in-law who were watching their children play, I was invited to sit at their table, where Uzun later joined us. Uzun had moved to Berlin from Varto, Turkey, in 1973 with her children (then five years old and six months old). They were joining her husband, who had arrived with the guest worker program six years earlier. By the time I met her, all of her family had left Varto, which she remembers as the most beautiful place she had ever seen, albeit full of tensions between the Kurdish Sunni and Alevi population. She started working in Berlin in 1974, first as a cleaner for a year, then in a can factory. She then took a break to look after her children, including two who had been born in Germany. In 1988, she started working again—this time as a state employee in a kindergarten—and continued to do so for eighteen and a half years. When she arrived in Berlin in 1973, she had lived with her husband and their two children in a back-facing one-room apartment with a small kitchen, a coal-burning stove, and no toilet in Kreuzberg's Dresdener Strasse, which she remembers as a "disaster."[104] A year later, they moved to a front-facing two-room apartment in the same building, which they had to share with an old German woman until she died.

It was a relief to move to Block 28, designed by Krier, where Uzun found an apartment in the early 1990s through her son's architect girlfriend, who had grown up there. Uzun still keeps in touch with her son's ex-girlfriend and her extended family, who are now neighbors in Block 28, and they occasionally get together in the garden for tea and snacks just like the day I met them. The architect has quite a few memories about growing up in this IBA building, where her family had been among the first tenants. As a matter of fact, she remembers coming with her parents to check out the apartment when it was still under construction; the stairs had not yet been built and they

Figure I.37 Views of Uzun's kitchen and living room in Block 28
for IBA-1984/87, photographed by Esra Akcan, Berlin, 2012.

had to find roundabout ways to see the bedrooms on the upper floor. Even as a child,
she could tell that this was a special place because of the many architectural tourists
who showed up on their doorsteps and in the Hof-garden (Figure I.34). She remembers visiting the child-friendly IBA-exhibition across the street from their building on
Lindenstrasse, where there was a big aquarium in front of the glass façade, and playful
swings for children. She also remembers the time when their neighbor cut her abusive
husband's body into pieces with the saw that she had borrowed from her mother.[105]

When I met her, Uzun was living in a unit facing one of the four streets of Block 28,
created by Krier's urban design and executed by a collaborating architect, but she had
previously lived in an apartment with a central *sofa* designed for the same block by
Krier himself. Every resident I talked to mentioned the fact that the floor plan of each
unit is different in Block 28, even though they look similar from the outside.[106] For
Krier, this insistence on making every apartment different was nothing short of reviv-
ing "the richness of our European cities" and a "culture of plans that is more or less lost
today," as confirmed by the "very rational and very boring" units jamming contemporary publications.[107] However, the residents do not find all of the apartments equally
successful: those with open bedrooms are unrealistic, it is impossible to take a shower
standing in some units because of their sloping ceilings, and some windows are inaccessible for cleaning from the inside.[108]

Uzun also thinks her current apartment compares poorly to her previous unit with
the central *sofa* designed by Krier at Alte Jakobstrasse. She put me in touch with the
Turkish family who moved into this apartment after she left, and I visited them on a
day when they were preparing to participate in the local street market. They were kind
enough to let me take photographs despite the hectic rush in the house and the mess
created by the cutting, chopping, and cooking of food to sell in the market. For some
reason, it was not the more carefully framed images showing the salient features of
the apartment—such as the big *sofa* used as the living room, the balcony that faces
both the outdoor garden and the inner courtyard, the view of the interwoven courtyard and Hof-garden from the living room, and the deep white beam voided with a

Figure I.38 View from Uzun's balcony in Block 28 for IBA-1984/87, photographed by Esra Akcan, Berlin, 2012.

circle and a square seen from the window (Figure I.35)—that captured my attention as I wrote these pages. Instead, it was a photograph that I took almost accidentally from the central *sofa* (Figure I.36). The first object that strikes the eye in this photograph is the high-definition television, whose screen shows a couple kissing each other in the famous Turkish TV show "Adını Feriha Koydum" (in English, "I named her Feriha"). Many other objects may also make one believe that this apartment is in Turkey, such as the *tespih* (rosary) hung on the back wall, the large carpets, the tulle curtains, the analog wall clock that looks like it has just escaped from an old movie set, and the family photos surrounding the TV screen. Almost all of the other objects are common enough to have come from almost anywhere, including the ceiling lamp, the white IKEA wardrobe and closet with neatly placed coffee mugs and plates behind its glass flaps, the vacuum cleaner, the surge protector, the artifical flowers, and the notebook on the dresser. Built-in features give away the location, though, including the thermostat and window frames that are characteristic of Berlin apartments. One can see that the three distinct rooms in the photograph are intertwined with each other by virtue of the fact that the central *sofa* serves as both the living room and the heart of the apartment because it connects the different parts. Krier referred to sociability as an attribute of the "Turkish house," and the residents did not fail to comment to me on the sociable everyday life created by passing through the central *sofa* to go from one room to another.

In contrast to her previous apartment, Uzun had a long list of complaints about her current unit and modifications she had to make with her own money. As she realized after moving in, the plastic floor had accumulated so much dirt over the years that it took her days to clean even with her professional skills. The toilet room was so misplaced that one could hear every detail happening inside from the living room. The kitchen was so small that no refrigerator would fit in, but it accommodated a useless small cellar (*Kammer*) inside. She enlarged the kitchen by demolishing this cellar with the help of her son, changed the kitchen door to make it possible to bring in large appliances, and painted all the cupboards. She built a floor-to-ceiling sliding partition out of white, delicate, semi-transparent fabric, cut into pieces of 50 centimeters in length, which provides a modifiable screen to separate her sleeping and living spaces (Figure I.37). She often sits on her narrow balcony to watch the street, and she has a view of the arched gate in Krier's Konzepta building (Figure I.38).[109] Using body language as well as words, she describes her ideal house, which is not too different from the type with a central *sofa* that she used to live in:

> If I were an architect like you, I would draw a beautiful plan. How would I draw it? First of all, the toilet and bathroom must be placed far away from the living room and kitchen. They would not be all muddled up like in here. The living room, the bedroom, and the kitchen would all have separate doors, opening up to the salon. In Turkey, they call the living room a salon; I call the circulation space a salon, and they don't understand me. This salon would be a large space, where all doors open up.[110]

That one would expect an architect and a resident have the exact same aspirations about an urban space is obviously unrealistic. At first sight, Krier's and Uzun's com-

Figure I.39 View of plinth with absent sculpture in Schinkelplatz of Rob Krier's Block 28 for IBA-1984/87 photographed by Esra Akcan, Berlin, 2016.

plaints about what is considered permissible at Schinkelplatz may also seem to imply a tension between their values. Krier is still spiteful for not having been able to install any of the sculptures planned for the piazza. A plinth still stands in the middle awaiting its artwork (Figure I.39). As a matter of fact, it was Krier himself who had financed, executed, and installed the crucifixion sculpture on the back façade of the Konzepta block, without the permission of any state authority (Figure I.40).[111] As an "illegal" object, this sculpture must be the first street art in the neighborhood, the graffiti inscribed on the façade by the building's architect himself. In contrast, the forbidden picnics in the shared open spaces are Uzun's biggest concern.[112] Krier's complaint about not being able to install sculptures in the urban plaza, and Uzun's not being able to have a picnic there may seem to indicate two unrelated worldviews, but both people have the same subversive instinct about the bureaucracies in urban spaces. Uzun still recalls the day when the police showed up the minute she tried to boil water to make tea at Schinkelplatz, and that memory prompts her to list all her other fears: the fear of being held by the police for having a picnic in a park, the fear of having neighbors call the police because she and her family make too much noise, and the fear of their children being taken by the police for disturbing Germans.[113]

Not even once do her words imply a sadness about poverty or homesickness, except when she talks about her children, and her regret about their education.[114] It may come as a surprise to the reader that few second-generation Turkish migrants have grown up to have important careers, compared to their German contemporaries. Like

Figure I.40 Rob Krier, Sculpture/street art and satellite dish on Rob Krier's Konzepta building, photographed by Esra Akcan, Berlin, 2016.

almost every other Turkish guest worker's child, Uzun's son was placed in the foreigner class at school, despite her attempts to find another school, agreeing to commute to a far neighborhood every day if he could only be placed in the same classroom with the citizens. Foreigner classes were common throughout West Germany in the 1980s as a way to separate citizen and noncitizen (especially Turkish) students. Even university professors endorsed this practice. In the Heidelberg Manifesto of 1982, for example, professors united against the "education problem of foreigners" ("especially those from the so-called Third World") wrote: "The integration of large masses of non-German foreigners is not possible without threatening the German people, language, culture, and religion. ... What hope do our own children have when they are being educated predominantly in classes with foreigners?"[115] Uzun's son was almost put in the class for children with learning disabilities because he could not speak proper German when they first immigrated. Had a Turkish teacher not prevented this assignment, he would not have been able to finish high school (the Gymnasium) and go on to a university college.

Uzun admits that she hardly ever goes anywhere in Berlin outside her immediate neighborhood and Kottbusser Tor in central-east Kreuzberg. When she was working, she had no free time anyway. The Cem House (the gathering place of the Alevis for religious and social activities) that she visits from time to time is also located in this area. Indeed Görlitzer Park is as far as she would go, and that is only because some old friends from Varto still lived there. She often got together with them when she used to live in Dresdener Strasse, and their children played together in the apartment—the Hof was too dangerous back then.[116] She tells me: "I feel as if I am in Turkey here [in Kreuzberg]. I came to this neighborhood when I was twenty-three and lived here for all [the rest of] my life. When I go to East Berlin, I feel like a foreigner arriving in the city for the first time." Having never lived in a big city in Turkey and with no acquaintances left in her hometown, she does not have a sense of homecoming when she visits Turkey either. Kreuzberg is the only place where she feels connected.

The evening I was returning home from my final meeting with Uzun, my ride on the U-Bahn (subway) got me wondering about who decides to become an immigrant worker. Someone who leaves her citizenship privileges by force or by choice, with the conviction that life must be better somewhere else? Someone who is ready to suffer working in tough conditions during her youth to be able to save enough for the future or to send money to her family back in her hometown? Someone who decides to live surrounded by a language that she hardly speaks, and who gradually leaves her own language as well? Someone who is optimistic enough to think that she will find more opportunities in another country, despite being deprived of citizenship rights, or someone who is pessimistic enough to prefer any unknown life to the one where she currently has rights? Someone who gives up the pleasure of ever being able to say "I often meet with my childhood friends," or someone who can be friends from a distance? Someone who regrets not having the possibility of finding a long-lost object in the house where she has lived all her life, or someone who does not want to be weighed down by such long-standing spatial memories? While any of these questions were valid, they only scratched the surface of the complex migrant experience.

1 Emine Sevgi Özdamar, *Aynadaki Avlu*, trans. Esen Tezel (Istanbul: YKY, 2012), 37. All translations from publications and interviews are mine unless otherwise indicated. **2** "Die Türken kommen: Rette sich wer kann," *Der Spiegel*, July 30, 1973. Translated as: "The Turks Are Coming! Save Yourself If You Can!," trans. David Gramling, in *Germany in Transit: Nation and Migration 1955–2005*, ed. Deniz Göktürk, David Gramling, and Anton Kaes (Berkeley: University of California Press, 2007), 110–11. **3** Rita Chin and Heide Fehrenbach, "What's Race Got to Do with It? Postwar German History in Context," in *After the Nazi State: Difference and Democracy in Germany and Europe*, ed. Rita Chin, Geoff Eley, Heide Fehrenbach, and Atina Grossmann (Ann Arbor: University of Michigan Press, 2009), 1–29. **4** Ruth Mandel, *Cosmopolitan Anxieties: Turkish Challenges to Citizenship and Belonging in Germany* (Durham, NC: Duke University Press, 2008), 99. **5** Rita Chin, *The Guest Worker Question in Postwar Germany* (Cambridge: Cambridge University Press, 2007), 16. **6** Ayhan Kaya, *Sicher in Kreuzberg: Constructing Diasporas: Turkish Hip Hop Youth in Berlin* (Bielefeld, Germany: Transcript Verlag, 2001); Mandel, *Cosmopolitan Anxieties*; Carla Elizabeth MacDougall, "Cold War Capital: Contested Urbanity in West Berlin, 1963–1989," PhD diss., Rutgers University, 2011. **7** In 1978, these focal points were declared to be Linden-/Ritterstrasse, Friedrichstrasse, Askanischer Platz, Kemperplatz, Mariannenplatz, Lützowplatz, Prager Platz, Hafen Tegel, Altstadt Spandau. "Vorlage – zur Beschlußfassung über die Vorbereitung und Durchführung einer Internationalen Bauausstellung in Berlin im Jahre 1984." Abgeordnetenhaus von Berlin. 7. Wahlperiode. Drucksache 7/1352. 30.06.1978. I take the translations from this text's translation by the Senate itself: Der Senator für Bau und Wohnungswesen, "Berlin: IBA" Report, Berlin. n.d. German version: 1978. 23–24. IBA-Akten, B 78/014, Landesarchiv, Berlin, Germany [hereafter Landesarchiv]. "Internationale Bauausstellung Berlin 1984," *Bauwelt*, vol. 69, no. 26 (14 July 1978): 1005. **8** Der Senator für Bau und Wohnungswesen, "Berlin: IBA,"18. **9** Ibid., 13–14. **10** Ibid., 11. Vittorio Magnago Lampugnani mentions a report prepared by Dietmar Grötzebach and Bernd Jansen in October 1977 that listed these six goals, which remained unchanged in the Senate's bill ("How to Put Contradiction into Effect," *Architectural Review*, September 1984, 25–27). **11** Vittorio Magnago Lampugnani, "Architectural Exhibitions: A Fragmentary Historical Survey for Europe and the USA," in *Erste Projekte: Internationale Bauausstellung Berlin 1984/87: Die Neubaugebiete – Dokumente, Projekte*, vol. 2 (Berlin: Quadriga Verlag, 1981), 30–55. Also see Vittorio Magnago Lampugnani, "Die Innenstadt als Wohnort: ein Modell für Metropolen," in *Das Neue Berlin: Für einen Städtebau mit Zukunft*, ed. Dankwart Guratzsch (Berlin: Gebr. Mann Verlag, 1987), 13–15, and "The Berlin Tradition of Architectural Exhibitions," *AD* 53, nos. 1–2 (1983): 10–14. **12** *Erste Projekte: Internationale Bauausstellung Berlin 1984/87: Die Neubaugebiete – Dokumente, Projekte*, vol. 2; Josef Paul Kleihues, *750 Jahre Architektur und Städtebau in Berlin: Die Internationale Bauausstellung im Kontext der Baugeschichte Berlins* (Stuttgart, Germany: Verlag Gerd Hatje, 1987); "750 Years of Archi-

tecture and Urban Planning," IBA Exhibition Brochure, 1987. IBA-Akten, B91/062, Landesarchiv; *750 Jahre Berlin. Das Programm*. IBA-Akten, A 87/054, Landesarchiv. **13** On April 12, 1983, the Senate released the following list of twenty-three exhibitions and events to take place in 1984 (thirty new venues were added in 1984): "Idee Prozeß Ergebnis" Martin Gropius Bau; IBA vor Ort; Städtisches Wohnen; Symposium: Architektur zwischen Individualismus und Konvention; Friedrich Gilly; Kreuzberger Mischung; Symposium & Ausstellung: Kooperatives Planen, Bauen und Wohnen im Kiez; Schöne neue Welt; Initiativen vor Ort; Die gebauten Beispiele; Internationaler Vergleich; Bestandssicherung von Wohnungen in gründerzeitlichen Stadtquartieren; Ein Städtevergleich; Internationaler Kongress Demokratie als Bauherr; Kooperatives Bauen; Stadtstruktur, Stadtgestalt, Bauforum; Innerstädtische Wohnquartiere der Dritten Welt im Vergleich; Die Zukunft der Metropolen: Das Beispiel Berlin; Vier Berliner Großsiedlungen der Weimarer Republik; UIA-Architekturwoche in Berlin; UIA-Ausstellung Studentenarbeiten; UIA-Ausstellung: Bauen mit einfachen Mitteln; Stadt-Analyse: Stadterneuerung; 7th Congress of UIFA (International Union of Architects and Planners). See "Internationale Bauausstellung Berlin Konzeption und Programm für 1984" *Bauwelt* 19, vol. 74, (May 1983): 733–34. For a list of the thirty venues added in 1984, see IBA, *Report Year '84. Idea Process Result* [Promotion Brochure], IBA-Akten, B84/036, Landesarchiv. **14** Many of these exhibitions also had extensive catalogs. See, for example, *Idee Prozeß Ergebnis: Die Reparatur und Rekonstruktion der Stadt* (Berlin: IBA, 1984); Vittorio Magnago Lampugnani, ed. *Das Abenteuer der Ideen: Architektur und Philosophie seit der industriellen Revolution* (Berlin: Frölich and Kaufmann, 1984); Karl-Heinz Fiebig, Dieter Hoffmann-Axthelm, and E. Knödler-Bunte, eds., *Kreuzberger Mischung: Die innerstädtische Verflechtung von Architektur, Kultur und Gewerbe* (Berlin: IBA, Verlag Ästhetik und Kommunikation, 1984); Josef Paul Kleihues, ed., *750 Jahre Architektur und Städtebau in Berlin: Die Internationale Bauausstellung im Kontext der Baugeschichte Berlins* (Stuttgart, Germany: Verlag Gerd Hatje, 1987). IBA also published extensive catalogs of the buildings designed and constructed for the building exhibition. See Josef Paul Kleihues, *Internationale Bauausstellung Berlin 1984/87: Die Neubaugebiete – Dokumente, Projekte* (Stuttgart, Germany: Verlag Gerd Hatje, 1981–93), 7 vols.; *In der Luisenstadt, Studien zur Stadtgeschichte von Berlin-Kreuzberg* (Berlin: IBA, 1983); Vittorio Magnago Lampugnani, ed., *Modelle für eine Stadt* (Berlin: IBA, 1984); *Remisen in der Stadterneuerung* (Berlin: IBA, 1985); Marco de Michelis et al., *La Ricostruzione della Città: Berlino-IBA 1987* (Milan: Electa, 1985); Heinrich Klotz and Josef Paul Kleihues, eds., *International Building Exhibition Berlin 1987* (New York: Rizzoli, 1986); *Internationale Bauausstellung Berlin 1987: Projektübersicht* (Berlin: IBA, 1987); Dankwart Guratzsch, ed., *Das Neue Berlin: Für einen Städtebau mit Zukunft* (Berlin: Gebr. Mann Verlag, 1987); Dieter Hoffmann-Axthelm, *Baufluchten: Beiträge zur Rekonstruktion der Geschichte Berlin-Kreuzbergs* (Berlin: IBA, 1987); Gernot Nalbach and Johanne Nalbach, *Berlin Modern Architecture: Exhibition Catalogue* (Berlin: STERN, 1989). **15** "150,000 interessierten sich für die Bau-Ausstellung," *Berliner Morgenpost*, August 29, 1987. **16** Günter Schlusche, interview by the author, November 8, 2016, Berlin, in English, 00:14:04–00:15:59, 01:21:30. Hildebrand Machleidt, interview by the author, July 12, 2012, Berlin, in German. Both audio and video recordings of these interviews are in the author's collection. **17** Josef Paul Kleihues, "Aspekte der Berliner Stadtplanung nach dem 2.Weltkrieg," *Baumeister* 84, no. 9 (1984): 29–37, "Die IBA vor dem Hintergrund der Berliner Architektur- und Stadtplanung des 20.Jahrhunderts," in *Modelle für eine Stadt*, ed. Vittorio Magnago Lampugnani (Berlin: IBA, 1984), 24–36, and "From the Destruction to the Critical Reconstruction of the City: Urban Design in Berlin after 1945," in *Berlin–NY: Like and Unlike*, ed. Josef Paul Kleihues and Christina Rathgeber (New York: Rizzoli, 1993), 395–409. **18** Kleihues, "From the Destruction to the Critical Reconstruction of the City," 399. **19** Josef Paul Kleihues, "Architektur als Sehnsucht: grenzenlos. Die Architektur, das wollte ich sagen, bedarf unser aller Pflege," in *Erste Projekte: Internationale Bauausstellung Berlin 1984/87: Die Neubaugebiete – Dokumente, Projekte*, vol. 2 (Berlin: Quadriga Verlag, 1981), 61. **20** Kleihues, "From the Destruction to the Critical Reconstruction of the City," 405. **21** Quoted in Vittorio Magnago Lampugnani and Gerwin Zohlen, "Città e utopia: Intervista a Wolf Jobst Siedler," *Domus*, no. 685, (July–August 1987), 20. **22** Tilmann Buddensieg, "Die Maße entscheiden. Zum Stadtbild der Internationalen Bauausstellung und des Neuen Bauens," in *Modelle für eine Stadt*, ed. Vittorio Magnago Lampugnani, (Berlin: IBA, 1984), 39–48. **23** Wolfgang Pehnt, "I B Aporien," in *Modelle für eine Stadt*, ed. Vittorio Magnago Lampugnani, (Berlin: IBA, 1984), 59. **24** Josef Paul Kleihues, "Zur Stadtentwicklung Berlins," in *Erste Projekte: Internationale Bauausstellung Berlin 1984/87: Die Neubaugebiete – Dokumente, Projekte*, vol. 2 (Berlin: Quadriga Verlag, 1981), 13–27. **25** IBA-1984, "Internationaler engerer Wettbewerb Berlin Südliche Friedrichstadt Wilhelmstraße." Competition Brief, Berlin, May 1981, p.94, 14. **26** Doug Clelland, "Berlin: An Architectural History," *AD* 53, nos. 11–12 (1983): 5–5; David Leatherbarrow, "Friedrichstadt: A Symbol of Toleration," *AD* 53, nos. 11–12 (1983): 22–31; Goerd Peschken, "The Berlin Miethaus and Renovation," *AD* 53, nos. 11–12 (1983): 49–57. **27** IBA, *Report Year '84: Idea Process Result* [Promotion Brochure], 6, IBA-Akten, B84/036, Landesarchiv. **28** "Das Abenteuer der Ideen," [Exhibition Brochure]. 1984, B 84/091, Landesarchiv. **29** Vittorio Magnago Lampugnani, *Architektur und Städtebau des 20.Jahrhunderts* (Stuttgart, Germany: Verlag Gerd Hatje, 1980). The English edition is Vittorio Magnago Lampugnani, *Architecture and City Planning in the Twentieth Century* (New York: Van Nostrand Reinhold Company, 1985). **30** Vittorio Magnago Lampugnani, ed., *L'Avventura delle Idee nell'architettura 1750–1980* (Milan, Italy: Electa 1985). **31** Lampugnani, ed *Das Abenteuer der Ideen*. **32** Lampugnani, *Architecture and City Planning in the Twentieth Century*, 8. **33** Kenneth Frampton, "The Architecture of Ideas," *Progressive Architecture* 1 (January 1985): 25–27. Quotation: 25. **34** Vittorio Magnago Lampugnani, "The Adventure of Ideas: Architecture and Philosophy since the Industrial Revolution," *A + U*, no. 177 (June

1985): 89–124. Quotation: 94. **35** Vittorio Magnago Lampugnani, "L'orizzonte del passato: La Südliche Friedrichstadt come modello virtual per una nuova cultura architettonica," *Casabella* 45, no. 471 (July–August 1981): 28–31, 63. Quotation: 63. **36** Vittorio Magnago Lampugnani, "Das Ganze und die Teile. Typologie und Funktionalismus in der Architektur des 19. und 20.Jahrhunderts," in *Modelle für eine Stadt*, ed. Vittorio Magnago Lampugnani, (Berlin: IBA, 1984), 83–117. Quotation: 116. **37** Kleihues, "Die IBA vor dem Hintergrund der Berliner Architektur- und Stadtplanung des 20.Jahrhunderts." See also Aldo Rossi, *Architecture of the City*, trans. Diane Ghirardo and Joan Ockman (Cambridge, MA: MIT Press, 1982); Wolf Jobst Siedler, Elisabeth Niggemeyer, *Die gemordete Stadt. Abgesang auf Putte und Straße, Platz und Baum* (Berlin: Herbig, 1964). **38** Claus Baldus, "Kein Leben'ges ist ein Haus, immer ist's ein Vieles," in *Josef Paul Kleihues im Gespräch* (Berlin: Ernst Wasmuth Verlag, 1996), 13–54. See also Jane Jacobs, *The Death and Life of Great American Cities* (New York: Random House, 1961). **39** Siedler and Niggemeyer, *Die gemordete Stadt*. **40** Rossi, *Architecture of the City*. **41** Josef Paul Kleihues, "Southern Friedrichstadt," in *International Building Exhibition Berlin 1987*, ed. Heinrich Klotz, and Josef Paul Kleihues (New York: Rizzoli, 1986), 128. **42** Claus Baldus, "Kein Leben'ges ist ein Haus, immer ist's ein Vieles," in *Josef Paul Kleihues im Gespräch* (Berlin: Ernst Wasmuth Verlag, 1996). Paul Kahlfeldt, Andres Lepik, and Andreas Schätzke, eds., *Josef Paul Kleihues: The Art of Urban Architecture* (Berlin: Nicolai, 2003). **43** Josef Paul Kleihues, "New Approaches to Life in the Inner City: The Row or the Block," *Architectural Design Profile*: Post-War Berlin, November–December (1982): 66–69. Quotation: 66. **44** Josef Paul Kleihues, "Architektur als Sehnsucht: grenzenlos. Die Architektur, das wollte ich sagen, bedarf unser aller Pflege," in *Erste Projekte: Internationale Bauausstellung Berlin 1984/87: Die Neubaugebiete – Dokumente Projekte*, vol. 2 (Berlin: Quadriga Verlag, 1981), 58. **45** The series ran in the *Berliner Morgenpost* from January 16 to September 30, 1977. Its articles were reproduced without images in *International Bauausstellung Berlin 1984/87: Die Neubaugebiete. Die Projekte*, vol. 7 (Stuttgart, Germany: Verlag Gerd Hatje, 1993), 324–67. Some of the original articles can be found in James Stirling Archives, AP140.S2.SS10. D1.P18, CCA, Montreal, Canada [hereafter CCA]. **46** Josef Paul Kleihues, "The IBA Influence," *Lotus* 41, no. 1 (1981): 18–20. Quotation: 20. **47** Anna Teut, "Die Stadt reparieren, nicht planieren," *Berliner Morgenpost*, January 16, 1977 (reproduced in *Internationale Bauausstellung Berlin 1984/87*, vol. 7 [Stuttgart, Germany: Verlag Gerd Hatje, 1993], 324). **48** "Modelle für eine Stadt," *Berliner Morgenpost* special edition, January 17, 1977. Meinekestrasse Folder, 1976. James Stirling Archives. AP140.S2.SS10. D1.P18. CCA. **49** Handwritten notes on paper in Meinekestrasse Folder, 1976. James Stirling Archives. AP140. S2.SS10.D1.P18. CCA. **50** An office memo indicates that Kleihues called to ask Stirling to finish the design before October 1976, so that Siedler could weigh in on the project. See Memo. 2.9.1976. Meinekestrasse Folder, 1976. James Stirling Archives. AP140.S2.SS10.D1.P18. CCA. **51** The drawings of this project can be found in James

Stirling Archives. AP140.S2.SS10.D45. CCA. **52** James Stirling and Partner, "Meineke Street, A Conceptual Remedy," Manuscript, London, October 1976. James Stirling Archives. AP140.S2.SS10.D1.P18. CCA. **53** Harry Rostock, "Meine Vorstellung von Berlin," *Berliner Morgenpost*, January 19, 1977 (reproduced in *Internationale Bauausstellung Berlin 1984/87*, vol. 7 [Stuttgart, Germany: Verlag Gerd Hatje, 1993], 331–334. Quotation: 332). **54** Ibid., 333. **55** The following items were published in the *Berliner Morgenpost* series "Modelle für eine Stadt" in 1977: J.P. Kleihues, "30 Jahre Bauen seit dem Kriege: Vorschlag für ein Reparaturprogramm" and "Programmvorschläge für eine internationale Bauausstellung zur Wiederbelebung des alten Berlins," Heinrich Klotz, "Aus den sinnlos herumstehendenden Fragmenten muss eine Imwelt werden," Wolfgang Pehnt, "Eine Reparatur aus dem Geist des Straßenraumes," and W.J. Siedler, "Nicht die Konkurse, die Fehlplanungen sind der Skandal der Baupolitik Berlins," all January 17; Ulrich Conrads, "Stadtplanung – mit Zorn und Trauer betrachtet," February 1; Carlo Aymonino, "Zentrum des Platzes mit einem Theater und baumbestandener Anhöhe," and J.P. Kleihues, "Die Chancen für eine neue Baupolitik nutzen," March 20; Heinrich Klotz, "Ruin der Berliner Baupolitik," Rob Krier, "Stadtraum-Architektur benötigt keine modischen Sensationen," Wolfgang Pehnt, "Prager Platz: Aus einer Leerstelle eine Lehrstelle machen," and W.J. Siedler, "Am Kreisel: Kunst für Fledermäuse," all March 22; Heinrich Klotz, "Stadtplaner scheuen das Wagnis: Statt Phantasie nur Mittelmaß", and Siedler, "Wo Funktionäre herrschen, erstickt die Stadt in planerischer Provinzialität," both August 13; J.P. Kleihues, "Neue Bauausstellung frei von Klischees eröffnet Berlin Chancen," Heinrich Klotz, "Die heroische Steinlandschaft im Kampf gegen eine spielerische Freizeitlandschaft," Charles Moore, "Ein Netz heiterer Wasserstraßen," Wolfgang Pehnt, "Hinweise auf ein verrottetes Industrie-Venedig," Aldo Rossi, "Vielfalt verschiedener Funktionen," and Peter Smithson, "Kletterpflanzen machen den Kanal zum Laubengang," all September 23. **56** Gottfried Wurche, "Modernisierung der Wohnviertel wird gefordert," *Berliner Morgenpost*, February 2, 1977 (reproduced in *Internationale Bauausstellung Berlin 1984/87*, vol. 7 [Stuttgart, Germany: Verlag Gerd Hatje, 1993], 337. **57** Kurt Andersen, "Rebuilding Berlin—Yet Again," *Time*, June 15, 1987, 48–50. **58** "Ergebnisprotokoll der Preisgerichtssitzung des internationalen städtebaulichen Ideenwettbewerbs 'Wohnen in der Friedrichstadt'," IBA report. B 80/029, Landesarchiv. **59** Rob Krier, *Urban Space*, trans. Christine Gzechowski and George Black (New York: Rizzoli, 1979). A short version was published as Rob Krier, "Typological and Morphological Elements of the Concept of Urban Space," *Architectural Design* 49, no. 1 (1979): 2–17. **60** Ibid., 15. **61** Ibid., 31. **62** Ibid., 170. **63** Rob Krier, interview by the author, May 29, 2012, Berlin, in English. Tape 1, 00:24:03–00:25:24. Both audio and video recordings of this interview are in the author's collection. **64** Ibid., 01:46:02. **65** Hielscher/Mügge, Gruppe 67, Rob Krier, and Planungskollektiv Nr. 1, *Experiment Wohnen – Konzepta Ritterstrasse* (Berlin: Archibook, 1981). **66** A Hof is the term used to refer to courtyards and areas surrounded by buildings in a Berlin block. One of major con-

tributions carried out in some IBA-1984/87 buildings was to turn the Hof into a large garden, even sometimes a neighborhood park. Therefore, this concept will be qualified with terms such as Hof-garden and Hof-park where appropriate. **67** Ibid., 36. **68** Rob Krier, "Städtebauliches Gutachten Berlin Südliche Friedrichstadt." Drawing Album, December 1977. B Rep 168 (Karten) IBA Neubau. 1036: Bl. 1–42. Landesarchiv. **69** Krier's "Ideal Plan" considered Mehringplatz and Unter den Linden together, ignoring the existence of the Berlin Wall. It proposed a green ring circling the area and absorbing the postwar buildings, as well as restrictions on building heights and minimum courtyard dimensions. See Rob Krier, "Berlin: South Friedrichstadt. Scheme of an "Ideal" project for the Friedrichstadt zone," *Lotus* 28, no. 3 (1980): 67–73. **70** Krier, interview by the author, 01:13:10. **71** Der Senator für Bau und Wohnungswesen, "Engerer Wettbewerb Lindenstraße-Ritterstraße-Nord Südliche Friedrichstadt Berlin-Kreuzberg," B 79/018, Landesarchiv. **72** Krier, "Berlin: South Friedrichstadt." **73** Krier interview by the author, 00:10:30–00:10:55. **74** The architects who collaborated on Block 28 under Krier's artistic direction were the partnerships of Dietrich Bangert, Bernd Jansen, Stefan Scholz, and Axel Schultes; Barbara Benzmüller and Wolfgang Wörner; Andreas Brandt, Thomas Heiss, Axel Liepe, and Hartmut Steigelmann; Eckhard Feddersen and Wolfgang von Herder; Joachim Ganz and Walter Rolfes; and Urs Müller and Thomas Rhode. For projects on Block 28, also known as Ritterstrasse housing or Schinkelplatz, see: IBA-Akten, 481 Bl 1–8, B Rep 167/865-867, 876, 1036, 1055, 1356, 1424, 1425, 1432, 1433, 1504, Landesarchiv. Rob Krier, "Ritterstrasse Housing," *Lotus* 41, no. 1 (1981): 30–41; "Grundsätze und Ziele der Internationalen Bauausstellung Berlin 1984," *Berliner Bauvorhaben* 31, no. 13 (5 May 1980): 1–9; "Wohnen in der Stadt," special issue, *Architektur + Wettbewerbe* 106, 1981; Peter Rumpf, "146 Wohnungen in Berlin, Ritterstrasse-Nord oder die gute alte Zeit des sozialen Wohnungsbaus," *Bauwelt* 74, no. 42 (11 November 1983): 1678–97; Alberto Ferlanga, "Rob Krier Schinkelplatz," *Lotus* 36, no. 3 (1983): 103–7; Joachim Ganz, "Einzelhausbebauung Linden-Ritterstrasse, Berlin-Kreuzberg," *Architektur + Werrbewerbe* 99 (May 1979). **75** Krier, "Städtebauliches Gutachten Berlin Südliche Friedrichstadt," 2. **76** Rob Krier, "City Divided into Building Plots: Dwelling on the Ritterstrasse Berlin," *Lotus* 28, no. 3 (1980): 74–82. Quotation: 75. **77** Krier, interview by the author, 00:50:46–00:55:00. **78** Gerald Blomeyer, "Robert Krier: The White House, Berlin-Kreuzberg, 1977–1980," in "Free-Style Classicism," ed. Charles Jencks, special issue, *AD* (January–February 1982): 62–67. **79** Alberto Ferlenga, "Rob Krier Schinkelplatz," *Lotus* 36, no. 3 (1983): 103–7. **80** Rob Krier, "Ritterstrasse Housing," *Lotus* 41, no. 1 (1981): 30–41. Quotation: 30. **81** Krier, *Urban Space*, 17. **82** Rob Krier, *On Architecture* (London: Academy Editions, 1982), 5. Krier exemplified his theses with one project each for Luxembourg, Stuttgart, Vienna, and Karlsruhe, but with seven projects for Berlin, home to by far the highest number of designs (three for Kreuzberg, two for Spandau, and one each for Prager Platz and Charlottenburg). **83** Ibid., 10. **84** Krier, "City Divided into Building Plot," 81. **85** Krier, interview by the author, 00:28:00–

00:32:10. **86** Ibid., 01:22:46. **87** Ibid., 00:36:00–00:39:00. **88** Krier, "Berlin: South Friedrichstadt." **89** Krier, interview by the author, 00:43:41. **90** Architekten und Ingenieur-Verein zu Berlin, "Gespräche im Reichstag zur Internationalen Bauausstellung," [also published in AIV zu Berlin zur IBA" *Baukultur,* no. 1 (1980): 51], Report. A79/028, Landesarchiv. **91** Ulrich Conrads, "betrifft," *Bauwelt* 70, no. 25 (6 July 1979): 1065. Conrads's other short pieces in *Bauwelt* were published in volume 74, numbers 14 and 15 (pages 609 and 61, respectively) and in volume 75, number 21 (page 873). **92** Meinhard von Gerkan, "Germany: Architecture from Frying Pan to Fire," *Architectural Review* 169, no. 1012 (June 1981): 331–333. Quotation: 332. **93** Matthias Sauerbruch, "Berlin," *Architecture Today,* no. 1 (September 1989): 14. **94** Marco de Michelis, "The Myth of Phoenix: The Case of the IBA 1984, Berlin," *Lotus* 33, no. 4 (1981): 5–19. Quotation:19. **95** Ibid., 11. **96** Bruno Zevi, "An Open Letter on the Internationale Bauausstellung Berlin 1984," *L'architettura* 27, no. 7 (1981): 386–89. **97** "Besorgnis und Genugtuung über die Entwicklung des Stadtbilds," *Der Tagesspiegel,* November 19, 1985; fa, "IBA-Bauten: Fensterlos und kurvig," *Berliner Morgenpost,* September 29, 1985. **98** Josef Paul Kleihues, "Wandering So as Not to Go Astray: Interview with J. P. Kleihues," *Domus* 623 (December 1981): 29–31. **99** Thomas Maldonado, "Berlino 1984," *Casabella* 471, Year: XLV (July–August 1981): 9. **100** Colin Rowe, "Ein offener Brief zur verschwundenen Öffentlichkeit," in *Modelle für eine Stadt,* ed. Vittorio Magnago Lampugnani (Berlin: IBA, 1984), 144. See also Hannah Arendt, *The Human Condition* (Chicago: University of Chicago Press, 1958). **101** Rowe, "Ein offener Brief zur verschwundenen Öffentlichkeit," 139. **102** Doug Clelland, "Architecture in Progress," *AD* 53, nos. 1–2 (1983): 2–4. **103** Kenneth Frampton, "The Status of Man and the Status of His Objects," in Kenneth Frampton, *Labor Work and Architecture* (New York: Phaidon, 2002, or. 1979), 24–44. **104** Hatice Uzun, interview by the author, May 26, 2012, Berlin, in Turkish, Tape 3, 00:01:11. Both audio and video recordings of this interview are in the author's collection. **105** Hatice Uzun, interview by the author (with Deniz G.), May 18, 2012, Berlin, in Turkish. Tape 2. **106** Gonca G., interview by the author, May 18, 2012, Berlin, in Turkish. Tape 1, 2:40 (an audio recording of this interview is in the author's collection); Uzun, interview by the author (with Deniz G.) Tape 2, 00:18:23. **107** Krier, interview by the author, 00:55:50– 00:56:00; 01:25:43. **108** Uzun, interview by the author (with Deniz G.), Tape 2, 00:18:23–00:20:20. **109** Uzun, interview by the author, Tape 3, 00:40:06–00:46:10. **110** Ibid., 00:56:35–00:58:20. **111** Krier, interview by the author, 01:31:21–01:34:09. **112** Uzun, interview by the author, Tape 5, 00:11:45. **113** Ibid., Tape 3, 00:25:00–00: 28:35. **114** Ibid., 01:00:46. **115** "Heidelberg Manifesto," trans. Tes Howell, in *Germany in Transit: Nation and Migration,* ed. Deniz Göktürk, David Gramling, and Anton Kaes (Berkeley: University of California Press, 2007), 111–13. Originally published in *Frankfurter Rundschau* (4 March 1982): 112, 113. **116** Uzun, interview by the author, Tape 5, 00:10:14.

STROLL 1

From Schinkelplatz to Checkpoint Charlie

That one could discover a microcosm of the contemporary Western architectural debates simply by taking a walk in a neighborhood is obviously quite rare. But sometimes a single conversation in a living room can present the entire history of many countries. Similarly, if one strolled through West Kreuzberg from corner to corner, one would come across a different architectural approach with each new building one passed, even though these ideas were all assimilated into IBA Neubau's strategy of critical reconstruction. Taking inspiration from and updating the genre of guidebooks, travel literature, and urban miniatures, the strolls in this book imagine a stroller moving physically (or an avatar moving virtually) in Kreuzberg with some kind of navigation technology at his or her reach. Ubiquitous today, navigation devices locate us on world maps by dislocating our bodies from physical space and relocating them onto the digital space of the navigation panel. By virtue of this localization through dislocalization, we see our bodies represented on smart-phone screens as colored dots with coordinates, moving or blinking on city maps, with easily accessible street views embodied in the maps' data. Our stroller is a dot in virtual space, but one who is also capable of dislocating in time, and one who is interested in archival sources and in traveling to a past when Kreuzberg's urban renewal took place.

Let's start our stroll from stop I, leaving Rob Krier's four perimeter blocks that created streets and a central piazza that he named Schinkelplatz. Turning south from this piazza on Lindenstrasse, one would immediately notice a white circular building on the other side of the street, a half-donut shape on the city map, whose façade is adorned with expressively placed balconies supported by thin round columns. This is the design for Block 30, prepared by the Dutch architect Herman Hertzberger in collaboration with contact architects Inken and Hinrich Baller (Figure 1.1 a).[1] Rather than filling in the gaps of the urban block to complete its perimeters, as usually required by IBA Neubau, Hertzberger designed a semicircular building in the middle of this site, joining it to the residential buildings along the long edges but separating it from the modernist church at the narrow tip of the triangular block. This urban design created qualities that were unique in the building exhibition: it resulted in the most intimate courtyard of all the IBA Neubau inner gardens—a paved circular ground interrupted by low-rise plants, which merge with greenery on private balconies, and a large sandbox that functions as the kindergarten's (located in the building) playground. In this way, the modernist church was not assimilated into the block but staged as a freestanding building on a platform. The heights of the semicircular building wings are carefully calculated to blend in with the heights of neighboring buildings and the church, smoothly dropping from five stories to four. Hertzberger designed the building entrances that rhythmically interrupt the façade and the vertical circulation cores that serve two apartments on each floor as fully glazed semi-open extensions of the street. Given that these spaces are not heated or cooled, each apartment is provided with a

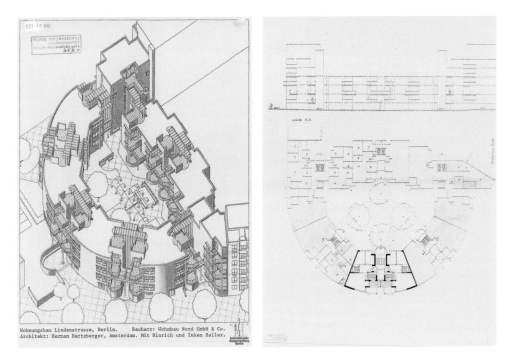

Figure 1.1a–b Herman Hertzberger with Inken and Hinrich Baller, Building in Block 30.

threshold room between the common core and the home interior (Figure 1.1b and 1.1c). The balconies supported by thin columns are arranged in a variety of sizes and positions so that they make it possible for neighbors to converse with each other, both across the building and between floors (Figure 1.1d). The playful arrangement of balconies differentiates this public housing sharply from the postwar standardized and homogeneous sets of units, both from the street and the courtyard (Figure 1.1e). One of the most noteworthy attributes of Hertzberger's building is its self-help nature: its construction was undertaken by the members of a cooperative.[2] The units were completed and administered by the members of the Selbstbaugenossenschaft Berlin e.G. (Berlin self-building cooperative) to reduce costs, but not much flexibility and adaptability seems to have been written into the design process—which would have been fitting for a self-help venture and made this building a unique example of open architecture. Overall, the building provided forty-eight dwellings units (six one-bedroom apartments, thirty-nine two-bedrooms, two three-bedrooms, and one four-bedroom) for the members of the cooperative, who have also been responsible for its maintenance.[3] The inner courtyard of this building remains one of the rare publicly accessible courtyards in Berlin.

If one continued walking south on Lindenstrasse after leaving Hertzberger's building, one would reach Block 33, which was the result of IBA Neubau's prestigious international open competition "Living in Friedrichstadt" of 1980 (also see stroll 6). As an outcome of this competition, Hans Kollhoff and Arthur Ovaska undertook much of the urban design of Block 33, which included fifteen units for the disabled and forty-five units for seniors (Figure 1.2a).[4] They were commissioned for the extra-long building

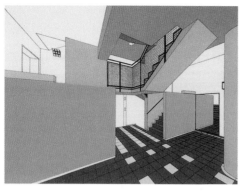

Figure 1.3 c Hans Kollhoff and Arthur Ovaska, Long building in Block 33.

made of red brick and white stucco with balcony balustrades of perforated metal, which a stroller walking south on Lindenstrasse would hardly miss. By itself the building creates a perimeter for a new street in front of it and one of Berlin's largest Hof-gardens behind it (Figure 1.2 b). One could enter this publicly accessible green space through the monumental gate carved into the long building and spend time in the neighborhood park, landscaped with orderly trees and playgrounds, or use it as a shortcut to go in various directions including toward the Berlinische Galerie (Figure 1.2 c and 1.2 d). In the spirit of IBA's collaborative urban design ideals, three different architectural offices designed the buildings in this perimeter block. Kollhoff and Ovaska's long building contained 102 apartments in different sizes (ranging from 48 to 149 square meters) and of diverse types (ranging from duplex units to gallery accessed dwellings. Figures 1.3 a and 1.3 b). The common circulation spaces and diversity of units were represented in colorful perspective drawings and typological matrices (Figure 1.3 c).[5] One of the finest discoveries for a stroller in this Hof-garden would be the building inside it designed by the Japanese architect Arata Isozaki, standing in the middle of the block and hence creating the boundary between the new and historical Hof-gardens. The building has a central entrance from both sides that connects the two gardens, a variety of two- and three-bedroom apartments, and smartly interlocking duplexes, and it is memorable for its vaults that run in the direction of two vectors (Figure 1.4 a).[6] Isozaki's design communicates with the existing buildings around the historical garden with its scale and tripartite façade structure and by integrating the remains of an old gate at its entrance (Figure 1.4 b). The age of the ruined brown stones contrasts with the freshness of the sharply cut and neatly executed white ones (Figure 1.4 c–d). If one went back to the new garden-Hof and looked toward the far end, one would see the white corner building with its rhythmic framed balconies overlooking the green area. This Janus-face terraced housing complex with common entrances from the street sides was designed by Dieter Frowein and Gerhard Spangenberg (Figures 1.5 a and 1.5 b). Finally, Kollhoff and Ovaska also designed the Tower House (*Turmhaus*), which one would immediately notice right across the Hof-garden after going through the gate. This building contains ten apartments (ranging in size from 41 to 74 square meters) and has a carefully proportioned façade composed of red-brick and white-stucco surfaces and perforated-metal balcony balustrades (Fig. 1.6 a).[7]

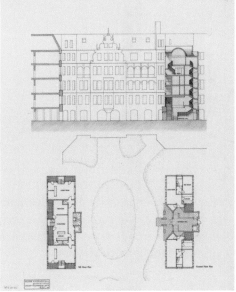

Figures 1.4 a–b Arata Isozaki, Building in Block 33.

I am invited into an apartment in the Tower House. The occupant—an immigrant from the former Yugoslavia (the part that is now Serbia) to Istanbul, who then immigrated to Germany for political reasons thirty years ago—prefers to be cited as "a resident." Having lived in Nuremberg and Bremen and studied political science in Munich, he has lived in Berlin for sixteen years, and in this apartment for six of those years. He has quite a few ideas about architecture and city planning in Germany. He appreciates Block 33's large Hof-garden for its ample playgrounds and location away from the street noise, and the entire complex's exterior appearance for its red bricks and repetitive balconies. He spends little time in the Hof-garden himself, but he enjoys sitting on his balcony and looking out into the garden with his elderly mother, who spends hours in the balcony (Fig. 1.6 b). However, he is less enthusiastic about the functionality of his apartment, citing problems such as the bathroom without natural ventilation, the small kitchen, the unheatable unit with three exterior walls, and the need to use a great deal of electricity to provide heat. He finds this subordination of the interior for the sake of the exterior appearance typical of architects nowadays: "This is the general syndrome of 'starchitects.' ... They want to draw attention with a blast."[8] He talks about Kreuzberg's gentrification after the 2008 financial crisis, and the city's "systematic policy to purge Kreuzberg of foreigners."[9] He mentions that many of the finest public housing complexes in Berlin were sold to big corporations after 2008 with appealing deals. "The burden of the economic crisis falls on public housing" and consequently on the immigrant population in this way, he concludes.[10] A resident has altered nothing in his apartment, as he thinks he will return to Turkey soon, once the political situation calms down—just as he has hoped for the past thirty years. He has changed apartments ten times, because he never considered himself permanent: "The syndrome of temporariness falls on the psyche of many migrant families. Frequent moves from place to place comply with the state of mind that one would never

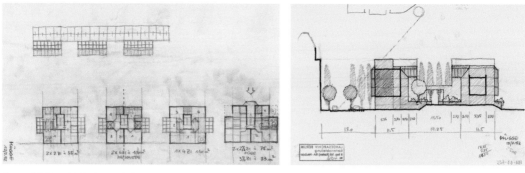

Figure 1.7 Horst Hielscher and Georg-Peter Mügge, study sketches for Block 33, 1982.

stay anywhere permanently."[11] He illustrates this condition by quoting the lyrics of a song composed by the Turkish musician, author, and filmmaker Zülfü Livaneli, who translated the words from Bertolt Brecht's poem "Gedanken über die Dauer des Exils" (Thoughts on the duration of exile):

> Bir çivi çakma duvara
>> Schlage keinen Nagel in die Wand
>>> (Don't drive a nail in the wall)
> iskemleye savur ceketi.
>> Wirf den Rock auf den Stuhl.
>>> (toss the jacket on the chair.)
> Üç günün telâşı niye
>> Warum vorsorgen für vier Tage?
>>> (Why the haste for three or four days?)
> Yarın gidersin buradan.
>> Du kehrst morgen zurück.
>>> (Tomorrow you will leave.)

Let's continue our stroll. If one left the Hof-garden defined by Kollhoff and Ovaska's long brick building, one could immediately visit the compound across the pedestrian street, also designed as part of Block 33. The twelve square urban villas (*Stadt-villa*)—freestanding, multistory, multifamily buildings in a garden—on the long sides and the two rectangular buildings on the short ones create an urban space whose scale is between that of an interior street and a Hof-garden (Figure 1.7). While one could easily assume that the twelve seemingly identical, freestanding white buildings are the work of the same architect, they were actually designed by three different architectural offices that doubtlessly followed the urban design. Franz Claudius Demblin designed the six urban villas with vaulted roof extensions and carved-in balconies; Horst Hielscher and Georg-Peter Mügge designed the four with balconies that jut out and attic windows; and Jochem Jourdan, Bernhard Müller, and Sven Albrecht designed the other four with circular balconies (Figure 1.8 a–d). Another example of IBA's collaborative urban design as a form of open architecture, albeit one with hierarchical rules, this narrow perimeter block contained two other buildings at the ends with white surfaces facing the Hof and brick façades on the street. The one designed by Werner

Figure 1.9a Werner Kreis and Ulrich and Peter Schaad, Building in Block 33.

Kreis and Ulrich and Peter Schaad would attract the attention of a stroller on Linden-strasse with its brick circular roofscape and frozen flag sculpture (Figure 1.9 a–b). The L-shaped building on the other edge undertaken by the Stavoprojekt Liberec collective from Czechoslovakia responds to its location at the street corner with an eye-catching, transparent stair tower where its two wings meet.

There is still more to see in Block 33. The "Living in Friedrichstadt" competition had asked the contestants to design a garden behind the Berlin Museum (now the Jewish Museum), which was housed in one of the last remaining baroque palaces of the city. Kollhoff and Ovaska designed a series of land sculptures with geometrically perfected shapes and on straight axes for this garden, referring to identifiable historical urban spaces and public parks (Figure 1.10). If one continued to walk south on Lindenstrasse, one would immediately recognize Daniel Libeskind's extension to the Jewish Museum, which was attained after an IBA competition, but was not built until long after because of delaying circumstances that included the fall of the Berlin Wall (Figure 1.11).[12]

If one made two right turns from Lindenstrasse and walked north on Friedrichstrasse, on both sides of the street one would see several IBA-1984/87 infill buildings that com-pleted Blocks 20 and 606, providing this major street with continuous perimeters. For instance, one could stand on the grass in the Theodor Wolff Park to view the south-ern edge of Block 20 and the IBA buildings that complete the perimeter block (Ralf Dähne, Helge Dahl, Rosie Grässler, Figure 1.12). From there one could also see Rave and Partner's tiny brick building on the corner of Wilhelmstrasse, which carves out a circular open space from the square ground plan. After receiving one of the first prizes for Block 20 as part of IBA's "Wilhelmstrasse" competition,[13] Rave and Partner were commissioned to design this building, which transformed the idea of a Berlin Hof from a courtyard behind buildings into an urban niche on the street front (Figure 1.13). From the park one could also see the Thomas-Weißbecker-Haus, previously occupied by squatters but renovated as a self-help project during IBA and turned into a com-munity house for homeless people. However, one would need to go to Wilhelmstrasse to see the expressive graffiti on this building's façade (Figure 1.14).[14] Continuing on Friedrichstrasse, one could take a peek inside Block 20 on the west through the gate created by John Hejduk's building (Stop VII). One could see the kindergarten in the middle of this Hof—the low-rise brick building defining a semicircular playground and

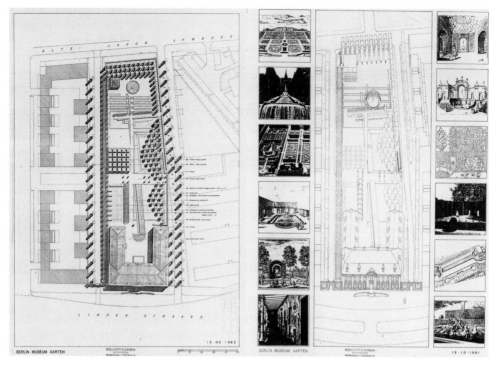

Figure 1.10 Hans Kollhoff and Arthur Ovaska, Berlin Museum Garden in Block 33.

outdoor stairs at the back, designed by Bassenge, Puhan-Schulz, and Partner of Berlin after the firm had received the other first prize for Block 20 as part of IBA's "Wilhelmstrasse" competition (Figure 1.15). Behind the kindergarten, one could see the other gate building across from Hejduk's—the building with triangular lines and memorable inner atrium designed by Hansjürg Zeitler, Helmut Bier, and Hans Korn (Figure 1.16). On the western side of Friedrichstrasse, in Block 606, one could see a building designed by Gino Valle, Mario Broggi, and Michael Burckhardt. Only the building's narrow façade would be visible during one's stroll, but it extends four fingers behind, creating promenades and sports fields that stretch toward Lindenstrasse, with a view of the Jewish Museum and other IBA buildings (Figure 1.17). The other infill buildings reconstructing the continuity of Friedrichstrasse (designed by Douglas Clelland, Mario Maedebach and Werner Redeleit, and Joachim Schmidt), whether seen from the street level during a stroll (Figure 1.18 a) or from above (Figure 1.18 b), testify to a typical IBA-1984/87 intent to hide big postwar buildings from sight, such as the Flower Market Hall of Block 606, unloved for its large scale and industrial aesthetic. Walking north a few more steps on Friedrichstrasse, let's stop at Checkpoint Charlie, where an astonishingly large number of established and emerging architects designed buildings in the four blocks surrounding this corner as a result of IBA's most prestigious competition.

1 For the buildings designed by non-German offices, there were "contact architects" working in Germany and therefore familiar with building codes and procedures. The drawings are in B Rep 168 (Karten) IBA Neubau, No. 268–277, Landesarchiv, Berlin. **2** Katerina George, "Selbsthilfe," in *Südliche Friedrichstadt: Internationale Bauausstellung Berlin 1984/87: Die Neubaugebiete – Dokumente Projekte,* vol. 3 (Stuttgart, Germany: Verlag Gerd Hajte, 1987), 310–11. **3** Hildebrand Machleidt, "Block 30/26," in ibid., 202–3. **4** Hildebrand Machleidt, "Seniorenwohnungen und -freizeitstätten," in ibid., 3:306–7; Katharina George, "Wohnungs- und Städtebau für Behinderte," in ibid., 308. The drawings of buildings in Block 33, including those by the offices of Kollhoff and Ovaska; Isozaki; Kreis and Schaad; Hielscher and Mügge; Demblin and Hanson; Jourdan Müller, and Albrecht; Stavoprojekt Liberec; and Frowein and Spangenberg are in B Rep 168 (Karten) IBA Neubau, No. 278–406, 889–890, 1313–1316, 1421 Bl. 1–10, Landesarchiv, Berlin. **5** *Internationale Bauausstellung Berlin 1984/87: Die Neubaugebiete Doku-mente Projekte,* vol. 3, 284–86. **6** Ibid., 288–89. **7** Ibid., 287. **8** A resident, interview by the author, June 22, 2012, Berlin, in Turkish, 00:06:34, 00:09:59. An audio recording of this interview is in the author's collection. **9** Ibid., 00:17:19–00:18:02. **10** Ibid., 00:15:40–00:16:17. **11** Ibid., 00:33:40–00:37:56. **12** For more about Libeskind's building in the IBA context, see Esra Akcan, "Apology and Triumph: Memory Transference, Erasure and a Rereading of the Berlin Jewish Museum," *New German Critique* 110 (summer 2010): 153–79. **13** Stefan Schroth, "Ergebnisprotokoll der Preisgerichtssitzung des internationalen engeren Wettbewerbs Berlin Südliche Friedrichstadt Wilhelmstraße." IBA Report. 9–11 December 1981 B 81/039, Landesarchiv. **14** For self-help projects, see Uli Hellweg, "Zwischen Ausweg und Irrweg: Sebsthilfe," in *Idee, Prozeß, Ergebnis: Die Reparatur und Rekonstruktion der Stadt,* 178–83; Gerald Blomeyer and Barbara Tietze, *Die andere Bauarbeit* (Stuttgart, Germany: Deutsche Verlags-Anstalt, 1987), 142–55.

STOP II

Buildings That Die More Than Once:
Open Architecture as Collectivity

The stories of an Italian architect, a Spanish architects' collective, a Turkish guest worker, and a Kurdish refugee meet at Checkpoint Charlie, the place that has become the iconic symbol of the Cold War in Germany because of its location at the border between West and East Berlin where the American sector ended. These four intertwined stories, which touch each other tangentially, are assembled in this chapter by tracing them from the 1960s till they all culminate at an urban corner in Berlin. While IBA-1984/87 operated as an organization between 1979 and 1987, the history of ideas behind its approach to urban renewal can be understood by looking closely at the construction of those ideas in the early and mid-1960s (the years when the first generation of guest workers moved from Turkey to Germany) and at their translation into building practice during the early 1980s (the years when many refugees arrived in Germany due to the 1980 coup d'état and its aftermath in Turkey).

Aldo Rossi was arguably one of the main theorists whose ideas were behind IBA-1984/87 and one of the principal architects who participated in it. Rossi took part in the *Berliner Morgenpost* debate in 1977 discussed in stop 1. In the catalog of the IBA exhibition *Modelle für eine Stadt* as well as his subsequent declarations, the Neubau director Josef Paul Kleihues reiterated that Rossi's *Architecture of the City* was a primary intellectual source for him.[1] This book (published in Italian in 1966 and translated into Spanish in 1971, German in 1973, Portuguese in 1977, French in 1981, and English in 1982) had inspired a sharp turn in architecture and informed the choices of IBA-1984/87 in differentiating its urban renewal policy from previous practices. Different but equally influential concepts are associated with Rossi's theory, including rational architecture, typological study, analogical architecture, and autonomous architecture, but not open architecture. In fact, many architects and scholars would probably see his repetitive and imitative forms that are unconcerned with creating a feeling of astonishment and his opaque texts that are insistent on collective memory as signs of something other than open architecture. Let's start the intertwined stories of this chapter, then, by tracing the emergence and co-optation of Rossian concepts between the early 1960s and late 1980s, which will also demonstrate the construction of networks of architects in Italy, Germany, Spain, and the United States.

What Comes before and after Form, according to Aldo Rossi

Architecture of the City was a culmination of Rossi's early writings, most of which had initially been published in the influential Italian journal *Casabella,* edited at the time by Ernesto Rogers.[2] Like the IBA team whose members were concerned about the preservation of the historical city, Rogers had long been deliberating about this topic that made him one of the earliest critics of the modern movement's early canonical reading.

Figure II.1 Cover of *Casabella* no. 255, 1961.

Figure II.2 Cover of *Casabella* no. 288, 1964.

For example, in a 1957 report titled "The Problem of Building within Existing Environments," Rogers urged architects to "establish continuity between past and present [for] the harmonious inclusion of new structures with the environments receiving them."[3] Criticizing contemporary architects for failing to preserve the past and ignoring the historical process, he introduced the concept of typology as a "restricting action" for a better engagement with the existing cities (Figure II.1). Rogers explicitly analyzed the contemporary urban problems in terms of the land policies of capitalist development: "private ownership of land assailed by speculative greed. One of our aims should be a substantial revision of the institution of property."[4] Throughout his tenure as the editor of *Casabella* (he left the publication in 1964), he made the journal a forum for publishing research (especially on European cities), rereading the modern movement by bringing to the fore its hitherto neglected architects and qualities, and elaborating Italian Marxist positions in support of the 1960s student movements.[5] Along with Carlo Aymonino, Vittorio Gregotti, Silvano Tintori, and Luigi Nervi (who joined the journal's stable of writers in 1959 to write about buildings with interesting structural engineering), Rossi contributed frequently throughout Rogers's tenure, initially as part of the study center team, and starting in 1961 as part of the editorial team.

In Rossi's articles during these years, his attraction to the books, architects, and cities of German-speaking countries is obvious. He reviewed books by Hans Sedlmayr on modern architecture, Emil Kaufmann on the eighteenth-century classicism of Étienne-Louis Boullée and Claude Nicolas Ledoux, and Roland Rainer on the planning of Vienna. He also wrote articles on Adolf Loos and Peter Behrens as part of a rereading of modernism; modern German architecture as it developed in Berlin, Frankfurt, Munich, Dusseldorf, and Mannheim; and Oswald Mathias Ungers as representative of the new German architecture.[6] When *Casabella* launched a series of special issues on big cities, with Aymonino working on Rome and Tintori on Milan, Rossi took on Berlin and published an extensive essay on the city's residential typologies that also appeared in

Architecture of the City (Figure II.2).[7] A couple of themes in Rossi's early articles that indicated his critical view of the modernist canon also prepared him for his major book.

The first theme was rediscovering modernisms in architecture, for which the *Casabella* authors assumed a revisionist historian's role and brought forward previously underacknowledged architects who respected the past more than the avant-gardes who searched for the shock of the new. In addition to Rossi's texts on Loos, Behrens, and the architects of the modern public housing complexes in Germany, Rogers wrote on Henry van de Velde, Giorgio Grassi on Hendrik Petrus Berlage, Tintoni on Tony Garnier, and Gregotti on Auguste Perret and expressionist architecture.[8]

Rossi's discovery of what I will call open architecture in Adolf Loos's work is particularly important for our purposes. Rather than focusing on Loos's famous manifesto "Ornament and Crime," Rossi used the architect's multiple essays to portray a much more nuanced figure.[9] In addition to Loos's complex response to the disappearance of crafts with industrialization and to the lessons of historical architects, Rossi took notice of his critical stance toward *Gesamtkunstwerk* (total work of art). In a series of articles, Loos had mocked his colleagues who advocated the design of environments from the largest to the smallest scale as a total work of art, giving the architect the role of an all-defining author while blocking the agency of users to design and change their living spaces.[10] Loos did not appreciate architects who imposed their taste on society and dictated how people should live to the minutest detail—a top-down approach that Rossi named and criticized as "moralism": "I believe Loos's position was the most critical stand taken against the moralism of the Modern Movement and its constantly redemptive attitude toward doing, as well as its optimism about how architecture could teach society how to live."[11] In a way, Rossi must have seen something of himself in Loos. Both architects designed buildings devoid of ornament or exaggeration, and using mere primary geometric forms, which were, in Rossi's words, attempts to "work day to day perhaps on small things, ... find morality again in the infinite complexities of the possibilities of life, ... make things wonderfully more intense."[12] At least occasionally, Rossi mentioned that his buildings were complete only with the life that emerged in them once they were inhabited. Speaking of his Gallaratese Housing in Milan just as its construction was finished, he commented on the insufficiency of the early photographs in communicating the project's intention before the public moved in: "Only very recently, walking in front of it, I saw the first open windows, some laundry hung out over the balustrades to dry ... those first shy hints of life it will take on when fully inhabited. I am convinced that the spaces intended for daily use—the front portico, the open corridors meant to function as streets, the porches—will cast into relief, as it were, the dense flow of everyday life, emphasizing the deep popular roots of this kind of residential architecture."[13]

If revising and diversifying the perception of the modern movement in architecture was one of the trajectories of the *Casabella* team, identifying the problems in contemporary cities caused by modern planning practices was another. In an editorial in 1959, Rogers clearly stated that *Casabella* was a journal of both international architecture and urbanism, one that looked at buildings in their urban context rather than in a vacuum.[14] Countless research articles on small, medium, or large cities in Italy and elsewhere were published, and there were frequent reminders of the need for urban reconstruction in European cities. Rossi identified the "immense task of reconstruction" as the main problem faced by German architects[15] and appreciated Ungers "as an architect of reconstruction … [of] that which lives in that place's history."[16]

Rossi's views on contemporary city planning and megastructures carried him into a controversy about open form, a term that was used occasionally but quite indecisively during this time. He defined himself in opposition to, on the one hand, the total plan espoused by Manfredo Tafuri, who was skeptical about architecture's ability to fight against capitalist land policies and who therefore advocated carrying architecture into city planning,[17] and, on the other hand, the large-scale architectural visions that erased the historical qualities of urban environments.

In an article that Rossi wrote with Francesco Tentori and Gian Ugo Polesello in *Casabella*, he took on the problem of the city peripheries—also the theme of the XIIth Milan Triennale —to criticize the tall and freestanding postwar housing blocks that mushroomed outside of city centers without the urban qualities of pedestrian historical environments. Not unlike the way proponents of IBA-1984/87 later complained about the massive freestanding housing blocks built on the outskirts of Berlin to address the postwar housing crisis, Rossi and his colleagues wrote about the "dullness" of the peripheries of Milan.[18] This controversy over current practices climaxed at the tenth meeting of the Istituto Nationale di Urbanistica in 1965. Projects that were proposed in the name of open plan and open form (*piano aperto* and *forma aperta*), such as Kenzo Tange's megastructure for the Tokyo Bay and Giancarlo de Carlo's ideas about the city as open structure, which Rossi had criticized in several venues, left him "perplexed."[19] Rossi and coauthors explained their perplexity by saying, "Only the presence of a closed and stable form permits continuity in producing actions and successive forms."[20] In the words of the scholar Mary Louise Lobsinger, the city as open form meant the "refurbishing of the modernist trope of the open plan dressed up in a politicized notion of the plan as process. Rossi and his colleagues insisted that the city had specific dimensions and that only closed forms could provide continuity in urban development and sponsor the kind of activities that produced new urban forms. … Architecture … was the concrete measure of the city."[21]

Rossi justified his defense of the "closed form" in the tenth meeting of the Istituto Nationale di Urbanistica by opposing the megastructures and postwar planning alternatives that were termed "open." However, in other instances, the *Casabella* team used the metaphor of the open city to contest total planning and bring back the architectural qualities of fragments in a city as zones of experimentation. In *Casabella*'s issue on Berlin in 1964, in which Rossi published his typological study of the city's residential districts for the first time, Aymonino published an article titled "Una Città 'Aperta'" (An 'open' city) that praised Berlin as a library of solutions to problems that were endemic in many European cities. Discussing the "Great Berlin Competition" and works of Bruno Taut, Hans Scharoun, the Luckhardt brothers, Ludwig Hilberseimer, and Walter Gropius among others, Aymonino pointed out the value of experimentation in designing a city in parts as long as a clear perspective was applied to all of the parts.[22]

Years later, Rossi explained that his interest in Berlin was due to the "cultural similarities between Italy and Germany," and for being a city "made in parts."[23] Berlin's fragmented nature that proved the ineffectiveness of the total plan also supported Rossi's proposal in *Architecture of the City* that the zone of urban operations should have been the limited city districts rather than the whole city.[24] Instead of total plans that falsely reduced the city to a single idea, the urban interventions could be made on an architectural scale (that is, on the scale of the building, street, or block), and architectural form with all its aspects could be remobilized to shape cities. It was this idea of the city district as an artifact to be preserved, reconstructed, or designed that also guided IBA-1984/87 in designating Kreuzberg as a zone of operation.

In the *Casabella* issue on Berlin, Rossi published his article on residential typologies, which also appeared in *Architecture of the City* two years later (Figure II.3).[25] This research anticipated Rossi's criticism of what he called "naïve functionalism." Canonical modernism had imprisoned architectural discourse in the assumption that function determined everything, including the house, the monument, and the city. Not only did dividing a city into the functional zones of industry, housing, leisure, and transportation—the guiding principle that came out of CIAM's 1933 meeting—reduce the diversity of urban experience, but categorizing urban artifacts (buildings, streets, districts) in terms of their functions also created a shortsighted view of a city's history. This overrated emphasis on function hardly took into account the fact that the function of urban artifacts changed over time.[26] The "primary elements" of a city that secured continuity in time, such as its monuments as "signs of collective will" and "fixed points in [an] urban dynamic," were valuable not because of but in spite of their changing functions. They continued to live even though their functions died.[27] Consequently, studying a city by categorizing it into functions was constricting.[28] Instead, Rossi categorized Berlin's residential types to account for the "city conceived together with its architecture:"[29] single-family houses, semidetached houses, and residential blocks.[30] Discussing the best practices of each type, he was particularly attentive to the set of architectural ideas coming out of the Weimar period *Siedlungen* (residential estates) designed by Taut, Martin Wagner, and Scharoun, among others. Rossi disagreed with critics such as Tafuri (although he was not mentioned by name) who viewed these public housing areas as "autonomous districts" in a city of divided sectors and as fragmented zones unable to address the problems of the greater metropolitan area. On the contrary, Rossi believed that these projects not only integrated their architecture with the city as a whole but also built on the existing residential models by making a "synthesis of the new and the old."[31]

How, then, did Rossi think that architects should engage with the city? A unique definition of open architecture comes out of *Architecture of the City*, which was relatively "closed" in the book's reception during the late 1970s and early 1980s as a work promoting autonomous architecture. The book was a manifesto against the hitherto canonical modernism in architecture and city planning that Rossi had been criticizing all along: top-down "moralism," the destructive impact on historical urban areas, "naïve functionalism," and total planning. The alternative proposal relied on a revised theory of typology.

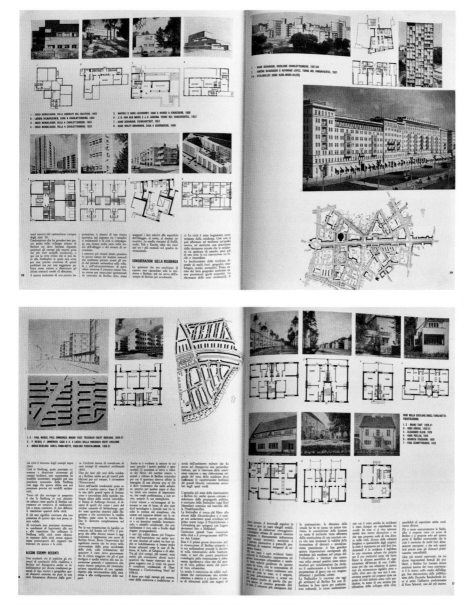

Figure II.3 Aldo Rossi's discussion of Berlin's residential types (Weimar period, IBA-1957 and Stalinallee housing) in *Casabella*, 1964.

Perhaps Rossi's theory is best summed up in the following obscure statement: "The City is a work of art ... a man-made object, architecture or engineering that grows over time."[32] How could a city be a work of art that is transformed over time? According to Rossi, collectively urban artifacts could create a work of art if they shared the idea of a type. When every architect, even those who lived at different times, designed artifacts in relation to the same type, the resulting city could be a unified work that grew over time in a continuous way.

Rossi revived the distinction between type and model made by Quatremère de Quincy, an eighteenth-century French architect, to ensure that his proposal would not restrict creativity. In Quincy's words, "the word type presents less the image of a thing to copy or imitate completely than the idea of an element which ought itself to serve as a rule for the model."[33] That is, rather than being copied uncreatively, type was to be imitated imaginatively: "moral imitation, imitation by analogy, by intellectual relationships, by application of principles."[34] This Aristotelian mimetic theory of art, rather than one that relied on the idea of the modern artist as a genius creator, helped Rossi distinguish himself from canonical modernism's association with tabula rasa, or a mind without memories. In contrast to the premise that a city or a building could be constructed from scratch and designed by a single architect whose mind was a tabula rasa, the typological design method ensured the continuation of the collective memory (a term for which Rossi relied on Maurice Halbwachs) and the collective intellect: "I believe instead that precisely because the city is preeminently a collective fact it is defined by and exists in those works that are of an essentially collective nature. ... The beauty resides both in the laws of architecture which they embody and in the collective's reasons for desiring them. ... The city itself is the collective memory of its people, and like memory it is associated with objects and places. The city is the locus of collective memory."[35]

Many scholars bring out continuity as the basic attribute of a city that would result from typological design. According to Pier Vittorio Aureli, for one, the theory of type sought to move architecture away from iconic, episodic, and consumable gestures.[36] Nonetheless, I would like to emphasize that Rossi's theory of type was completed only when "type" was paired with the concept of the "event" and "collective memory" paired with "collective will." Rossi defined "the concept of type as something that is permanent and complex, a logical principle that is prior to form and that constitutes it."[37] While type came before form, event came after it and granted each urban artifact its own singularity, or identifying character: "Where does the singularity of urban artifacts begin? ... We can now answer that it begins in the event and in the sign that has marked the event."[38] In other words, type transmitted the collective memory, and history made the event. Throughout the life of cities, the political choices of citizens and the "collective will" determined the events and their physical signs on form: "We not only affirm the relevance of politics but even maintain that it is of primary importance, and indeed, decisive. *Politics constitutes the problem of choices*. ... [Cities] are the signs of collective will."[39] What makes Rossi's theory a unique interpretation of open architecture is its emphasis on design as a product of the collective mind (including collaboration with dead people) on the one hand, and the acknowledgment of future transformation through the physical signs of the event on the other hand. What makes typological design method open architecture is not the fixed type that comes before form (even if type is open to multiple formal iterations) but the acknowledgment of the collective mind in the constitution of the type, and of the fact that past and future events are signs of collective human agency on architecture, not necessarily signs of the single architect.[40] Rossi even rejected the concept of urban design to define his approach, because such a term would have assumed that an individual plan shapes a city, rather than the collective memory that constitutes type and the collective will that is reflected in the event.[41] In that way,

Rossi gave the architect his or her due position in the life of cities: not as an all-determining author, but as an agent participating in collective memory and collective will.

An idiosyncratic conviction about death and life emerges from Rossi's writings, drawings, and projects that will help me elaborate on open architecture. Reflecting on *Architecture of the City* years after its publication, Rossi drew an analogy between autobiography and death (defined as the "continuation of energy") and declared that he had identified a similar problem in his book "with the relation between form and function: form persists and comes to preside over a built work in a world where functions continually become modified."[42] In his introduction to the German translation in 1973, Rossi had summarized his argument in similar terms, by pointing out the openness of form in the sense of its adaptability to different situations and functions: "These buildings are seen as structure[s] that have formed and are still forming the city, offering the maximum adaptability to new functions over time. … The broadest adaptability to a multiplicity of functions corresponds to an extreme precision of form."[43] The pair of death and life was mirrored in the pairs of type and event, permanence and adaptability, unchanging architectural principles and their reflections in actual situations, "rational" laws of architecture and the contingent history of buildings: "The principles of architecture are unique and immutable, but the responses to different questions as they occur in actual situations, human situation[s], constantly vary. On the one hand, therefore, is the rationality of architecture, on the other the life of the works themselves."[44] Even though forms continued to live, buildings died repeatedly and acquired new functions and new physical signs with each new historical event. Rossi proposed that cities were made up of urban artifacts that died more than once. If *Architecture of the City* were adapted into a novella or movie, it would have depicted a perpetually reincarnated city with zombie buildings. Or perhaps the book anticipated the "Zombie Manifesto," in which Sarah Juliet Lauro and Karen Embry suggested a new interpretation of the zombie as a "thought experiment" in the name of the posthuman subject of global capitalism. The zombie's "irreconcilable body (both living and dead)" suggests that "the only way to truly become posthuman is to become antisubject." A spin on Donna Haraway's "Cyborg Manifesto," Lauro and Embry's work presented the zombie—with its mythic origin in the Haitian revolution—as a body that was raised from death to labor in the fields and associated it with the brain-dead factory worker, who not only is a slave (to capitalism) but also embodies a slave rebellion.[45] Rossi's proposal to view the city as made up of urban artifacts that die more than once is also a call for the city to refuse to die or admit its ephemerality. Such a city could not be destroyed, as something that is both living and dead cannot be killed. Unlike the capitalist city that, with its endless consumerism, perpetually destroyed existing forms to build new ones, the city with zombie artifacts would have refused to go to the grave.

The metaphor of death appears in a number of Rossi's works. The San Cataldo Cemetery in Modena, Italy, a building that he designed with Gianni Braghieri, is composed of a cube (a brick building with windows but no floors or roof that functions as the communal grave of those who died in war), a cone (a building for the remains of the people who were abandoned in insane asylums, hospitals, and jails), a U-shape building, and a set of blocks that form a triangle in the site plan with streets between them. From

Figure II.4 Aldo Rossi, Cataldo Cemetery in Modena, Italy, 1971.

above, this city of the dead looks like a corpse lying on the ground, with its head being the cube without a roof and open to the "Blue of the Sky" (the competition project's title), ribs being the blocks that make a triangle, arms being the U-shape building, and phallus being the cone (Figure II.4).[46] In this building complex, Rossi sought to revive the communal function of commemoration and reminded us that there used to be no real distinction between the tomb and the house.[47] It is therefore no coincidence that Rossi's architectural designs for a cemetery and public housing look alike. The Modena Cemetery resembles the IBA and the Gallaratese housing blocks: the same colonnades, the same square windows, the same proportions, and the same brick. The similarity of Rossi's buildings is further emphasized in his famous "La Città Analoga" (Analogous city) drawing (Figure II.5), prepared with Bruno Reichlin, Fabio Reinhart, and Eraldo Consolascio for the 1976 Venice Architecture Biennale, curated by Gregotti. Rossi made a collage of his own buildings in a drawing that referred to ancient, Roman, and medieval cities and works of Michelangelo, Francesco Borromini and Karl Friedrich Schinkel, all unified in the composition. The drawing implied the collective making of a physical environment, rather than the individuality of any one of its pieces.[48] For instance, the plan of the Modena Cemetery in this drawing seamlessly continues the streets of Cesare Cesariano's reconstruction of the Vitruvian city, the combination making a radial urban composition. The plans and façades of Rossi's housing projects are interwoven with the drawings of primary shapes, classical orders, and historical monuments.

In a number of striking drawings for the Modena Cemetery, Rossi exaggerated the rendering of the shadows, and in some drawings shadows are cast on the south. A dark shadow of a human body is obvious in the "Analogous City" drawing as well, placed off to the left and cast on the city fabric. But there is no body to cast the shadow. It is drawn on the city like a ghost without a body, another fictional creature that lives after death and refuses to die. This ghost shadow is a trope for architecture itself. As the scholar Eugene Johnson has emphasized, while explaining the Cemetery in Modena, Rossi once defined architecture (referencing Boullée) as "what remains of man," just like graves and the shadows of their stones remain after the natural cycle of life and death is completed. Diogo Seixas Lopes has commented on this city of the dead as the "fixed setting of perpetual dwellers," testifying to Rossi's melancholy that casts buildings as "signs of isolation ... renouncing the ideal of transformation."**49**

In my opinion, a unique definition of open architecture, instead, emerges from Rossi's association of death and architecture, one that views the generational cycle of death and life as analogous to the dynamic between fixed type and constantly occurring events, unchanging form and ever-changing function, memory and history, and permanence and adaptability. The type as a logical principle constitutes form, and form constantly restores itself as a different building (or street or district) whenever its function and inhabitants change. Buildings die more than once, while types and forms remain. Types that are established collectively, and thus hold the collective memory, and zombie urban artifacts that constantly remain open to their own reiterations through the collective will constitute what I mean by Rossi's theory of open architecture as collectivity.

Of all the interpretations of Rossi, it seems that the ones by Bernard Huet and Val Warke detect a quality in Rossi's work that is similar to a quality that I detect in open

Figure II.5 Aldo Rossi with Bruno Reichlin, Fabio Reinhart, and Eraldo Consolascio, "La Città Analoga" (Analogous city) drawing, 1976, Venice Architecture Biennale.

architecture. Huet highlighted Rossi's proposal to reconstruct architecture as a collective discipline, and saw Rossi's "Analogous City" drawing as a metaphor for the European city that is continuously reconstructed over itself. This confirms Rossi's interest in architecture that is perpetually transformed by people and over time.[50] In the heyday of poststructural theory, Huet also attributed a "semantic openness" to Rossi's geometrical elements: "They are 'floating' signs, open to meaning. Rossi is fully aware that recourse to such elementary, non-figurative and archaic geometrical figures was not only a way to escape the garrulity of 'speaking' architecture to achieve, through silence, the effect of great architecture of the past, but at the same time to open the gates of the collective imagination, the memory attached to these forms."[51] Similarly, Warke interpreted this silence in Rossi's forms as a sign of their unfinalizability, in much the same way as Mikhail Bakhtin talked about dialogical imagination: "Fundamental to unfinalizability is a work's open-endedness, which initiates the dialogic opening of a work so as to provide an addressee with the opportunity to join the author in effectively coauthoring a work, if not an opportunity to create another work."[52]

In spite of all this openness, however, Rossi barely speaks about an alterity that would come out of the collective memory and the collective will. The continuity with the past and the unity in the city to be secured through typological design method relies on the premise that the historical forms create one homogeneous and harmonious whole. Rossi seems to assume that the collective memory and the collective will lead to the same ideal. His theory is based on the premise of a society that reaches consensus easily and has no real tensions, dialectics, radical others, or room for the possible otherness of the newcomer or the noncitizen. Only in a few cases does Rossi think through the cosmopolitan hospitality of cities such as Venice and New York, and even then he forecloses the possible alterity that could come out of this hybridity:

> Venetian architecture itself is an example of what "analogous city" means. Venice, during its economic and commercial expansion, brought home elements of architecture from distant cities and used them to give birth to a new composition. In this respect, NYC [New York City] is similar to Venice: its neighborhoods, such as Chinatown, Little Italy, the Ukrainian quarter, are attempts at reproducing a certain environment. Put all together, they form a city which is different from, but at the same time analogous to, previous ones. Thus strolling along the streets of this city, one sees elements of the lifestyles and forms of German, Latin, Jewish, Eastern cities, which are translated into this new form which is the NYC. Similarly Venice, which was independent from the Pope and the Empire, was a city where Turks, Jews, Lombards, and Slavs could live together, and everything melted into its language, its civilization, its unique architecture.[53]

Rossi seems to assume that districts reflecting ethnic and national diversity in cities like Venice and New York create a new unity effortlessly. Rossi's analogous city is made up of open architecture, but one that assumes harmonious dialogue and does not confront historical and current inequalities, power relations, or the erasures and oppressions resulting from class-based and geopolitical hierarchies. However, in reality the voice of the victor has often subordinated the collective memory and the

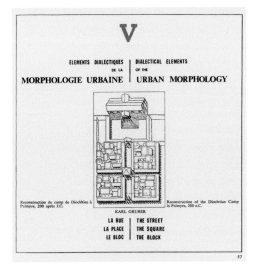

Figure II.6 A cover page of *Rational Architecture:*
The Reconstruction of the European City. Catalog of
the exhibition curated by Leon Krier, 1978.

collective will, rather than integrating into them the voice of low-income residents or
noncitizens.

In his subsequent practice, Rossi came to be associated increasingly with rationalism
and autonomous architecture. He curated the *Architettura Razionale* (Rational architecture) exhibition for the 1973 Milan Triennale, which brought together works associated with historical rationalism[54] and representing what was called the "new rationalism" of contemporary architects, including Grassi, Leon Krier, Rob Krier, Rossi,
Giuseppe Samona, James Stirling, Ungers, and the NY Five architects (Peter Eisenman,
Michael Graves, Charles Gwathmey, John Hejduk, and Richard Meier), as well as texts
by Aymonino, Ezio Bonfanti, Colin Rowe, and Massimo Scolari.[55] This exhibition thereby connected architects in Germany, Italy, and the United States with the concept of
rationalism. A few years later, the IBA Neubau would invite most of these architects
to reconstruct Berlin.

Rationalism as a movement gained instant recognition. *Rational Architecture: The Reconstruction of the European City*, a 1978 exhibition curated by Leon Krier, included the
work of many of the IBA architects, as well as conceptual tools that would frequently
be used to discuss a new urban renewal policy (Figure II.6).[56] In one of the introductory essays in the catalog, Robert Delevoy declared that the exhibition's aim was to "fill
the gap" between what had been endorsed by CIAM's functionalist urban theory and
its practical results, including, for instance, the gap between "masterly demonstration and striking failure of a way of town-planning thought" exemplified by Brasilia.[57]
Krier launched rational architecture as a "critical" alternative, rooted in the "study
of the history of the city … as the history of the types."[58] "Urban morphology" was a
term used frequently in the exhibition catalog and a chapter conceived as a manual
for architectural design in which buildings created geometrically identifiable urban

voids, such as ordered streets and squares, rather than random leftover spaces. The exhibition's central concern was the integration of new structures into an existing urban fabric. It displayed new housing, public buildings, monuments, quarters (cities within a city), highways, and gardens as constituent elements of existing and new but continuous urban fabrics.

The exhibition catalog also included Anthony Vidler's influential essay "The Third Typology," in which Vidler suggested a relationship between the rationalists of three distinct periods in Western architecture.[59] There were the eighteenth-century rationalists who imitated nature, such as Marc-Antoine Laugier, whose idea of the primitive hut had its architectural origin in tree trunks and branches; the twentieth-century architects who imitated the machine to respond to industrialization as the spirit of the age; and finally the new rationalists, for whom historical architecture was the model to imitate imaginatively. This relationship placed Rossi and the typological design method in the realm of the increasingly dominant discourse of autonomous architecture. The third period of rational architecture was different from the first two because, Vidler argued, it required no validation outside of architecture, whether natural or artificial: "No longer is architecture a realm that has to relate to a hypothesized 'society' in order to be conceived and understood; no longer does 'architecture write history' in the sense of particularizing a specific social condition in a specific time or place. The need to speak of the nature of function, of social mores—of anything, that is, beyond the nature of architectural form itself—is removed. ... [Architecture is] released into its own autonomous and specialized domain."[60]

Rossi had used the word "autonomous" in *Architecture of the City*, but he had done so to advocate the birth of a discipline to study the city architecturally, and to be able to account for the irreducible complexity of the factors that actually shape the city—not to claim that architectural design is autonomous or devoid of political, social, technological, or psychological concerns.[61] Vidler had also preemptively declared that autonomy does not make architecture apolitical, because historical architectural forms from which the new rationalists distilled typological lessons were already political. Nonetheless, especially in the United States and as the English translation of his work spread worldwide, Rossi increasingly came to be known as an architect who promoted design autonomy. The Institute for Architecture and Urban Studies in New York, which Eisenman and Vidler had helped found, translated, exhibited, and discussed Rossi's work. As early as 1976, the institute's journals *Oppositions* and *Skyline* included numerous articles on type and typology by de Quincy, dal Co, Moneo, Rossi, and Vidler; Rossi's *Architecture of the City* and *Scientific Autobiography* were translated into English as part of the institute's book series; and the institute organized an exhibition of Rossi's projects, presenting them with an introductory essay by Eisenman.[62]

In 1984 the exhibition *Autonomous Architecture* at Harvard University was launched with *Harvard Architecture Review's* special issue with the same title.[63] The essays constructed a temporal and spatial lineage between historical and contemporary European architects, as well as American practitioners associated with "rationalism" and "autonomy"—usually using these words interchangeably. *Architecture of the City* was presented as the most influential book on architects who turned to architecture's "autonomous conception, ... [who] discovered the specificity of architecture and its laws, ... abandoned interdisciplinary myths and no longer believe[d] that architecture is born from the marriage between the analysis of functions and the solids of Euclidean geometry."[64] The exhibition brought together eight architects—Agrest and Gandelsonas, Mario Botta, Eisenman, Machado, Ungers, and Silvetti, and Rossi—identifying their approach this way:

> The term autonomous architecture refers to the notion that architecture has a particular quality, an essence, which is specific to it and which distinguishes it from the other arts. Architecture is regarded as a separate endeavor, a discipline, complete with principles and norms internal to itself. ... Those architects who subscribe to this approach strive to design buildings that represent only the consistency and logic of a chosen formal organization. Consequently, the form, which is generated from strictly formal considerations, may not appear to have been determined by the usual factors that relate architecture to man and context: function, scale, site, symbol, and so on. The architecture becomes an independent object, complete within itself, autonomous.[65]

By 1984, the year when the first IBA-1984/87 building exhibition opened, Rossi's assimilation into the autonomous architecture discourse was complete, turning him into an architect of autonomous formalism at the expense of his own political, social, and psychological contributions to understanding the lives and agency of the human beings who reside in a city. Autonomy, as we will see in stops III and V, was highly endorsed by the IBA Neubau team as well, to differentiate its policy of "critical reconstruction" from IBA Altbau's participatory "gentle urban renewal." In a comprehensive historical survey, Vittorio Magnago Lampugnani, a consultant for IBA, contrasted typology and functionalism as two major thought models in the previous three hundred years, with the first signifying an independent discipline with invariable principles and the second signifying a design approach that responds to specific conditions. The difference between typology and functionalism was thereby constructed as the one between autonomy and contingency, placing Rossi on one side of the binary.[66] It was therefore no coincidence that when IBA Neubau launched its most renowned architectural competition, known as the "Kochstrasse/Friedrichstrasse Competition," Rossi was one of the architects invited to submit a proposal.

A Refugee and a Spousal Migrant: Çetiner and N.Y.

As Rossi was working on his theories and buildings in the 1960s through the 1980s, two separate lives were simultaneously unfolding in Germany and Turkey that eventually crossed in neighboring IBA Neubau buildings that had been constructed as a result of the "Kochstrasse/Friedrichstrasse Competition."

Even though they were the same age (seventy at the time of my interviews), Günsel Çetiner and N.Y. came to Berlin at different times and for quite different reasons. Çetiner arrived in 1972 from Istanbul, following her husband, who had arrived in 1969 with the guest worker program. N.Y. arrived as a refugee in 1994 from Mardin, after

Figure II.7 Günsel Çetiner, interviewed by Esra Akcan, Berlin, 2012.

fleeing from Turkey due to the Kurdish situation. Neither woman ever worked outside the home, and both told me that they had never learned German—for reasons that will become clear as their stories unfold in the following pages. "I was a very socially active girl in Turkey, but my life had to change after I moved here,"[67] Çetiner says (Figure II.7). The apartment that she moved into in Kreuzberg when she first arrived in Germany was in sharp contrast to her parents' "relatively heaven-like," three-story wooden house surrounded by a garden in Istanbul, where she recalls living a stress-free life, frequently going out to movies and concerts, and enjoying the late afternoon snacks her mother prepared for her when she returned from school.[68] She tells me that "when I arrived [in Berlin] in 1972, the buildings were not modern like this. All the walls were full of bullet holes, the buildings were dull [ruhsuz] and in ruins. There used to be the [Berlin] wall at that time … [which was] unmaintained."[69]

She characterizes her first apartment in Kreuzberg as dull, impractical, and small. The walls were covered with wallpaper, and the floors were rough wood that they painted themselves. There was no hot water, and the apartment was heated with a coal-burning stove that was so complicated only her husband could get it to light. She used to dry the laundry on those beautiful stoves that she now misses, since they did not make the air as dry as the modern central heating in her current apartment. Like everyone else, she remembers the outdoor toilets with particular disgust. Theirs were in the Hof, and she had to share it with the men who used to work in the furniture workshop across their building: "I was afraid to go out to the toilet at night, and—forgive me for saying this, but I kept a thing in the kitchen. If someone killed you at the door, no one would even notice. … I could never live in a place like that again. I don't know how I did it at the time. I was frightened."[70] There was no bathtub in their apartment either, and she and her husband used to go to a *hamam* (public bath), she says before rapidly correcting her choice of words—as there were only a couple of showers there. They lived in a few other Altbau apartments, all located in Kreuzberg, which they renovated with their own means, before she eventually moved into the building designed by Rossi.

An event on a day in 1991 made such an impact on her that it colors everything that she tells me years later, and she constantly finds a way to direct our conversation to a time before that day. Everything she says about her apartment and daily life after the event are also affected by it. Her husband was a strong, 190-cm-tall, hard-working man who was not ashamed of his labor. He renovated even the smallest details of the Altbau buildings, he added a bathroom, he loved to live in beautiful houses, and he let her buy whatever she wanted. Nobody could have imagined what would happen to him. After having had a bad headache for four or five days, he fell down while taking a hot shower, which was followed by an operation from which he never recovered. Totally paralyzed, he was housebound for the last fourteen years of his life. This event, which functioned as the chronological marker of our whole conversation, meant that she became his caretaker in the apartment, refusing the help of the nurses that she found redundant and even disruptive, as they messed up the house by entering in without taking off their shoes. She tells me that "if he was German, this would not have happened. He should have been sent to rehabilitation. There was a chance that he could get better. … If he was German, they would have sent him there. They discriminated."[71] Çetiner supports this claim by referring to her conversation with a Turkish-speaking doctor who explained to her afterward that there must have been a mix-up, because the hospital reports recommended rehabilitation for her husband. Left with her two sons and daughter, without work, and unable to receive her husband's benefits, she felt that her life had been turned upside down. It became only slightly more sustainable when she found out that she had a right to receive social welfare.

She finds racism and her husband's paralysis responsible for the rupture in her son's education as well. After her son started high school as the only Turkish student in his class, he came home offended and frustrated every day because he felt discriminated against regardless of how well he did.[72] He left school, and after his father's paralysis, discontinued his formal education to help at home. Çetiner often refers to the aftermath of the fall of the Berlin Wall in 1989 to explain the hostility toward her family, confirming the views of scholars who have attributed the rise of xenophobia after the unification of Germany to some politicians' campaigns that targeted migrants and refugees as causes of the country's economic crisis and political instability.[73]

Even though Çetiner complains about racial discrimination, race and ethnicity function as a basic category in her mind as well, revealing hostility directed both toward and from her. She finds Germans responsible for her husband's situation, and East Berliners for her son's. "I don't like the Arabs, and not much the Kurds either," she declares moments later, without noticing a paradox in her use of categories based on race and ethnicity, but she stops and checks immediately to see whether I am either in order to make a correction if necessary. "The difficulties of life change people, humanity vanishes," she reconciles in conclusion.[74] She suspects that her blond hair and green eyes helped her get a residence permit in spite of the fact that she did not speak a word of German—which annoyed many of her friends who had been denied a permit despite their hard work in preparation for the exam. "Nobody believed I was Turkish, and they whined about the Turks to me," she says, and I cannot tell whether she is internalizing or subverting a common stereotype.[75]

This common stereotype is that of the so-called Turkish bride, which has continued to color media representations of the thousands of women in Çetiner's legal situation since the mid-1970s. In 1973, the guest worker program in its original state came to a close, and the Family Unification Law was passed, which allowed immigrant workers to bring their spouses and under-aged children to Germany. Supported by the governing coalition of Social Democrats and Free Democrats, the new law was meant to restrict the arrival of new immigrant workers while simultaneously facilitating the "integration" into German society of existing ones.[76] The common simplistic portrayal of the spousal migrants who arrived after this law, known as Turkish brides, emphasized their otherness and difference, depicting them as victims of forced marriages and patriarchal husbands.[77] In a typical text from 1978, Susanne von Paczensky described them as women who "live amongst us, [and are] far from invisible, on the contrary: thanks to head scarf and floral pattern trousers, gestures and behavior they are visible, evidently strangers. Strangers, that is to say, strange. … Now they live in our cities as indigestible foreign bodies … [T]hey stand close together all muffled up, speak an incomprehensible language, cook unfamiliar dishes. They walk submissively two steps behind their husbands."[78]

I think that, as an individual rather than an informant representing her ethnicity and gender, Çetiner tells her story in a way that challenges both the stereotypical view of Turkish brides as merely passive victims of their husbands and the thinking of people who are ready to turn a blind eye to patriarchy for the sake of dismantling the stereotype. As her husband believed he could make enough money, Çetiner never worked professionally, but she now regrets this decision because if she had worked she would have learned German and met new people. Her husband "both did good and bad to me," she concludes.[79]

Çetiner could not visit Turkey after her husband's paralysis in 1991, as she had chosen to take care of him in their apartment. N.Y. could never go back to Turkey either, once she had officially taken refuge in Germany in 1994. While Çetiner is one of the tens of thousands of spousal migrants whose arrival was legalized by the Family Unification Law in Germany, N.Y. is one of the similarly large number of refugees who left Turkey as a consequence of the violent coup d'état in 1980 and its aftermath (Figure II.8). As a result of this military coup, 7,000 Turkish citizens were charged with death penalty offenses (517 were sentenced to death, of whom 50 were executed); 300 died in prison, possibly because of torture; 1,683,000 were listed as "suspicious"; 650,000 were taken into custody; 230,000 were taken to court; 30,000 were fired; 23,677 professional organizations were forced to disband; and 937,927 publications were closed down.[80] Due to the same coup, 14,000 people lost their Turkish citizenship, and around 30,000 people—predominantly those associated with the Turkish and Kurdish left—are said to have sought asylum.[81]

"In my hometown in Mardin," N.Y. tells me, the political situation got so out of hand that "lumpen young idealists" found themselves joining in violent armed battles. After the coup on September 12, 1980, many of N.Y.'s comrades were placed in the Diyarbakır Prison, now well known as one of the most violent punitive institutions in history, where torture was frequently practiced. Due to the lack of space, "people were jammed into horse stables like animal herds," N.Y. says, and she holds this prison responsible

Figure II.8 View from N.Y.'s apartment, photographed by Esra
Akcan, Berlin, 2011.

for the violence that followed, as it turned even moderate individuals into flaming rad-
icals.[82] Her husband, who had had a high-level job in the municipality, was confined
for two years and four months in Diyarbakır. She has a vivid memory of his condition
after being released: "Due to uninterrupted torture, the flesh in between his fingers
was cut throughout. He had walnut-size wounds all over his body that were reswollen
with uncontrollable inflammation every year. ... He had no teeth left in his mouth."[83]
He never wanted to flee to Germany with her, and he stayed in Turkey.

The aftermath in Mardin of the coup convinced N.Y. to move to one of the big metrop-
olises in western Turkey: She had seen people "set villages on fire, burned the villagers, stripped men naked in freezing snow in front of their children. ... You cannot put
everything into words. Leave it. I saw guerrillas whose eyes were taken out and ears
cut off. I saw guerrilla girls' corpses being raped. You either had to take a gun in your
hand or run away. We ran away, we migrated."[84] However, it became clear to her that
fleeing to a big metropolis did not provide a solution, because discrimination against
her continued there.

After spending all her savings to bribe policemen to get a fake passport for her son and
visas for both of them, she came to Berlin to stay temporarily with German friends
in Kreuzberg. "The state actually helped us emigrate," she says, as if it had wanted to
throw them out of the country.[85] After an unsuccessful attempt, her other children,
their spouses, and her grandchildren escaped through illegal means, on foot and on
trains so cold that water in bottles instantly froze.

N.Y. remembers how pleasantly surprised she was when she first arrived to see police
officers without weapons and capable of smiling—"at least trying to seem like a dem-
ocrat"—and how she felt a relative sense of freedom to wander around the city, even
its periphery.[86] She continued being committed to world events in Germany. We have
lengthy conversations about the Kurdish population in Germany, Turkish politics since
the 1970s, domestic violence in both immigrant and German families, noncitizens' lack

of willingness to fight against hidden racism in Germany, and the difference between the immigrants of the first, second, and third generations. She explains that a refugee's situation is even more difficult than that of a guest worker: the latter migrates in a relatively prepared way with some resources, while the refugee escapes secretly, leaving her house for the last time as if she was going out on an ordinary day. The stories that she tells about the architectural spaces where she lived confirm.

Immediately after arriving in Germany, she and her children were placed in three different *Heim* buildings (hostels or dormitories)—in Neukölln, Tegel, and Spandau—despite her requests that they be allowed to stay together. She still remembers the New Year's Eve when her son could not join their celebrations due to the strict *Heim* rules.[87] The conditions in the *Heim* buildings were so disagreeable that they changed six places in two and a half years:

> There are all sorts of people in the *Heim*. Always a fight, always an ambulance on the front door. *Heim* life is really difficult. You need to adjust. Twenty families share a kitchen, the toilets are common. They kept the Muslims on a separate floor. ... I used to stay in one room with my two children. ... We stayed in a *Heim* for German homeless people for a year. In the refugee *Heim*, the kitchen always used to be occupied, and we waited hungry for hours for it to be free. In the *Heim* for the German people, it was the opposite, nobody cooked. ... There was a woman wearing merely a T-shirt and no panties. I was raising my children there and did not want to stay due to cultural differences.[88]

She did not accept the apartments that the Housing Office showed her on the peripheries of East Berlin and Wedding, either: "There were a lot of [neo-]Nazis at the time in East Berlin and they did not want the foreigners. I told the Housing Office that I ran away from the fascists in Turkey, and now they were trying to put me together with their own fascists. ... They found me a place in Wedding, but I refused to take it, as Wedding was full of [Turkish] ultranationalists [ülkücü] at the time."[89] Eventually, she saved for key money to pay someone who informally found her an apartment in Kreuzberg—where she could easily adjust, as she could speak Turkish in all of the grocery stores, butcher shops, and other stores: "Turkish people lived in Kreuzberg, but they were Turkish democrats."[90]

A Synergetic Architectural Competition

Both Çetiner and N.Y. live in IBA Neubau apartments built as a result of the organization's prestigious "Kochstrasse/Friedrichstrasse Competition," launched in September 1980. When IBA divided Kreuzberg into four study zones, it had named the war-torn area bordered by Hallesches Tor on the south, Checkpoint Charlie on the north, Potsdamer Platz and railways on the west, and postwar housing blocks on the east South Friedrichstadt. Covering an area of 125 hectares, 80 percent of which belonged to the city, and containing 12,000 inhabitants and 20,000 work places when IBA was launched,[91] South Friedrichstadt had been the topic of a study seminar in 1979 in which fifty internationally respected planners, architects, scientists, and politicians participated.[92] Part of South Friedrichstadt, the "Kochstrasse/Friedrichstrasse

Competition" area consisted of four large building blocks (Blocks 4, 5, 10, and 11) that intersected at the junction of the two streets mentioned in its name and was bordered by the Berlin Wall and Checkpoint Charlie, which divided the American sector of West Berlin from East Berlin. The symbolic importance of the site cannot be overstated. Dieter Hoffmann-Axthelm, an expert on the history of Berlin and a frequent IBA consultant, compared it to Pearl Harbor and Mount Rushmore.[93]

IBA divided the "Kochstrasse/Friedrichstrasse Competition" area into four subcompetitions, one for each of the city blocks, and six architects or architect groups were invited to submit proposals for each of the parts. The twenty-four invited participants and the jurors (seven, together with four alternates) represented nothing less than a who's who of Western architecture. The participants included Raimund Abraham, Hans Kammerer, Rem Koolhaas, Kisho Kurokawa, Rossi, and the offices of Bohigas, Mackay, and Martorell, Eisenman and Robertson, Kollhoff and Ovaska, Reichlin and Reinhart, and Venturi and Rauch, to name a few, turning this Berlin corner into the hot spot of architectural debates.[94]

In addition to working on their own designated blocks, the twenty-four architects were expected to develop visions for the other three city blocks as well. This unusual organization reflected IBA's urban renewal policy. Due to the paranoia of homogenized megablocks and in the spirit of collaborative urban design, IBA organizers must have hoped the competition would result in four different commissions, whose architects would nevertheless be in synergistic dialogue with each other. In this way, the architects were asked to develop their visions for their city blocks by considering not only the block's context in Kreuzberg, but also the urban fabric to be created by their interventions, if their visions were to be extended to neighboring blocks. Rafael Moneo had defined the notion of type as "a concept which describes a group of objects characterized by the same formal structure," and the typological design method as "the act of thinking in groups."[95] The competition asked the architects to think in precisely this way: in groups, and even as a collective. During the competition, the jury selected a winner for the general urban design concept for a block but determined that three or four other invited architects who had not won should also collaborate by designing buildings in the same block under the artistic direction of the winner of the first prize. In other words, inviting architects to participate in a closed competition turned out to be IBA's step toward stimulating collaborative urban design—a form of open architecture, as discussed in stop 1 but, in this case, one that was staged by a central authority.

From the initial steps, IBA managed the competition so that it could create synergies through the interaction of acknowledged and up-and-coming architects. In the evaluation reports for the jury meetings, the architectural teams were not anonymous. When the competition was launched, all of the participants were invited to attend two full-day briefings and go on site tours on September 21 and 22, 1980.[96] In these briefings, Kleihues—the Neubau director and competition juror—explained IBA's general aims and principles, Kreuzberg's historical development, and the competition's procedures; and Senator Hans Christian Müller presented his perspective on the potential of reconstructing perimeter blocks. The participants were assured that they were not simply being asked to repeat the historical town plan, but the existing buildings were nevertheless considered fixed, unless there were "exceptional, well-founded cases to alter" them.[97]

In his introduction to the competition brief, Kleihues informed the competitors about the 1979 study seminar, especially its recommendation that "the remains of the historical urban ground plan, i.e., the geographical and spatial characteristic features of the area should form the basis for organization and planning."[98] Kleihues used the phrase "collage d'histoire" to describe the area, composed of three historical layers: the baroque plan of the eighteenth century; the intensive construction of the nineteenth and early twentieth centuries, the results of which are referred to as the Stone Berlin; and the destruction of World War II. In Kleihues's eyes, in addition to Friedrichstrasse, there were many other baroque city axes that could be repaired by preserving their scale and geometry.[99] Even though the war had erased much of this history, and even though the area was in a much more dilapidated condition than the IBA Altbau areas, it was possible to critically reconstruct the ground plan (as the competitors were asked to do). Kleihues concluded his introduction by criticizing the buildings constructed in the 1960s and 1970s and pointing instead to Taut and his public housing projects as the model that exemplified the "social and artistic commitment of the twenties as well as the rational tradition of the city," confirming IBA's rereading of the history of modern architecture.[100] Other tips for the competitors included returning the streets to their original width; ensuring that large building blocks were fragmented and footpaths provided in between them; designing public green areas and open spaces with ample playgrounds, squares, and parks; and combining different city functions and diverse social and ethnic groups.

As was the case for all of IBA competitions, the brief for this one also included an extensive section written by Thomas Biller and Wolfgang Schäche and illustrated with ample maps and photographs of the "still perceptible" baroque ground plan laid out by Philipp Gerlach, and developments of the Kaiserreich era (1871–1918), which was identified as the "most decisive period," when the area "took on its characteristic architectural physiognomy."[101] The authors unambiguously stated that this "character and architectural expression" had to be "considered as providing the sole historical premises on which new urban planning must in future be based."[102] The brief gave detailed information about the existing buildings in each of the four blocks, their functions and property status, cultural facilities around the area, traffic, and vegetation. The major competition requirement was to provide public housing units, but the planning guidelines clearly listed a mixture of everyday functions connected to work, education, and leisure; "the need for social integration for various age brackets, social classes and nationalities"; and the requirements to provide facilities for the disabled, as well as for community formation.[103]

There is a convenient contradiction in the competition's requirements. Even though this site in Kreuzberg was acknowledged in passing as an area of "various age brackets, social classes and nationalities," the otherwise detailed brief surprisingly made no mention of the immigration or "guest worker" issue. My interview with David Mackay of Martorell Bohigas Mackay Architects (MBM) confirmed the fact that IBA evidently did not see international immigration as a relevant topic for this competition, as it was not discussed with the participants, even though Mackay suggested that it must have filtered into the things they were told.[104] Additionally, the functional requirements were such that noncitizen families' chances to move into the newly constructed buildings were reduced. The competition required that 70 percent of the dwellings be reserved for units with two or three rooms (that is one- or two-bedroom units) for 1–3 people living inside, while limiting four-bedroom dwellings to 5–10 percent of the whole—thereby commissioning public housing unsuitable for a majority of noncitizens with big families.[105] The implied strategy here (intentional or mandated by the Senate) was to change the percentage of the noncitizen population in the area, especially of those from Turkey—a population who accounted for 50 percent of the inhabitants in some sections of Kreuzberg.

While these requirements were quite similar to those of the other IBA Neubau competitions, the site's location at Checkpoint Charlie gave this competition an added significance in Cold War politics. The participants, especially those working on Block 4, were required to include in their designs the customs, the Allies and the police functions.[106] Although hardly anyone then anticipated the fall of the Berlin Wall a decade later, IBA was indeed quite forward looking. The brief noted in passing: "The basic urban planning ideas put forward by the Internationale Bauausstellung for the area near the wall are based on possible future integration of the two parts of Berlin, East and West. The prerequisite for such integration among other factors involves restoration of the historical structure."[107] In other words, in IBA's eyes, the critical reconstruction of the historical ground plan would also be fitting for a reunified city in the future, under the possibility that the Wall fell, as Berlin's urban fabric would then be restored to its condition before division. Among the participants, only Rem Koolhaas proposed buildings for the east side for a condition without the Berlin Wall, albeit not in a way that met IBA's expectations (stop VI).

On January 9, 1981, the twenty-three remaining participants (Venturi and Rauch had withdrawn from the competition) submitted their proposals, and on February 5–7, 1981, the jury composed of Max Bächer, Werner Düttmann (replacing Müller), Gregotti, Kleihues, Rob Krier (replacing Hejduk), Lampugnani (replacing Ungers), and Paolo Porthogesi met. A preliminary examination report prepared for the jury analyzed the projects in relation to their "urban design concept" and "block concept."[108] The examiners prepared comparative charts for floor space index and the breakdown of dwellings in terms of number of rooms, and especially figure-ground maps that showed that almost all of participants—the only exceptions were Koolhaas, and Eisenman and Robertson, (whose proposals will be discussed in stop VI)—followed IBA's suggestion that they fill in the perimeters of the blocks, in at least three if not all four blocks (Figure II.9). While almost all architects suggested perimeter buildings with varying degrees of perforation along the street edges, Bohigas, Mackay, and Martorell, Kurokawa, and Schürmann left the Wilhelmstrasse edge unbuilt to provide strong physical and visual access to the school in the middle of Block 10. Not surprisingly, the first criterion of the evaluation report categorized the proposals by determining whether or not they

Figure II.9 "Kochstrasse/Friedrichstrasse Competition," IBA-1984/87, figure-ground relations of the projects submitted to the competition, Berlin, 1981.

closed the block peripheries. The examiners seemed particularly concerned about the accentuation of the Friedrichstrasse and Kochstrasse junction by building up the corners of all four blocks.

Rossi's entry followed his own collective design ideals.[109] In his explanation report for the competition project, Rossi advocated the subordination of the individual architect's ego for the sake of the unity and continuity in the city:

> The problem of building in Berlin and within a block in the center of Friedrichstadt is a problem of urban architecture. This is to say that personal invention, architecture elevated but at a personal level, is not valid for the architectural and urban problems of the large town. ... [T]the edges of the block seem more important than the architecture. ... The error of modern architecture is to have not conformed to the streets, stripping the town of all vivacity and compactness. ... The first point of the project was then to respect the alignment of the street. Buildings were constructed along the perimeter of the area, thus reconstructing Friedrichstadt.[110]

The subordination of the new buildings and the architect's ego to the collective voice of the city was quite agreeable to IBA, which had been praised for ending an era of "arrogant city planning."[111] Rossi also paid homage to Schinkel, Taut, Mies, Behrens, and Hans Poelzig for considering the city as "an ensemble of architectural proposals where style took second place with respect to the urban system," and he criticized the Hansaviertel, where "good works of architecture do not succeed in covering the erroneous planning decision."[112] In his overall urban design drawing, Rossi proposed perimeter buildings for all of the blocks except, curiously, Block 5—where he inserted a figure-ground proposal that seemed to be the same as Eisenman and Robertson's.

For Block 10, Rossi completed the perimeters with a continuous building, which extended along the street edges but was rhythmically interrupted with his signature steep-roofed towers and which allowed several access points to the large protected Hof-garden at the back (Figure II.10). In addition to providing these portals, he broke the continuity of the building to preserve the existing trees along the street and collaged trees from Schinkel's engravings on his own façade drawings (Figure II.11). All of the dwellings had balconies and were accessed through the connecting galleries on upper floors, while a portico welcomed the city's pedestrians on the ground floor. The combination of red brick and green steel lintels, multistory glazed surfaces, and the elaboration of the corner with a fat round column were the most memorable aspects of the building. On the choice of brick, Rossi referred to Schinkel, who had predicted that brick would replace stone in the modern industrial city (Figure II.12).[113] On the white column at the corner, he referred to the Filarete column in Venice as a "sign of urbanization, of civic life, of history. ... This column also has an auspicious meaning: it ignores the physical existence of the Wall and belongs to the two cities"[114] (Figures II.13) Just next to the Berlin Wall, the building sought to deny the wall with its fat, round, white column (Figure II.14). The jury commended Rossi's entry for being based on "classical elements" and found it "of high artistic quality" and "convincing" in both urban design and building scale.[115]

Raimund Abraham, who was also competing for Block 10, proposed that a big structure like a thick, long brown wall encircled all of the edges of the blocks, with frequent breaks to provide views to the back through different variations of large and high frames. All the corners of the blocks were treated in the same way, with a diagonally carved out cubic volume that contained an open staircase (Figure II.15).[116] Despite its perimeter block conception, the jury found this proposal "of remarkable aesthetic quality" but "self-asserting" and "problematical" for this area.[117]

For Block 4, Oriol Bohigas, David Mackay, and Josep Martorell proposed two long, parallel buildings on a slight curve that created a wide, tree-lined, inner street connecting Friedrichstrasse and Wilhelmstrasse (Figure II.16).[118] In their explanation report the architects declared two primary objectives: to base the reconstruction of the city on the "historical validity of the street" and to consider the Berlin Wall as a "temporary accident that should not devalue the façade."[119] Accordingly, the buildings and the inner public pedestrian road connecting the two-towered monumental gates at both ends ran parallel to the wall, and the Kochstrasse was altered to make a curve. This curve was introduced to break the monotony of the façade and to regulate the angle with Wilhelmstrasse so that the two sides of this street were better integrated and the continuity of the city was reestablished.[120] The housing units proposed along the wall had access from the garden, which was another reason to ensure that this space remained public between the suggested curved buildings (Figure II.17). Additionally, the architects wanted all dwellings to be connected to a street (in the air), either the covered walkways on the ground moving toward the monumental gates or galleries on the upper levels. The wide street in the air (the gallery) with rhythmic slender columns carrying the roof was one of the most memorable spaces and façade elements of the proposal. The new organization of the streets created a triangular space between the proposed buildings and the Berlin Wall, which was designed as a green area over a multistory garage that could be turned into offices if the wall came down. This public park contained a stepped outdoor seating area and a serpentine "Gaudi bench" with convex and concave curves for extroverts and introverts, similar to the one at Park Güell in Barcelona (Figure II.18).

Despite the relatively rule-bending site plan, the façades of the competition project with the tower portals, large arched gateways, small square windows, and steep roofs gave it a revivalist, heavy, and monumental air that was accentuated by the dark brown color used in renderings. In my interview with him years later, Mackay admitted: "I think we went too far in the initial project to be German. We tried to pick up what we thought were Prussian elements in architecture. ... For the style, we found [it] very curious that there were water towers, all over Berlin, and we felt that was something we could pick up."[121] Overall, the environment to be created by this proposal with its streets, Hof-gardens, galleries, and parks looked like a hybrid of the medieval and classical, and Nordic and southern, architecture of Europe. The jury found the suggested curve on the Kochstrasse absolutely unacceptable,[122] so much that another project and model of the same proposal, but one with straight streets, was immediately produced under Kleihues's orders (Figure II.19).[123]

Among the other proposals for Block 4, the jury found those by Kollhoff and Ovaska and by Koolhaas undesirable because the former divided the block into small units, and the latter suggested different urban models for each block (stop VI). In other words, neither followed IBA's obsessive mandate for the perimeter block.

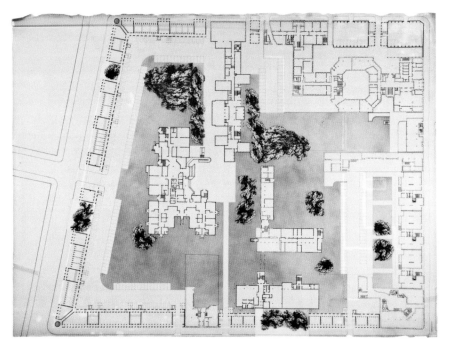

Figure II.10 Aldo Rossi, "Kochstrasse/Friedrichstrasse Competition" project, IBA-1984/87, Berlin. Plan.

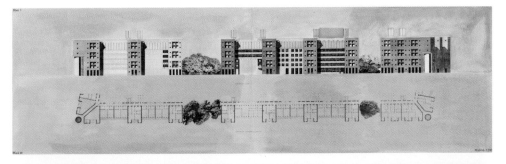

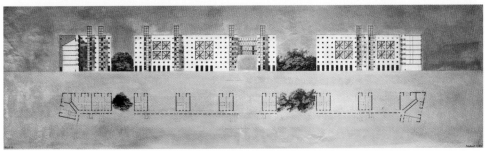

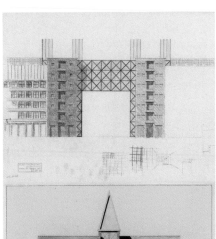

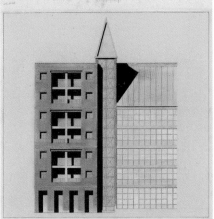

TOP: Figure II.11 Aldo Rossi, "Kochstrasse/Friedrichstrasse Competition" project for Block 10, IBA-1984/87, Berlin. Façades. LEFT: Figure II.12 Aldo Rossi, "Kochstrasse/Friedrichstrasse Competition" project for Block 10, IBA-1984/87, Berlin. Façade details. RIGHT TOP: Figure II.13 Aldo Rossi, "Kochstrasse/Friedrichstrasse Competition" project, IBA-1984/87, Berlin. Studies of the façade and round column at the corner. RIGHT BOTTOM: Figure II.14 View of Aldo Rossi's building in Block 10, photographed by Esra Akcan, Berlin, 2010.

For Block 5, Eisenman and Robertson also broke the competition rules, by refusing both to offer an overall urban design concept that involved the other three blocks and to provide public housing in favor of a monument (stop VI). Kammerer's relatively quiet proposal for this block, which provided for continuity of the façade between the historical and new buildings, was received favorably. Kurokawa proposed an inventive project with creative conceptual and spatial suggestions such as the city door, city window, and city veranda; external mirrors that reflected the city in a way that created an illusion of continuity between East and West Berlin (the architect made a reference to the Japanese tradition of reflecting the surrounding landscape); and intricate inward-looking dwellings organized around a network of smaller courts and two pedestrian levels (Figure II.20). The jury judged it "too complicated."[124]

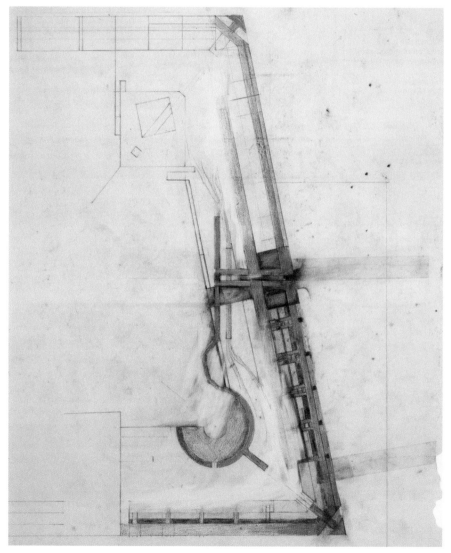

Figure II.15 Raimund Abraham, "Kochstrasse/Friedrichstrasse Competition" project for Block 4, IBA-1984/87, Berlin.

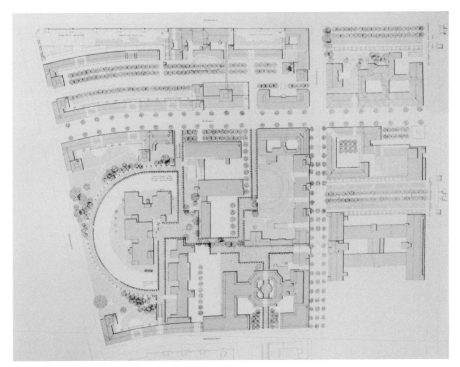

Figure II.16 Bohigas, Mackay, and Martorell, "Kochstrasse/Friedrichstrasse Competition" project for Block 4, IBA-1984/87, Berlin. Site plan.

Finally, for Block 11, Reichlin and Reinhart, who were no other than the collaborators of Rossi in the preparation of the "Analogous City," proposed three buildings that created a big Hof-garden and a smaller courtyard at the corner. Instead of having a unified pattern, the three proposed buildings responded to their immediately adjoining or opposite buildings, thereby creating a collage of dissimilar historical references.[125] "No formal hegemonic design, but an operation to 'sew up' the buildings facing each other. The unifying factor works at a deeper level," the architects explained, seeing this as reminiscent of the historical episodes of Berlin itself (Figure II.21).[126] As a result, the Kochstrasse elevation, for example, was composed of the rhythmically spaced octagonal towers of an L-shape corner building, on the one hand, and the shoulder-to-shoulder, obliquely placed pointed roofs of a young people's hostel, on the other hand. In the architects' eyes, the latter created an "allusion to the Gothic city, but an imaginary one, a dream city: an obsession with towers in the fortified city" (Figure II.22).[127]

The competition participants were invited to stay at Hotel Berlin during the jury meetings. While waiting for the results, Eisenman must have found the following handwritten note from Koolhaas: "Peter, I am not sure—they say they still have to fight for it—but I *think* that you won the 1st prize. Aldo too, and Reichlin and Reinhart, Bohigas. I am nowhere to be seen. Too gothic. [Something was scratched out]. See you later. Congratulations if it is true. Rem."[128] Koolhaas did indeed have the correct information. In addition to choosing the first prize winners, the jury decided that some of the other competitors should also design buildings in their designated blocks in accordance

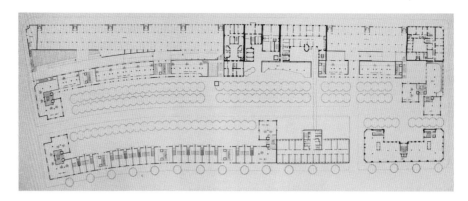

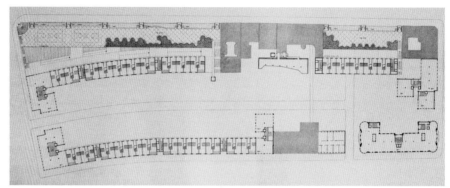

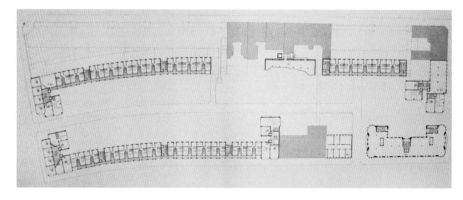

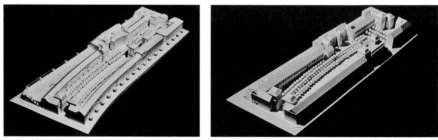

TOP: Figure II.17 Bohigas, Mackay, and Martorell, "Kochstrasse/Friedrichstrasse Competition" project for Block 4, IBA-1984/87, Berlin. First, third, and fifth level ground plans and façades. BOTTOM: Figure II.19 Bohigas, Mackay and Martorell, "Kochstrasse/Friedrichstrasse Competition" project for Block 4, IBA-1984/87, Berlin. Comparison of the models of competition and revised version.

Figure II.18 Bohigas, Mackay, and Martorell, "Kochstrasse/Friedrichstrasse Competition" project for Block 4, IBA-1984/87, Berlin. Perspective from Hof-park, street in the air and Gaudí bench.

with the winning urban design concept. For Block 10, where Rossi won first prize and hence was responsible for the overall site, the three other competitors—Abraham, Ante Josip von Kostelac, and the team of Dietmar Grötzebach and Günter Plessow—were commissioned to design buildings at specific addresses.[129] For Block 4, the Bohigas, Mackay, and Martorell group was appointed to design the overall framework but asked to involve other architects in consultation with IBA and the Senate. Soon afterward, it was decided that Koolhaas, Joachim Schürmann, and Peter Faller-Hermann Schröder would carry out parts of the project.[130] Additional teams were brought in later.[131] Even though the jury decided that Block 5 would be "constructed in accordance with the conceptions of" Eisenman and Robertson,[132] the team was later commissioned to design something else at one corner of the site (stop VI), while another building in the same block was given to Kammerer (Figure II.23). For the corner of Block 11, Reichlin and Reinhart proposed a U-shape building with rhythmically arranged octagonal extension bays and a partially closed courtyard defining an elliptical floor pattern. The owner of this site refused to accept the project endorsed by IBA and used a different

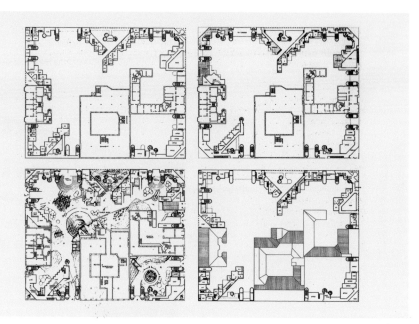

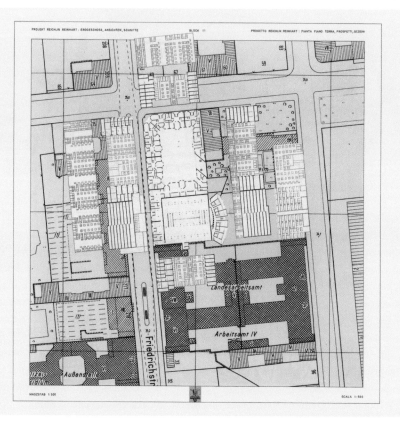

TOP: Figure II.20 Kisho Kurokawa, "Kochstrasse/Friedrichstrasse Competition" project for Block 5, IBA-1984/87, Berlin. BOTTOM: Figure II.21: Bruno Reichlin, Fabio Reinhart, "Kochstrasse/Friedrichstrasse Competition" project for Block 11, IBA-1984/87, Berlin. Composite drawing of site plan and sections.

Figure II.22 Bruno Reichlin, Fabio Reinhart, "Kochstrasse/Friedrichstrasse Competition" project for Block 11, IBA-1984/87, Berlin. Façade detail.

architect to construct a different building with public subsidies. A structure with a glass circular tower at its corner stands on the site today (Figure II.24). In the view of IBA coordinator Günter Schlusche, this created a serious crisis when Kleihues realized that he might not be able to realize his vision unless he had local politicians, owners, and developers on board. This led to the competitions among the developers, which required the developer with the winning bid to comply with IBA's design to receive public subsidies.[133] John Hejduk's Berlin Tower Housing was also constructed at the southern edge of this block (stop VII). Overall, the "Kochstrasse/Friedrichstrasse Competition" must have been so important for IBA's public relations that the results appeared immediately in various newspapers and other publications in German, Spanish, French, and other languages.[134] What eventually got built, however, was quite different from what had been proposed.

From Vision to Reality and Back Again with Bohigas, Mackay, and Martorell

It might not have been just a coincidence that the experiences of Block 4's architects Bohigas, Mackay, and Martorell and the building's resident N.Y. were connected. Apart from the fact that one lived in a space designed by the other, the Catalan-Spanish tensions that concerned the architects and the Kurdish-Turkish tensions that subjugated the resident were intertwined at a level that exposes the conduct of the modern state's institutions, which are themselves predicated on the restraining definitions of citizenship. Soon after the end of the fascist regime in Spain with Francisco Franco's death in 1975, Bohigas published an article in the influential Italian journal *Lotus* on the future

TOP: Figure II.23 Hans Kammerer, Building commissioned as a result of the "Kochstrasse/Friedrichstrasse Competition" project for Block 11, IBA–1984/87, Berlin. BOTTOM: Figure II.24 View of the corner of Koch- and Rudi-Dutschke-Strasse at Checkpoint Charlie, photographed by Esra Akcan, Berlin, 2011.

of Catalan architecture, and on the long road to the democratization of architectural institutions, including the city government and the university (where Bohigas later became the dean of the Faculty of Architecture). He wrote:

> The present shift in the political situation in Spain has opened up the way for a transformation of social and cultural structures destined to hold great significance for the evolution of Catalan architecture. … Such changes will affect … the social and political role of the architect in the ambit of a new political structure that will allow him the possibility of participation.

> Up to now Catalan architecture has been distinguished by its … relative capacity to carry out the role of independent cultural witness, without "dirtying its hands" in a political participation which was felt to be alien …

> It is therefore possible that in the next few years the majority of architects, whose works up to now could only be revealed in sophisticated international reviews, will dedicate themselves to the thankless, but fruitful, task of structuring the new institutions.[135]

Bohigas and Josep Martorell Codina—both born in Barcelona—had teamed up in 1951, and Mackay, who had been educated in London, joined their office as a full partner in 1962. Before being invited to participate in IBA's competition, the office had almost exclusively designed collective housing projects and urban housing blocks, though it had also designed a few schools, single-family houses, and parks.[136] In Mackay's words, this made them as a perfect candidate for IBA's commission: "We spent a lot of time designing fitting into existing buildings. So we were very conscious that we had to relate to the existing buildings and the street. And we were always conscious that whatever building we were doing was part of a city."[137]

Just as they did in their IBA competition project, the architects had worked on breaking up monotony and creating surprising vistas in their designs for large blocks in urban contexts, such as the Marti l'Huma block in Sabadell (1974–79) that generated a new curving street. Another of their projects, La Salud block in Barcelona (1969–73), was composed of a perimeter building that exactly followed the trapezoidal street lines and another perimeter building that defined a square courtyard in the middle. The two perimeter buildings resolved the tension between the irregular geometry of the existing urban lot and the ideal geometry of the new inner courtyard, or the imperfection of the found urban condition and the order of the proposed architectural form. The looping street between the buildings changed in width and form, thereby creating exciting vistas and varying outdoor spaces. When the team exhibited eight of these urban blocks (including the competition design for IBA) in the influential architecture gallery Aedes in Berlin in 1988, the architects introduced them as "almost closed" city blocks and "almost corridor streets" to reconstruct the nineteenth-century street-square-block structure of European cities, without turning a blind eye to the valid modernist critique of this urban fabric on the grounds of health and hygiene (Figure II.25).[138]

The office was probably invited to participate in the "Friedrichstrasse/Kochstrasse Competition" because of the architects' ties in Italy, just as the other winners, Eisenman and Robertson and Reichlin and Reinhart, were connected to this country through Rossi. Bohigas had defended the creation of a discipline that studied the city in relation to its architecture, recognizing that problems of form are as important as social, political, and psychological ones and that a city is made up of "collective representation"—ideas in accordance with those advocated by Rossi in *Architecture of the City*.[139] Bohigas had also joined the editorial board of *Lotus* in 1975; the office had curated the Spanish Pavilion in the Venice Architecture Biennale of 1976 (curator: Gregotti); and, as Mackay confirms, they had known the Italian architect Gregotti, a juror for IBA's

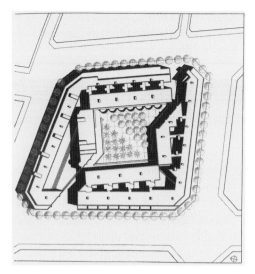

Figure II.25 Bohigas, Mackay, and Martorell, La Salud block, Barcelona, 1969–73, exhibited in Aedes Gallery in Berlin in 1988.

competition.[140] Even though the team had not known Kleihues before the competition, they saw themselves as in agreement with his objectives.[141] Simultaneously, the municipal authorities in Barcelona chose the office as the planners and architects of the Olympic Village in Barcelona, which gave the architects the rare opportunity of being at the forefront of the urban renewal of two major European cities. While reconstruction of the European city must have signaled a break from the fascist era in Barcelona in the architects' minds, reconstruction in Berlin took a more conservative approach to the immigration politics in that city.

In the late 1980s, Bohigas openly criticized international architectural discourse, which he found too cynical and too obsessed with autonomy and style, and he continued to defend the political relevance of architecture for the broader public:

> The disciplinary autonomy and stylistic eclecticism which were the first buttresses of the attempt to transcend modernism are now the excuse for an architecture whose purpose is purely rhetorical, an architecture which resembles the oratory of the old rhetoricians with its extravagant formal luxury and strategically placed jokes so that the audience didn't … notice that the speaker had nothing to say. But, has architecture really nothing to say today? Is it no more than an artistic form which has spent itself and cannot adopt any critical attitude other than that of witticism, … a flight which is at the same time both irresponsible and a defense against possible accusations of irresponsibility?[142]

The story of Block 4 in Berlin represents one of the most interesting cases of open architecture as collaborative design. Bohigas, Mackay, and Martorell's office structure suggests that this process must have come almost naturally to them. As a three-partner office, Mackay explains, they designed everything from the largest to the smallest

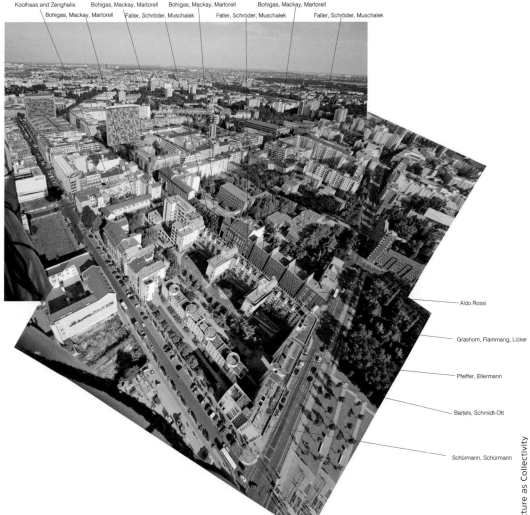

Koolhaas and Zenghelis   Bohigas, Mackay, Martorell   Bohigas, Mackay, Martorell   Bohigas, Mackay, Martorell

Bohigas, Mackay, Martorell   Faller, Schröder, Muschalek   Faller, Schröder, Muschalek   Faller, Schröder, Muschalek

Aldo Rossi

Grashorn, Flammang, Licker

Pfeiffer, Ellermann

Bartels, Schmidt-Ott

Schürmann, Schürmann

Figure II.26 Collaborators of Block 4 commissioned as a result of the "Kochstrasse/Friedrichstrasse Competition" project, IBA-1984/87, photographed by Esra Akcan, Berlin, 2011.

scale together, the three of them looking at the same piece of paper, discussing the project, and never settling on a solution through vote-by-majority but changing it until they reached a stage that all three of them fully agreed on. If there was a distribution of tasks, it involved their roles in the team, so that they could bring different perspectives to bear in the common discussion: Mackay concentrated on the project stage in the office; Martorell oversaw construction on site, when the design often continued to evolve as they adapted their projects to take account of new criteria emerging out of the sites; and Bohigas performed "as their biggest critic," connecting them to current intellectual discourses as a university professor and a public figure.[143] In this context, the discussions with Kleihues on even the minutest details and the consequent design changes must have never seemed to them as interference with their creativity. "You

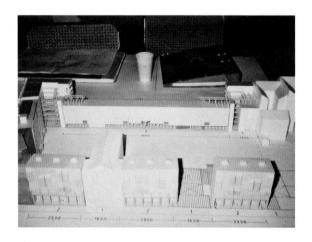

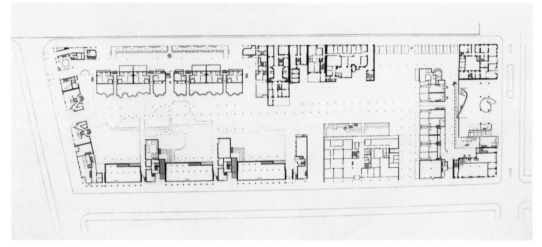

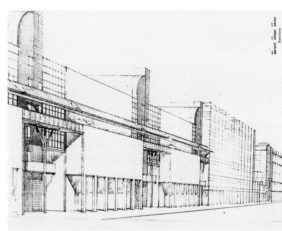

TOP: Figure II.27 Bohigas, Mackay, and Martorell, Study model for Block 4 commissioned as a result of the "Kochstrasse/Friedrichstrasse Competition" project, IBA-1984/87. MIDDLE: Figure II.28 Bohigas, Mackay, and Martorell, Plan for Block 4 commissioned as a result of the "Kochstrasse/ Friedrichstrasse Competition" project, IBA-1984/87. BOTTOM: Figure II.29 Bohigas, Mackay, and Martorell, Block 4, IBA-1984/87, street-in-the-air.

have to remember that we always work with three partners together, and we are used to discussing our designs," Mackay says. "We like it, because you learn from people looking at the building differently, and it is richer. You have your ideas, and it is nice to be challenged, to make sure they are valid."[144]

Nonetheless, I use the term "open architecture" in discussing the collaborative design for Block 4 in a different sense than team work in a single office or deliberations with a client or director (Figure II.26). After the competition, IBA commissioned Bohigas, Mackay, and Martorell to design four nonadjacent sites along Kochstrasse and the green area inside the block, and asked them to coordinate the designs for the other lots that were produced by six other architectural firms. The team wrote general guidelines for the participating architects.[145] Mackay, who oversaw the Berlin project from its initial competition stage to the end of its construction, remembers that the collaboration between the architects came together in Stuttgart in a meeting that lasted all day and into the night. The photographs of study models crammed in between sketches, folders, and coffee mugs confirm that the architectural teams must have worked on their parts that infilled the overall perimeter block, and the group must have deliberated on the collective effect of their individual contributions (Figure II.27).

Mackay suggested integrating elements that connected the buildings of different architects in ways that would be more than typically taking account of buildings in adjacent sites. Unlike the stylistic guidelines that regulated the continuity of the row houses in the collaborative design directed by Rob Krier (stop I), these buildings also shared inner circulation paths and unbroken façade elements. A continuous arcade on the ground floor created a pedestrian walkway for the shops at that level, while a continuous street in the air like a cornice on the façade connected the dwelling units (Figure II.28). Mackay says that "we all agreed that this cornice will bring down the scale [of the building], and it would be a community creator"[146] (Figure II.29). The other architectural offices, especially that of Faller, Schröder, and Muschalek must have worked with Mackay on the common entrances and circulation paths of their adjacent buildings (Figure II.30). Bohigas, Mackay, and Martorell's three identical but separated buildings functioned as gateways into the block, because the architects integrated the entrances both to the buildings and the green area inside the block with outdoor stairs climbing up to the back terraces and the street in the air. These triplet buildings shared a promenade that brought together multiple circulation paths: those from the street to the park inside the block; from the street or park to the urban terrace facing the park; from the street, park, or terrace to the street in the air that connected the buildings along Kochstrasse; and from all these common outdoor spaces to individual apartments. These triplets were placed perpendicularly to the green area, thereby creating smaller niches in the large neighborhood park inside without dividing it up (Figure II.31).

The collaborative design process for the Friedrichstrasse edge with Koolhaas's OMA (Office of Metropolitan Architecture) was further complicated because of the demands of the American Cold War forces related to their checkpoint. The original competition design had suggested an inner street between Friedrichstrasse and Wilhelmstrasse,

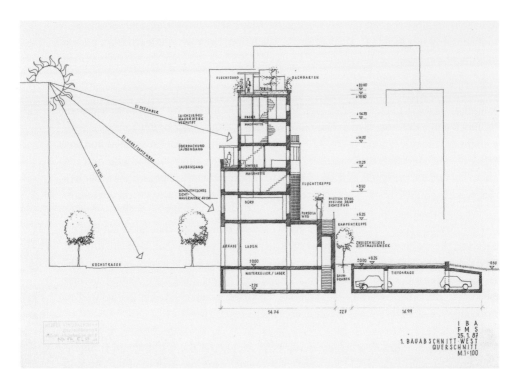

TOP: Figure II.30 Faller, Schröder, and Muschalek, Building in Block 4, IBA-1984/87. BOTTOM: Figure II.31 View from Hof-garden in Bohigas, Mackay, and Martorell's Block 4 for IBA-1984/87, photographed by Esra Akcan, Berlin, 2011.

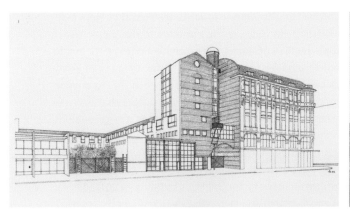

TOP: Figure II.32 Bohigas, Mackay, and Martorell, Building in Block 4 commissioned as a result of the "Kochstrasse/Friedrichstrasse Competition" project, IBA-1984/87. BOTTOM: Figure II.33 Views of Hof-garden with "Gaudí bench" and urban terrace in Bohigas, Mackay, and Martorell's Block 4 for IBA-1984/87, photographed by Esra Akcan, Berlin, 2011.

with big portals at both ends. However, the American allies insisted that OMA's design prevented an open gate, thereby eliminating the entrance to the public street in between. Even though multiple public entrances were provided to the park inside Block 4, its character as a complete passage was impaired, and the opening to Friedrichstrasse was completely blocked.[147] There was a controversy when the Americans refused to contribute to the buildings' public housing budget, a debate that was carried into daily newspapers.[148] There was an additional crisis when the American allies demanded that armed vehicles and small tanks had to be able to come through OMA's building and go out of the building designed by Bohigas, Mackay, and Martorell without being seen.[149] It must have been this secret underground passage in between the buildings that I used with a former resident to enter OMA's building in 2012, after it had been vacated because of gentrification. The two offices worked closely together, meeting in Berlin and London and sharing the stages of design with each other.[150] As a result, OMA, represented by Elia Zenghelis and Matthias Sauerbruch for this project, designed the building along Friedrichstrasse (stop VI), and Bohigas, Mackay, and Martorell designed the L-shaped building on the eastern edge of the block, which communicated with both their triplets along Kochstrasse and OMA's building (Figure II.32).

Finally, the collaboration of the architects who designed the block edges along the Berlin Wall and the Wilhelmstrasse was enabled through several meetings in Berlin, where Mackay—who by then was going to the city every two months—was asked to comment on the design stages.[151] His biggest disagreement with Kleihues—on the space and façade facing the wall—occurred at this point. While Mackay was worried about the wall's effect, Kleihues seems to have been certain that the wall would come down.[152] The long building along the wall, designed by Bartels and Schmidt-Ott, had private gardens facing the green area inside Block 4. Rather than proposing a fence to divide the private gardens from the public park, Bohigas, Mackay, and Martorell used their competition project's Gaudí bench—which was already being prefabricated in Barcelona—here to function both as a retaining wall to protect the private gardens and as a seat for the community in the park (Figure II.33).

During this design process, the appearance of the block changed tremendously as well. Gone were the monumental stone façades, small windows, arched porches, and heavy entrance towers that had reminded some Berliners of concentration camps rather than water towers, as the architects had intended. The style that the architects had chosen for the block's perceived reminiscence of "Prussian elements" was replaced with whitewashed walls, flat roofs, and large windows: "As we worked on, we did a self-criticism. ... We became conscious of Berlin architecture in the twentieth century as a leader of social housing. We had much more dialogue than [during] the competition times."[153] The triplet buildings along the Kochstrasse that punctuated the long façade with their slightly higher vaulted towers were in dialogue with the towers of Rossi's design across the street, as were the uses of brick and green steel elements to carry and cover the street in the air (Figure II.34).

Despite the significant changes, Bohigas, Mackay, and Martorell insisted on two design elements that had already been established in the competition stage: the street in the

Figure II.34 View of Block 10 by Aldo Rossi (left) and Block 4 by Bohigas, Mackay, and Martorell (right) for IBA-1984/87, photographed by Esra Akcan, Berlin, 2011.

air and the continuous green area inside the block. Mackay believes that streets in the air, where neighbors can talk to each other, are one of the main contributions that architecture can make to immigrants' lives.[154] Another type of space to build solidarities and networks is obviously the neighborhood park. The green area inside Block 4 is one of the largest in Berlin, comparable to the city's canonical horseshoe-shape park in Britz Housing, designed by Taut and Wagner. While the other IBA Neubau buildings introduced a scale that turned the cramped and dark Hof spaces of Berlin's nineteenth-century Mietskasernen into large and pleasant Hof-gardens, the area in Block 4 is much bigger, on the scale of a large neighborhood park. Mackay says: "We believe in neighborhood parks [that are] common property for everybody living around [them]. …We are very much influenced by the original nineteenth-century Cerda plan [in Barcelona] who provided gardens in the center of each block."[155] Some of the landscape architects proposed to divide the area up into separate smaller gardens, but Bohigas, Mackay, and Martorell insisted on its unity and continuity, so that it would be a large park and a connecting urban element between the streets.[156] While the architects used the term "closed city block" for their projects that physically defined streets and inner gardens to differentiate them from the freestanding, prismatic, open blocks of the postwar period, they provided open access to the areas inside the blocks through large and inviting urban gates.

Figure II.35 View of the entrance to the Hof-garden of Bohigas, Mackay, and Martorell's Block 4 for IBA-1984/87, photographed by Esra Akcan, Berlin, 2009.

Even though I had heard some complaints from residents about the lack of privacy, the neighborhood park inside Block 4 had worked quite well before the iron gates closed it up around 2012 (Figure II.35). Children used to play safely inside, and neighbors used to have regular meetings on the Gaudí bench. N.Y. confirms: "It was better without the gates. Neighbors from other blocks also came in, everybody met there, we used to drink our tea there, got to know each other."[157] She used to take a shortcut through the Hof-garden to go to the grocery store and other such common destinations, but now that she has the key to only the iron gate that is the closest to her apartment, she can no longer do that. As a result, she finds herself using the neighborhood park less and less: "It [adding the gates] might have been better for the security of the kids, but the kids from neighboring apartments can no longer come in to play. It is no longer pleasant. It is too official. One feels as if entering someone else's garden."[158]

Even though having an apartment of her own is infinitely better than living in a *Heim*, N.Y. thinks the Berlin apartments compare poorly to those in her hometown in Turkey. If her family had designed these apartments, they would have made the kitchen much bigger, included a large separate pantry, added a dining room, and made the rooms bigger—instead of what she calls "half rooms," which she compares to graves.[159] What N.Y. appreciates the most about her apartment in Block 4 is the open view of the Topography of Terror (an indoor and outdoor history museum) across from her building, another important IBA competition site that used to be the Nazi headquarters

Figure II.36 View from N.Y.'s apartment overlooking the Topography of Terror Museum, photographed by Esra Akcan, Berlin, 2011.

before it was bombed, and for which John Hejduk designed his unbuilt "Victims" project (stop VII) (Figure II.36). Over the years, N.Y. watched out of her window as this site was transformed from a pile of debris so high that she could see only the top floor of the Martin Gropius Bau Museum at the other end of the site, to a memorial and documentation center for the victims of World War II. She still remembers the morning when the cellar of the Gestapo headquarters for torturing and executing political prisoners was discovered: "There, in that corner, over an area of forty square meters, they found many rubber tires placed side by side. I assume they were used to isolate the sound of torture."[160] It is not that she, a Kurdish refugee escaping from Turkish state violence, had deliberately chosen to live in an apartment that overlooks a site that reminds her of the Jews tortured by the Nazi German state, that is in a building block designed by a Catalan architectural firm whose members criticize Spanish fascism, and that is located in a neighborhood in which German discrimination against foreigners from Turkey is a frequent topic of conversation. But she is certainly apt to notice urban signs of state brutality and racism that intertwine the histories of multiple places and peoples throughout the twentieth century.

Across the street in Block 10, Rossi—with his partner Braghieri and contact architects in the Berlin office of Grötzebach, Plessow, and Ehlers—constructed a building that soon became one of the most cited examples of the architects' oeuvre (Figure II.37). Of the offices that were commissioned to design buildings in this block as a result of the

Figure II.37 View of Block 10 by Aldo Rossi (front) and Block 4 Bohigas, Mackay, and Martorell (back) for IBA-1984/87, photographed by Esra Akcan, Berlin, 2012.

competition, only Rossi's eventually got to realize its project, which meant that IBA's collaborative urban design strategy was not used in this iconic site. This must not have mattered much to Rossi. What he meant by collectivity in architecture had little to do with collaborative urban design, anyway. Typological design method to Rossi involved communicating with the collective memory of the city, including with architects who were long dead, rather than designing an urban district together with colleagues.

During the competition, the jury had found the gallery connecting the apartments on upper levels to be inappropriate for this site. Rossi had declared that galleries, or "open corridors to function as streets," that he had used in Gallaratese Housing were remarkable attributes of public housing as a type. However, following the jury's demands, Rossi and Braghieri turned their L-shaped corner building into terraced housing with rhythmically placed separate entrances and vertical circulation cores, which indeed accentuated the signature towers. This also meant that unit balconies faced the Hof-garden, and these balconies are among the most pleasant spaces in the building, according to Çetiner (Figure II.38). The other memorable façade elements in the competition version remained: the fully transparent glass walls along the east-facing Wilhelmstrasse extended to the entire height of the façade, with their green metal frames dividing the surfaces into squares and the sloping glass roofs giving them the appearance of greenhouses. From the inside, this striking gesture on the façade created quite idiosyncratic spaces, defining winter gardens as narrow as 175 centimeters, and at several points 55 centimeters wide (Figure II.39). Though I doubt that anyone uses these

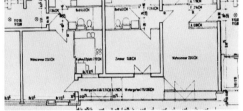

Figure II.38 View of the rear façade of Aldo Rossi's Block 10 for IBA-1984/87, photographed by Esra Akcan, Berlin, 2010.

Figure II.39 View of the winter gardens (also includes detail of plan) in Aldo Rossi's Block 10 for IBA-1984/87, photographed by Esra Akcan, Berlin, 2011.

narrow spaces as living room extensions, the winter gardens invite residents to use their imagination: some use it for plants, others as a smoking area, and still others for storage, others as a void and children always find a way to play there (Figure II.40). The fat round column reminiscent of the Filarete column in Venice also remained, defining a public entrance to the garden inside the block through a narrow passageway. However, it has been quite easy to close this hidden gate with an iron fence, which turned the Hof-garden into a private outdoor space to be used only by the residents of the building.

If we were to follow Rossi's analogy between architecture and theater, which he used to explain his design for Teatro del Mondo that sailed on the waters during the 1979 Venice Architecture Biennale, architectural form is like a fixed stage that becomes the site of a theatrical experience only when the actors are present.[161] Similarly, a form becomes an architectural experience, a building, with the cycles of life and death that take place in it. The first thing Çetiner says about living in an Aldo Rossi building is that "it is a very functional apartment, especially its kitchen," even though this may not come as a compliment to an architect who built his reputation by criticizing naïve functionalism.[162] She especially enjoys the cross-ventilated kitchen with big windows, which she decorated using special white lattice curtains that become a frequent topic of our conversation (Figure II.41). What she appreciates the most is the apartment's brightness and open view over the large Hof-garden, which allows light to enter throughout the day and her plants to grow (Figure II.42).[163] She hardly

Figure II.40 View of the use of a winter garden in
Aldo Rossi's Block 10 for IBA-1984/87, photographed
by Esra Akcan, Berlin, 2011.

spends time in the Hof-garden, meeting friends and family members instead in the
park across the street, in the interior of the block designed by Bohigas, Mackay, and
Martorell—because her daughter used to live in one of the apartments facing the big
urban terrace there, before having to leave due to the high rent. "Now the rich, the
lawyers and doctors, live in that building," Çetiner says, confirming the anxiety of
N.Y. and others about the termination of the IBA buildings' public housing status and
Kreuzberg's gentrification.[164] As a matter of fact, high rents constitute the most frequent topic of our conversations about architecture, exposing yet again the agonizing
burden of capitalism on residents of public housing, as well as on architecture itself.
In contrast to N.Y., however, Çetiner thinks that the iron gates privatizing the neighborhood park in Block 4 have improved it: "Many outsiders used to come in, … drunken
people—we were afraid to go out there at night."[165] Perhaps one democratic way to
take into account different residents' views would have been to keep it public during
the day but semiprivate at night, as Mackay suggests—just like "public parks that close
at night."[166]

Unlike all of the other residents discussed in this book, neither Çetiner nor N.Y.
changed much in their respective apartments. After her husband passed away, Çetiner stopped using the bedroom, freezing the space at the time of his death.[167] Similarly,
N.Y. explains that she has never identified herself with an architectural space, as she
has constantly lived with a sense of temporality, the almost certain feeling that as a
refugee she would soon have to move again for some reason.[168] Probably as a coincidence, my conversations with both women end with an indication that they actually

Figure II.41 View of the lattice curtains in Çetiner's apartment in Aldo Rossi's Block 10 for IBA-1984/87, photographed by Esra Akcan, Berlin, 2016.

spend their time somewhere different than the physical space they inhabit. Çetiner's days are taken up with the episodes of quite a few Turkish TV shows that she can now watch, due to the legalization of satellite dishes in Germany[169] (See Figure VII.24). She wears a high-tech headset that receives the sound when she is cooking in the kitchen, sitting on the balcony, or even is outside the building to run a quick errand. Her son, a self-taught computer expert, brought the headset for her.[170] N.Y. also uses modern technology that lets her fly to her hometown even if she is not legally allowed to physically cross the border. With the invention of phones with cameras, she can now see her daughter whom she had left behind in Turkey and then not met for eighteen years. "We try to get to know each other like this," she says.[171] She also watches, over and over again, the tapes. "The tapes?" I asked. It turns out that her friends and family members who can visit Turkey bring back videotapes on which they have recorded funerals, weddings, dinners, occasional get-togethers, or individual messages from her family members, as well as views of the mountains and trees, shepherds and lambs, and the changing city of Mardin. Sometimes she orders a tape of some of her favorite places before they depart, just as her-son-in-law recently ordered a video of an acorn tree—which reminds me of the artwork by Emily Jacir titled "Where We Come From" (2001–3), composed of the photographs of the places that the Palestinian refugees reported as sites they wished to be able to experience one more time. The tapes do not have to show N.Y.'s own relatives or her own former house and garden; she borrows and watches others' tapes, too. She mentions a couple of times the videos that show the imaginary graves of her dead relatives.[172] Enforced disappearance, a crime according to the United Nations, has been a common act of military juntas, including the one

Figure II.42 View of plants in Çetiner's apartment in Aldo Rossi's Block 10 for IBA-1984/87, photographed by Esra Akcan, Berlin, 2016.

in Turkey—which resulted in 750 disappeared people in 1994–95 alone.[173] The lack of real graves for N.Y.'s relatives raises again a question that Judith Butler has asked: "What makes for a grievable life?"[174] Why does the state apparatus consider some lives mournable but others so unmournable that it denies them graves? If architecture is what remains after death, as Rossi said, how are we to think of the architecture for refugees who are denied a grievable death?

1 Josef Paul Kleihues, "Die IBA vor dem Hintergrund der Berliner Architektur- und Stadtplanung des 20. Jahrhunderts," in *Modelle für eine Stadt*, ed. Vittorio Magnago Lampugnani (Berlin: IBA, Siedler Verlag, 1984): 24–36; Claus Baldus, "Kein Leben'ges ist ein Haus, immer ist's ein Vieles," in *Josef Paul Kleihues im Gespräch* (Berlin: Ernst Wasmuth Verlag, 1996), 13–54; Josef Paul Kleihues, "From the Destruction to the Critical Reconstruction of the City: Urban Design in Berlin after 1945," in *Berlin—NY: Like and Unlike*, ed. Josef Paul Kleihues and Christina Rathgeber (New York: Rizzoli, 1993), 395–409. See also Aldo Rossi, *Architecture of the City*, trans. Diane Ghirardo and Joan Ockman (Cambridge, MA: MIT Press, 1982). **2** Rossi declared that he wrote *Architecture of the City* in the early 1960s—the years when he was simultaneously publishing articles in *Casabella*. See Aldo Rossi, *A Scientific Autobiography*, trans. Lawrence Venuti (Chicago: Graham Foundation, 1981), 15. For a collection of Rossi's early writings, see Aldo Rossi, *Scritti scelti sull'architettura e la città 1956–1972* (Milan: Clup, 1975). For thorough discussions of Rossi's early writings, see especially Carlo Olmo, "Across the Texts," trans. Jessica Levine, *Assemblage* 5, February (1988): 90–121; Bernard Huet, "L'Heritage d'Aldo Rossi,"

AMC 84 (November 1997): 58–61; Mary Louise Lobsinger, "The New Urban Scale in Italy: On Aldo Rossi's 'L'architettura della città,'" *Journal of Architectural Education* 59, no. 3 (2006): 28–38; Pier Vittorio Aureli, "The Difficult Whole," *Log*, no. 9 (2007): 39–61. **3** Ernesto Rogers, "The Problem of Building within Existing Environments," *Zodiac* 3 (April 1990): 8–11. Quotation: 8. Historians have pointed out the Gramscian position of the members of Rogers's circle in criticizing capitalist greed as an influence on the young Rossi. See Micha Bandini, introduction to Micha Bandini, David Dunster, and Aldo Rossi, *Aldo Rossi: Architecture, Buildings and Projects* (London: Institute of Contemporary Arts, 1983). **4** Rogers, "The Problem of Building within Existing Environments," 10. **5** This does not mean that the journal failed to follow the contemporary work of canonical Western European and North American architects, accompanied with occasional reportage on non-Western architecture in dialogue with the Western centers. For example, in the period 1958–64, the journal reported on the work of Alvar Aalto, Louis Kahn, Le Corbusier, Mies van der Rohe, Paul Rudolf, and Frank Lloyd Wright; the work of Felix Candela in Mexico, Oscar Niemeyer in Brazil, and Kenzo Tange in Japan; and the work of the European émigrés Josep Lluis Sert and Walter Gropius in Iraq. **6** In chronological order, Aldo Rossi, "Una critica che respingiamo," *Casabella*, no. 219 (1958): 32–35, "Emil Kaufmann e l'architettura dell'illuminismo," *Casabella*, no. 222 (1958): 43–47, "Adolf Loos," *Casabella*, no. 233 (1959): 5–11, "Aspetti dell'architettura tedesca contemporanea," *Casabella*, no. 235 (1960): 27–32, "Peter Behrens e il problema dell'abitazione moderna," *Casabella*, no. 240 (1960): 47–48, "Un giovane architetto tedesco: Oswald Mathias Ungers," *Casabella*, no. 244 (1960): 22–35, and "Un Piano per Vienna," *Casabella*, no. 277 (1963): 3–21. **7** Aldo Rossi, "Aspetti della Tipologia Residenziale a Berlino," *Casabella*, no. 288 (1964): 11–20. The Rome issue was *Casabella*, no. 279 (1963), and the Milan issue was *Casabella*, no. 282 (1963). **8** Vittorio Gregotti, "L'architettura dell'Espressionismo," *Casabella*, no. 254 (1961): 24–50. **9** Aldo Rossi, "Adolf Loos," *Casabella*, no. 233 (1959): 5–11. **10** Adolf Loos's "Furniture for Sitting" (1898) and "The Poor Little Rich Man" (1900) are reprinted in Adolf Loos, *Spoken into the Void: Collected Essays 1897–1900* (Cambridge, MA: MIT Press, 1983), 28–33 and 124–29, respectively. His "Interior Design: A Prelude" (1898) and "The Interiors in the Rotunda" (1898) are reprinted in Adolf Loos, *Ornament and Crime: Selected Essays* (Riverside, CA: Ariadne, 1997), 51–56 and 57–62, respectively. **11** Aldo Rossi, "Modernism's Trajectory: Rossi on Loos," *Skyline*, April 1982, 18–22. Quotation: 19. **12** Ibid., 20–21. **13** Aldo Rossi, "Thoughts about My Recent Work," *A + U*, vol. 65, no. 5 (1976): 83. **14** Ernesto Rogers, editorial, *Casabella*, no. 223 (1959): 1. **15** Rossi, "Aspetti dell'architettura tedesca contemporanea," 31. **16** Rossi, "Un giovane architetto tedesco: Oswald Mathias Ungers," 22. A partial English translation of the essay appeared in *Casabella*, no. 654 (1998): 18. **17** See Esra Akcan, "Manfredo Tafuri's Theory of Architectural Avant-Garde," *Journal of Architecture* 7, no. 2 (2002): 135–70. **18** Gian Ugo Polesello, Aldo Rossi, and Francesco Tentori, "Il Problema della periferia nella città moderna," *Casabella*, no. 241 (1960): 39–55. **19** A. Rossi, E. Mattioni, G. Polesello, and L. Semerani, "Città e territorio negli aspetti funzionali e figurativi della pianificazione continua," reprinted in Rossi, *Scritti scelti sull'architettura e la città 1956–1972*, 289–297. Quotation: 290. In this article Rossi and his co-authors criticize Tange's project for Tokyo for not offering any alternative to current living forms, despite its new look. For Rossi's comments on Giancarlo de Carlo, see Aldo Rossi, "Nuovi problemi," *Casabella*, no. 264 (1962): 3–6. **20** Rossi, Mattioni, Polesello, and Semerani "Città e territorio negli aspetti funzionali e figurativi della pianificazione continua," 291. **21** Lobsinger, "The New Urban Scale in Italy," 34. For other articles that have mentioned the Istituto Nationale di Urbanistica speech as an important juncture in Rossi's thinking, see Bernard Huet, "Aldo Rossi or the Exaltation of Reason," in *Aldo Rossi: Tre città / Three Cities: Perugia, Milano, Mantova* (New York: Electa / Rizzoli, 1984), 10–13; Olmo, "Across the Texts"; Aureli, "The Difficult Whole." **22** Carlo Aymonino, "Una Città 'Aperta'," *Casabella*, no. 288 (1964): 53–54. **23** Aldo Rossi, "La diversità di Berlino," *Casabella*, no. 632 (March 1996): 22–25. **24** Rossi wrote: "My convictions of the following: 1. With respect to urban intervention today one should operate on a limited

part of the city … 2. The city is not by nature a creation that can be reduced to a single basic idea" (*Architecture of the City*, 64). **25** Rossi, "Aspetti della Tipologia Residenziale a Berlino" and *Architecture of the City*, 72–82. **26** Rossi, *Architecture of the City*, 46–48. **27** Ibid., 22. **28** To demonstrate alternative ways of categorization, Rossi mentioned Jean Tricart (who employed economic categories such the precapitalist, capitalist, paracapitalist, and socialist houses), Marcel Poete (who believed that the street, the monument, and their permanence were what made a city unique) and Milizia (who classified urban artifacts in relation to their private and public functions, location in the city, form and organization). See ibid., 48–55. **29** Ibid., 53. **30** Ibid., 72–82. **31** Ibid., 82. Rossi contrasted the Weimar *Siedlungen* in Berlin to the postwar housing on the city's periphery. "What a loss that the lesson of these modern architects went on deaf ears after World War II!" Polesello, Rossi, Tentori, "Il Problema della periferia nella città moderna." **32** Rossi, *Architecture of the City*, 32 and 34. **33** Quatremère de Quincy, "Type," *Oppositions Reader: Selected Essays 1973–84*, ed. Michael Hays (New York: Princeton Architectural Press, 1998): 618. **34** Ibid., 619. Midway between the extremes of rigidity and fancy, this theory of architecture based on type appealed to its promoters because it allowed for ordered, controlled, and disciplined imagination. **35** Rossi, *Architecture of the City*, 126 and 130. **36** Aureli, "The Difficult Whole." **37** Rossi, *Architecture of the City*, 40. **38** Ibid., 106. **39** Ibid., 161–62. **40** Ibid., 116. **41** Ibid. **42** Aldo Rossi, *A Scientific Autobiography*, trans. Lawrence Venuti (Cambridge, MA: MIT Press, 1981), 1. **43** Rossi, *Architecture of the City*, 179. **44** Ibid., 116. **45** Sarah Juliet Lauro and Karen Embry, "A Zombie Manifesto: The Nonhuman Condition in the Era of Advanced Capitalism," *boundary* 235, no. 1 (2008): 85–108. Quotation: 87. See also Donna Haraway, "A Cyborg Manifesto: Science, Technology, and Socialist-Feminism in the Late Twentieth Century," *Simians, Cyborgs and Women: The Reinvention of Nature* (London: Routledge, 1991). **46** For an engaging reading of this building, see Eugene Johnson, "What Remains of Man—Aldo Rossi's Modena Cemetery," *Journal of the Society of Architectural Historians* 41, no. 1 (1982): 38–54. **47** Aldo Rossi, "The Blue of the Sky," *Oppositions* (Summer 1976): 31–34. The article was reprinted in *AD* 52, no. 2 (1982): 39–41. **48** Aldo Rossi, "Analogous City: Panel," *Lotus* 13, December (1976): 1–9. For interpretations of the drawing, see Peter Eisenman, "The House of the Dead as the City of Survival," in *Aldo Rossi in America: 1976–1979* (New York: Institute for Architecture and Urban Studies, 1979); Johnson, "What Remains of Man"; Micha Bandini, David Dunster, and Aldo Rossi, *Aldo Rossi: Architecture, Buildings and Projects* (London: Institute of Contemporary Arts, 1983); Carsten Ruhl, "Im Kopf des Architekten: Aldo Rossis La città analoga," *Zeitschrift für Kunstgeschichte* 69, no. 1 (2006): 67–98. **49** According to Johnson, Rossi was influenced by Boullée, who was inspired by the shadow of his own body in the moonlight while designing funerary buildings as an architecture of extreme sadness. Building on Boullée, Rossi defined architecture whose "cycle is natural, like the cycle of man," as "what *remains* of man" (quoted in Johnson, "What

Remains of Man," 54). Diogo Seixas Lopes, *Melancholy and Architecture. On Aldo Rossi* (Zurich: Park Books, 2015). Quotation: 168, 205. **50** Bernard Huet, "L'Héritage d'Aldo Rossi," *AMC* 84 (November 1997): 58–61. **51** Bernard Huet, "After the Glorification of Reason: Aldo Rossi: From National Abstraction to Emblematic Representation," *Lotus* 48–49 (1985–86): 209–15. Quotation: 212. **52** Val K. Warke, "Type—Silence—Genre," *Log* 5 (Sprıng / Summer 2005): 122–29. Quotation: 124. See also Mikhail Bakhtin, *The Dialogical Imagination: Four Essays* (Austin: University of Texas Press, 1982). **53** Diana Agrest, interview with Aldo Rossi, *Skyline*, September 1979, 4. **54** These works were designed by Adolf Behne, Le Corbusier, Garnier, Mosei Ginzburg, Ludwig Hilberseimer, I. I. Leonidov, Loos, Taut, and Giuseppe Terragni. **55** E. Bonfati, R. Bonicalzi, G. Branghieri, F. Raggi, A. Rossi, M. Scolari, and D. Vitale, *Architettura Razionale*, 4th ed. (Milan: Franco Angeli Editore, 1979). **56** *Rational Architecture: The Reconstruction of the European City* (Brussels: Archives d'Architecture Moderne, 1978). **57** Robert Delevoy, "Towards an Architecture," in ibid., 14–22. **58** Leon Krier, "The Reconstruction of the City," in ibid., 38–42. Quotation: 41. **59** Anthony Vidler, "The Third Typology," in ibid., 28–32. **60** Ibid., 31. **61** Rossi wrote that "we can study the city from a number of points of view, but it emerges as autonomous only when we take it as a fundamental given, as a construction and as architecture; only when we analyze urban artifacts for what they are, the final constructed result of a complex operation, taking into account all of the facts of this operation which cannot be embraced by the history of architecture, by sociology, or by other sciences" (*Architecture of the City*, 22). **62** Eisenman, "The House of the Dead as the City of Survival." Eisenman also wrote the introduction to the English translation of Rossi, *Architecture of the City*. **63** "Autonomous Architecture," special issue, *Harvard Architecture Review* 3 (Winter 1984). **64** Claudio d'Amato, "Fifteen Years after the Publication of the *Architecture of the City* by Aldo Rossi: The Contribution of Urban Studies to Autonomy of Architecture," in ibid., 83–92. Quotation: 83. **65** "Autonomous Architecture," special issue, *Harvard Architecture Review* 3 (Winter 1984): 93. **66** Vittorio Magnago Lampugnani, "Das Ganze und die Teile: Typologie und Funktionalismus in der Architektur des 19. und 20. Jahrhunderts," in *Modelle für eine Stadt*, ed. Vittorio Magnago Lampugnani (Berlin: IBA, Siedler Verlag, 1984), 83–117. **67** Günsel Çetiner, interview by the author, June 29, 2012, Berlin, in Turkish, Tape 1, 00:27:53. Both audio and video recordings of this interview are in the author's collection. **68** Ibid., Tape 1, 00:49:00–00:54:00. **69** Ibid., Tape 1, 00:28.27. Also at 00:30:51. **70** Ibid., Tape 1, 00:21:34–00:24:00. **71** Ibid., Tape 1, 00:36:00–00:39:04. **72** Ibid., Tape 2, 00:00:54–00:01:30. **73** See, for instance, Gökçe Yurdakul, *From Guest Workers into Muslims: The Transformation of Turkish Immigrant Associations in Germany* (Newcastle, UK: Cambridge Scholars Publishing, 2009). **74** Çetiner, interview by the author, Tape 2, 01:12:33. **75** Ibid., Tape 2, 00:51:00. **76** Ulrich Herbert, *Geschichte der Ausländerpolitik in Deutschland* (Munich: Beck, 2001). **77** Elisabeth Beck-Gernsheim, "Turkish Brides: A Look at the Immigration Debate in Germany," in *Migration, Citizenship, Ethnos,*

ed. Y. Michal Bodemann and Gökçe Yurdakul (New York: Palgrave Macmillan, 2006), 185–95. **78** Quoted in ibid., 187. **79** Çetiner, interview by the author, Tape 1, 00:12:51–00:13:08. **80** Accessed January 2010, http://www.belgenet.com/12eylul/12092000_01.html. For more documents, see accessed January 2010, http://www.belgenet.com/12eylul/12eylul.html. **81** For interviews with eighteen male refugees in Europe who sought asylum because of the coup, see Emin Karaca, *12 Eylül'ün Arka Bahçesinde Avrupa'daki Mültecilerle Konuşmalar* (Istanbul: Siyah Beyaz, 2008). **82** N.Y., interview by the author, summer 2012 (also in 2011), Berlin, in Turkish. Tape 1, 00:03:56. Both audio and video recordings of this interview are in the author's collection. **83** Ibid., Tape 1, 02:21:25. **84** Ibid., Tape 1, 00:06:59–00:08:15. **85** Ibid., Tape 1, 00:11:00. **86** Ibid. **87** For the *Heim* buildings of the first generation of guest workers, see Metin Uyaner, "Arbeiterwohnheime für die Migraten in NRW—Eine historische Darstellung der 60er und 70er Jahre," Essen, 1996. In Domit Index. www.domit.de. **88** N.Y., interview by the author, Tape 1, 00:29:36–00:39:58. **89** Ibid., Tape 1, 00:22:03–00:24:34. **90** Ibid., Tape 1, 00:24:22. **91** The figures are taken from Gernot and Johanne Nalbach, *Berlin Modern Architecture: Exhibition Catalogue* (Berlin: STERN, 1989); and *Josef Paul Kleihues im Gespräch* (Berlin: Ernst Wasmuth Verlag, 1996). **92** Senator für Bau und Wohnungswesen, "Städtebauliche Studie Kochstraße Südliche Friedrichstadt," Berlin, Report of July 1979, IBA Documents / Drawings, B 79/001, Landesarchiv; Alfred Buch and Hans Brachetti, "Gutachten zur Planung Fernwärmeversorgung Kreuzberg-West." Report of December 1979, IBA Documents / Drawings, B91/191, Landesarchiv; Katharina George-Barz, "Die Südliche Friedrichstadt," Report. Undated, IBA Documents / Drawings, B91/188, Landesarchiv. **93** Dieter Hoffmann-Axthelm, "Keine Kreuzung wie jede andere," *Bauwelt* 81, no. 15 (20 April 1990): 752–63. **94** The invited architects or groups were: Dieter Baumewerd (Münster); Oriol Bohigas, Josep Martorell, and David Mackay (Barcelona); Peter Faller et al. (Stuttgart); Hans Kollhoff and Arthur Ovaska (Berlin); Rem Koolhaas (Amsterdam), and Joachim Schürmann (Cologne), for Block 4; Ernst Bartels and Christoph Schmidt-Ott (Berlin); Peter Eisenman and Jaquelin Robertson (New York); Hans Kammerer et al. (Stuttgart); Kisho Kurokawa (Japan); Gerhard Spangenberg and Dieter Frowein (Berlin); and Werner Wirsing (Munich) for Block 5; Raimund Abraham (New York); Peter Berten (Berlin); Burghard Grasshorn (Dortmund); Dietmar Grötzebach and Günter Plessow (Berlin); Aldo Rossi (Milan), and Ante Josip von Kostelac (Darmstadt) for Block 10; and Klaus-Theo Brenner and Benedict Tonon (Berlin); Jochem Jourdan and Bernhard Müller (Darmstadt); Herbert Pfeiffer (Lüdinghausen); Bruno Reichlin and Fabio Reinhart (Zurich); Heinz Schudnagies and Uwe Hameyer (Berlin), and Robert Venturi and John Rauch (Philadelphia—who withdrew) for Block 11. The jurors were Max Bächer (Darmstadt), Vittorio Gregotti (Milan), John Hejduk (New York), Josef Paul Kleihues (Berlin), Hans Christian Müller (Berlin), Paolo Porthogesi (Rome), and Oswald Matthias Ungers (Cologne). During the evaluations, Werner Düttmann replaced Müller, Rob Krier replaced Hejduk, and Lampugnani replaced Ungers. The "technical advisors" included the art historians and architects Tilmann Buddensieg, Bernard Huet, and Heinrich Klotz. See "Internationaler engerer Wettbewerb Berlin Südliche Friedrichstadt Kochstraße/Friedrichstraße," competition brief (Berlin: Internationale Bauausstellung Berlin 1984, 1980): 14–17. Copies of the competition brief can be found at IBA Documents/Drawings, Landesarchiv; AP.142.S1.D63, 142-0089T, Rossi Papers, CCA; and DR 1991:0018:940, Eisenman Papers, CCA. **95** Rafael Moneo, "On Typology," *Oppositions* 13 (1978): 22–29. Quotation: 23. **96** "International Restricted Competition Kochstrasse/Friedrichstrasse: Minutes of Participants; and Juror's Colloquium," Minutes of the Meeting, IBA 644-1, MBM Archives, Arxiu COAC; Letter from IBA to all participants, jurors, alternate jurors, technical advisors, preliminary advisors and guests, IBB 644-6, MBM Archives, Arxiu COAC. **97** Ibid., 5. **98** Kleihues noted that "the four building blocks meeting at the junction of Kochstrasse and Friedrichstrasse represent a model project to which the recommendations put forward by the Friedrichstadt seminar and the basic principles of Internationale Bauausstellung 1984 apply." See Josef Paul Kleihues, "Introductory Remarks," in "Internationaler engerer Wettbewerb Berlin, Südliche Friedrichstadt Kochstraße/Friedrichstraße" competition brief (Berlin: Internationale Bauausstellung Berlin 1984, 1980), 10. **99** "Josef Paul Kleihues, interviewed by Lore Ditzen," *Architectural Review* 176 (September 1984): 42–44. **100** Kleihues, "Introductory Remarks," 10. **101** Thomas Biller and Wolfgang Schäche, "Appendix," in "Internationaler engerer Wettbewerb Berlin, Südliche Friedrichstadt Kochstraße/Friedrichstraße" (Berlin: Internationale Bauausstellung Berlin 1984, 1980), 70–110. **102** Ibid., 78. **103** "Internationaler engerer Wettbewerb Berlin, Südliche Friedrichstadt Kochstraße/Friedrichstraße," 24. **104** David Mackay, interview by the author, July 9, 2012, Barcelona, in English. Tape 1, 58:23–58:48. Both audio and video recordings of this interview are in the author's collection. **105** "Internationaler engerer Wettbewerb Berlin, Südliche Friedrichstadt Kochstraße/Friedrichstraße," competition brief, 46. The breakdown of dwelling units was also one of the questions in the participants' Q & A before the submission. See "International Restricted Competition, Kochstrasse/Friedrichstrasse: Reply to Inquires," DR 1991:0018:940, Eisenman Papers, CCA. **106** "Internationaler engerer Wettbewerb Berlin, Südliche Friedrichstadt Kochstraße/Friedrichstraße," 56. **107** Ibid., 44. **108** The preliminary examiners were Rainer Döring, Heinz Jürgen Drews, Christian Neeße, Regina Poly. "Internationaler engerer Wettbewerb Berlin Südliche Friedrichstadt Kochstraße/Friedrichstraße. Bericht der Vorprüfung," AP.142.S1.D63. 142-0089T, Rossi Papers, CCA. **109** The competition drawings can be found at AP.142.S1.D63, Rossi Papers, CCA; and IBA Documents/Drawings, 989–996, 1029–1035, Landesarchiv. **110** Aldo Rossi, "Premise: The Architecture of Berlin and the Project," Explanation report for entry project in the competition for Kochstrasse/Friedrichstrasse, 1–2. AP.142.S1.D63, 142-0089T, Rossi Papers, CCA. **111** Wolfgang Pehnt, "I B Aporien," in *Modelle für eine Stadt*, ed. Vittorio Magnago Lampugnani (Berlin: IBA, Siedler Verlag, 1984), 59–68. **112** Rossi, "Premise: The Architecture of Berlin and the

Project," 2. **113** Ibid., 1. **114** Aldo Rossi, "Looking at These Recent Projects: Housing at Kochstrasse, Berlin and Shopping Center in Parma," *Lotus* 57, no. 4 (1987): 7–29. Quotation: 9. **115** "Internationaler engerer Wettbewerb Berlin, Südliche Friedrichstadt Kochstraße/Friedrichstraße. Preisgerichtsprotokoll," IBA Documents/Drawings, B 81/041, n.p, Landesarchiv. **116** The official name of the office came to be Martorell Bohigas Mackay Architects (MBM). As Bohigas was invited to IBA competition, and Mackay worked on the Berlin building, I will use the architects' names in alphabetical order. The drawings can be found at IBA Documents/Drawings, 422 Bl. 1–7, also see 423, 424, 425 Bl. 1–5, Landesarchiv. **117** "Preisgerichtsprotokoll," n.p. **118** The competition drawings can be found at Martorell Bohigas Mackay Architects Archives [hereafter MBM Archives], Arxiu COAC, Barcelona; and IBA Papers and Documents 537 Bl. 1–12, 538, 1047, Landesarchiv. **119** "IBA Urban Design for Kochstrasse 65/Zimmerstrasse 19 Berlin Kreuzberg," manuscript, IBA 769-3, p.1, MBM Archives, Arxiu COAC, Barcelona; "Aspectos Generales," manuscript, IBB 644-1, MBM Archives, Arxiu COAC, Barcelona. **120** This point was also discussed by Mackay, interview by the author, Tape 1, 27:00–29:00. **121** Ibid., Tape 1, 00:29:07. **122** "Preisgerichtsprotokoll," n.p. **123** David Mackay to Klaus Groenke, March 16, 1981, IBB-644-6, MBM Archives, Arxiu COAC, Barcelona. The letter mentions conversations with Kleihues on March 6 and 12 in Berlin, where this decision was discussed. In the architects' archives, there is also a sketch that says "very important … Kleihues" and in which the site plan is schematically drawn with straight buildings. See IBB 644-1, MBM Archives, Arxiu COAC, Barcelona. **124** Confirmed by Mackay, interview by the author, Tape 1, 00:33:20–00:34:40. "Internationaler engerer Wettbewerb Berlin Südliche Friedrichstadt Kochstraße/Friedrichstraße. Bericht der Vorprüfung," Manuscript. AP142.S1.D63. 142-0089T, Rossi Papers, CCA. The preliminary examiners were Rainer Döring, Heinz Jürgen Drews, Christian Neeße, Regina Poly, "Vorprüfung" and "Preisgerichtsprotokoll," n.p. **125** The drawings can be found at IBA Documents and Papers, 1426 Bl. 1–16, Landesarchiv. **126** B. Reichlin et al., "Evocative Passion: Project for Kochstrasse," *Lotus* 32 (March 1981): 61–62. Quotation: 61. **127** Ibid., 62. **128** Handwritten note probably from Rem Koolhaas to Peter Eisenman. Folder DR1991:0018: 939, Eisenman papers, CCA. **129** "Preisgerichtsprotokoll," n.p. **130** "Feinprogramm." Manuscript of the building program of Block 4. Date 22.12.1981., IBB 644-6 MBM Archives, Arxiu COAC, Barcelona. **131** The added teams were Grashorn, Flammang, and Licker; Bartels and Schmidt-Ott; and Pfeiffer and Ellermann. Also see Mackay, interview by the author, Tape 1, 00:49:00. **132** "Preisgerichtsprotokoll," n.p. **133** Günter Schlusche, interview by the author, November 8, 2016, Berlin, in English. 00:23:00–00:30:00. Both audio and video recordings of this interview are in the author's collection. **134** "Wohnen in der Stadt," *Architektur + Wettbewerbe* 106 (1981); "Konzepte und Ideen: Wohnen und Arbeiten in der südlichen Friedrichstadt: Ergebnisse eines internationalen Wettbewerbs," *Baukultur*, no. 3 (1981): 29–31; Lluis Domenech, "Berlin, gran padrino de la arquitectura," *La Vanguardia*, March 12, 1981; Lore Ditzen, "Die großen Konzepte setzen sich durch: Ein internationaler Architektur-Wettbewerb an der Berliner Mauer," *Süddeutsche Zeitung*, no. 49 (1981): 107; Rosa Maria Pinol, "Premi de Berlin al tándem Bohigas-Martorell-McKay," *AVUI*, February 18, 1981, 24; "Premio internacional para el arquitecto Martorell," *dilluns*, March 16, 1981, 10; François Chaslin, "Berlin: Raccommoder la ville," *Le Monde*, April 7, 1981. The competition projects remained at the forefront of much of the writing on IBA. See, for example, Dietmar Grötzebach, "Norm und Individualität in der Südlichen Friedrichstadt," *Baumeister* 84, no. 9 (1984): 53–56; Luis Fernandez-Galiano, ed., "Berlin, IBA '87 (2)," special issue, *A & V Monografías de Arquitectura Vivienda*, no. 2 (1985); Carlo Aymonino, "Berlin as Example," *Casabella*, no. 480 (May 1982): 36–37; Kenneth Frampton, "Habitation à Berlin: Notes sur L'IBA," *Silo*, nos. 2–3 (fall 1987–spring 1988): 14–16. **135** Oriol Bohigas, "Catalan Architecture: The Process of Democratic Institutionalization," *Lotus* 23, no. 2 (1979): 5–8, Quotation: 5 and 7. **136** For a comprehensive list of the office's projects, see Kenneth Frampton and Adolf Martinez, *Martorell, Bohigas, Mackay: Trente ans d'architecture, 1954–84*, trans. Raymonde Coudert (Milan: Electa, 1985). **137** Mackay, interview by the author, Tape 1, 00:23:18–00:24:00. **138** Martorell, Bohigas, Mackay, "Eight Experiences: City Blocks Almost Closed and Almost Corridor Streets," in Martorell, Bohigas, Mackay, *Der Baublock 1958–86* (Berlin: Aedes, 1988), 14–20. **139** "Entretien avec Oriol Bohigas," *AMC* 38 (1976): 59–66. **140** Mackay, interview by the author, Tape 1, 00:18:34. **141** Ibid., Tape 1, 00:19:40–00:20:16. **142** Oriol Bohigas, "Architecture: Extravagance and Witticism," in Martorell, Bohigas, Mackay, *Der Baublock 1958–86* (Berlin: Aedes, 1988): 4–5. Quotation: 5. **143** Mackay, interview by the author, Tape 1, 00:11:10–00:15:11. **144** Ibid., Tape 1, 00:54:17–00:54:25. Mackay confirms that Kleihues was involved in even the minutest details: 00:53:59. Countless letters between Kleihues and Mackay in the office's archives also suggest that the Neubau director was involved closely at every stage of the process and in all design and administrative questions. **145** Mackay to Kleihues, Letter of 29.9.81; Kleihues to Mackay, Letter of 07.10.81. Box: IBB 644-6, Bohigas, Mackay, Martorell Archives. Arxiu COAC, Barcelona. **146** Mackay, interview by the author, Tape 1, 00:45:12. **147** Bohigas, Mackay, Martorell architects, Manuscript "I.B.A. Urban Design for Kochstrasse 65, Zimmerstrasse 19. Berlin-Kreuzberg," Box: IBA 769-3, Bohigas, Mackay, Martorell Archives. Arxiu COAC, Barcelona. **148** C. v. L., "Streit um künftige Mieten am Checkpoint Charlie," *Der Tagesspiegel*, September 18, 1986. **149** Mackay, interview by the author, Tape 1, 00:45:40–00:46.47. **150** Matthias Sauerbruch (OMA) to David Mackay, Letter of 17 July 1985;

Attachment of OMA Project as it stands on 12 July 1985. IBA, Box: 769-3, Bohigas, Mackay, Martorell Archives. Arxiu COAC, Barcelona; Mackay, interview by the author, Tape 1, 00:36:27. **151** Mackay, interview by the author, Tape 1, 00:48:41–00:49:00. **152** Reiner to Mackay, June 25, 1985. A drawing that says "Version Kleihues" sent along this letter comments on the "Zimmerstrasse problem" and the Berlin Wall. IBA, Box: IBA 769-3, Bohigas, Mackay, Martorell Archives. Arxiu COAC, Barcelona; Mackay, interview by the author, Tape 1, 00:50:43–00:52:55. **153** Mackay, interview by the author, Tape 1, 01:10:26. Perception that towers reminded some of concentration camps: 01.09:31. **154** Ibid., Tape 1, 00:58:23–00:59:50, 01:10:00–01:11:07. **155** Ibid., Tape 1, 01:15:54–01:16:26. **156** Ibid., Tape 1, 01: 24:47–01:25:12. **157** N.Y., interview by the author, Tape 1, 01:04:26. **158** Ibid., Tape 1, 01:07:36. **159** Ibid., Tape 1, 02: 41:48. **160** Ibid., Tape 1, 00:55:00. **161** Rossi wrote: "The theater is very similar to architecture because both involve an event—its beginning, development, and conclusion. Without an event there is no theater and no architecture"; "I have always claimed that places are stronger than people, the fixed scene stronger than the transitory succession of events. This is the theoretical basis not of my architecture, but of architecture itself. In substance, it is one possibility of living. I liken this idea to the theater: people are like actors"; and "In time and place I have found an analogy for architecture, what I have called 'the fixed scene of human events.' And this too has focused my interest on the theater and the *locus* it constitutes" (*A Scientific Autobiography*, 48, 50, and 78; see also 29–31). **162** Çetiner, interview by the author, Tape 1, 00:03:18. **163** Ibid., Tape 1, 00:08:39. **164** Ibid., Tape 1, 00:11:59. **165** Ibid., Tape 1, 01:04:38, 01:07:14. **166** Mackay, interview by the author, Tape 1, 01:20:16. **167** Çetiner, interview by the author, Tape 1, 00:09:30. **168** N.Y., interview by the author, Tape 1, 02:41:19–02:42:00. **169** After a Turkish immigrant family won its appeal to the German Federal Constitutional Court in 1993 (207 C 171/93), the residents gained legal permission to install satellite dishes as part of their constitutional right to freedom of information. **170** Çetiner, interview by the author, Tape 2, 01:21:01. **171** N.Y., interview by the author, Tape 1, 00:17:39. **172** Ibid., Tape 1, 02:24:05–02:30:00. **173** Özgür Sevgi Göral, Ayhan Işık, and Özlem Kaya, "Executive Summary: The Unspoken Truth: Enforced Disappearances," Truth Justice Memory Center, 2014, accessed August 7, 2015, http://yeni.hafiza-merkezi.org/wp-content/uploads/2015/04/Unspoken_Truth_Exec_Summary.pdf. **174** Judith Butler, *Precarious Life: The Powers of Mourning and Violence* (New York: Verso Books, 2006), 20.

STROLL 2

From Checkpoint Charlie to Potsdamer Platz

After stopping at the neighboring buildings in Blocks 10 and 4 designed by Aldo Rossi and by Bohigas, Mackay, and Martorell, let's continue our stroll from the corner. If one walked south on Wilhelmstrasse, one could hardly miss the two brick skyscrapers holding the two corners of Block 9. This block was part of IBA's urban design competition for the triangular area between the Berlin Wall and the Hallesches Tor, and between Wilhelmstrasse and Stresemannstrasse. As was the case in the "Kochstrasse/Friedrichstrasse Competition" (stop II), the architects invited to participate in the competition for Wilhelmstrasse were asked to develop both general plans for an area that covered several blocks (in this case, Blocks 9, 19, and 20) and architectural designs for their designated blocks. The architectural offices that won the competition shared the commissions for buildings in Block 9 (Figure 2.1).[1] Walking south from Rossi's building, one would pass in front of the brick tower with a square ground plan and a low-rise wing extending along Wilhelmstrasse, designed by Grupo 2c (Figure 2.2). Jochen Brandi and Partner designed the wing along the Anhalter Strasse of this L-shaped compound that constitutes the perimeter block's corner. If one continued the stroll, the localization indicator on one's navigation screen would hit Pietro Derossi's tower. The street view would be of a high-rise building resembling a modernized medieval castle, memorable for the surfaces of its façade that are half of brick and half of stucco, the truncated slope of its roof, and the open balconies surrounding its circular stair tower (Figure 2.3a). If one could discreetly enter this stair tower and climb up, one could see the views that neighbors have of other IBA buildings (Figure 2.3b–c). Turning right, one would walk along the "Self-Help Terraces" housing, based on an idea of Dietrich von Beulwitz. Twenty-nine unfinished apartments were provided in this building, to be completed by occupants themselves under professional supervision as a way to reduce costs. The built-in terraces offered the possibility of extension in the future (Figure 2.4a–b). By prioritizing self-help and anticipating future change, this building is a forerunner of a special type of open architecture that was popularized in the 2010s by Alejandro Aravena.[2] If one made a right turn on Stresemannstrasse and reached the northwest corner of Block 9, one would see at a distance on Anhalter Strasse the former KukuCK (Kunst und Kulturzentrum Kreuzberg [Kreuzberg's culture and art center]) building. In 1981, squatters had moved into this industrial building, turning it into an underground arts and music center. After initial attempts to legalize their residence and renovate the building through a self-help program had failed, police forces expropriated the building and drove the squatters out in 1984.[3]

Continuing the stroll along Stresemannstrasse, after passing the site where the Topography of Terror Museum now stands and walking behind the Martin Gropius Bau Museum, one would reach Zaha Hadid's building of Block 2 at the Dessauer Strasse corner of this street. Situated in what was commonly called the women's block, where two of the buildings in the compound were designed by Myra Warhaftig and Christine

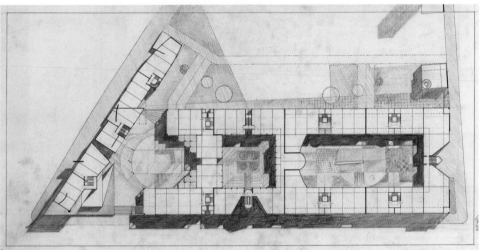

TOP: Figure 2.5 Romuald Loegler and W. Dobrzański, Proposal for Block 2, 1986. BOTTOM: Figure 2.6 Proposal for Block 2, 1986–87.

Jachmann in addition to the one by Hadid, the completion of this block was delayed till after IBA's closing and passed over to DeGeWo. In the view of Günter Schlusche from the IBA team, it was only after the 1981 crisis that Josef Paul Kleihues, the IBA Neubau director, "was willing or rather forced to give his approval to this type of housing." Only then did Kleihues find himself being pushed to listen to members of local groups, provide units that would be appropriate for multiple lifestyles, and consider issues such as gender and disability—which made Block 2 possible.[4] The design process for this block was a tokenist response to the demands of the feminist groups FOPA and UIFA to integrate more women into the IBA process, as well as the current discussions about women's architecture and women's emancipation (Stop IV).[5] While Hadid's building rightly attracts the most attention, quite a few unrealized ideas were created for this block over the course of 1986 and 1987.[6] A workshop was organized for April 10–11, 1986, and a series of 1:500 concept diagrams and three-dimensional

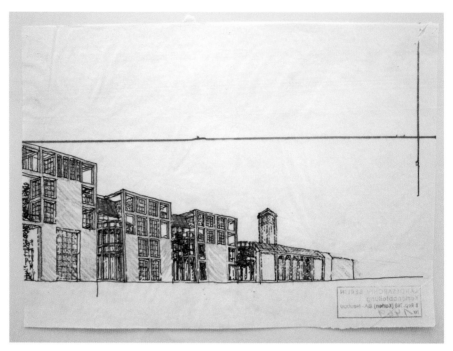

Figure 2.10 b Daniel Karpinski, Romuald Loegler and W. Dobrzański, and Peter Blake, St. Lukas church, Block 2, view of Bernburger Strasse (sketch of 1986).

massing studies were produced in July 1986, comparing each other in relation to buildable area, parking places, and ratio of commercial and residential places. While some of these alternatives proposed a U-shaped building, completing the perimeter block by fully constructing the Dessauer Strasse edge and filling in the unbuilt half of Stresemannstrasse and Bernburger Strasse, others proposed to turn the same area into a network of smaller courtyards.[7] Romuald Loegler and W. Dobrzański from Poland worked on an alternative block structure, and their colored drawings include features such as a walkway from the museum area and a shortcut between Stresemannstrasse and Bernburger Strasse that would provide a monumental urban front on the path traversing the block (Figure 2.5).[8] Later, more detailed 1:200 site plans of these alternatives were produced (Figure 2.6).[9]

Finally, a collaborative scheme completing the block edges and forming a network of three inner courtyards was implemented: Warhaftig built the L-shaped building that, together with Hadid's building, creates the triangular courtyard (Figure 2.7 a–b). Warhaftig's building is notable as a demonstration of her ideas for emancipatory types of residences for women that she had worked on in her 1982 dissertation, such as units designed for single mothers, the "living-area kitchen" (*Wohnraumküche*) that was placed in all of the twenty-four units with one to four bedrooms, and the storage room for baby strollers provided next to each common stairwell. The IBA controversy and resolution over emancipatory types of residences for women were even discussed in daily newspapers.[10] Jachmann built the U-shaped building that was attached to Warhaftig's and creates the second courtyard (Figure 2.8). The Polish architects Wojciech

Figure 2.10 c Daniel Karpinski, Romuald Loegler and W. Dobrzański, and Peter Blake, with St. Lukas church, Block 2, view of Bernburger Strasse (sketch of 1986).

Obtułowicz and Daniel Karpinski and Loegler Dobrzański built two L-shape buildings separately that were attached to each other and to Jachmann's, creating the third courtyard. While Hadid's, Warhaftig's, Jachmann's, and Obtułowicz and Karpinski's buildings together reconstruct the continuity of Dessauer Strasse (Figure 2.9 a–b), Obtułowicz and Karpinski's and Loegler and Dobrzański's buildings complete the unbuilt areas on Bernburger Strasse (Figure 2.10 a). Peter Blake designed the building adjacent to the existing St. Lukas church (built in 1859–61 and rebuilt in 1951 after being destroyed in World War II) on this street. When one compares the preliminary sketches showing the integration of proposed buildings with the existing church and the built version, one realizes that many of the collaborative ideals and much of the architectural imagination spent on this block could not be translated into the real world (Figure 2.10 a–c).

Hadid was openly critical of IBA for suppressing her creativity and giving her only a small project, which she defined as a "struggle on two fronts, first against the IBA strategy of infill and repair, secondly against the tight building regulations of social housing."[11] Nonetheless, her building has many qualities and is a fine example of disabled and public housing. Hildebrand Machleidt from the IBA Neubau team recalls the discussions about whether to invite Hadid to participate. She had just won the "Hong Kong Peak Competition," but Kleihues was skeptical that she could actually construct a building, given her gravity-defying, tempestuous designs communicated in technically unspecific drawings with shooting lines. Machleidt remembers speaking to both Hadid and Kleihues, convincing the former to join a public housing collective and the

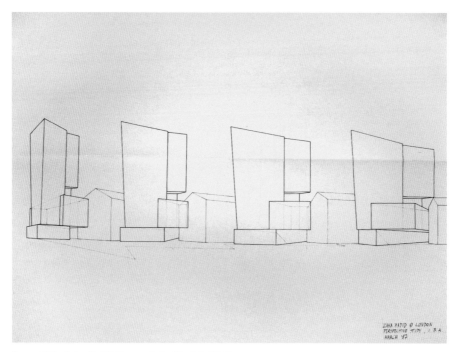

Figure 2.11a Zaha Hadid, Proposals for Block 2, 1987.

latter that a good collaborating contact architect from Berlin would ease his worries.[12] Hadid's IBA project was published at that time, along with her "Hong Kong Peak Competition" project, giving her a chance to prove that she was not merely a "paper architect." "I wouldn't go through all the trouble it takes to do the drawings if I didn't fundamentally believe my proposals could be built," she declared.[13] Accepting the IBA commission, despite complaining that she had been cornered into a "women's block," which she described as like "being told you have leprosy," Hadid divided her project into an eight-story tower and three-story horizontal housing as her own way of subverting the strict building height regulation that required five stories on average.[14] Her preliminary sketches in 1987 of the corner building with a vertical and a horizontal wing illustrates that she was part of the renewed modernist takeover of IBA by architects who opposed making historical references (stops VI and VII). Hadid developed expressive sketches for circulation diagrams and massing studies, thinking of the building in terms of interlocking volumes or hovering slabs sandwiched in between flying vertical planes (Figure 2.11 a–b). The built version maintained the flying planes concept. The angular tower carried by load-bearing planes is veiled with a bronze-color flying surface on the street corner (Figure 2.12 a). Turning onto Dessauer Strasse, one would enter the triangular Hof in the back by passing underneath the high narrow opening at the point where Hadid's building meets Warhaftig's (Figure 2.12 b–c). While climbing the few steps to pass through this urban gate, one would hardly anticipate the intimate garden behind the blocked view, landscaped mostly with grass surfaces and low bushes (see Figure 2.7 b). One could observe the freestanding planes of the tower from this side as well, which are accentuated with different colors. The continuous balcony on the first floor and the interrupted balcony on the second, with

154

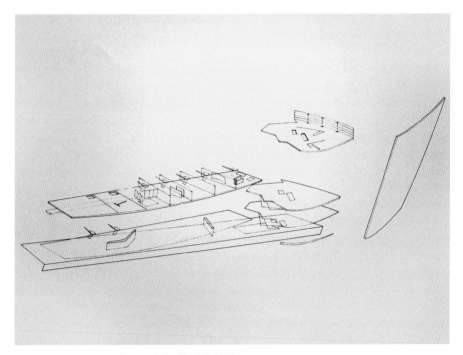

Figure 2.11 b Zaha Hadid, Proposals for Block 2, 1987.

perforated metal balustrades, constitute much of the façade elaboration of the horizontal wing (Figure 2.12 d). This wing is partially raised to allow pedestrian access between the museum area and the Hof.

I am invited to two apartments in Hadid's building, one in the tower and the other in the low-rise wing. All of the units in the tower are for families with a handicapped member, and V. lives in one of them (Figure 2.12 e). Having arrived in Germany from Gaziantep, Turkey, in 1992, she is determined never to go back, as she does not think her handicapped daughter would receive the same quality of care anywhere else but in Germany. Her daughter spent a year and a half in the hospital after her birth, without which V. believes her child would not have survived, and the daughter was entitled to live in this public housing. The entire building is designed for handicapped access: one can conveniently enter the building both from the street and the Hof; a wheelchair-accessible path takes residents to the Hof; the circulation area on each floor around the elevators is big enough for the storage and rotation of three wheelchairs (Figure 2.12 f); all units have an additional bathroom for handicapped people; the kitchen is designed so that one could cook sitting in a wheelchair; all rooms are equipped with multiple buttons to sound an alarm; and all light switches, doorknobs, and doorbells are kept low on walls (Figure 2.12 g). In addition to these features, V. appreciates her kitchen and bathroom, and especially the common balcony on each floor at the elevator entrance where she can spend time as if it were an extension of her apartment—washing the rug or simply looking out at the view (see Figure 2.7 and 2.8). Every afternoon in the adjacent Hof (the one defined by Warhaftig's and Jachmann's buildings), she meets other women from this block, who have been an immense help in raising her handicapped child. The Hof has definitely enabled her to get to know her neighbors, she says; she has met most of her friends there.[15]

Sakine Albayrak chose to live in the low-rise wing of Hadid's building the minute she saw the large elongated balcony, which is now nothing short of a well-kept garden filled with her plants (Figure 2.12 h). She cites the building's central location, small but functional rooms, and ventilated toilet as other assets. She had not insisted on an open kitchen during her apartment search, but she frequently mentions how this arrangement allows her to be part of the conversations with her family and guests rather than being confined into a small space while cooking, and how it has helped her children learn to share the housework. Her husband equally appreciates the contribution of the open kitchen to the sociability of their everyday life, but he adds that this would not have been as pleasant if the architect had not designed a cross-ventilated apartment.[16] However, the pleasures of the balcony are impaired because of the small triangular Hof, which she identifies is more like a passageway (*Durchgang*). Due to the proximity of the neighboring buildings, neighbors can overhear others' conversations and see into each other's apartments. As she wears a headscarf in public, she feels it a burden to step out onto the balcony only when she is fully dressed—something she did not have to do in her previous apartment's balcony, which was shielded better. Moreover, she cannot see the sky from inside the apartment due to the nearby building.[17] She connects her desires for privacy to her sense of freedom, and her definition of an ideal apartment to her career as well as her political self. She arrived in Kreuzberg from Turkey when she was six years old to join her parents, who had already arrived with the guest worker program. She remembers her parents' apartment going through the IBA Altbau renovation, which she finds positive in principle, but raises her hesitation because the residents were not able to make a choice of keeping the beautiful stoves that brought the family together.[18] She criticizes the segregation of German and Turkish students into different classes at school, and the fact that she was not sent to Gymnasium even though her grades were good enough, because "neither were the teachers attentive, nor the parents conscious of possibilities." "I was a victim of the first generation," she concludes,[19] but she took her education into her own hands, enrolled herself at schools and took special courses, and now she is the director of a kindergarten following the Montessori system. For that kindergarten, she raised the money to buy the expensive materials of a fully equipped school. She traces her determination back to the day she witnessed the head nurse shouting at her mother at work: "I took offense at this and told myself that I will not let anyone shout at me and will not shout at anyone."[20] She and her husband, who has also studied pedagogy, find the Montessori system the most successful of the reform pedagogies, because it places the child's freedom at the center and strikes a good balance between individual freedom and social solidarity—two opposite ends they find exaggerated in the traditional German and Turkish education systems, respectively.[21] Her ideal apartment, she says, would let the residents feel a similar sense of freedom.[22]

Before moving to Hadid's building, Albayrak lived across the street in Block 6, in an apartment whose private balcony and large garden she greatly appreciated. We take a walk together to Block 6, which is bordered by Bernburger, Dessauer, and Köthener

Strasse and Hafenplatz. The block was built by multiple architects from Berlin, including the offices of Rave and Partner; Borck, Boye, and Schaefer; Christoph Langhof; and Grötzebach, Plessow, and Ehlers. However, what is most noteworthy about this block is its contribution to ecological planning, overseen by Schlusche and AG Ökologischer Stadtumbau, in a garden designed by the landscape architect Hans Loidl.[23] Albayrak was one of the people who successfully passed an interview required to determine her eligibility for renting an apartment here. She had to promise to follow the specific recycling and waste-management regulations employed in IBA's experimental block for ecological living.[24] The gates underneath the buildings that lead one into the inner garden are painted with leafy patterns (Figure 2.13 a), but this block is green for other reasons, too. The inner garden contains a 900-square-meter water-purification plant, which recycles gray water used in the buildings of the block. The plan was to purify and recycle water from the bathrooms and kitchens of 70 of the 106 new apartments. The enterprise is an early model for Berlin's water-recycling program. The IBA exhibition *Water and Living* was held in one of these buildings in the summer of 1987, in which an empty apartment was also exhibited as a result of Schlusche's initiative—an anomaly, as most IBA buildings were exhibited only from the outside in 1987.[25] During the first years, the tenants formed an association and met regularly to discuss the maintenance of the garden and share their experiences with recycling and water use.[26] Unlike the orderly manicured landscapes in other IBA Hof-gardens, the green area in Block 6 is more like a jungle, memorable for the full-grown plants and the bridge over the artificial lake used for recycling (Figure 2.13 b–c).

If one left the jungle in Block 6 by crossing underneath the gate carved into the building along the Dessauer Strasse, one would find oneself in the Fanny-Hensel-Weg. Checking the localization indicator on the navigation panel, one would recognize that this is a new pedestrian path cutting across the middle of Block 7. It is created by Kleihues's housing on one side and Peter Brinkert's kindergarten building on the other side. Even though he had earned a reputation for inviting postmodernist architects to Berlin, Kleihues's own building looks like a textbook example of housing from the Weimar period. The long curving building is whitewashed and covered with balconies and galleries whose balustrades run continuously along the entire façade (Figure 2.14 a–b). At the back, two-thirds of the building leans against the solid wall of the existing Altbau building, which created a challenge that the architect resolved by designing striking common circulation spaces and apartment units oriented toward only one direction (Figure 2.14 c–d). On the other side of the Fanny-Hensel-Weg, one would see the red and brown brick buildings designed by multiple architectural offices working in perfect harmony to create a perimeter block with curving lines on the southern half of Block 7 (Figure 2.15 a). The office of Nalbach and Nalbach designed the corner buildings on both sides of Brinkert's kindergarten as well as another infill building on Dessauer Strasse, Georg Kohlmaier and Barna von Sartory designed the curving building with repetitive brown brick frames on the Hafenplatz (Figure 2.15 b), and Kelp, Ortner, and Ortner designed the structures along the Schöneberger Strasse. After circling around this block, let's turn left on Bernburger Strasse and stop at the building designed by Oswald Mathias Ungers for Block 1.

1 Stefan Schroth, "Ergebnisprotokoll der Preisgerichts-sitzung des internationalen engeren Wettbewerbs Berlin Südliche Friedrichstadt Wilhelmstraße," IBA Report, B 81/039, Landesarchiv. 2 Katerina George, "Selbsthilfe," in *Südliche Friedrichstadt: Internationale Bauausstellung Berlin 1984/87: Die Neubaugebiete— Dokumente, Projekte*, vol. 3 (Stuttgart: Verlag Gerd Hatje, 1987), 310–11. 3 W. Süchting, "Gebäudesanierung für das Kunst- und Kulturzentrum Kreuzberg," in ibid., 139. 4 Günter Schlusche, interview by the author, November 8, 2016, Berlin, in English, 00:19:39–00:21:20, 01:02:57–01:06:03. Both audio and video recordings of this interview are in the author's collection. 5 Josef Paul Kleihues, "Block 2," in *Südliche Friedrichstadt: Internationale Bauausstellung Berlin 1984/87: Die Neubaugebiete—Dokumente, Projekte*, 88–89. 6 The drawings for different projects undertaken for Block 2 are in B Rep 168 (Karten) IBA Neubau, No: 407–418, 924, 1358 Bl. 1–7, 1359 Bl. 1–7, 1374 Bl. 1–9, 1427 Bl. 1–9, 1428 Bl. 1–6, 1436–1439, 1440–1462, 1463–1472, 1473–1478, 1479–1489, 1490–1491, 1492–1501, Landesarchiv. 7 B Rep 168 (Karten) IBA Neubau, No: 1374 Bl. 1–7, 1479–1489, Landesarchiv. 8 B Rep 168 (Karten) IBA Neubau, No: 1492–1501, Landesarchiv. 9 B Rep 168 (Karten) IBA Neubau, No: 1490–1491, Landesarchiv. 10 C. v. L., "'In emanzipatorischen' IBA-Häusern soll die Küche im Mittelpunkt stehen," *Der Tagesspie-gel*, April 20, 1986. 11 Zaha Hadid, "IBA Housing," *A + U* 299, no. 8 (1995): 38–45. Quotation: 38. See also Heide Moldenhauer, interview by the author, May 28, 2012, Berlin, in English, 01:10:56. Both audio and video recordings of this interview are in the author's collection. 12 Hildebrand Machleidt, interview by the author, July 12, 2012, Berlin, in German, 01:49:30–01: 52:20. Both audio and video recordings of this interview are in the author's collection. 13 Deborah Dietsch, "Beyond the Peak: Three Projects by Zaha Hadid," *Architectural Record* 175, no. 7 (1987): 118–29. Quotation: 118. 14 Ibid., 120. 15 V., conversation with the author, summer 2012, Berlin. 16 Sakine Albayrak, interview by the author, June 26, 2012, Berlin, in Turkish, 00:15:30–00:17:21. Both audio and video recordings of this interview are in the author's collection. 17 Ibid., 00:20:00–00:28:00. 18 Ibid., 01:10:00–01:18:21. 19 Ibid., 00:44:26–00:46:36. 20 Ibid., 00:49:38–00:50:03. 21 Ibid., 00:52:10–01:02:30. 22 Ibid., 01:58:28. 23 Günter Schlusche, "Block 6," in *Südliche Friedrichstadt: Internationale Bauausstellung Berlin 1984/87: Die Neubaugebiete—Dokumente, Projekte*, 90–91. 24 Albayrak, interview by the author, 00:03:51–00:10:25. 25 C. v. L., "Pflanzen und ein 'Schönheitsteich' sollen Trinkwasser sparen helfen," *Der Tagesspiegel*, May 19, 1987; Schlusche, interview by the author, 01:53:17–01:55:11. 26 Albayrak, interview by the author, 00:35:02.

STOP III

Opened after Habitation

Oswald Mathias Ungers's Berlin

I decided to revisit the square brown building near Berlin's Potsdamer Platz on June 5, 2012, to converse informally with the residents whom I had interviewed in the past two years as part of the research for this book. Little did I know that this was an unordinary day in the building's life, and that the shocking news I just received about a murdered woman in Kreuzberg had taken place here.

During my research, I had heard neighborhood residents referring to the building as the Asihaus (asocial house) with a sense of dark humor, but I had not previously heard about an event as traumatic as this murder. The night before, one of the residents had been violently murdered by her husband in front of her six children. Her head and one of her breasts was cut off and thrown into the Hof, where a memorial with flowers and her photograph stood the next morning. Soon after I arrived at the building, the Hof was filled with neighborhood residents and members of civil society groups, who had gathered to mourn and protest domestic violence, as well as local journalists (Figure III.1).

The building is located today adjacent to the unified Berlin's Potsdamer Platz, but it hardly enjoyed such a centrality when it was originally constructed in the middle of a ruined neighborhood, just steps away from the Berlin Wall (Figure III.2). Designed by the German architect Oswald Mathias Ungers, the six-story structure incorporates itself smoothly into the city fabric, complying with the principles of IBA-1984/87, in which it participated. Ungers was one of the masterminds behind IBA Neubau, and he had initially been considered for the post of director responsible for the South Friedrichstadt area. He declined the position, probably because he wanted to build rather than administer and because of his differences of opinion with Josef Paul Kleihues. Ungers had already established himself as one of the most important internationally recognized architects of postwar Germany, a participant in postwar public housing construction but also one of the first critics of high modernism for its lack of attention to historical context, and an influential professor at the Technical University of Berlin and Cornell University in the United States. Ungers was invited to develop an overall urban plan, act as a jury member in architectural competitions, and design two building complexes for IBA. He had already theorized about what would become known as critical reconstruction; coined the term "urban villa" with his team of students; and shown, in one of his projects for Charlottenburg, how empty Berlin lots could be reconstructed by completing them, rather than destroying the remaining buildings and starting from scratch (Figure III.3). Nonetheless, Ungers's ideas were not totally in agreement with those of Kleihues. Rather than treating the perimeter block as the "gene of the city," he referred to his building near Potsdamer Platz as "a block within a block," a derivative of his urban theory which was improved since the mid-1950s.[1]

Figure III.1 June 5, 2012 Memorial in Oswald Mathias Ungers's Block 1 for IBA-1984/87, photographed by Esra Akcan, Berlin, 2012.

Figure III.2 Aerial view of Oswald Mathias Ungers's building in Block 1 (center) and Zaha Hadid's in Block 2 (bottom left) for IBA-1984/87, photographed by Esra Akcan, Berlin, 2010.

After building a large-scale housing project in Märkischesviertel, which was criticized by IBA proponents, Ungers aligned himself with the new generation of architects that approached high modernist values critically. A participant in the 1954 CIAM conference that was marked by the split between the old and the new generations, Ungers took the side of the young Team X, and opposed the tabula rasa approach and functional zoning principles of Le Corbusier and others. He also supported a deeper appreciation of historical architectural forms: "It became clear to me that architects must recognize contexts and the historical continuity which determines the identity of any specific site and from which a new architecture necessarily develops. It would be pointless once again to search for some sort of universal style which exists only in the abstract, independent of time and place."[2] Ungers's Grünzug Süd project in Cologne in 1962, presented at the Team X meeting in 1966, was a manifestation of this shift, proposing to understand the local context as a heterogeneous environment. Ungers photographed the two sides of a section of the main street to analyze the morphology—that is, the pattern of open and closed spaces and the type and rhythm of urban artifacts (Figure III.4). Moving to Berlin in 1963 to teach at the Technical University, Ungers produced self-published books and pursued typological and morphological studies of the city with his students until he moved to Cornell University in 1969, where he was chair of the Department of Architecture until 1975. During that period he clarified his urban theory by differentiating it from other contextualist approaches in the department and architectural discourse in general. The three Cornell summer studios organized under the themes of the urban block, the urban villa, and the urban garden (1976, 1977, 1978) provided a particularly productive forum for architectural invention.

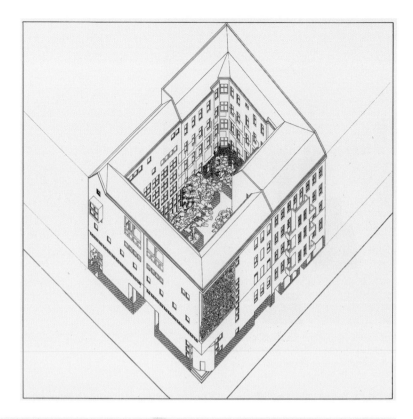

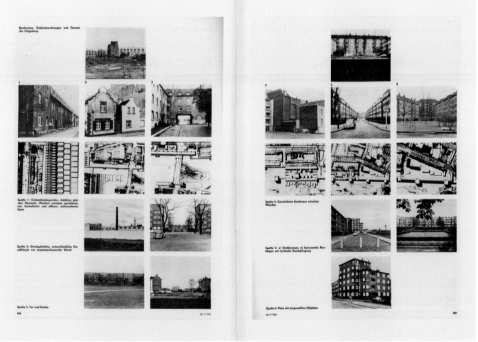

TOP: Figure III.3 Oswald Mathias Ungers, Reconstruction of perimeter block in Charlottenburg, Berlin, 1978.
BOTTOM: Figure III.4 Oswald Mathias Ungers, Grünzug Süd, Cologne, 1962.

Figure III.5 Oswald Mathias Ungers, *MAN transFORMS*
exhibition at Cooper Hewitt Museum, New York, 1976.
Collaborators: Simon Ungers, László Kiss, Henri Ferretti.

The *MAN transFORMS* exhibition at Cooper Hewitt Museum curated by Hans Hollein
in 1976 inspired a method of designing with metaphors rather than assuming the designer's mind was a tabula rasa. Juxtaposing 128 sets (each consisting of two images
and a concept that had morphological affinities with each other), Ungers made a case
for the mimetic imagination rather than designing from scratch. The exhibition was arranged like a city street, with rows of square images placed across from each other, juxtaposing a city plan or diagram, a natural organism or artifact, and a concept (written
in four languages on four sides of the square). Cut-out human silhouettes that openly
alluded to René Magritte's figures were mounted on the floors and jutted out from the
walls to create the simulation of a street (Figure III.5).[3] Ungers explained this initiative
as follows: "The main point of reference or the essential meaning is not the perception
of reality as it is, but rather the search for a higher idea, general substance, a coher-
ent thought or a general concept that ties together all the pieces."[4] Making an analogy
between a city and an artificial or natural artifact, and conceptualizing this affinity
with one term, was meant to help the audience see all three from a new perspective.
In this tripling action, Oscar Niemeyer and Lucio Costa's master plan for Brasilia was
brought together with a photograph of an airplane under the concept of stretching,
Bruno Taut's sketch in *Dissolution of Cities* was coupled with a rose under the concept
of blooming, and a map of Venice was combined with two interlocking hands under
the concept of encounter (Figure III.6).

When Ungers named his own approach "architecture as theme," he was referring to the
annihilation of functionalist or stylistic concerns in favor of a conceptual drive that
guides the design process:[5]

If one takes the history of architecture into consideration from this point of view, one comes across themes that recur in different cultures and that have been utilized for totally diverse functional and building purposes [for example, the atrium]. … The tired formula "form follows function" or the theory that architecture should be nothing but the representation of functions, is not, in my judgment, a teaching of architecture, but, at best, a technicist interpretation of architecture, and one, moreover, that is easily refutable. … The project should derive instead from a theme, from the theoretical conception of a particular architectural work set in a specific context. The history of architecture should be seen as a history of ideas and not—as it has been seen up to now—as a chronological enumeration of styles.[6]

Pedagogically, Ungers depended on a similar method, inviting his students to learn from the typological and morphological qualities of precedents.

Ungers eventualy coined the term "dialectical city" for his overall approach to urban design—a term that meant, on the one hand, the acknowledgment of the modern city as an accumulation of fragmented zones, each with its own character, as opposed to a single whole, and, on the other hand, the architect's engagement with the existing context in a dialectical fashion without aspiring for a reconciliation or synthesis.[7] He wrote: "The first criterion of my design is the dialectical process with a reality as found. … [Some call this contextualism.] It is also the rationalization of an existing reality."[8] His project for Tiergarten in 1973 (with Rem Koolhaas and P. and D. Allison), for

Figure III.6 Pages from Oswald Mathias Ungers's *City Metaphors*, 1982.

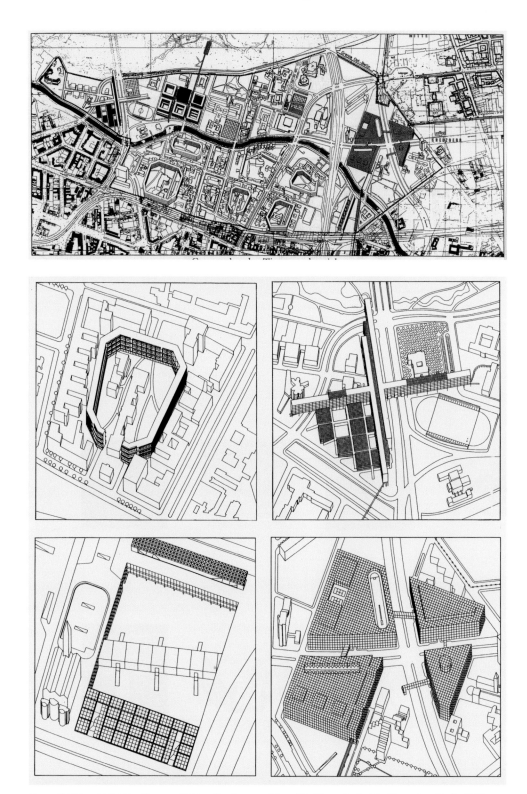

Figure III.7 Oswald Mathias Ungers with Rem Koolhaas and P. and D. Allison, Project for Tiergarten, Berlin, 1973.

example, illustrates this idea in a war-torn area that would become one of the subsections of IBA six years later (Figure III.7). He chose five sites that were close to each other and proposed urban improvement projects based on an observation of what was existing, lacking, and potentially present in each case. The five cases ended with different forms: in one, Ungers intensified the density by completing the edge and building inside the blocks; in another, he proposed a cross-shape building to mark the transition from a park to an urban area; and in yet another, he proposed a sunken plaza so as not to compete with the existing landmarks nearby—particularly Mies van der Rohe's National Gallery and Hans Scharoun's Library. At this point, Ungers explained that his projects were "better characterized as fragments and partial solutions of a very specific area, than an ideal realization of a platonic idea. They can be seen as an attempt to get away from the myth of the perfect plan."[9] In Kenneth Frampton's words, Ungers strove to achieve a "dialectic between place-form and placelessness" in applying his "bounded forms" to the chaotic metropolis, and he used this method to search for architecture's order "without falling into the acritical rigidity of making both an untenable closure and an idealistic exclusion."[10] Many members of the IBA Neubau team considered Ungers much more open to diversity than Kleihues, and hence they saw Ungers's refusal of the directorship position as a missed opportunity. In Günther Schlusche's words, "Ungers was also a prima donna, … but he had a more open mind to different views and models of architecture. But Kleihues always wanted to influence architecture; he tried to change architects' design."[11]

Let us not be misguided by Ungers's use of the term "dialectic." He rejected the understanding of the city as a social space, and his ideas increasingly moved away from a latent open architecture that would have made the inhabitants' voices audible. This can already be sensed in his early projects, despite his ideas that implied an openness to a city's multiple constituencies. The Cities within a City/Archipelago project for Berlin (1977), a collaboration with young Koolhaas, Hans Kollhoff, and Arthur Ovaska (see stop VI for Koolhaas's contributions), the drawings for which were made by Peter Riemann under Ungers's supervision, assumed that Berlin's population would drop (Figure III.8).[12] The project's manifesto with eleven theses as published in *Lotus* advocated the pluralist city instead of a single total plan: "The pluralistic project for a city within the city is in this respect the antithesis to the current planning theory which stems from a definition of the city as a single whole."[13] Many ideas in this manifesto reemerged when Ungers presented the project to the Berlin authorities for a future building exhibition (that eventually became IBA-1984/87): "The problem is no longer posed as the designing of a completely new environment, but rather as the rebuilding of what already exists. Not the discovery of a new order for the city, but the improvement of what is already there; not the discovery of new conceptions, but the rediscovery of proven principles, not the construction of new cities, but the re-organization of old ones—this is the real problem for the future. There is no need for a new Utopia, but rather to create a better reality."[14]

To accomplish these intentions in a presumably shrinking city, the team of designers proposed to choose the city districts with identifiable and typologically interesting features, and let the rest disappear. Museum Island, Friedrichstadt, the area around

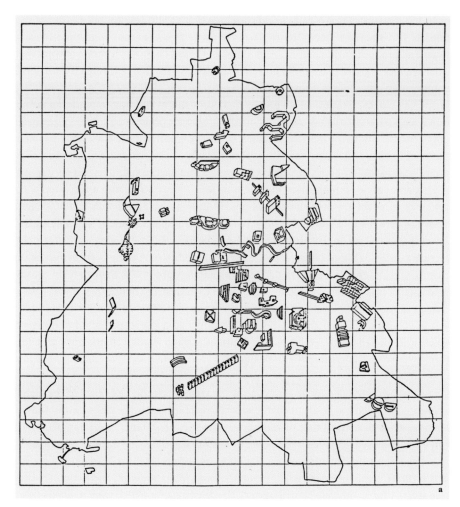

Figure III.8 Oswald Mathias Ungers, in collaboration with Rem Koolhaas, Hans Kollhoff, Arthur Ovaska, and Peter Riemann, Cities within a City/Archipelago Berlin, 1977. Map of Berlin.

Görlitzer station, Schlossstrasse, Horseshoe Siedlung, Gropiusstadt, Siemensstadt, Onkel Toms Hütte Siedlung, and Tempelhof made the list of urban areas with identifiable and morphologically compelling features (Figure III.9). If the project had been constructed, Berlin would have turned into islands swimming in a sea of green, a nonunified agglomeration of identifiable urban areas, and an ensemble of "cities within a city."

There might be several influences behind this project, including ruinomania, or Moses Ginzburg and M. Barshch's "Green City" of 1930, which proposed a socialist reconstruction of Moscow in line with the ideas of the "deurbanists". This project had proposed the evacuation of Moscow and the resettlement of its population as well as the dispersal of its industries all over U.S.S.R. "Thus Moscow would finally be left as a huge park containing only the administrative facilities and a sort of museum of the 'city' consisting of the most characteristic neighborhoods and monuments."[15] Ungers himself, on several occasions, criticized people who would turn the city into a countryside, but Archi-

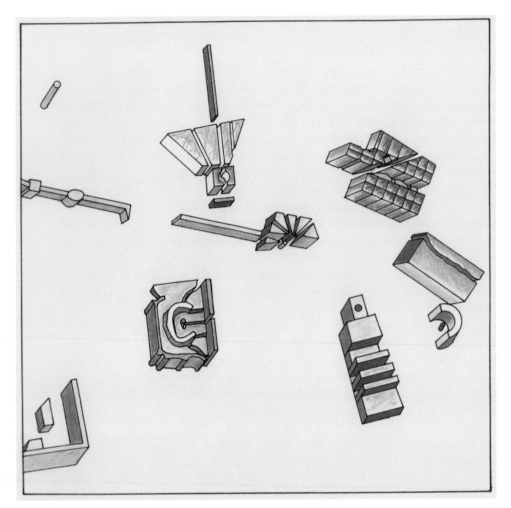

Figure III.9 Oswald Mathias Ungers, in collaboration with Rem Koolhaas, Hans Kollhoff, Arthur Ovaska, and Peter Riemann, Cities within a City/Archipelago Berlin, 1977. Remaining city districts.

pelago holds a central place today for many critics, including Pier Vittorio Aureli, who found in it a conceptual inspiration for rescuing the city against the forces of endless urbanization (that is, capitalist expansion),[16] and Reinhold Martin, who revealed the ghost of modernist utopian thinking in postmodernism.[17] Seen from the perspective of the immigrant population, however, the project's assumption that Berlin needed to shrink with the erasure of its nondescript parts ignored the pressing housing shortage and turned a blind eye to the urgent need for low-cost housing in areas like Kreuzberg (stop IV). At the time, Berlin's immigrant population was actually increasing due to the several governmental measures (it rose from 8.6 percent in 1973 to 12.5 percent when IBA was finished). Berlin's population as a whole also grew by 440,000 people between 1978 and 1993, and half of this growth is attributed to noncitizen families.[18] Archipelago was therefore more of a formal experiment in urban design than a response to the city's actual population or its needs. The manifesto cited the fact that Berlin had one of the highest percentage of foreigners in its population of all German cities as evidence to support the argument that the city was shrinking, implying that Ungers hardly saw the "dialectic city" as a social space or immigration as a relevant matter for the future of the city.[19]

Ungers's projects for IBA intervened in Berlin in relatively more restrained ways, even though he suggested implementing the Archipelago project in a couple of other venues in the early 1980s.[20] Even at Cornell University's second eight-week summer studio on Berlin in 1978, which culminated in the book-length report "The Urban Garden" edited by Ungers, Hans Kollhoff, and Arthur Ovaska (which appropriated the "Ideal image of Belle-Alliance Platz" on its cover, see Figure I.11) one could sense a transformation from the Cities within a City project despite the continuation of themes.[21] According to a list in this report, numerous scholars made appearances in the summer studios, including Carlo Aymonino, Peter Cook, Peter Eisenman, Heinrich Klotz, Ettore Sottsass, Koolhaas, and Anthony Vidler. The report contained Ungers's, Ovaska's, and Kollhoff's as well as the students' projects for an area in West Kreuzberg, the same site that was to be named IBA Neubau's South Friedrichstadt (Figure III.10). The three editors of the report each wrote articles as part of the report, advocating to varying degrees the pluralistic design that they conceptualized as the architectural translation of the democratic ethos.

Of the three, it was Ovaska who suggested the crispest theorization of the Cities within a City/Archipelago project, describing it as "the notion of seeing the city as analogous to a Picturesque garden" and associating the intervention with the pluralistic ideals of democratic society. After summarizing the history of gardens in "The City as a Garden, The Garden as a City," Ovaska suggested:

> This theme, in sum, presents the following ideals for the Greening of the shrinking city:
>
> **1** The establishment or preservation of certain extreme "places of reason," each independent in its impression and content, as set pieces in the otherwise wilderness of the city
> **2** The provision of a city concept which enhances the opposite and divergent conceptions inherent to the Metropolis. That is, the pluralist city, which consists of multiple viewpoints and sheds the Unitary Truth myth which has plagued Modern Architecture for half a century
> **3** The establishment of a city concept which allows for the common expression of memory and prophecy
> **4** The provision of symbolic statements of this theme through the Architectural Greening of the City and the merging of Landscape and Urban Design.[22]

In his text "The Architecture of Collective Memory" in the same report, Ungers referred to the story by Italo Calvino in which a traveler finds a memory of the past he did not know he had ever had at each new place he reaches. Like many of his contemporaries, and Walter Benjamin in his discussion of the Angel of History, Ungers argued that one had to walk toward the future by turning one's face to the past: "Journeys to relive your past" are also the "journeys to recover your future."[23] Hadrian's Villa was the perfect example of a collection of places and the "first evidence of an architecture of memory, collecting set-pieces from history, ... [that] resembles the idea of an ideal city, a humanist city, a place for the arts and sciences, a miniaturized Universe, where humanist ideals are gathered in a "classical" environment. ... It was a pluralist concept, every building conceived, designed and built following its own rules and orders."[24] Ungers presented his own projects, including the Student Hostel in Enschede (1963), Tiergarten Museum (1964) and Archipelago as translations of the pluralist ethos of Hadrian's Villa into contemporary architecture. Finally, Kollhoff wrote "City of Places" in the report that culminated from Cornell University's second summer studio in Berlin, where he also criticized the "anachronistic attempt of urban planning to create a homogeneous environment, devoid of any 'irritating' historical remnants," and he defended a pluralistic design as the reflection of the democratic ethos. This would be achieved by interpretatively analyzing the existing site conditions and engaging with them in a creative dialogue while designing new buildings without covering over differences and collisions: "Since variety and collision of points of view are characteristics of democratic society, we might [as well] accept this collision and form it."[25] The potential paradox in choreographing plurality through architecture alone, or relying on a single profession to "form" democracy single-handedly remained unresolved—which might explain Ungers's future career which, I argue, evolved to erase these necessary questions about democracy.

Ungers refined his ideas about the dialectical city in the following years. Faulting the high modernists for their anachronistic attempt to find a "complete and self-contained urban system," he stated: "Unlike the village, the town, or the ideal city, the present-day metropolis no longer has a unified form. It is a heterogeneous aggregation of different elements, systems and functions ... of fragments. The present-day city is dialectical; it is thesis and antithesis at the same time."[26] "The art of urban design consists

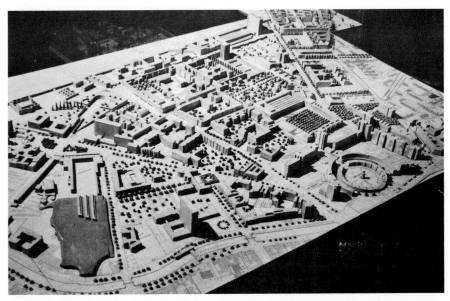

Figure III.10 Model of a study for South Friedrichstadt prepared during Cornell University's Berlin summer studio, 1978.

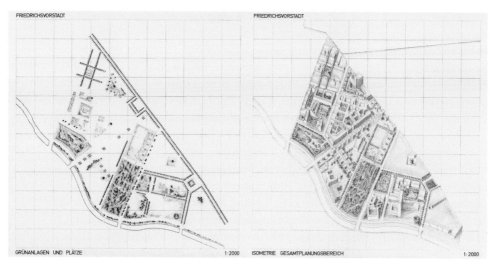

Figure III.11 Oswald Mathias Ungers, Project for Friedrichsvorstadt, Berlin, 1981. Planning of green areas and building.

of identifying the places within the urban chaos, naming them, and discovering their special features. Thus, urban design is the art of discovery, not invention."[27] Many of these ideas were akin to IBA's goals, which also rejected high modernism's tabula rasa approach. What Berlin needed was no longer city planning but piecemeal interventions on manageable sites, no longer master plans but district plans. Ungers was commissioned to develop one such district plan for South Friedrichstadt for IBA in 1981. As noted above, he had already created a project for the same site four years earlier, albeit in a bigger territory, in which he had explored the morphological potentials of the block structure by filling in gaps and mimicking the existing buildings but proposing many variations. The IBA version of this project zoomed in a little closer and repeated the dialectic city concept but reduced the number of variations somewhat. Ungers had analyzed the area when it had reached its maximum development in the past, documented the erasure of the fabric in World War II and the postwar planning, and finally proposed solutions to critically reconstruct it (Figure III.11).

Zooming in still further, Ungers designed the overall structure of IBA's Block 1 as well, in collaboration with Bernd Faskel and Hans Müller (1982). In the dialectic between the as-found conditions of the site and his "rational" interventions, he divided the block into a square grid, of which his building filled in the southwestern corner square (Figure III.12). The dimensions of the grid were defined by the adjacent square lot, where the only remaining prewar neoclassicist building, the Meistersaal (1910–13), is located. Originally square, this building had been partially destroyed in the war. By restoring the square grid, Ungers intended to reconstruct the collective memory of the site. The result was not exactly a perimeter block, as Kleihues would have preferred. Instead, it hollowed out the southwestern edge to accommodate a park that disrupts the continuity of the street front and lets the building stand free as an object in city space. It is rather one of those open blocks that Kleihues criticized, in contrast to the closed perimeter blocks in the core of Berlin.[28]

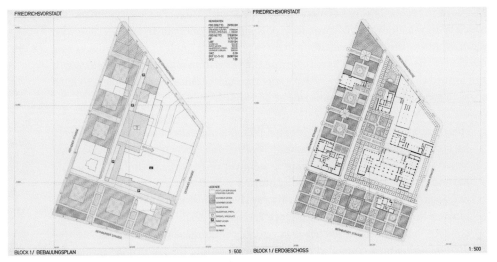

FRIEDRICHSVORSTADT

FRIEDRICHSVORSTADT

BLOCK 1/ BEBAUUNGSPLAN 1:500 BLOCK 1/ ERDGESCHOSS 1:500

Figure III.12 Oswald Mathias Ungers, in collaboration with Bernd Faskel and Hans Müller, Block 1, IBA-1984/87, Berlin, 1982.

Block 1 and Autonomous Architecture

If the city was an open system, Ungers must have seen his own task as introducing order and endorsing closed form in this "dialectic." Ungers is usually considered to be one of the fathers of autonomous architecture. According to Martin Kieren, "At stake [in his work] is the right of architecture … to evolve within the confines of its own methods and systems of belief … to develop free from the control of other disciplines."[29] Ungers's ideas on the autonomy of architecture in comparison to his response to the socio-economic needs of a given building's habitants seem to have grown more and more doctrinaire over time. In 1976, he was theorizing an open architecture in terms of the adaptability of space in anticipation of users' requests. Closely resembling Mies's concept of the open plan, the minimalism of design would have allowed for the maximum flexibility of use of a space. Ungers wrote:

> The designer is faced with the problem of choosing between precision and adaptability in his plan, of defining fixed and non-fixed organizational elements. If it is the purpose of production to provide tools to serve the needs of man, environments should be adaptable enough to respond to human needs and changes. Therefore the principle of adaptability should be made one of the basic conditions of design … This approach means the opposite of what designers are used to doing, which is searching for a maximum planned solution for the most elaborate and deterministic formal order, fixing every function of use or predetermining any move in space. A design concept with an orientation toward adaptable systems of order, however, searches for a minimal design in which the organization of elements in space will be minimized to allow or even provoke a maximum participation of those who are using the space. Such a concept requires the exploration of a design matrix for an open-ended and self-generating process. … In reality adaptability in architectural design means a transformation from an authoritarian act to an act of participation.[30]

It is hard to reconcile these sentences, however, with Ungers's later statements, in which he increasingly moved away from participatory concerns. In an interview with Heinrich Klotz, Ungers defended his insistence on right angles and orderliness as a reaction to the doctrine of Scharoun during the years immediately after World War II and argued that variation in regularity was the right architectural approach to open space to meet human desires, differences, and idiosyncrasies:

> [The] fundamental principle of design which distinguishes many of my projects ... [is] strict regularity which allows for rich variation. ... [W]e forget that man cannot be optimized. For if we were to assume architecture could be optimized, we would have to assume that man could be optimized as well. But human wishes, dreams, and desires are so important and so diverse that we must provide a certain amount of space to accommodate them. ... When I arrived in Berlin in the sixties to study architecture, Scharoun's influence was virtually tyrannical and unchecked. ... [A]ny architecture which employed right angles and rationally determined forms was attacked as being "inhumane." That was a polemic I could not accept.[31]

During the IBA years, Ungers repeated the antifunctionalist reaction of his generation. He stated in *Architecture as Theme*: "An architecture that starts out from a theme places man at the center, since man is more than a functional being, more than a 'user'—as he is so often called today. ... [T]he functionalist Siedlungen of the twenties no longer form an element of attraction for the present generation."[32] This book rationalized Ungers's projects to date in relationship to some themes, rather than to a program, location, style, or other possible categories such as the themes of transformation, assemblage, incorporation, assimilation, and imagination. In 1981, Ungers published his article on the right of architecture to an autonomous language, a translation of which had already appeared in the catalog of the Venice Architecture Biennale of 1980.[33] The theory of autonomous architecture depended on the assumption that there was a distinct divide between internal and external concerns of architecture. The autonomous language was nothing but the language of form, architecture's intrinsic value—as opposed to the allegedly external concerns of, for example, sociology, ecology, economy, and technology:

> Architecture nowadays is mostly conceived as an ecological, sociological and technological function. Economical problems like effective usefulness, profitability and economizing, are brought to the forefront by the operators and are declared to be the theme and content of architecture. ... However, it is useless continuing to discuss architectural problems [as] if it is only a question of satisfying the existing requirements in the most rational way. ... It is equally difficult to derive a formal structural project from mere social conditions, since one cannot trust sufficiently either in the behavior and habits of a single person's life or in the general public's feelings. ... The pretensions of Economy and Sociology are joined by those of Technology. There can be no doubt that the invention of new materials and the arrival of new building methods have enriched the world of construction. This fact, however, must not lead us to overestimate the thinking about construction, which is the case with those who spread the mistaken vision of the engineer as the artist-build-

er of the future. … Let's take this formula to its limit: architecture is not dependent on the end. … After a long period of doctrinal dependence on the dogmas of modern architecture, what counts nowadays is that architecture should be accepted again as an art. … Like all other arts, architecture is capable of freeing man's surroundings and existence from gray banality and from the vulgarity of reality, it can transcend the constraints of material necessity.[34]

By 1998, Ungers's ideas had crystalized in defense of autonomy at the expense of openness to the user's voice and adaptability of form: "Architecture is not a function of something else. … It is autonomous. … Any building that has as its theme something other than itself is … trivial. It may fulfill legitimate purposes and needs, but if it does not fulfill itself as an idea …, it remains banal, incapable of satisfying the claim of architecture to be an expression of spiritual universality."[35]

The Asihaus, the brown square building built for IBA-1984/87, had a special place in the immigration policies of the Berlin Senate, IBA's employer, which in 1975 had barred any additional noncitizen families from moving to Kreuzberg and in 1978 had imposed a quota on every building of West Berlin, limiting the share of its residents who were foreigners to 10 percent. As discussed above, these housing laws were transposed into the functional program of the IBA Neubau buildings by limiting the percentage of large apartments, which would have been appropriate for the stereotypical big Turkish families. Justified as deghettoizing and desegregation measures, these regulations deliberately targeted the guest workers' families, as it was technically impossible for them to have become citizens, and sought to change the proportion of the noncitizen population in the area. While reducing noncitizens' chances to move into the new buildings, IBA Neubau designated some formal experiments specifically as "foreigner zones." The Asihaus was one of them. Once Ungers's design was selected for this remote edge of Kreuzberg, he was given a functional program with an unusually high number of apartments with five to seven rooms, which must have been intended for guest workers with many children.[36] There are twelve apartments with two rooms, eleven with three rooms, fourteen with four rooms, four with five rooms, and even three with seven rooms, altogether 44 flats. While in the rest of Kreuzberg the Senate made sure that immigrant families in each building did not account for more than 10 percent of the residents, the number of big apartments in this building at the margins of the city confirm that it was designed to accommodate a majority of immigrants.

The building is a rigorous geometrical experiment of sorts. Ungers extended the site's square grid onto the building itself and designed a square in a square. It is possible to argue that the concept of the block within a block was an offspring of concepts of the urban villa and doll within a doll that also occupied Ungers's mind at that time. Ungers explained many of his influential projects, including the Hotel Berlin (1977) and the Architecture Museum in Frankfurt (1979–84) with the concept of a house within a house, which he compared to the traditional Russian dolls that emerged from inside a larger doll: "The theme of the doll inside a doll or of the house within a house has operated over the course of time, and therefore more or less by chance. But it can be consciously

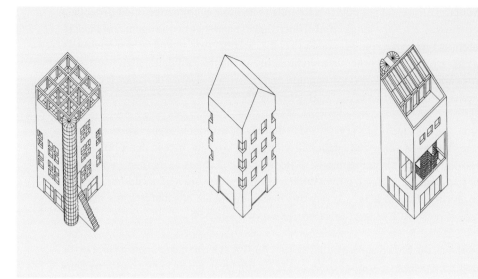

Figure III.13 Oswald Mathias Ungers in collaboration with Hans Kollhoff and Thomas Will, Housing Complex, Marburg, 1976.

introduced into architecture as a principle of design, a principle that makes differentiation and variety possible in very diverse fields."[37] The urban villa (*Stadtvilla*)—a freestanding, multistory, multifamily building in a garden—was a term that Ungers, his students and teaching associates used quite often during those years, usually defending it as a typological invention. The term had already appeared in Ungers's competition project for the 4th Ring Berlin-Lichterfelde (with Koolhaas and K.-L. Dietzsch, 1974), which attracted the attention of IBA's initial supporter at the Berlin Senate, Hans Christian Müller.[38] In Ovaska's recollection, the first reiteration of the hybrid between the urban villa and the city within a city came about when Ungers's team was preparing for the "Roosevelt Island Competition" (1975) and explored the possibility of designing a miniaturized Manhattan with a shrunken Central Park surrounded by a number of shrunken urban blocks that would therefore have become urban villas: "I think of that moment as the first combination of the urban villa and the city in the city...and a real 'creative leap.'"[39] The urban villa was the official theme of Cornell University's Berlin summer studio where the Cities within a City/Archipelago project emerged. The Housing Complex in Marburg (1976), prepared in conversation with Heinrich Klotz, and designed by Ungers with Kollhoff and Thomas Will who had been educated in Germany but had arrived at Cornell, was the most effective visualization of the theme and variations that could be achieved through the use of an urban villa. The team proposed a variety of alternatives for the perimeter block (including an L-shaped building, parallel blocks, and a square courtyard) and then settled on the five-tower scheme composed of semi-independent buildings placed to make an L-shape and define an urban area in between its wings. Calling this step of the process as the construction of a "vocabulary," they developed thirteen variants for each tower, with variables of exterior stairs, stairs at the core, carved in terraces, roof gardens, corner windows, oblique extension bays, and so on (Figure III.13). This project is noteworthy also because it exposes the distance between where Ungers started and ended, when one views his career in

176

  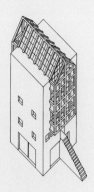

terms of the level of hospitality toward residents in open architecture. In the Marburg project, the anticipation of the user's voice motivated the extensive number of variations on the theme—a concern that would disappear from Ungers's lexicon by the time his IBA buildings were built:

> The construction proposal made here need not necessarily be regarded as a definitive result. It in fact reveals scope for morphological development. The alternatives put forward give the idea of a multiplicity capable of satisfying as wide a reality as possible, without being tied down for the time being to any one solution. … All these steps taken to date have been decided and carried out without the participation of a possible occupant. They are so to speak free inventions of possibilities without a direct or real cause. … The next logical step to be taken would be the further development of concrete phases, i.e., the cooperation of a future user, which development would then lead to a third series of standard buildings.[40]

Referring to Berlin's Tiergarten as an area formerly occupied by many villas, IBA-1984/87 planned urban villas—especially in the South Tiergarten area, where Ungers designed two projects and acted as a jury member in important architectural competitions (stroll 3). These urban villas were multifamily apartments collected in a freestanding structure with a square plan, usually based on a four-square scheme with a central vertical core. For instance, Werner Goehner, who was one of Ungers's graduate students in 1971–73 and later a fellow professor at Cornell University, prepared a competition project with urban villas for Block 234, near Lützowplatz. The project, which won an honorable mention, displays the number of variations that could be employed with this diagram, by introducing different balconies, winter gardens, rooftop terraces, and skylights for the central core (Figure III.14)[41]

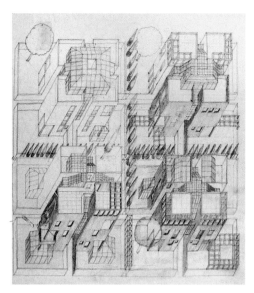

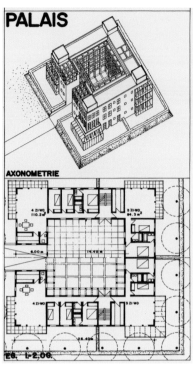

LEFT: Figure III.14 Werner Goehner, "Residential Park at Lützowplatz Competition" project for Block 234, near Lützowplatz, IBA-1984/87, Berlin. Urban villas.
RIGHT: Figure III.15 Werner Goehner, "Residential Park at Lützowplatz Competition" project for Block 234, near Lützowplatz, IBA-1984/87, Berlin. Palais.

In Ungers's Marburg project, the square within a square was derived from the urban villa by hollowing out the cube at its center and turning the inner vertical circulation core into a courtyard. Later, the four-square scheme would turn into a nine-square scheme. A similar variation named "Palais" was also suggested as one of the four urban types in Goehner's competition project for Block 234, even though this project differed from Ungers's in that it had only one gate into the inner courtyard, two vertical circulation cores, and one continuous glazed gallery that circled around the courtyard and connected all of the units together (Figure III.15). Ungers had already coined the term "city palace" (*Stadtpalais*) in an article in *Deutsche Bauzeitung* in 1979 in introducing his multifamily housing in Charlottenburg, where he added a new U-shaped building to turn the existing building into a compound with a rectangular courtyard.[42]

The nine-square plan of the Asihaus creates a square courtyard at the center of a square building composed of eight square towers, served by four square stairwells, all placed in a city block divided into a square grid; all four façades are composed of square windows, and the eight freestanding square towers are bridged on the fourth floor, above the square surface with nine square perforations on three floors (Figure III.16). Ungers crafted a masterful ground plan to accomplish the geometric ambitions of his scheme (Figure III.17). Almost no two apartments are the same, so that they could be accommodated in this form, in stark contrast to the standarized dwellings of generic mass housing projects. Residents of an apartment on the ground floor in the middle wings access their units directly from the courtyard, dropping into their living rooms abruptly from a public space. These units are duplexes. Some of these spaces were reserved

Figure III.16 Oswald Mathias Ungers, Building in Block 1, IBA-1984/87, Berlin. Axonometric.

for a kindergarten and meeting rooms, but they barely functioned so. Residents of a corner ground-floor apartment enter their units after passing through the common building entrance. These are also duplexes. Residents of apartments above enter from the corner wings and take the common stairway. For example, residents of third-floor apartments in the middle wings need to cross the bridge upon entering their apartments, and they can enter from the bridges on both sides—an unnecessary organization dictated by the symmetry of the plan. Residents of sixth-floor apartments have private terraces, and some of these apartments are duplexes accessed from the fifth floor. Each apartment has a winter garden, which cannot be detected from the outside

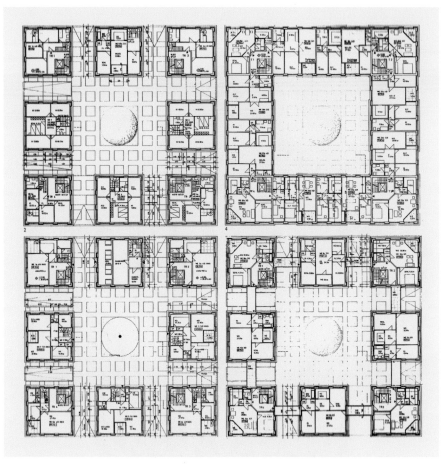

Figure III.17 Oswald Mathias Ungers, Building in Block 1, IBA-1984/87, Berlin. Plans and elevation, version October 1985.

because its opening is the same as the other windows. In other words, to achieve the building's strict regularity in form, Ungers had to include rich variation in the apartment plans.[43] Ungers's preoccupation with Kreuzberg and fascination with the square continued in the later stages of his career. His competition project for Berlin's Kulturforum included a skyscraper as an homage to Mies van der Rohe which was composed of variations on a square (Figure III.18).

Ungers ignored his building's role in the discriminatory integration policies, and he was explicitly cynical about social concerns and participation in architecture in the later stages of his career. Not a member but a target of the 1960s student movements in Berlin, leaving the Technical University to teach at Cornell as a result, Ungers reflected on the experience in an interview with Koolhaas and Hans Obrist in 2004: "I wanted to develop the students' ability to think, and all they cared about was to organize a revolution. ... Social problems cannot be resolved in architecture."[44] While these words can be interpreted as representative of Ungers's later career, they are not too inconsistent with his theory of architecture as a closed system in dialectical relation with the

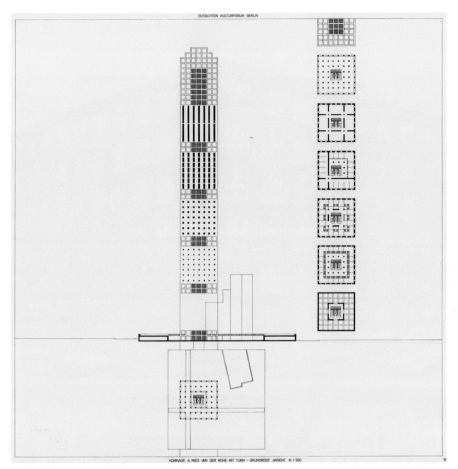

HOMMAGE A MIES VAN DER ROHE MIT TURM – GRUNDRISSE ANSICHT M 1:500   19

Figure III.18 Oswald Mathias Ungers, Homage to Mies van der Rohe, "Kulturforum Competition" project, Berlin, 1987.

fragmented and open metropolis. His words in another interview shortly after the IBA buildings were completed confirm this:

> There can't be [a dialogue between the public and the architect]. The process of being creative … is a dialogue between you and your fantasy, your intellect, your ratio, your mind, and your potential. … The public is not my concern, and it will never be. If, later on, people enjoy looking at and living in my buildings, that would be enough. You cannot do more. … Of course I believe in a democratic system, but in one that would secure the right of the individual. The democratic system doesn't mean the great majority. It means the protection of the extreme, the individual.[45]

This end was a tragically different point from where Ungers had said he started. While some of his colleagues in IBA Altbau were promoting radical participation of inhabitants, Ungers advocated a radical denial of participation for the integrity of architecture, which he treated as a higher mode of engagement with the individual and the human condition.

STOP III   Opened after Habitation

181

Figure III.19 Views of Oswald Mathias Ungers's building in Block 1 from the outside and inner courtyard, photographed by Esra Akcan, Berlin, 2009.

At this point, we might ask how fitting was Ungers's choice of this architectural design for lodging large noncitizen families. The oral histories I have conducted with the occupants of Ungers's building indicate the mixed opinions about living in a building like a passageway open at all sides, and organized around a small paved courtyard with no playground for the many children who would grow up there (Figure III.19 and III.20). "The problem is not the architecture, it is the users," says Mr. Karaoğlan, who lives in an apartment with a terrace. Şenay X., who lives in a duplex that is accessed directly from the courtyard, partially agrees, and so does Fatma Barış, who lives with her four children and husband in one of the largest units on the third floor. Residents fault each other, but some of the tensions must have been augmented because of the building's design and dimensions.[46]

Take the courtyard. Nobody spends any amount of time in this small courtyard, as all the residents I spoke to confirmed, except the children who played football there. While the IBA was proud of providing ample space for playgrounds inside the large courtyards of the perimeter blocks, in this building designated as housing for noncitizen families with many children, the fact that children played in the courtyard was a constant source of controversy (Figure III.21). Apart from the noise they made, their balls frequently broke windows. Some residents refused to return a ball after it had shot into a living room and broke a vase or two, which frustrated the children so that they threw eggs at the windows in return. Once a neighbor even processed a police order against the children who played in the courtyard.[47] When people enjoyed grilling on their terraces on the sixth floor, others complained that the smoke was entering their apartment directly across (Figure III.22). While friendly neighbors liked talking to each other from one window to another across the small courtyard, it disturbed people who worked the night shift and tried to sleep in the mornings. The curtains covering the windows of all units are so opaque that being in the courtyard feels more like entering a cube with solid walls than experiencing a social space defined by the life around it.

Even though Ungers did not welcome alterations in his designs, residents left their marks on the building beyond those of usual repairs and maintenance, to reduce the limitations that the geometric ambitions of his floor plans imposed on the everyday use of space. The Barış family's unit is a case in point. I conversed with Fatma Barış and her son Bekir at length in 2011, and I also interviewed the family on the day of the murder and the two sons in 2012. Originally from Urfa, Turkey, the family had lived in a couple of German towns before moving to Berlin. Fatma Barış still remembers each of the houses they lived in vividly. They had so little financial resources and her husband had to work so many shifts that she had volunteered to do all the heavy construction and fine-tuning involved in renovating the apartments. Her husband frequently tells me that I would not believe my eyes if I could see how magically she changed dumps into warm homes. The first of their houses was in a deserted hilltop in South Germany near the Swiss border, which was large and decent enough but so isolated and felt so lonely that she insisted on moving after three months. They were not allowed to install satellite dishes back then, which eliminated the possibility of television characters

TOP LEFT: Figure III.20 View of the urban gate to Oswald Mathias Ungers's building in Block 1, photographed by Esra Akcan, Berlin, 2011. TOP RIGHT: Figure III.21 View of Oswald Mathias Ungers's building in Block 1, photographed by Esra Akcan, Berlin, 2011. BOTTOM: Figure III.22 View of terraces in Oswald Mathias Ungers's building in Block 1, photographed by Esra Akcan, Berlin, 2009.

serving as companions. "People need people more than beautiful houses," she says, recalling how devastated she had felt.[48] They found a worn-out apartment in a dark and cold basement where mice considered themselves at home, spiders had left their webs all around, ceilings were so low that family members could easily touch them while standing on the floor, and windows and doors were so poorly constructed that it was impossible to heat the space in winters. Nonetheless, she worked on that apartment for months, moving all of the furniture out of one room so that she could fix, paint, and decorate, one room at a time. In the end, the visitors could not believe they were entering the same apartment.[49] Her husband does not hide the established patriarchic comment that it is to the advantage of a woman to prepare a livable home to keep her man, even though they both giggle at this comment.[50] Before they decided to move to Berlin, they lived in a couple of other places, all of which she renovated and decorated—even though that meant living for six years without enough money to take a vacation.

They found their unit in Ungers's building after a lucky coincidence and through a network of friends who saw it advertised on the street. They still remember the woman at the housing office who understood their difficult situation and helped them in getting the unit. When they first arrived, all of the members of the familiy remember that the corridors smelled disgusting, the unit was dirty, the kitchen was unusable, and the floor was covered with a worn-out plastic. Now, there is a kitchen with new cupboards and appliances, the floor is parquet, the walls have been painted and decorated, and the house is always clean, in sharp contrast to the building's corridors. During their stay, Fatma Barış purchased the matching furniture year after year. She brought the curtains all the way from Austria. Her husband bought the wallpaper and installed it so that the pattern was upside-down, which became so popular that all of their friends did the same at their own homes. The children chose their own furniture, and Bekir suggested the placing and orientation of the dining table, so that the living room would be more spacious (Figure III.23).[51] As I was taking interior photographs upon my first visit, the mother and the son made sure to stage their place in its perfect form, removing anything temporary that would have accidentally fallen into the frame.

The Barış family resides in a unit with two entrance bridges on both sides, as a result of Ungers's uncompromising symmetric plan. Rather than respecting the integrity of this symmetry, Fatma Barış decided to use only one entrance bridge and turn the second into a bedroom for her daughter (Figure III.24). With four children and a limited budget, she prioritized giving her daughter a room of her own above the symbol of cosmic order. Like many of her neighbors, she turned the winter garden into an additional bedroom for her youngest child (Figure III.25). The family is ambivalent about the small courtyard and the resulting proximity between apartments. On the one hand, it forces them to keep the translucent curtains closed at all times, while on the other hand, Fatma's husband says "this is something we are used to in our culture in Turkey. There too, the streets are narrow, we are used to living with curtains closed." She is more critical, as she thinks a courtyard closed from all sides blocks ventilation, if not keeping the sunlight out.[52]

Figure III.23 Views of Barış's living room in Oswald Mathias Ungers's building in Block 1, photographed by Esra Akcan, Berlin, 2011.

Figure III.24 Views of Barış's appropriation of entrance bridges as arrival space (left) and daughter's bedroom (right) in Oswald Mathias Ungers's building in Block 1, photographed by Esra Akcan, Berlin, 2011.

With a tradition that goes back to the days of the Berlin Wall, the Kreuzberg neighborhood is famous for its ubiquitous graffiti. The Asihaus is also full of predesigned images placed precisely by artists in the square niches between architectural axes, as well as ad hoc texts scribbled anonymously on walls in common areas, which most residents consider vandalism. This street-art culture has inspired Bekir Barış, the family's teenage son, who has painted the walls of his youngest sibling's room with cartoon characters. And at her elder sister's request, he drew Kitty characters and hugging figures on a pink background, and flowers around her circular mirror. In contrast, black-and-white geometrical figures define his own room, where he not only painted on the walls, but also added some touches to the lamp and mirror, working with graphics that match the bathroom fixtures and the color of his mother's carefully chosen furniture (Figure III.26). Bekir Barış somewhat underestimates his wall paintings. "I don't even take them seriously," he says in our interview, even though he undertook a few similar painting jobs after being in demand as a result of his previous work. However, he stopped making wall images in private apartments, because he felt being cornered into drawing merely for children, and he does not find much meaning in redrawing a cartoon character that someone else created. Instead, he loves to do inventive pencil drawings on paper, a talent that was first noticed when he was in kindergarten.[53] When I hear that he throws his older drawings out because he finds them imperfect and learn that he does not pay much attention to schooling that would lead him to a university education, I find myself breaking my own no-intervention rule and lecturing him about studying.

With Fatma's design sensibilities and Bekir's wall images, the Barış family's apartment has become an extraordinary example of the voice of resident-architects in shaping and improving Kreuzberg's living spaces. When I ask for permission to use our interview and photographs in this book, I understand that Fatma Barış is proud of her creation, as many designers would be.[54]

Figure III.25 View of Barış's appropriation of the winter garden as a bedroom in Oswald Mathias Ungers's building in Block 1, photographed by Esra Akcan, Berlin, 2011.

When I visited the building a couple of years after the murder, I noticed that a lot of face-lifting had taken place, which went against many of the original design ideas. The building was now enclosed with fences and gates, leaving only one opening as the official entrance to the courtyard and the units. Other formerly public entrances had been closed and were being used as places to park bicycles. The tree in the courtyard now had a wooden platform around it. There were signs all around banning children from playing in the courtyard, telling parents to guard their children, and reminding people that the place is surveilled with security cameras. New and benign wall paintings decorated the square surfaces. Street lamps had been installed at all corners, making the courtyard bright at all times. The user profile also seemed to have changed with the rising rents (Figure III.27).

The day of the murder in the Asihaus also prompted me to prepare "Adding a Layer under the Mercator Grid" as part of the 2012 Istanbul Design Biennale, a multimedia installation that carried ongoing research into visual forms (Figure III.28, see also stop VI). While the drawings, archival documents, photographs, and interviews revealed many aspects of Kreuzberg's urban renewal, it proved to be difficult to include the experience of immigrant women who were subject to domestic violence. These women's voices disappeared between German discrimination from one side and their Turkish husbands' machismo from the other.

This installation consisted of a set of staged photographs in which I tried to represent the invisible and the inaudible. Gathering information mostly from court translators and neighbors, I reenacted six traumatic stories in an apartment in housing designed by Peter Eisenman and Jaquelin Robertson for IBA-1984/87—a commission they re-

Figure III.26 Views of Bekir Barış's wall paintings in his sister's, brother's and own room in Oswald Mathias Ungers's building in Block 1, photographed by Esra Akcan, Berlin, 2011.

ceived after a competition project that exposed the complexities of victimization and exclusion in the context of postwar Germany trying to come to terms with anti-Semitism (stop VI). Each story was represented by a staged photograph that froze one moment before the event and a quotation from a translator or resident who had spoken to me about the event. For example, a quotation from Fatma Barış referred to the murder in the Asihaus:

> "He made her work like a slave even when she was nine months pregnant; last night he cut her throat and breast in front of his six children and threw them into the Hof from the balcony" (Neighbor F. B. on Semanur S., Berlin, June 5, 2012).

The other quotations were:

> "Some time after walking out on the marriage, he secretly went in with his old keys to stab her while sleeping" (translator under oath Y.Ö., Berlin, June 3, 2012).

Figure III.27 View of Oswald Mathias Ungers's building in Block 1 with new murals and penalty signs, photographed by Esra Akcan, Berlin, 2014.

"He set the bed on fire to leave the past behind him and then walked out" (translator under oath Y.Ö., Berlin, June 3, 2012).

"We showed him the photograph of his dead wife's head with red lines indicating where he shot her and where the bullets went out; he did not show any reaction, neither sorrow, nor regret, like a solid wall" (translator under oath Y.Ö., Berlin, June 3, 2012).

"I used to wait for my husband in front of the window all night; we then found out that he had married a second woman in the Ost [East Berlin] and had a kid" (interview at Kreuzberg's Kotti e.V. Family-garden, Berlin, May 30, 2012).

"A great many Turkish kids who were born and grew up here are drug addicts; men steal, women prostitute themselves to find the money; they have to sell 5–10 grams every day to meet their own needs." (F. M., Berlin, May 28, 2012).

"Adding a Layer under the Mercator Grid" was a cautionary reminder about the mistake of idealizing the victim as the synonym of the good, just as Friedrich Nietzsche warned that the victim—the slave, in his case—is not necessarily the embodiment of the good simply by virtue of being the opposite of the master. Being a target of discrimination is not a guarantee of immunity toward exerting discrimination over others. In the case of Kreuzberg, multiple layers of race, ethnicity, and gender functioned as categories of exclusion, including those between Germans and Turks, Turks and Kurds, Turks and

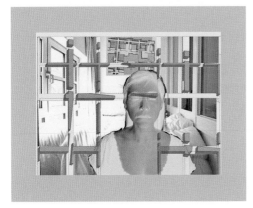

Figure III.28 Esra Akcan, "Adding a Layer under the Mercator Grid," Istanbul Design Biennale, 2012.

Arabs, and women and men. In extreme cases, hostility between groups turned into physical violence and murder, as had occurred in the Asihaus. Ms. Karaoğlan told me that day: "We complain about others, but such a crime happened in our community. You are doing research. Please also conduct research about our Turkish women and Turkish marriages. I asked my neighbors who knew her [the murdered woman]: didn't you ever tell her that she lives in a social welfare state, that she has many rights, she could go to the police? ... She constantly lived in fear; she probably did not know her rights."[55]

Karaoğlan's emphasis on rights resonates with Kreuzberg's urban renewal, because it was not only the inability of women to exercise their rights but also the lack of sufficient noncitizen rights and the continuing paradoxes of human rights that affected this process. As the world witnesses the most extreme refugee crisis since World War II, which exposes the radical crisis of the current human rights regime today, Berlin's experience with housing for former guest workers and refugees becomes increasingly relevant.

Working on public housing and urban renewal in a noncitizen district of the city has therefore carried me to a theory of open architecture. Ungers's square brown building in Kreuzberg is part of the story of an architect who started out defending plurality and democracy against unitary planning, and contextual design against the tabula rasa approach, but the story tragically ended in his advocating design's rule over the environment and his displaying little interest in the contextual problems of discrimination and immigration. The new hospitality of the open architecture to come would therefore be at its best when directed toward the noncitizen, particularly the refugee and the stateless, because nothing exposes the unresolved contradictions of modern international law and the current human rights regime as effectively as the refugee. The stateless person throws into question the very limits of the human rights defined with the precondition of being a citizen of a state. This new hospitality toward the noncitizen has to constantly evolve as long as the current definition of citizenship enforces conditional and limited hospitality, and as long as refugees and global migrants continue to remain rightless.

---

1 The bibliography on Ungers is extensive. For a recent comprehensive biography, see Jasper Cepl, *Oswald Mathias Ungers: Eine intellektuelle Biographie* (Cologne, Germany: Verlag der Buchhandlung Walter König, 2007). For Kleihues, referring to the perimeter block as the "gene" of Berlin: Josef Paul Kleihues, "Southern Friedrichstadt," in *International Building Exhibition Berlin 1987*, ed. Heinrich Klotz and Josef Paul Kleihues (New York: Rizzoli, 1986), 128. **2** "Excerpts from a Dialogue between Heinrich Klotz and O.M. Ungers" (1977), in *O. M. Ungers: Works in Progress 1976–1980*, ed. Kenneth Frampton and Silvia Kolbowski (New York: Institute for Architecture and Urban Studies, 1980), 20–23. Quotation: 20. **3** Oswald Mathias Ungers, *City Metaphors* (Cologne, Germany: Walther König, 1982); Wallis Miller, "Circling the Square," in *O. M. Ungers: Cosmos of Architecture*, ed. Andres Lepik (Berlin: Hatje Cantz, 2006), 97–107. **4** Ungers, *City Metaphors*, 7. **5** Oswald Mathias Ungers, *Architecture as Theme* (Milan: Electa, 1982). **6** Oswald Mathias Ungers, "The Doll within the Doll: Incorporation as an Architectural Theme," *Lotus* 31, no. 3 (1981): 15–21. **7** Oswald Mathias Ungers, "Planning Criteria," in Oswald Mathias Ungers, *The Dialectic City* (Milan: Skira 1997); Heinrich Klotz, ed., *O. M. Ungers 1951–1984: Bauten und Projekte* (Frankfurt: Friedrich Vieweg & Sohn, 1985); Wilfried Kühn, "The City as Collection," in *O. M. Ungers: Cosmos of Architecture*, 69–81. Also see Ungers, *Architecture as Theme*. **8** Oswald Mathias Ungers, "Planning Criteria," *Lotus* 11, no. 1 (1976): 13. **9** Ibid. **10** Kenneth Frampton, "O. M. Ungers and the Architecture of Coincidence," in *O. M. Ungers*, 1–5. Quotation: 2. **11** Günter Schlusche, interview by the author, November 8, 2016, Berlin, in English, 00:37:38–00:38:40. Both audio and video recordings of this interview are in the author's collection. **12** O.M. Ungers with Summer Academy for Berlin, "Cities within the City," *Lotus* 19 (1978): 82–97. Also see Florian Hertweck and Sébastien Marot, eds., *The City in the City: Berlin: A Green Archipelago* (Zurich: Lars Müller Publishers, 2013). For Riemann's contributions, see ibid., 166–67. **13** Ungers with Summer Academy for Berlin, "Cities within the City," 86. **14** Ibid., 96. **15** Anatole Kopp, *Town and Revolution: Soviet Architecture and City Planning 1917–1935*, trans. Thomas E. Burton (London: Thames and Hudson, 1970). Quotation: 179. I would like to thank Kenneth Frampton for pointing out this publication to me. **16** Ungers said: "When I arrived in Berlin in the sixties to study architecture,

Scharoun's influence was virtually tyrannical and unchecked. ... Scharoun denied the idea of the city. This was most obvious in his design for the capital city, Berlin ["Hauptstadt Berlin"]. There he interpreted the city as a countryside and spoke of the 'park city' and the 'countrified area of culture.' I on the other hand was much more interested in creating clearly defined urban spaces and propagating an urban architecture, and this led me to oppose the Scharoun school. ... I opposed the dissolution of the city into countryside with my formulation of strictly delineated urban spaces and the definition of clearly determined forms" (in "Excerpts from a Dialogue Between Heinrich Klotz and O. M. Ungers," 22–23). Also see Oswald Mathias Ungers, "Interview with Rem Koolhaas and Hans Obrist," *Log* spring–summer (2009): 50–95; Pier Vittorio Aureli, *The Possibility of an Absolute Architecture* (Cambridge, MA: MIT Press, 2011). **17** Reinhold Martin, *Utopia's Ghost: Architecture and Postmodernism, Again* (Minneapolis: University of Minnesota Press, 2010). Also see Kühn, "The City as Collection." **18** Hartmut Häussermann, "The Integration of Immigrant Populations in Berlin," in *Immigrants, Integration and Cities: Exploring the Links*, p.137, accessed September 21, 2011, https://books.google.com/books/about/Immigrants_Integration_and_Cities.html?id=KI6bAwAAQBAJ&printsec=frontcover&source=kp_read_button#v=onepage&q&f=false **19** Florian Hertweck, Sébastien Marot (eds.), *The City in the City: Berlin*, 90. **20** See, for instance, Oswald Mathias Ungers, "Berlin: A Morphological History," *Urban Design International* 6 (1981): 21–25 and 40. **21** O. M. Ungers, Hans Kollhoff, Arthur Ovaska, "The Urban Garden: Student Projects for the Südliche Friedrichstadt, Berlin Summer Academy for Architecture '78 in Berlin" (Berlin: Studio Press for Architecture, 1978). B Rep 168, Landesarchiv. **22** Arthur Ovaska, "The City as a Garden, the Garden as a City," in "The Urban Garden," n.p. **23** O. M. Ungers, "The Architecture of Collective Memory," in "The Urban Garden," n. p. **24** Ibid. **25** Hans Kollhoff, "City of Places," in "The Urban Garden," n. p. **26** O. M. Ungers, "Aphorisms on Architecture," in *Oswald Mathias Ungers: Works and Projects 1991–1998*, ed. Francesco dal Co (Milan: Electa, 1998), 11. For a different translation, see Ungers, *The Dialectic City*, 19–20. **27** Ungers, *The Dialectic City*, 21. **28** Josef Paul Kleihues, "Housing Blocks," *Lotus* 19 (1978): 62–76. **29** Martin Kieren, "Architecture as an Existential Problem," in *Oswald Mathias Ungers* (Zurich: Artemis, 1994): 9–34. Quotation: 9. **30** Ungers, "Planning Criteria," *Lotus*, 13. **31** "Excerpts from a Dialogue between Heinrich Klotz and O.M.Ungers," 20, 21, and 22–23. **32** Ungers, *Architecture as Theme*, 125. **33** Oswald Mathias Ungers, "Das Recht der Architektur auf eine autonome Sprache," in *Kunst und Gesellschaft: Grenzen der Kunst*, ed. Heinrich Klotz (Frankfurt, Germany: Umwelt und Medizin Verlagsgesellschaft, 1981), 69–93. **34** Oswald Mathias Ungers, "Architecture's Right to an Autonomous Language, 1979," in *The Presence of the Past: First International Exhibition of Architecture La Biennale di Venezia 1980* (Venice: Edizione La Biennale di Venezia, 1980), 319 and 324. **35** Ungers, "Aphorisms on Architecture," 10. **36** "Feinprogramm Block 1," IBA-Akten B Rep 168, Nr. 705, Landesarchiv. **37** Ungers, "The Doll within the Doll," 15. **38** Cepl, *Oswald Mathias Ungers*, 311. **39** "An Exhibition Concept: Arthur Ovaska in Conversation with Sébastien Marot, August 2010," in *The City in the City: Berlin: A Green Archipelago*, ed. Florian Hertweck and Sébastien Marot (Zurich: Lars Müller Publishers, 2013), 144–52. Quotation: 146. **40** Oswald Mathias Ungers, Hans Kollhoff, and Thomas Will, "A Vocabulary," *Lotus* 15 (1977): 88–97. Quotation: 92. **41** Werner Goehner, correspondence with the author, March 16, 2017, in English. Letter and PowerPoint presentation in Goehner's and the author's collections. **42** Oswald Mathias Ungers, "Wohnbebauung Schillerstraße, Berlin-Charlottenburg," *Deutsche Bauzeitung*, October 1979, 28–29. See also Cepl, *Oswald Mathias Ungers*, 424–25. **43** Ungers stated this as the "fundamental principle that distinguishes my projects" ("Excerpts from a Dialogue between Heinrich Klotz and O. M. Ungers," 20). **44** Ungers, "Interview with Rem Koolhaas and Hans Obrist," 50–95. **45** "Le style, c'est l'homme: A Conversation with Oswald Mathias Ungers," in *The Invisible in Architecture*, ed. Ole Bauman and Roemer van Toorn (London: Academy Editions, 1994): 52–65. Quotation: 55 and 57. **46** My conversations with these residents took place in 2011 and 2012. More formal interviews with members of the Barış and Karaoğlan families are cited below. **47** Bekir and Yunus Barış, interview by the author, June 2012, Berlin, in Turkish, 00:24:00–00:27:21. Both audio and video recordings of this interview are in the author's collection. **48** Fatma Barış, interview by the author, July 5, 2012, Berlin, in Turkish, 00:05:12–00:05:54. An audio recording of this interview is in the author's collection. **49** Ibid., 00:05:24–00:07:03. **50** Ibid., 00:08:03. **51** Ibid., 00:25.00–00:30:00. **52** Ibid., 00:47:36–00:49:29. **53** Bekir and Yunus Barış, interview by the author, 00:00:00–00:15:00. **54** Fatma Barış, interview by the author, 00:58:11–00:58:32. **55** Karaoğlan family, interview by the author, June 5, 2012, Berlin, in Turkish, 00:23:00–00:27:00. An audio recording of this interview is in the author's collection.

STROLL 3

From Potsdamer Platz to Tiergarten

Back in the days when IBA buildings were launched as an exhibition in 1987, it would have been difficult to perceive the eastern and western sides of the deserted Potsdamer Platz as continuous parts. After the fall of the Berlin Wall in 1989 and the exhaustive building construction carried at and around the Potsdamer Platz, it is now much easier to walk from Block 1 to the Landwehr canal. Before the destruction of World War II, the area between the Tiergarten and the canal had been famous for its expensive villas and for being the former diplomatic quarter. Walking on the northern banks of the canal in the late 1970s, one would have passed such epoch-making buildings as Mies van der Rohe's National Gallery, seen Hans Scharoun's State Library and Philharmonic, and August Stüler's Matthäi Church at a distance, and walked along Emil Fahrenkamp's Shell Building. As a public building designed next to these masterpieces, the Science Center predictably became IBA-1984/87's major showpiece. After an invited competition, James Stirling and Michael Wilford—who won over Mario Botta and Dietrich Bangert, Bernd Jansen, and Axel Schultes—received the commission to design the building. The winning architects integrated the two existing historical buildings within the borders of the site into their composition, which looked like a campus of independent but connected buildings with a central courtyard in between (Figure 3.1a). Nicknamed the Cake because of the blue and pink layers on the façade of its round shape, the architects had aimed to produce a "friendly, charming, unbureaucratic place—the opposite of an 'institutional environment'" (Figure 3.1b).[1] The German public must have already been familiar with Stirling's late practice, particularly the Staatsgalerie in Stuttgart, which has become one of the most iconic buildings of postmodernism as a style. Together with the houses at Tegel, this building was responsible for IBA's reputation as an exhibition of postmodern architecture, even though the building exhibition included a much bigger array of approaches—as would have become clear to any stroller by now. Vittorio Magnago Lampugnani, an IBA consultant, had identified this building as a strong example of the new "architectural historicism" with links to the work of Robert Venturi and Robert Stern in the United States and of the participants of the Venice Architecture Biennale of 1980, curated by Paolo Portoghesi.[2]

Behind the Science Center, one could see the apartment complex with four parallel fingers designed by Kurt Ackermann from Munich. If one crossed the bridge to continue the stroll on the southern banks of the Landwehr canal, taking a glimpse from a distance at the pedestrian bridge undertaken by IBA and designed by Brenner and Tonon (Figure 3.2), one would come across the energy houses on Lützowufer in Block 647: five similar but non-identical six-story buildings (each designed by a different architect) that are connected by two-story wings and collectively contain sixty-nine energy-efficient units. Walking in this direction, one would see buildings by the offices of Faskel and Nikolic; von Gerkan, Marg, and Partner; Pysall, Jensen, and Stahrenberg; Kilpper and Partner, and Schiedhelm, in that order (Figure 3.3 a–c). If one followed

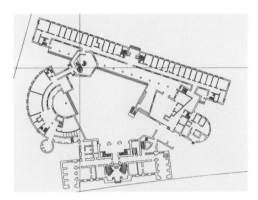

Figure 3.1a James Stirling and Michael Wilford, Science Center.

the curve on Lützowufer, one would reach the freestanding square building by the Turkish architect Zeki Dikenli and his partners Erich Schneider and Hanno Lagemann, all based in Cologne (Figure 3.4 a). The four units on each floor of this building are organized diagonally in the square ground plan, giving each apartment a corner view. The preliminary sketches for the projects in 1985 and 1986 indicate that the architects experimented with multiple schemes before settling on this one (Figure 3.4 b).[3]

Dikenli and Schneider-Wessling had also been invited to IBA's prestigious "Lützow-strasse Competition" for Block 647 in 1980, along with Vittorio Gregotti, Alison and Peter Smithson, Office of Metropolitan Architecture (OMA), Georg Heinrichs, and Johannes Uhl (stroll 6). The jury for the competition was composed of equally celebrated names: Botta, Josef Paul Kleihues, Leon Krier, Hans Müller, Rolf Rave, and Bruno Reichlin. The competition had involved connecting the Landwehr canal and Lützowstrasse by integrating the already designed row houses and the old pumping station, as well as designing a youth center.[4] After deliberation, the jury found no entry worthy of the first prize but recommended that Gregotti be commissioned to design the project. As a matter of fact, Bernd Penack, the representative of the Housing Construction Financing Society who examined the projects from the perspective of their economic feasibility had resigned from the jury because "there appeared to be no respect of a basis for support within the framework of social housing programs."[5] Gregotti had envisioned gate buildings on both ends of the row houses, which had posts made out of bricks and lintels made out of glass and metal frames.[6] He had designed a youth center for the triangular site where Lützowstrasse meets the canal (Figure 3.5 a). The posts and lintels of the gate buildings made out of predominantly solid and predominantly light materials interlocked with each other. The glass and metal frames capped the brick surface in the competition version (Figure 3.5 b–d). The jury criticized Gregotti's urban design for exceeding the limits of the competition by "deviating from the given task" and the inner organization of the apartments for including north-facing units, having inadequate access to living rooms, and lacking outdoor spaces such as balconies. Nonetheless, they found the project "sober and almost hard, and … simultaneously very clear, reserved and congenial."[7] The jury also had doubts about the privacy of the inner gardens, which could be why Gregotti deleted the monumental gate buildings on the

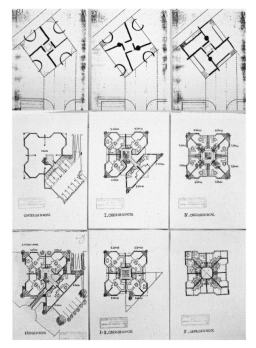

Figure 3.4 b Zeki Dikenli, Erich Schneider and Hanno
Lagemann, Building in Block 647.

river side in the built version. Continuing our stroll, if one took the pedestrian path
from Dikenli's building on the canal and walked along one of the quiet streets between
these row houses, one would reach Gregotti's gate building (Figure 3.6 a). The gate
frames the buildings around the area from both sides (Figure 3.6 b–c). Only part of the
project was executed, a fact that Kenneth Frampton found unfortunate. He endorsed
this building, along with Hans Kollhoff and Arthur Ovaska's urban design for Block
33, as "the most consistent and sensitively detailed residential complex to be realized
under the auspices of IBA to date," but one that revealed that "warfare" not only destroyed buildings but also necessitated the struggle with the "misguided bureaucratic
and speculative" forces.[8]

If one went through one of the Gregotti gates onto Lützowstrasse, one would immediately see another IBA building extending along the street. Block 234 across the street
from Gregotti's building is one of the largest undertaken by IBA, bordered by Lützowplatz, Lützow-, Einem-, Kurfürsten- and Derfflingerstrasse. Even though this would
not be readily apparent to a stroller from the street, this block is noticeable on the city
map for its character as a block within a block. IBA had launched an open "Residential
Park at Lützowplatz Competition" (Wohnpark am Lützowplatz) for this site in 1981, for
which there were 464 applications and 142 final submissions. After four rounds of discussion and elimination between June 3 and 19, 1981, the jury—composed of Kleihues,
Christian de Portzamparc, Arieh Sharon, and Salvador Tarragó Cid, and joined by Oswald Mathias Ungers and Müller in later rounds—had awarded first prize to Herbert
and Siegfried Gergs from Stuttgart and second prize to Bernd Hellriegel and Hermann

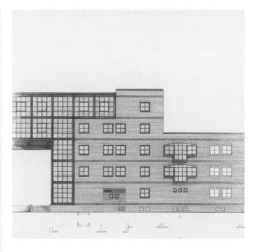

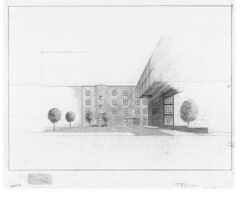

Figure 3.5 a–d Vittorio Gregotti, Urban design of Block 647, 1980.

Neuerburg from Cologne.[9] The Gergs' scheme had divided the area into separate perimeter blocks, while Hellriegel and Neuerburg had proposed an outer perimeter block and a series of urban villas in the inner garden—a plan that was closer to the executed version despite their winning only second prize (Figure 3.7). The jury's praise for their project sounds like it was written by Ungers himself: "In keeping with urban design concept of closing the outer edge, thereby restoring the alignment of the streets with infill architecture, and in keeping with the arrangement of individual structures in the inside of the block, living is also seen in a dialectical field of tension: the contiguous, more anonymous living form on the edge of the block and largely personalized and differentiated living form in the inside of the block. The design lives from this emphasized contrast."[10] The jury had proposed that each urban villa be designed by a different architect, as the typology allowed for such plurality. This was indeed the case in the built version. The inner block is composed of freestanding five-story urban villas, and the outer ring is made up of a solid perimeter building encircling the entire area and creating continuous streets on the front. Among the architects who designed segments of this continuous building on the outer perimeter were Botta, who planned the corner with two detached brick-texture surfaces standing on round metal-clad columns

STROLL 3   From Potsdamer Platz to Tiergarten

197

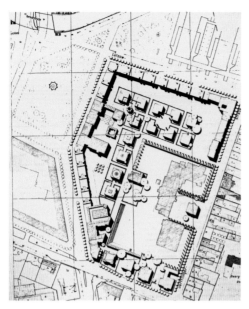

Figure 3.7 Bernd Hellriegel and Hermann Neuerburg,
"Residential Park at Lützowplatz Competition" project
for Block 234 at Lützowplatz, 1981.

and making a crack for the entrance to the building in between (Figure 3.8 a–b);[11] and
Peter Cook, whose white building contained two bays that were capped with vaults
and complemented by a web of cantilevering winter gardens climbing up the white
stucco surface (Figure 3.9 a–b). The Hof-garden of Block 234 no longer functions as
an unbroken public space or a penetrable block within a block, since iron gates have
closed previously public entrances and hedges now divide the area into sections (Figure 3.10 a). Nonetheless, if one could enter this Hof-garden either by finding an open
door along Lützowstrasse or by going through the gate at the corner of Einem- and
Kurfürstenstrasse, one would see glimpses of the open spaces intended for neighbors'
gathering in this area (Figure 3.10 b–c). Nine urban villas create pedestrian walkways
and gardens between the villas, all of which are variations on the nine-square ground
plan and have the same size and number of floors. Among the architects who designed
one or more of these urban villas are Siegfried Gergs, Werner Goehner, and the office
of Bartels and Schmidt-Ott (Figure 3.11). The Hof-garden includes a low-rise brick
kindergarten designed by Klaus Baesler and Berhhard Schmidt (Figure 3.12). According to Goehner, who had participated in the competition for Block 234 and won an
honorable mention, Kleihues had initially asked him to develop a perimeter building
along Kurfürstenstrasse, but it was Gergs who later invited him to design the urban
villa at the southern edge inside the block. Having proposed urban villas as one of the
four types for his competition project, Goehner thinks that "it was almost logical that
[he] got one of the urban villas of the final outline."[12] The Housing Association mandated brick facing, four stories, and one apartment per floor, but otherwise gave him
a free hand with the design. The designers of the urban villas collaborated through
Gergs for the east-facing sides of their façades, the location of their buildings and their
entrances on the site.

Leaving Block 234 from an open door, let's walk towards Lützowplatz and Lützowstrasse to see the compound designed by Ungers for Block 220.[13] If this stroll was taking place during IBA's exhibition opening, one would have seen that this building compound, composed of a front and a back wing, responded to two distinct scales: it provided a monumental front for Lützowplatz with an assertive six-story wing, and it created an intimate walkway inside the block with one-story row houses. The front building contained terrace houses and created a roofscape with three pitched parts on the plaza side, as if multiple buildings were combined under one set of urban design principles. At the back, the scale of this front wing carefully dropped into the scale of the row houses, creating a green, pedestrian path between it and the identical row houses across the path (Figure 3.13 a). This scheme allowed for a variety of outdoor spaces, including large terraces on multiple layers for apartments on the upper floors and front gardens for the row houses on the ground floor (Figure 3.13 b–c). However, if this stroll was taking place a few years ago, one would have discovered that the back wing had been pulled down, thereby destroying much of the original design (Figure 3.13 d). Just before the publication of this book, the stroller would even find that the entire complex had been pulled down. There are reports that the apartment units in this compound could not survive the real estate pressures on this central and valuable city lot.

Leaving the site of Ungers's building, let's turn west on Lützowufer, walk along the canal, and cross the first bridge on the way to Rauchstrasse. If one stood in the middle of Rauchstrasse and looked left and right to Blocks 189 and 192, respectively, one would see the results of two completely different conceptions of open architecture. It is hard to believe that Frei Otto's Öko-Haus in Block 192, an agglomeration of three buildings between Rauchstrasse and Corneliusstrasse, could be carried out as an IBA-1984/87 project under Kleihues's control. An open architecture in the postwar sense, analogous to the growing buildings of Japanese Metabolists, this complex was imagined by Otto as a tree-like set of open platforms on multiple levels, connected with exterior stairways, to be built onto and completed with the designs of different architects.

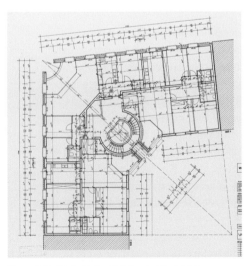 

Figure 3.8 a Mario Botta, Building in Block 234.

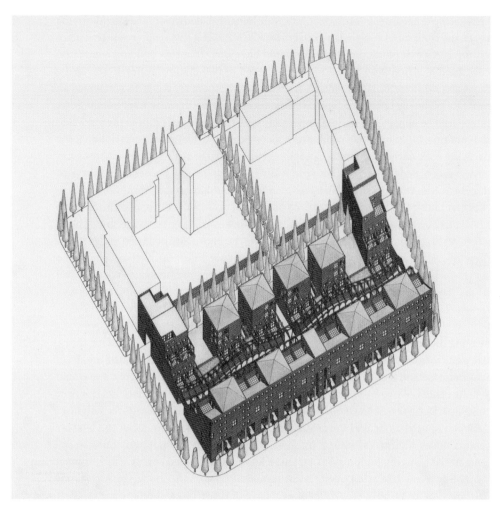

Figure 3.13a Oswald Mathias Ungers, Building at Lützowplatz for Block 220.

The result has created a cosmos in the midst of overgrown plants, which feels outside of Berlin—actually, outside of this world—like an agglomeration of multiple dream worlds in no hurry to interfere with each other. During the construction process, tenants and architects applied to build their own houses, as a version of a self-help initiative. Architects including Torsten Birlem, Jürgen Rohrbach, Manfred Ruprecht, and Ute Schulte-Lehnert designed the dwellings.[14] The twenty-four houses on multilevel "platforms" have been designed in an ad hoc manner, with a different form and program for each resident, out of an uncountable number of dissimilar materials, including different types and colors of wood, metal, brick, stone, and glass. No house, window, door, balcony, greenhouse, doorknob, or ornament seem alike; many are quite idiosyncratic. This open architecture celebrated individualist expression to the ultimate degree, with no motivation for harmonization (Figure 3.14 a–d).

In contrast, it is hard to imagine that eight different architects designed the eight freestanding buildings of Block 189 across the street at the southern edge of Tiergarten.[15]

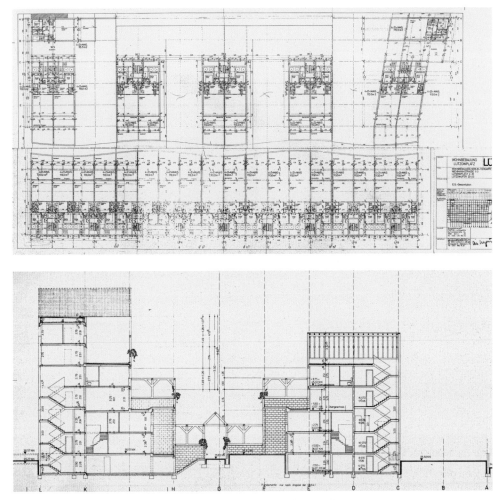

Figure 3.13 b–c Oswald Mathias Ungers, Building at Lützowplatz for Block 220.

Rob Krier carried out the urban design and invited the architects (Figure 3.15 a): Aldo Rossi and Krier built the two buildings on the short edges (Figures 3.15 b-c); the offices of Brenner and Tonon, Giorgio Grassi, Hans Hollein, Krier, Henry Nielebock, and Valentiny and Hermann designed the six detached urban villas on the long edges with the same square ground plan and same number of floors (Figure 3.15 d), creating a nice garden inside the penetrable block. Much like Krier's urban design at Ritterstrasse (stop 1), this was another variation of IBA's perimeter blocks and an example of open architecture as collaboration, but one that created a hierarchy between the chief architect and those under his subordination. Krier defined the design regulations and micromanaged this block to such a degree that he even drew the ground plans of the building allocated to Hollein, which was a substitute on the collective drawing until Hollein submitted his overdue design.[16] Built in one of the most prestigious locations in Berlin for evidently higher-income residents, this VIP "public" housing did not go uncriticized in the German media for "suppressing social problems" in favor of "architects' exhibitionism," and for postmodernist takeover (Figure 3.15 e-f).[17] In the daily newspapers,

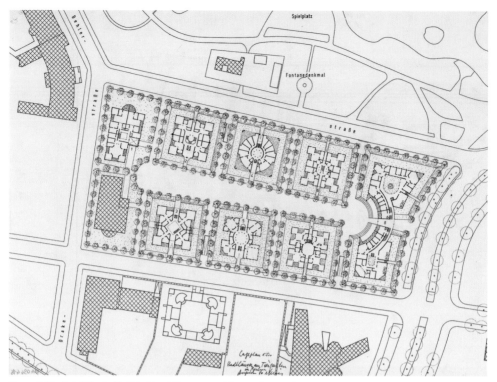

Figure 3.15a Rob Krier (with Aldo Rossi, Brenner and Tonon, Giorgio Grassi, Hans Hollein, Henry Nielebock, and Hermann & Valentiny), Urban design and individual buildings in Block 189.

IBA's initiatives in Tiergarten in general were endorsed as living in a garden of Eden but scrutinized for their functionality and feasibility.[18] The contrast between Otto's and Krier's modes of hospitality toward their co-designers helps us understand the two ends of open architecture as collaboration: one fetishizes individual freedom to such an extent as to ignore the need for a social contract, and the other mandates unity and harmony to such degree as to leave little room for individual expression and equal standing between architects.

Now that we have reached the western end of IBA's demonstration area, let's drop a pin in a navigation device to Kottbusser Tor, and stroll, walk, drive, or take the train to the IBA Altbau areas.

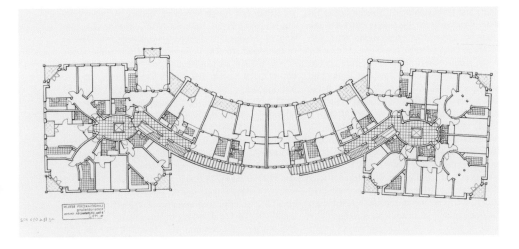

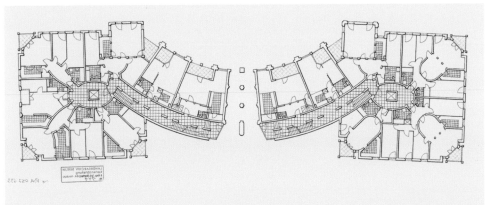

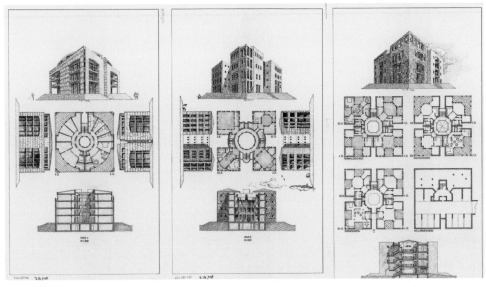

Figure 3.15 b, d Rob Krier (with Aldo Rossi, Brenner and Tonon, Giorgio Grassi, Hans Hollein, Henry Nielebock, and Hermann & Valentiny), Urban design and individual buildings in Block 189.

1 James Stirling and Michael Wilford, "Science Center," in *Erste Projekte: Katalog einer Austellung 1981 IBA Die Neubaugebiete,* vol. 2 (Berlin: Quadirga Verlag, 1981), 186. **2** Vittorio Magnago Lampugnani, "The Origin of Truth: Reflections on the New Historicism in Architecture. James Stirling's Science Center for Berlin," "Post War Berlin," ed. Doug Clelland, special issue, *AD* 25 (1982): 62–66. **3** For drawings of this project, see B Rep 168 (Karten) IBA Neubau, No: 193 Bl. 1–7, 194 Bl. 1–21, 195 Bl. 1–3, 196 Bl. 1–9, 197 Bl. 1–4, 198, 199 Bl. 1–33, 440 Bl. 1–4, Landesarchiv. **4** "Restricted International Competition Lützowstrasse Southern Tiergarten Quarter of Berlin," IBA Competition Brief. Berlin, September 1980, Berlin B 80/19, Landesarchiv; Questions and Answers report (Rückfragenbeantwortung): B 95/019; Jury Meeting Minutes report (Bericht der Vorprüfung), B 81/065, Landesarchiv. **5** "Restricted International Competition Lützowstrasse Southern Tiergarten Quarter of Berlin. Preisgerichtsprotokoll," Berlin, 1981, B 81/034, n.p. Landesarchiv. **6** B Rep 168 (Karten) IBA Neubau, No: 463 Bl. 1–2, 464 Bl. 1–3, 916 Bl. 1–2, 917, 456, 457 Bl. 1–2, 458 Bl. 1–5, 459 Bl. 1–5, 460–461 Bl. 1–2, 462, 200–204, Landesarchiv. **7** "Restricted International Competition Lützowstrasse Southern Tiergarten Quarter of Berlin. Preisgerichtsprotokoll," n. p. **8** Kenneth Frampton, "Construire in zona di guerra," *Casabella,* no. 525 (1986): 54–64. Quotation: 54 and 63. **9** "Internationaler Wettbewerb Wohnpark am Lützowplatz Berlin Südlisches Tiergartenviertel. Report of preliminary examination," Berlin, 1981. B 81/037, Landesarchiv; "Report of the Jury," B 81/035, Landesarchiv. **10** "Report of the Jury," 26. **11** For drawings of this project, see B Rep 168 (Karten) IBA Neubau, No: 168–172, 173 Bl. 1–3, 174–177, 178 Bl. 1–4, 179 Bl. 1–7, Landesarchiv. **12** Werner Goehner, correspondence with the author, March 16, 2017, in English. Letter and PowerPoint presentation in Goehner's and the author's collections. **13** For drawings of this project, see B Rep 168 (Karten) IBA Neubau, No: 227, 228 Bl. 1–2, 229, 230 Bl. 1–6, 231 Bl. 1–10, 232 Bl. 1–6, 233 Bl. 1–2, 234 Bl. 1–4, 235 Bl. 1–2, 236–240, Landesarchiv. **14** For interviews with participating architects and tenants, see "Dreaming of a Tree House—The Ecological Housing Project of Frei Otto in Berlin," accessed April 12, 2017, https://www.youtube.com/watch?v=xCpmfBWRPPM. **15** For drawings of this project, see B Rep 168 (Karten) IBA Neubau, No: 648, 901 Bl. 1–8, 902, 130–132, 133 Bl. 1–4, 134–151, 1370 Bl. 4–5, Landesarchiv. **16** Rob Krier, interview by the author, May 29, 2012, Berlin, in English, 00:25:30–00:28:00. Both audio and video recordings of this interview are in the author's collection. **17** Gerhard Ullmann, "Wohnen am Berliner Tiergarten: Träume der IBA Wunschbilder der Vergangenheit—Kritik 1," *Deutsche Bauzeitung,* September 1986, 14–19 and 181. **18** Roland Mischke, "Wie bewährt sich der Garten Eden?" *Frankfurter Allgemeine,* July 17, 1985.

Part 2
Open Architecture as Democracy

STOP IV

Gentle Urban Renewal:
Participation and Radical Democracy

Who were these men, who
built these kinds of streets? These houses,
these walls that come out of each other,
these roofs fallen over the top of another,
these sleepy windows under the roofs
that face the pumps on street edges?
Who were they, with their diggers and shovels,
with their rulers, who built all these?
If they knew these were for us
surely they would have done differently: opening the window
the sky would have filled inside forthwith. ...

Façades of flats facing the Naunynstrasse
have turned their asses to you,
like deaf transportation workers
indifferent to the loads they carry.
...
What else do they remind you of,
these façades with fallen plasters,
these grinning bricks, these scars?
Who would you say are those who live here?
Who plant sardinias in these miserable balconies;
these old people, who drag their rheumatic feet
to go shopping?

Aren't they those who asked for their rights
against the state who claimed
rights over them, risking their lives
for the foundations of today's democracy?

Aren't you living in these houses now
who will take on, carry on the days of struggle
In the rotten courtyards at the back?[1]

Two images empower these selected lines from Aras Ören's poems, written as a series in Turkish but first published in German between 1973 and 1979: the destitute
conditions of Kreuzberg's apartments and the struggles for the right to the city. Ören's
poems provide nonromanticized depictions of the daily life of Turkish guest workers in

their interaction with their German neighbors, whose lives are equally stark. His "Berlin Trilogy" takes us into the living spaces of Kreuzberg's habitants in the 1970s, as if the characters parade before our eyes one after another, carrying not only their personal baggage but also their apartments and streets. They include Niyazi, an immigrant from Turkey, who witnesses his neighbors' daily lives in Naunynstrasse with constant flashbacks of Istanbul; his downstairs neighboor, the sixty-seven-year-old widow Frau Kutzer, who longs for the days when she could enjoy Café Bauer and other prestigious socialite spaces in Berlin's other boroughs; Atıfet, an activist for worker's rights, who now lives in the corner of Naunynstrasse and Oranienplatz after escaping domestic abuse in Turkey and surviving her only son's death, following a police beating due to his anti-capitalist views; Halime's naughty children, who spend the entire days in the Hof and throw snowballs at Frau Kutzer's window after their mother goes to work in Telefunken to support them and her imprisoned husband; Kazım Akkaya, the skillful, apolitical carpenter who moved to Berlin due to the declining employment in his small town in Turkey, and who now works eleven hours a day to make as much money as possible; Sabri Şen, a worker who often calls in sick and walks Kreuzberg's streets deserted by adults but filled with children, and who dreams of opening a shop but soon finds himself at a bar in Skalitzer Strasse talking to Niyazi about class consciousness; Klaus Feck, the obsessive shopper, a victim of consumer culture, who turns his apartment into a small shop by endlessly buying new furniture and appliances; Emine, who escapes to Istanbul to leave behind her apartment with its three box-shape rooms and the streets that are too distant from home; Dieter, the exhausted construction worker, who tries to keep things clean and decent in an extremely rough and filthy Kreuzberg, and who has a bad dream about being evicted due to urban renewal, which will destroy his old building to erect a new one whose rents will be 25 percent higher.[2] As an author whose work goes beyond recording the guest worker's experience to imagining a multicultural Germany, Ören has been a central figure for scholars analyzing migration literature in Germany.[3] The intertwined stories in his work exemplify what Leslie Adelson called "touching tales"—a concept she proposed against the dominant trope of "between the worlds" in order to "suggest that Germans and Turks in Germany share more culture than is often presumed"—; or in Rita Chin's words, "His poems insisted on the interconnectedness of workers' economic and ethnic identities; and finally, challenged the fundamental dichotomy of native and foreign that had long served as the ideological bedrock for West German conceptions of citizenship."[4] The lines quoted above render a typical architectural scene: the typology of the nineteenth-century rental buildings creating networks of courtyards behind the streets with their walls "that come out of each other" and roofs "fallen over the top of another," the unrenovated walls that are still punctuated with bullet holes from World War II; the façades with "sleepy windows" that are stripped of their ornaments; and the cramped Hof-spaces where Ören hopes the revolutionary right-to-the-city movement will begin. Ören's poems paint Kreuzberg's main dilemma during the late 1970s: it was a worn-out immigrant neighborhood in need of urban renewal but threatened by the contemporary renewal policy itself, which would have destroyed the buildings and displaced the residents. The poems end with images of characters struggling for their social rights: Niyazi and Emine write separate letters to the Berlin Senate, the former requesting a two-room apartment, and the latter asking for her own passport so that she can claim her identity as a resident of Berlin.

Figure IV.1 Screen shots from some of the video-interviews carried out by Esra Akcan with the architects, tenant advisors, and residents of IBA Altbau, Berlin, 2009–2016.

Hardt-Waltherr Hämer and Participatory Urban Renewal without Displacement

It was precisely these problems that the IBA Altbau team took to heart during Kreuzberg's urban renewal. At the time that IBA Neubau was commissioning internationally famous architects to design attractive buildings for West Kreuzberg, IBA Altbau, under the direction of Hardt-Waltherr Hämer,[5] was pursuing a quite different labor-intensive venture a few streets apart, in the areas depicted in Ören's poems. In Ahrenshoop, Germany, on March 24, 2012, I interviewed Hämer—a figure of whom I had heard countless architects and tenant advisors speak with a rare sense of admiration and respect (Figure IV.1). Born in 1922, Hämer had spent some of his childhood in Samarkand and

(Left to right: Hämer, Arın, Nişancı, Eichstädt, Öncü, Moldenhauer, Machleidt, Ercan, Schlusche, Böhm, Çelik, von Davier, A., Düleç, Domschat, Kleff)

Tiflis, then in Russia—which he recalls as having made a great impact on him, particularly due to his architect father's mentorship.[6] Soon after his architectural education in the Hochschule für bildende Künste (HfbK, 1946–49), he designed a church (Ahrenshoop, 1951) in the form of a triangular prism that created a nonfamiliar worship space inside. It was during the design and realization of the Ingolstadt Theater as part of the remodeling of that city in the 1960s that Hämer says he formed most of his ideas about participatory design and citizen involvement. With its centralized stage in the concert hall, brutalist aesthetic, and generous circulation spaces, the building stands as one of the finest but least acknowledged works of the 1960s in Germany (Figure IV.2). The

Figure IV.2 Hardt-Waltherr Hämer, Ingolstadt Theater, c. 1960.

model reconstruction in Putbusser Strasse in Wedding (1968) and the renovation of Block 118 in Charlottenburg (1973–78), both in Berlin, earned Hämer his reputation and probably the directorship of IBA Altbau. At a time when the areas composed of nine-teenth-century rental buildings were perceived as unhealthy and unusable, he argued for their importance in Berlin's history. The pilot project for Block 118 in Charlotten-burg falsified all established opinions about contemporary urban renewal. This project proved that restoring a war-torn building cost only 62 percent of the cost of demolish-ing it and building something new, that residents did not need to be displaced due to urban renewal, and that the rents increased only two-thirds with a restored building, as opposed to constructing a new one.[7] In explaining the project, Hämer noted the se-verity of the housing crisis in Berlin by pointing out that 60,000 entitled families were waiting for public housing and that 240,000 units were still substandard, with no toilet or bath (Figure IV.3). In this context, the Berlin Senate's measures—including the *Auto-bahn* project in Kreuzberg called the Turbine (see stop I), which would have destroyed 100,000–150,000 more apartments and displaced their residents—were anything but a possible solution. Instead, the pilot project at Block 118 could serve as a new model for urban renewal that would avoid previous mistakes.[8]

Hämer's assertions about war-torn areas in Berlin are confirmed by the testimony of many inhabitants, including Cihan Çelik who grew up in Kreuzberg, and whose family was one of the first to move into an IBA-Altbau renovated unit in Block 76 (Figure IV.4 and IV.5). I met her for a scheduled interview in her apartment on July 2, 2012. Having arrived in Germany in 1978 from Erzincan, Turkey, and in Berlin in 1980, Çelik remem-bers vividly both the housing shortage and the dreadful living conditions in Kreuzberg.

TOP: Figure IV.3 View of Waldemarstrasse, Kreuzberg, before renovation, photographed by Heide Moldenhauer, Berlin, c. 1980. BOTTOM: Figure IV.4 View of Block 76/78, renovated by IBA Altbau (team-architect: Heide Moldenhauer), photographed by Esra Akcan, Berlin, 2012.

Figure IV.5 Views of Block 76, renovated by IBA Altbau (team-architect: Heide Moldenhauer), photographed by Esra Akcan, Berlin, 2012.

Berlin attracted many workers who earned extra payment for living in this city (a payment known as *Berlinzulage*) and young people who were exempt from military service for the same reason. "There were a lot of jobs, you could be employed in any company you wanted. But there were no apartments, no kindergartens. These two [shortages] were horrible. None, none, none,"[9] Çelik tells me. Many families had to bribe officials, she assumes, in the Housing Office to rent an apartment of their choice. She apologetically narrates how happy she was to move into a big apartment in Dresdener Strasse after its previous resident died at the age of ninety. When Çelik was pregnant, she had offered to exchange apartments with this woman, who was then living alone in a unit with five rooms, but the landlord did not want to tear the old woman from her memories. Once the apartment was vacant due to her death, Çelik and her family worked for a month to make the place suitable for them, including changing the "wallpaper that dated back to Hitler's times."[10] As a matter of fact, Çelik could well have been one of the characters in Ören's poems about Kreuzberg in the 1970s, who often try to find a slightly better and bigger apartment. They rely on social networks, they put in requests with the Senate as soon as they are politically motivated to expand their rights, and they wait for old residents to die so that they can move into the newly vacated apartments:

> What kind of a process is this
> that we stand
> by stepping on someone else's corpse?
> Who knows how many
> want the same thing
> and dig the grave of another
> without even realizing.[11]

The lack of indoor toilets and baths is a frequent topic of conversation for people who remember the times before the urban renewal. "The toilet was outside," Çelik recalls. "How hygienic can that be, how much can you clean it? No one would live like this unless [they were] absolutely hopeless, but when one must, one puts up with everything.

For taking a bath, we had to leave the house here, take the train for two *U-Bahn* stops to the *Stadtbad* [city bath], carrying our clothes, towels, shampoo, and all that—can you imagine? What a mess. It was quite an ordeal. We were so happy to move to this apartment with an indoor toilet and bath."[12]

Hämer does not remember exactly how he was chosen to direct this urban renewal, as he knew Josef Paul Kleihues and Oswald Mathias Ungers only slightly and did not think that they were particularly supportive of renovation, as they had directed their attention to new buildings.[13] Several initiatives for alternative urban renewal had already begun in the Altbau areas, such as the "Strategies for Kreuzberg Competition" (1976–78), which involved 129 participants, 34 jury members drawn from the Senate and community, and 11 winners, and which recommended the participation of current residents.[14] Citizen Initiative SO36 was prepared to take dramatic measures to put pressure on the City, such as "rehab" squatting in the empty buildings to prevent their demolition, which soon turned into an effective urban protest movement.[15] The Senate's bill on the initiation of IBA-1984/87 mentioned the Strategies for Kreuzberg as a promising participatory model.[16] When IBA introduced itself to the public in a brochure in 1980, it promised to carry "the concept of citizen participation" beyond the "customary forms of institutionalized participation without ignoring already existing approaches." The brochure continued: "Special importance is to be placed on working with those who seem poorly organized and whose interests are generally not appropriately defined, such as women, children, elderly, foreigners and others." The brochure also claimed that a "frustration" was connected to the Strategies for Kreuzberg, as citizens felt that their "chance to participate imaginatively in the renewal of their own neighborhoods has been threatened and suppressed due to the protracted and complicated planning process."[17]

In contrast to conventional city planning implemented from above, Hämer coined his approach as "gentle urban renewal" (*behutsame Stadterneuerung*, usually translated as "careful urban renewal") and openly promoted the use of a participatory model in which the people directly affected by the renovation would become the decision makers. In explaining his struggles in IBA Altbau, Hämer stated that he had to fight against the expectations of the politicians who wanted to turn Kreuzberg into an upper-middle-class neighborhood.[18] To deliver its promises, the IBA Altbau team identified twelve principles that were meant to serve as nothing less than a constitution, written in a demanding and activist tone. These were:

> **1** Gentle urban renewal is a factor of the needs and interests of the present residents and businesspeople of the district. Existing structures will be used wherever possible, not destroyed. ...
> **2** Gentle urban renewal requires a very large degree of agreement on objectives and methods between the residents and businesspeople and the developers or sponsors of projects. Technical and social planning and execution must go hand in hand.
> **3** The inherent vitality of the quarter, its typical features ... must be preserved and developed. ... The security of residents and businesspeople requires firm, long-term tenancy agreements and leases. ...

4 The renewal of houses and apartments will be carried out in progressive phases. …Do-it-yourself [self-help] measures on the part of the residents will also play a role.

5 The existing residential superstructure will be explored for opportunities to create new dwelling forms, for example, by adaptation and reorganization of ground plans.

6 The surroundings of dwellings will be improved step by step via "minor" strategies, such as provision of greenery in interior courtyards, embellishment of façades and fireproof walls by decorative measures and plantings, and in exceptional cases via the demolition of buildings.

7 Public facilities must be renewed and added to. Streets, squares and parks [must be expanded]. …

8 A prerequisite for gentle urban renewal is the establishment of generally binding principles of social planning. These will define affected persons' rights to be heard and their rights to material compensation.

9 The procedure of discussing and taking decisions…should not go on behind closed doors. Delegations of interested parties will have more rights; decision-making commissions will meet locally.

10 A program of gentle urban renewal should enjoy the confidence of all concerned. This necessitates that funding for the district in question be guaranteed for a period of several years. …

11 …Advisory and supportive functions (sponsors) need to be kept separate from construction-related functions (operative agents).

12 Gentle urban renewal is a continuous process. All measures taken must be so designed as to permit further urban renewal on the lines of this concept after…1987.[19]

These principles demanded the democratization of the design and renewal process; the consideration of current residents' needs and interests; the protection of their rights and financial security through legal measures; the protection of the current mixed population usually called the Kreuzberg mixture; the phasing of renovation steps; and the improvement of common spaces in a building, open spaces in a block, and public spaces in the neighborhood.[20] When the *Idee Prozeß Ergebnis* (idea process result) exhibition opened in Martin Gropius Bau Museum in 1984, the different design methods of IBA's Neubau and Altbau segments became clearly visible.[21] The directors and teams of both segments respected the historical city and wanted to preserve it, and both had a passion for renewal. However, the audience could hardly have missed the contrast between the drawing-oriented Neubau exhibition and the photographs in the Altbau section of residents, immigrants, protesters, squatters, shopkeepers, and tenant meetings—a contrast that existed in all exhibitions, events, and publications throughout IBA-1984/87. Like the Neubau segment, the Altbau one commissioned scholars such as Kristiana Hartmann and Dieter Hoffmann-Axthelm to conduct rigorous historical research into the physical development of the area.[22] In addition, IBA's accounts of historical and current conditions always recorded Kreuzberg as a neighborhood of working-class mobilization, squatting culture, and international immigration. The *Kreuzberger Mischung* (Kreuzberg mixture) exhibition in the fall of 1984 and the accompanying catalog under the conceptual guidance of Hämer made a strong case for

Figure IV.6 Cover of *Kreuzberger Mischung* (Kreuzberg mixture). Catalog of the IBA-1984/87 exhibition at the BEWAG Halle in 1984, curated by Hardt-Waltherr Hämer.

the hybrid nature of the area (Figure IV.6). "Kreuzberg mixture" signified not only the presence of diverse architectural types, but also the proximity of work and residential spaces as opposed to modernist functional zoning, as well as the coexistence of different nationalities and lifestyles.[23] In their contributions to the exhibition catalog, Yalçın Çetin and Olcay Başeğmez included a few portraits of Turkish migrants working in repair shops and food retail establishments.[24] As this publication illustrated, Kreuzberg was an extremely hybrid neighborhood composed of small shops, workshops for crafts, squatters, radical art and music groups, and immigrants.[25]

Çelik also identifies "multiculturalism" as the main reason she still chooses to live in Kreuzberg and as a protection against racism:

> I like to live in a multicultural way. People from all over the world live in Kreuzberg. Foreigners are more comfortable among foreigners. If they accidentally move somewhere else, they suffer. ... There are a few neighborhoods in Germany that the foreigners would be very uncomfortable in, such as Marzahn, where immigrants cannot survive. I would never live in or go to such places. We see what they do to people coming from Turkey all the time on TV. Nothing like that would happen in Kreuzberg.[26]

In an area of 310 hectares with 56,000 dwellers, an area composed of many abandoned buildings and blocks some of which (e.g., Block 76) had 25 % single-room flats, and where 48% of units had no private toilets,[27] a participatory model on a unit-by-unit basis required the mobilization of many working groups and mediating agencies. In addition to IBA's own team, numerous advisory groups were established as civil initiatives to represent the tenants' interests.[28]

Figure IV.7 Aerial view of Block 81 in Kreuzberg before urban renewal, photographed by Cihan Arın, Berlin, 11.2.1980.

Residents of Block 81, Cihan Arın and Noncitizen Rights to the City

Of all the groups living in Kreuzberg, this stop focuses on the noncitizen residents from Turkey to provide an in-depth account of the urban renewal process through oral histories of those involved. The site in question consisted of two blocks in the Kottbusser Tor area, "the Bronx of Kreuzberg" as the *Deutsche Bauzeitung* called it.[29] When the Senate's bill for IBA-1984/87 introduced this area, the "integration" of noncitizens was presented as a major architectural goal: "There will be a search for possible ways to support political efforts to integrate foreign families through architectural projects."[30] A report about IBA Altbau's progress between 1978 and 1980 identified discrimination against the Turkish population in the housing market as a major problem and confirmed that immigrant families needed and wanted modernly equipped apartments as much as Germans did.[31] Another report in 1981 identified all projects block by block and documented their existing situation, needs, and current standing to determine the amount of renovation needed.[32] Still another report warned about previous and existing initiatives, criticizing them for being exclusionary despite claiming otherwise, and called for more dialogue with the immigrant population, institutionalization of advisory groups, and establishment of counseling programs that would protect noncitizens' rights. The same report listed the lack of outreach to immigrant residents, the lack of communication between residents and authorities, and the number of grievances as major problems.[33]

While these reports that survived in the archives have no individual authors, it is possible to identify through oral histories the members of the IBA team who were critical of the mainstream integration policies, including members of the conservative and social democratic political parties. Among them was the Turkish architect Cihan Arın, who was responsible both for noncitizen participation in Altbau and Block 81 at Kottbusser Tor (Figure IV.7).[34] I met him several times in addition to conducting two formal interviews with him, on July 15, 2009, and July 4, 2012. Educated in Istanbul, Arın started working for IBA immediately after submitting to the Berlin Technical University his doctoral dissertation on the Turkish guest workers living in this area. He took part in both the Green Alternatives and Initiativkreis Gleichberechtigung Integration (IGI) civil society groups during the late 1970s and 1980s and appeared on German media speaking about issues connected to the impact of immigration in Germany (Figure IV.8).[35] For IBA, he edited a book and wrote several reports on the conditions and restoration of noncitizens' apartments.[36]

IGI exposed the housing discrimination in Berlin in its brochure "What Foreigners Think About Foreign Politics," written in both Turkish and German and released in May 1981.[37] IGI demanded to be a "discussant" in the German integration debates, not just the "object of discussion."[38] It reported that, as noted in the Introduction, landlords and housing bureaus consistently turned down foreign families' applications to rent apartments, which subsequently pushed them into ghettos made up of rundown buildings with small, substandard units. "The apartment will not be rented to foreigners" was a common phrase in newspaper advertisements.[39] Taking advantage of immigrants' lack of rights, landlords failed to perform legally required maintenance, since foreign families could hardly make official complaints about the decaying state of their apartments. There is a general consensus that Turkish guest workers did not invest much in improving their apartments during the early 1970s to save money for an early return back home. By the 1980s, however, many families had decided to stay in Germany permanently.

Figure IV.8 Brochures and booklets against the Senate's housing laws and regulations for noncitizens.

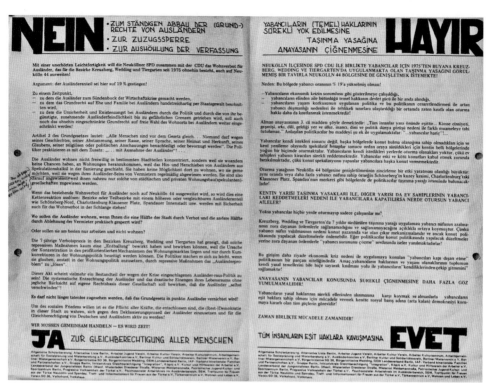

Figure IV.9 Bilingual flyer protesting the ban on entry and settlement, Berlin, c. mid-1970s.

IGI also outlined a set of urban and architectural strategies to improve the housing situation of the immigrant population. Rather than building new housing, the group argued that it would be more effective to repair existing units without a concurrent steep rent increase: this renovation (*Modernisierung* in German, and *yenileme* in Turkish) should proceed with the authorization of the buildings' current tenants and in accordance with their incomes; buildings should be demolished only in very urgent cases and with the approval of the residents; and rental applications should be reviewed by municipalities together with renters' organizations whose members could speak up for the rights of foreigners. These suggestions quite compellingly overlapped with the principles outlined by IBA Altbau.

Members of IGI also organized the *morgens Deutschland abends Türkei* exhibition that took place in Kunstamt Kreuzberg at Mariannenplatz between May 26 and August 23 in 1981. Filled mostly with Gert von Bassewitz's full-page street photographs (some of which were reused in IBA Altbau's major *Kreuzberger Mischung* exhibit) that were accompanied by texts written by IGI members including Arın, Safter Çınar, Necati Gürbaca, Hakkı Keskin, and M. Niyazi Turgay, the catalog of the exhibition reserved half of its pages for the political, economic, and religious structure of Turkey and the other half for the guest workers' working conditions, their children's schooling and leisure activities in Kreuzberg. In other words, the exhibit aimed both to document the guest workers' place of arrival and inform the German public about their place of departure. The critique of the recent 1980 coup d'état in Turkey and an article comparing the rise of fascism and political criminalization in Turkey and rightist extremism in Germany signaled IGI's political orientations and how the group's members were applying their left-wing ideas to the contexts of both countries.[40]

Arın often criticizes IBA as the outcome of "authoritarian social-liberal politics" and advocates the work of the IBA Altbau team as a subversive intervention.[41] He sees the division between the Neubau and Altbau sections as an "opportunistic duality" that was invented to make room for the "conservative, right-leaning" politics and aesthetic choices of Kleihues, as opposed to the "participatory, progressive" wing of urban renewal.[42] Debunking the myth that Berlin's population was shrinking, he confirms that the housing shortage was a major problem and that when an inhabitable apartment became available, 30–50 people would apply to rent it. In addition to Hämer's exemplary renovation of Block 118, Arın identifies the participatory housing in the Netherlands as a major precedent and influence on the Altbau team.[43]

Arın contributed to IBA Altbau's urban renewal principles on two major fronts: the criticism of the Senate's housing regulations and the encouragement of noncitizen participation. Between 1975 and 1978, the social democrat-liberal coalition in the Berlin Senate had passed a series of housing laws and regulations for noncitizens that coalition members defended as desegregation and integration measures, including the *Zuzugssperre*, the "ban on entry and settlement" (1975, known as *taşınma yasağı* among the Turkish migrants) that prohibited additional foreign families from moving into Kreuzberg, Wedding and Tiergarten, and the desegregation regulations (1978) that suggested that only 10 percent of the residential units be rented to noncitizens all over West Berlin. These restrictions caused the fabrication of fraudulent documents and bribery,[44] and were perceived by noncitizens themselves as restrictive measures intended to prevent them from living close to their relatives and forming social networks (Figure IV.9). Arın spent a considerable amount of energy in publicly criticizing and mobilizing protests against these regulations, and he had some success in getting the daily newspapers to report on the regulations' discriminatory nature.[45] In my interview, he summarized: "The Social Democrats were retaining the *Zuzugssperre*. This was a very authoritarian and racist approach. If the intention was to provide the even distribution of the city land among the population, then they should have passed moving bans on the rich and on the German citizens who received housing subsidies. [The ban] was unconstitutional."[46]

Officials and newspapers at various points on the political spectrum did indeed deliver ambiguous statements on immigration. One could condemn prejudice and hostility against noncitizens and then endorse anti-immigration measures in the same sentence. For instance, a state publication in which the Berlin Senate promoted IBA and its architectural program said:

> In his government address, Dr. Richard von Weizsäcker, the Governing Mayor [president of West Germany, 1984–94], [had] already set forth the guidelines of this process of integration in 1981. "Those who are willing to promote the integration of foreigners must receive help in every conceivable way. The Senate will give preference

to integration programs that provide space for the cultural independence and particular need of foreigners. But we Berliners must be prepared to approach foreigners openly and with good intentions. Prejudice and hostility among different groups of the population must no longer increase in the free part of the city." ... In addition he said it was only by taking effective measures against a further influx of foreigners that good citizenship relations based on a high standard of human dignity could be established with the foreigners remaining in Berlin.[47]

During the IBA years, only the Green Alternative group (which had not yet become a major political force) suggested a third option, between the forced integration policies of the social democrats and liberals, and the anti-immigration policies of the Christian Democrats. In a pamphlet on immigration and asylum whose writers included Arın, the Green Alternative group raised its objections to the *Zuzugssperre* and proposed measures that rejected residents' displacement and rent increases.[48] According to Arın,

> We [IBA Altbau] ran into conflicts with the Senate in the beginning. The Senate was financially supporting us, but they had an authoritarian approach. While they claimed to know how to do public housing and insisted on their own methods, we wanted to talk to the residents. It would have been very easy to discard us in the midst of this conflict, but we immediately took on the streets and established tenant consulting agencies; we advised the tenants and gained their support. Our good relations with the tenants prevented the Senate from dismissing us. It wouldn't be wrong to state that the participatory model was made possible despite the social authoritarian policies of the time.[49]

Hans-Günter Kleff worked in one of these newly founded tenant consulting agencies, whose mobilization and cooperation with IBA was decisive in preventing noncitizen displacement during the urban renewal. Architects working in the Altbau segment

Figure IV.10 View from a tenant meeting for an IBA Altbau renovation, IBA-1984/87, photographed by Heide Moldenhauer, Berlin, 1980.

Figure IV.11 View of Block 81, renovated by IBA Altbau (team-architect: Cihan Arın), photographed by Esra Akcan, Berlin, 2011.

often reported having difficulty communicating with tenants, since many first-generation immigrants did not speak German.[50] In addition to the four Turkish employees of the IBA Altbau team (Cihan Arın, Yavuz Üçer, Bahri Düleç, and Yalçın Çetin), it was the bilingual tenant advisors and translators in tenant consulting agencies who became the mediators between architects and residents. Kleff worked as a tenant advisor in the Altbau area SO36 (and briefly as part of the IBA team), and using language skills that he had acquired by living in and visiting Turkey after 1972, he counseled many Turkish-speaking residents. In 1984, he published a comprehensive book on the transformation of rural workers in Turkey into industrial workers in Germany, analyzing immigrant movements from economic, political, and religious perspectives. He devoted a section of this book to guest workers' housing conditions, using statistics and published work to provide ample evidence of the discriminatory practices and ghettoization in several cities of West Germany, including Berlin. For instance, seven out of seven advertisements of vacant apartments published in the *Berliner Morgenpost* on January 17, 1980, stated that only German applicants would be considered.[51] Out of every hundred substandard apartments in Berlin, fifty-six were inhabited by noncitizens from Turkey, and only eight by German citizens.[52]

To qualify for state subsidy to finance the renovation, building owners and developers had to get residents' approvals, and the tenant consulting agency SO36 functioned as a liaison between the municipal administration, owners, tenants, and IBA. When I met with Kleff in 2012 in Berlin, he identified noncitizens' hesitation to speak up for their rights as one of the biggest problems at the time and the cause of his main contribution as a tenant advisor.[53] The rents in rent-controlled apartments were unlawfully raised for noncitizen residents who did not know the regulations, and required maintenance was not performed as non-German speaking tenants could hardly ask for their rights. Kleff remembers one time when he could get the heating fixed in a building with frozen

Figure IV.12 Views of the protest against high rents in Kreuzberg, Berlin, July 6, 2012, photographed by Esra Akcan.

pipes in an icy cold Berlin winter only by threatening the "racist" officer with exposing his name in the press. He also remembers organizing a meeting with city officials and angry tenants, at which the officials finally agreed to meet rightful but long-neglected demands after "a lot of shouting."[54]

I met the tenant advisor Benita von Davier, who consulted with residents in Block 81, in 2012 in Kreuzberg. This block—a triangle at the entrance of the Kottbusser Tor formed by Dresdener, Adalbert-, and Oranienstrasse—is still known as an emblematic area full of immigrant residents and their shops, restaurants, and other small businesses. As of October 1978, 50 percent of the residents of Block 81 had been born in Turkey, with an even higher density on Dresdener Strasse.[55] Arın was responsible for this block on behalf of the IBA team, and the office of Dähne and Dahl had been commissioned to renovate most of the units.[56] After spending a year in Turkey, von Davier wanted to use her language skills to help immigrants, and she joined the tenant consulting agency on Dresdener Strasse, also known as K.O.T.T.I. She continued working as a social worker in the area after 2007, helping immigrants from several countries with problems such as unemployment, alcohol abuse, and domestic violence. During IBA's urban renewal, she remembers residents requesting bigger kitchens, indoor toilets, more rooms for their children or separate units for their extended families, and inexpensive heating. She often visited units with an architect and sometimes talked to residents over a drawing, but she usually demonstrated projected changes physically in space (Figure IV.10).[57] She recalls working with IBA as a "very positive, very constructive" experience, because it provided the current residents with good, affordable apartments and subsidized housing status for about three decades, which allowed them to continue living in the neighborhood.[58] "This is their *Dorf* (village)," she tells me. "There are people who have lived in the same apartment for thirty years and they do not want to leave."[59]

Suzan Nişancı remembers von Davier as one of the extremely caring tenant advisors who helped her with translations.[60] When I met Nişancı in 2012, she had been living in the same apartment on Dresdener Strasse in Block 81 for twenty-seven years (Figure IV.11). She explains, with a dark sense of humor, why she could never master the German language. "I worked as a cleaner all my life alone. The walls and ceilings did not speak to me in German."[61] Nonetheless, speaking up for one's rights in some language is the most frequent topic of our conversation. Even though she remembers going to the *Hausversammlungen* (tenant meetings) and having architects and tenant advisors visit her apartment during the urban renewal, she does not identify IBA as a particularly participatory process as far as she was concerned. "Nobody asked what I wanted," she says. But she immediately adds: "We also did not know how to ask, as we were under the impression that we did not have rights. I did not know my rights. … In the past, we blindly accepted it when someone told us that we did not have rights, that this was not our country, that something was forbidden for us."[62] For example, she regrets not being demanding enough to get her children out of the "foreigner class" that was filled exclusively with Turkish students, unlike her neighbor Ahmet who strategically demanded a "Kurdish class" for his child and managed to place the boy in the class with German citizens.[63] When I met her, she was preparing to participate in a march to protest rising rents on July 6, 2012 (Figure IV.12). She complained about her neighbors' reluctance to speak up for their rights and the tenant consulting agencies' disinterest in gentrification, which betrays the ideals on which they were founded in the 1980s:

> We [have] stayed silent. Even those associations and agencies that protest against everything stayed silent about [the rising rents]. They must be benefiting from them too. … After 1984, there were many Turks in Kreuzberg, but now they want to throw us out … so that rich people can move to Kreuzberg. They think we are not worth this place, but aren't we human? We worked and renewed this place, and now they will live happily here? … We paid for all this renovation with our rising rents, we fixed many of the crumbling parts ourselves—that means we did the renewal.[64]

Figure IV.13 View of Kreuzberg renovated by IBA Altbau, photographed by Esra Akcan, Berlin, 2009.

Figure IV.14 A tenant meeting for an IBA Altbau renovation, IBA-1984/87, photographed by Heide Moldenhauer, Berlin, 1981.

As a matter of fact, many immigrants take ownership of Kreuzberg's urban renewal and its symbolic significance in the global imagination by pointing out their own financial and cultural contributions in making the area a pleasant place to live, now found charming by the wealthy (Figure IV.13). These comments ignore IBA's role in delaying Kreuzberg's gentrification by virtue of the subsidized housing status given to the renovated buildings. Yet the residents do have a point. "The German state should know this," Çelik says. "If Kreuzberg is so beautiful now, it is thanks to the Turkish community. Nobody used to sit outdoors in Berlin. Once we started having cafes and shops on the ground floors, everyone followed."[65] While Çelik emphasizes Kreuzberg's multiculturalism, Nişancı prioritizes its neighborly character as her reason for living there. She remembers the first Turkish grocery in Berlin, opened by Saim *ağabey* (brother) on Dresdener Strasse, which was followed by doctors' offices, butcher shops, open-air markets, and so on: "I came to Kreuzberg directly from Istanbul when I was sixteen. I do not know anywhere else. When I go out on the street, I would recognize and say hello to eighty out of ninety people. There is neighborliness, everyone knows each other. You would not starve here no matter what time it is at night. You would not be afraid on the streets at night. I cannot live in Spandau if I had to move there now. ... I need to be able to ring bells unattended if I suddenly fall sick."[66]

The memories of going door-to-door, ringing every bell, introducing himself, and informing residents about the urban renewal and asking for their approval are still fresh in the mind of Martin Domschat, who worked as a tenant advisor on Dresdener Strasse with von Davier. He also remembers Hämer and Arın, and he met with me in 2012 in Kreuzberg. He vividly described these participatory meetings: At least six or seven people from different associations and interest groups would sit around a table, including an IBA team member, a tenant advisor, architects, and tenants—usually including both men and women. The first meeting, when the team would document the apartment's conditions and the residents' needs, would last for two or three hours, and many more meetings would be organized as needed during the renewal (Figure IV.14).[67] The biggest wishes of noncitizen families included having an indoor toilet and bath, better but affordable heating (which meant that many preferred coal-burning stoves to central heating) and more rooms.[68] Domschat also recalls a tension between "idealist" architects and "pragmatic" tenant advisors.[69]

As happened in other blocks renovated by IBA Altbau, families living in Block 81 were temporarily moved into other apartments in the area during the renovation and were given the option of coming back or staying at their new places. The Demir family on Dresdener Strasse, for instance, did not want to leave the building during the renovation due to the difficulties of moving back and forth with their new baby. The IBA team agreed to renovate the flat next door first, so that the family could use it while waiting for the renovation of their own apartment.[70] N. K., who had been living in the same building on Dresdener Strasse since 1976, mentions that she wanted to return to her original apartment after renovation, because she would have had to move out of Kreuzberg due to the *Zuzugssperre* if she had opted for another place.[71]

IBA strengthened the structural beams, renovated the mechanical and electrical equipment, added toilets and baths, fixed the infrastructure for kitchens (but did not provide kitchen equipment), added double windows for insulation and unit-based heating, redid the stucco façade and repainted interiors, replaced wood floors with a plastic-based material for easy maintenance, and in some cases lowered ceilings for easier insulation. While these last two activities must have saved money, they changed the spatial character of the renovated buildings. One of the most contested issues was the coal-burning stoves that were used to heat the apartments, which many families preferred to central heating to avoid a steep increase in rent.[72] The ceramic stoves were beautiful, colorful and came in a variety of sizes and shapes. (Figure IV.15). For example, Çelik has fond memories of living with a stove. When she was a child, her family used to keep the wood and the coal in the Hof and carried them upstairs on the weekends. For warmth, the whole family used to sit around the stove rather than alone in their colder rooms, which made the space near the stove a natural meeting point for everyone.[73] Some families dried laundry, boiled water, and even cooked on these stoves. However, Kleff disliked the idea of continuing to use them. "These old stoves have a very special operating system that the foreign families were not acquainted with," he says, pointing to the misuse of wood and garbage that broke the ovens and the frequent accidents involved with their use.[74]

Mindful that over-renovation would displace the immigrants due to a sudden rent increase, IBA Altbau handled modernization by fixing only what the current families could afford. In Germany, there was a fine distinction between renovation and modernization, and the latter typically caused a rent increase of 11 percent. In determining the rent increase after renovation, the IBA team wanted to categorize many gray areas as renovation rather than modernization in order to protect tenants. For example, Arın

Figure IV.15 Views of stoves in Altbau buildings in Kreuzberg before renovation, photographed by Heide Moldenhauer, Berlin, 1980–1981.

tells me how he cut the price of a double window in half by making an argument to the contractors that it was replacing an existing single window.[75] The big developer firms must have agreed to these profit-decreasing demands for the sake of the prestige they earned by working for IBA, which they must have balanced by raising prices in other housing developments around or outside Berlin.

In Block 81, a unit was enlarged by combining it with the adjacent flat so that the large family currently residing in the building could be accommodated.[76] The Nişancı family requested that the kitchen be placed as an open kitchen in their second living room (a separate living room exists in the apartment). After an agreement between the two tenant families, they were given an additional room from the adjacent building, which is a couple stairs higher due to the sloping street (Figure IV.16).[77] Among all of the residents I had conversations with, Nişancı has the biggest criticism of the design: She appreciates the central heating, as the coal-burning stoves created dirt, but she would have preferred the sink and oven to be placed on the other side in the kitchen, the doors to be placed to the side or made to open in the other direction so that the room could be used uninterrupted, and the entrance corridor to be made larger by taking away space from the kitchen or living room.[78] Another resident requested that a sink be installed in the living room to make ablutions before Muslim prayers more practical.[79] Mr. Ipek remembers his parents' biggest complaints about living in Block 81 as overcrowding and the outdoor toilets. He appreciates the way their two-room apartment was enlarged into a four-room one during the renewal by removing a wall and integrating it with the neighboring unit, so that he and his two siblings could each have a room of their own.[80]

Figure IV.16 View of Nişancı family's apartment in Block 81, renovated by IBA Altbau (team-architect: Cihan Arın), photographed by Esra Akcan, Berlin, 2012.

In Kleff's assessment, such reshuffling of apartments in the same and sometimes even neighboring buildings was IBA's biggest success: "The best effect of IBA was that people could stay where they lived at the time. … Most of the families could not only stay in their building, but [they] also got larger apartments, and many moved to the front building of the block. The flats were no longer too crowded. We gave some families two to three flats so that their newlywed son and daughter also got separate flats. We could solve the overcrowding of the flats, and this was IBA's greatest success."[81] Some of these requirements turned Kreuzberg apartments into quite special, at times idiosyncratic, units. The Altbau team tried to make optimizations so that they could respond both to the specific requirements of residents living in an apartment during the renewal and make sure the unit would still be marketable once the family left the building.[82] Aldo Rossi, one of the IBA Neubau architects, would have probably identified this design process as "naïve functionalism" (stop 2), but it was this process that let IBA Altbau avoid immediate gentrification, unlike most urban renewal projects around the world—something Rossi would have appreciated from a political perspective. In fact, the overdetermination of units by noncitizens was one of the major criticisms directed at IBA Altbau. In my interview, Hildebrand Machleidt, the IBA Neubau coordinator, asked: "Does user-oriented architecture happen only when you talk to the residents, or when you are a good architect and when the apartment is good? IBA was public housing and the responsibility was to the public, not only the residents currently living in the apartment. One had to think of the users in twenty to thirty years. IBA Altbau was only thinking of the present. If the apartment is too specific for a person, this would be a mistake."[83] This comment raises a series of important questions: Who determines the design of an apartment in public housing: those who will live in it right away; those

Figure IV.17 View of an outdoor toilet in an Altbau building in Kreuzberg before renovation, photographed by Heide Moldenhauer, Berlin, 1980.

Figure IV.18 View of a Hof in Adalbertstrasse in Kreuzberg before renovation, photographed by Heide Moldenhauer, Berlin, 1981.

who are expected to live in it in the near future; or those who are defined as abstract, timeless, and universal users whose requirements will remain the same at all times and wherever they moved from? Who are the legitimate representatives of urban renewal? Is participatory design necessarily a synonym of democracy in architecture? I will return to these questions at the end of this chapter.

Residents of Block 76/78, Heide Moldenhauer and One Woman at a Time

"I was afraid to go out to the toilet," Mr. Tuğrul remembers several times during my interview with him in 2012 (Figure IV.17). He was four or five years old when his family used to live at the back side of the Hof, before the urban renewal. Both of his parents worked for long hours during the day, leaving him alone in the apartment with a banana—a fruit he recalled as a treat at the time. After the day he ran into drunken men on the stairs speaking a language he could not understand, he never again dared to open the door and go to the toilet located outside the apartment, even if that meant he had to pee in his pants.[84] Other unpleasant details were equally vivid in his memory about growing up as a Turkish immigrant in Kreuzberg in the 1970s: everything was worn out; the Hof was not paved but muddy and dirty, covered with piles of black coal on the ground (Figure IV.18); the apartment was heated with a big stove; walls were stained with water leaks; and the window and door frames were broken. Perhaps he did not realize, but the damage caused by World War II had not been erased from the streets; city lots where the buildings had been destroyed were kept empty and full of

Figure IV.19 View of an Altbau apartment in Waldemar-strasse in Kreuzberg before renovation, photographed by Heide Moldenhauer, Berlin, 1981.

debris; bullet holes remained in the walls of the buildings that had survived the war; and a dangerous type of mold was slowly destroying structural wooden beams and threatening to make the ceilings fall (Figure IV.19). In the beginning, there were only a few children he could play with, and one of them, the older daughter in a neighboring family, killed herself by jumping out of a window into their Hof.[85] Even though he does not know or say whether his parents moved to Germany from Dersim, Turkey, for political or economic reasons, he remembers his father instructing him not to tell anyone at school or in the Hof that their hometown was Dersim.[86] Practicing their Alevi customs occasionally, they can now freely go to the Cem House around the corner (Figure IV.20). But his memories about the living conditions in Kreuzberg in the 1980s keep returning, even though one would expect him to have forgotten them by now—after having gotten good grades in school and having a good job and a good apartment that he does not want to leave. Thanks to Leyla Kubat, an activist teacher who also participated in IBA's seminars, he was taken out of the foreigner class and registered in citizen schooling.[87] "The first generation suffered a lot. We, the second generation, learned to say *Warum* (why); the next, third, generation learned to say *Nein* (no). They talk to us about integration now. You have not taught German to my mother and father, you have made them work like a dog, aren't we supposed to talk [about these things while discussing] integration now? That is why please talk to the elderly and record the living conditions of the past,"[88] he says, approving my research. After a while, at the end of the 1970s, there were more children in the area. In those days, up to five or six of

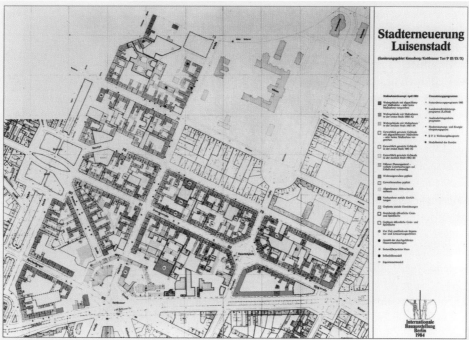

TOP: Figure IV.20 Cem House in Kreuzberg, photographed by Esra Akcan, Berlin, 2009. BOTTOM: Figure IV.21 "Blue plan." Urban renewal program of IBA Altbau, Kreuzberg, Berlin, 1981.

them used to sleep together in a room on the floor (only parents had a bed). His family moved to his current apartment in the front building of the same block, but back then, each room was occupied by a different family, and his family could witness every drama in their many neighbors' lives. This was when an architect rang their doorbell to inform his parents about the urban renewal project of Kreuzberg, hereafter to be known as IBA-1984/87.

This architect was probably Heide Moldenhauer, responsible for IBA's Block 76/78. One of the very few women professionals in the urban renewal project, she took up dancing later and had her first public performance at Kreuzberg's Ballhaus Naunynstrasse on her sixtieth birthday.[89] Having studied architecture in Stuttgart and sociology in Berlin, she worked for five years in DeGeWo housing in Wedding, which made her critical of the raze-and-build approach that was typical in urban renewal at the time. Soon after she quit that job due to her frustration, she received an invitation from IBA, but she was skeptical at first and reluctant to work in another Senate-sponsored urban renewal project. She changed her mind when she learned about Hämer's earlier work and his commitment to working with current residents, and when the Altbau director praised her reports on urban renewal. As she had been in a communist organization and had worked on the pro-abortion bill, she recalls that after she was hired IBA received an anonymous letter demanding that she be fired, but Hämer and Werner Orlowsky, the mayor of Kreuzberg, protected her.[90]

The participatory architecture, self-help projects, photographs, building programs, public art installations, exhibitions and events that Moldenhauer designed, produced, and organized during this process not only stand as unique examples of feminist practice, but also avoid the common forms of imperial feminism and ethnographic authority during the period. After working on the general planning (and coloring the big master plan referred to as the "blue plan," Figure IV.21), she became responsible for Blocks 76 and 78, in the Kottbusser Tor area, between Oranien-, Waldemar-, Naunyn-, and Adalbertstrasse and the Oranienplatz. She took about 3,500 diapositives on the streets, in the Hof-spaces and apartments, and during the tenant meetings and the renovation process, amassing a collection which now stands as nothing less than a sophisticated city archive of the period.[91] Recently, photographs that Candida Höfer took in her early career of Turkish guest workers in Germany have attracted the attention of scholars, who have praised them for their intimacy and dialogical nature (subjects look at the camera)—in contrast to images representing the patronizing ethnographic gaze.[92] In this sense, Moldenhauer's collection is a much more comprehensive *oeuvre*, as most of her photographs show the many levels of the agency of the residents she worked with, rather than catching them with the confidence of a photographer who feels entitled to intervene in the most private spheres of individual lives (Figure IV.22). The first empty unit renovated under Moldenhauer's responsibility in Block 76 served as a model apartment, used to gain the public's trust. Block 76 was also the exemplary project introduced in IBA's most visible *Idee Prozeß Ergebnis* exhibition catalog, where its 424 out of 551 occupied units accommodating collectively 1165 residents out of which 770 were noncitizens and 456 were children illustrated the housing problem in numbers, while Moldenhauer's photographs provided the same evidence in images.[93]

Figure IV.22 Heide Moldenhauer's photographs of residents in Adalbertstrasse, Kreuzberg, Berlin, 1981.

"I was a bit shy in the beginning with the Turkish people," Moldenhauer says during our interview. "Every day, I was confronted with one of my presuppositions."[94] During IBA, she regularly directed *Hausversammlung* (tenant meeting) for each building and went door-to-door to each and every apartment in her two blocks with her translator Necla, a young Turkish immigrant whom she had met in the neighborhood, spent many hours and prepared an exhibition with. During those group and one-to-one meetings, Moldenhauer communicated with residents through her translator to determine the best distribution of rooms among families and discuss the necessary renovations in each apartment, including the installation of indoor toilets, kitchens, and central heating and the use of construction materials (Figure IV.23). She avoided excessive modernization that would have raised the rents and displaced the current residents.

Moldenhauer was especially attentive to women's empowerment. She cautioned about the difficulty in hearing noncitizen women's voices, since it was the husbands who often participated in the tenants' meetings during IBA.[95] Even though many tenant advisors say that men communicated their wives' requests with the oft-pronounced idiom "Hanım istemiyor" (my wife does not want that) in participatory meetings, they also felt the need to talk to women directly in one-to-one meetings in their apartments.[96] There were a few organizations at the time in the eastern part of Kreuzberg that focused on gender equality. An architectural group called *Frauenprojekte* (women's project) was founded under IBA in 1979 and worked in areas near the Görlitzer Park, which had relatively smaller percentages of noncitizen residents—especially in Blocks 133, 108, and 109.[97] *Otur ve Yaşa* (reside and live), one of the biggest tenant consulting associations, wrote a report to IBA, informing them of the Turkish women's skepticism about a building exhibition, but also their cautiously optimistic comments. The association noted their requests for more parks and playgrounds.[98] Elişi Evi (house of crafts) was a civil society group with a common meeting space, initiated by German women, but nonetheless in collaboration with Turkish women. Announcing their goal as "integration" in a bilingual booklet published by IBA, they offered classes in German, help with children's homework, and lessons on cooking and home management and enabled women to practice crafts (such as sewing, knitting, folklore, flower arranging, glasswork, painting).[99] Despite the call for dialogue, the booklet shows that the association conceived of integration as a process that required Turkish women to change their customs and lifestyles, rather than resulting in a possible hybrid after a dialogical procedure. It read as follows:

Turkish young girls and women live under the dominance of lifestyles that belong to a rural and unindustrialized society. These behaviors are usually discordant with the social context they exist in. The education of many Turkish families is shaped by the Islamic traditions in their country. The status of Turkish women professionally and at home, their inadequate German, and the separation of women's and men's worlds, make it difficult to establish social bonds for women and young girls whose living space is largely bounded by the house. As a result, women and young girls have to live isolated from each other. We must understand the special condition and problems of these women in order to prevent their seclusion and complications that rise as a result. Only then we may find an opportunity to find solutions together, develop suggestions to their liking, and create social and cultural integration.[100]

In contrast, Moldenhauer was careful to report both about domestic violence and about the solidarity between women and men that prevented such acts in Turkish families. One day, she saw a young boy beaten by his father and convinced the mother to seek help from a social worker; on another day, she listened to a neighbor asking her husband to speak to the man in the next-door apartment and get him to stop beating his wife.[101] During the urban renewal of her two blocks for IBA Altbau, Moldernhauer helped transform an old stable in the Hof into a Kita (day care center, Figure IV.24)—which Mr. Tuğrul still remembers—and another old workshop building into a family garden, which I find still functioning as a meeting place for women, where they can take courses in several crafts or share stories of domestic violence. Block 76 also included a building only for women, which Moldenhauer and I visited in the summer of 2012 (Figure IV.25). Surely, it was not only Turkish women who

Figure IV.23 A tenant meeting during IBA Altbau, Kreuzberg, photographed by Heide Moldenhauer, Berlin, c. 1981.

were oppressed. Even though IBA considered itself to employ more women architects than was common in Germany at the time, the women's numbers were still small.[102] Moldenhauer talks about her visit to the United States to study the works of Julia Morgan, an architect whose unfair treatment in the canon is still telling.[103] Moldenhauer organized a panel with women architects in 1984, including Zaha Hadid (who canceled on the morning of the event, confirming the predictions of many people who had said the "diva" would not show up). Having interviewed Hadid—who had communicated her frustration with IBA's confining her to the design of a small building and giving her no freedom—Moldenhauer herself made a presentation about Hadid.[104] With her translator, Necla, Moldenhauer created an exhibition in 1984 on woman as architects in SO36, which included a display she created that was composed of her own photographs pinned over pieces of typical Berlin wallpaper, a low table, and two cushions that Necla's mother had knitted and sewed for the display (Figure IV.26).[105] Moldenhauer does not turn a blind eye to inconvenient truths of history. She made a special effort to find women architects to work in the renovation, "but they were not very professional," she says with disappointment. She had to fight with them about their depictions in their renderings of women in bikinis sunbathing in the Hof, or their complaints that Turkish women increased the dampness of the kitchen because they always had tea boiling on the stove.[106]

"The most disappointing for me," Moldenhauer continues, "was that the architects had no sense for beauty. Sometimes you can keep something and use it again." Many wooden doors and colorful coal-burning stoves were thrown out.[107] Instead of disregarding beautiful objects, she convinced the German-Turkish artist Hanefi Yeter to design mural reliefs on the façade of the building at the corner of Adalbert- and Waldemarstrasse in Block 76. Yeter's work is composed of humans made out of colorful three-dimensional tiles shown in everyday life scenes with a twist of unfamiliarity (Figure IV.27).[108] The erased mural on Dresdener Strasse 10 is also attributed to Yeter, which was one of the first representations of migrants' everyday life objects and memories of home, made

Figure IV.24 Heide Moldenhauer, Kita (day care center) in Block 78, Kreuzberg, Berlin, when built in 1984, and in 2012.

Figure IV.25 View from a Hof in Block 76, renovated
by IBA Altbau (team-architect: Heide Moldenhauer),
photographed by Esra Akcan, Berlin, 2012.

visible on the scale of an urban façade (Figure IV.28).[109] Yeter was also one of the three
Turkish artists who were featured in the bilingual *Mehmet Berlin'de/Mehmet aus Anatolien* exhibition around the corner at Kunstamt Kreuzberg between September 6 and
November 9, 1975 (the other two were Mehmet Çağlayan and Mehmet Aksoy). Just like
the *morgens Deutschland abends Türkei* exhibit in the same space six years later, which
involved some IBA Altbau members, this show had two foci: a long chronological overview of Turkey's economic, political, and cultural history, and information about the
bureaucratic details of immigration such as requirements for residence and working
permits, demands for democratic rights, photographs of Kreuzberg's streets, and guest
workers' conditions and leisure activities.[110] There is a long tradition in Kreuzberg of
murals and other forms of street art. Çelik, who lives in Block 76, remembers the day a
woman painted the mural on the façade of the old stable in their Hof: it showed three
children on a green hill looking at the smiling sun and blue sky (Figure IV.29).[111]

In addition to the Kita, family garden, and art projects, Moldenhauer was influential in
turning the Heile House in Block 76, occupied by squatters, into a self-help project that
supported public service. According to her recollections, the squatters and the Turkish
immigrants coexisted with neither tension nor co-operation. As Hämer, Moldenhauer,
and Kleff all mention, the squatters were initially skeptical of participating in IBA's
self-help projects, as they thought the organization represented the voice of the state.
There were a couple of tense incidents, such as the time when the squatters occupied
the Altbau office and tried to wreck the computers. Nonetheless, Hämer and the IBA
Altbau team eventually gained most of the squatters' trust and accepted many of their
demands, and the self-help projects were handled relatively successfully.[112] Today
Heile House still functions as a place where passersby can use a public bathroom and

toilet, and lunch is served in the common dining room almost every day (Figure IV.30). Additionally, after discovering how Necla's family had turned the roof of their building into a garden to grow their own food, Moldenhauer organized self-help events where noncitizen residents and children planted greenery in their Hof.[113]

Some residents still use the Hof-spaces in Block 76 to grow vegetables. For example, F. Güler, who lives on the top floor of a building on Waldemarstrasse, often goes down to the Hof to water the plants in her relatives' vegetable garden (Figure IV.31).[114] Her father had moved to Germany from Turkey in 1964, and she immigrated in 1973 to work in a hotel first, and then a chocolate factory, for a total of twenty-five years. She has been living happily in this apartment since 1982, but she confirms the difficulties of finding a decent place to live in the late 1970s. Echoing other residents, she recalls, "I was afraid to go out to the toilet." She also remembers the public-bath in Prinzen-strasse; the big washbowls her family kept in the house; the overcrowding; the small apartments they had to change one after another; and the ban on foreigners moving to Kreuzberg.[115] After she sought help from a tenant consulting agency as someone living in one room with four children, the advisor was very emphatic and found her this IBA Altbau apartment, whose renovation her family completed by finishing the wall-paper and painting. Her apartment is indeed unique, with a separate living room in addition to the central open living kitchen that leads to another wing, with bedrooms a few steps above. Evidently, this wing previously belonged to the neighboring building and was included in this apartment during the urban renewal to provide a much larger unit for the needs of her big family (Figure IV.32). She appreciates the "boundless" (*engin*) high ceilings, noting that a low cramping ceiling is the first thing she notices in many Neubau apartments.[116] She had the curtains made in Turkey and installed in Germany to cover the high windows under those high ceilings. Her most intense regret seems to be the fact that her children were not well educated—a fact that her son

Figure IV.26 Exhibition in SO36, prepared by Heide Moldenhauer, Berlin, 1984.

Figure IV.27 View of the murals by artist Hanefi Yeter on the corner of Adalbert- and Waldemarstrasse, renovated by IBA Altbau (team-architect: Heide Moldenhauer), photographed by Esra Akcan, Berlin, 2012.

confirms, but without failing to notice the political structure that caused this outcome: "The German politics for the Turks were harsh. The schooling policies were harsh. For instance, they could have mandated that employers give German classes to the guest workers. All these were criminal neglects (*ihmal*)."[117] The Güler family often leaves Kreuzberg, going to Alexanderplatz, Kurfürstendamm, and Neukölln and nearby villages in Germany, but they would not give up their apartment in this neighborhood. As a matter of fact, they estimate that around 2000 people live in Kreuzberg from the Sarılar village of Antep, where they come from, whom they meet often and have established solidarity networks. When I ask how they manage to create an agglomeration of this magnitude, given that I cannot find an apartment in Kreuzberg as a newcomer, they explain: "Whenever we learn that an apartment will open up, we have an agreement with the previous tenant to let the lease to our own friends. Whenever someone dies in an apartment, we immediately go to the housing office and request the unit for our relatives."[118]

Radical Democracy and the Limits of Hospitality

The examples above prove that the Senate's discriminatory housing regulations directed at noncitizens were subverted in IBA Altbau areas by a group of professionals employed by the Senate itself. The Altbau team prepared countless handouts to explain the renewal process and organized *Hausversammlungen* for each and every building in order to record and negotiate neighbors' conflicting and complementing requirements; the tenant advisors working in newly established tenant consulting

Figure IV.28 Erased mural on the façade of a building in Dresdener Strasse 10 (attributed to Hanefi Yeter).

agencies went door-to-door to each and every apartment to discuss the residents' needs and budgets; the translators found on the streets or in universities were employed; the architects removed or added walls, combined or divided units, and added stairs and service spaces to optimize the neighboring tenants' differing needs within their budgets; the developers agreed to some low-profit deals for the prestige of participating in IBA; the residents agreed to move temporarily to another apartment or to put up with the construction in their apartment during the renewal process; and the authorities agreed to give public housing status to residents for approximately twenty-five years, so that no single noncitizen family was unwillingly displaced from their apartment, keeping the original percentage of noncitizens in the area intact (Figure IV.33). This percentage was well above the Senate's 10 percent threshold. As Hämer said in my interview toward the end of his life: "We were against anything top-down, so we ignored those rules by the Senate, we did not care about these rules. And we managed to get around them. ... We were working with the leftist people from Turkey. We did not accept the authoritarian rules that were given to us. We went with our own rules."[119]

However, the residents from Turkey did not participate in matters outside the ones for which they were directly asked for their approval (their own apartment or shop). Few of them attended the participatory meetings about "infrastructure" buildings, public and vehicular transportation, and the organization of public parks and semipublic gardens inside the blocks.[120] The fact that men represented their families in tenant meetings also limited noncitizen women's participation. Turkish families did not take

Figure IV.29 View of the mural on the façade of a stable in a Hof in Block 76, renovated by IBA Altbau (team-architect: Heide Moldenhauer), photographed by Esra Akcan, Berlin, 2012.

advantage of self-help projects either, which attracted many squatters. Reasons for this are hard to determine. While many admittedly voiced their disinterest in or skepticism about the projects, Arın commented that IBA's participation model was geared toward the citizens and squatters rather than taking into account the cultural habits of the noncitizen population.[121] Many citizens and squatters made the most out of participation, always wanting to expand their rights, while the noncitizen families were too timid to ask for more.[122] Arın sees this as related to the question of owning the city: "Whose is this city? At the time, the foreigners did not see Berlin as their own city."[123] Nonetheless, different participation models could have been developed, and more translations during the meetings could have been provided to find ways to hear more noncitizen voices for the urban renewal decisions about public areas.

One of the examples of this impenetrableness was exposed when the Berlin Islamic Federation's official request to IBA that a mosque be built near the Görlitzer train station was rejected.[124] Newspapers reported that members of the "Fatih-prayer space" who were squatting in a warehouse near the Görlitzer train station were to be evacuated after the decision was made to demolish the warehouse.[125] The Turkish architect Kemal Berker, who had an office in Berlin with Bernd Seidel, designed a project with a glazed dome and blue glass minaret, which was put "off the table" for planning and architectural reasons, according to Werner Orlowsky. The authorities found the idea of constructing a mosque over a "shopping mall" to be "comical," but the architect defended the project as a "bazaar" whose proximity to a mosque was quite consistent

Figure IV.30 Views of the Heile House in Block 76, renovated by IBA Altbau (team-architect: Heide Moldenhauer), photographed by Esra Akcan, Berlin, 2016.

with traditional architecture.[126] According to Wulf Eichstädt, members of the Social Democratic Party (SPD) were the biggest critics of the plan to build a mosque with usual symbolic elements, such as a dome and minaret.[127] Kleff remembers the controversy as chiefly about building a mosque with state-subsidized funds.[128] Such an argument in the name of secularism that state should not be involved in the building of any religious spaces disregards the fact that the same state had historically been central to the institutionalization of Christianity in this context. Arın recalls Orlowsky's hostility and Dieter Hoffmann Axthelm's argument that a mosque was unnecessary, as abandoned warehouses and factories already fulfilled the purpose. In Yalçın Çetin's memories, Orlowsky told them that supporting the building of a mosque did not make political sense for him. Given the noncitizen status of Turkish migrants, his electorate was composed exclusively of Christians.[129] Even though a small number of Turkish professionals working under IBA, including Arın and Çetin, raised their voices against this rejection, they soon had to drop the idea, since they prioritized their own commitment to secularism.[130] Thus, the one time when some Turkish residents tried to participate in IBA matters beyond those related to their own dwellings and officially requested to make themselves more visible in the city, IBA determined that those noncitizens could not speak. It is thus plausible to argue that IBA wanted noncitizens to participate only if their desires were commensurable with the organization's values.

IBA Altbau's success in empowering inhabitants vis-à-vis the state was partially dependent on the protesters who often filled the streets of Kreuzberg, in rallies initiated by German squatters. Nonetheless, the relationship between the squatters and immigrants calls for a closer look. Carla MacDougall has pointed out that members of the squatting movement in Kreuzberg during these years failed to recognize that most of them maintained the same racialized structure as the state that squatters rejected, which in her view "prevented radical left and progressive activists from maintaining a sustained critique of what it meant to be German. ... Literally occupying the same physical space in a neighborhood synonymous with public fears around immigration and heterogeneity, Kreuzberg's activists in the 1990s reproduced instead of challenged static images of migrants from Turkey, often drawing upon the same vocabulary and stereotypes used in mainstream public debate."[131] Despite the cases that suggest ad

TOP: Figure IV.31 View of a vegetable garden in a Hof in Block 76, renovated by IBA Altbau (team-architect: Heide Moldenhauer), photographed by Esra Akcan, Berlin, 2012. LEFT: Figure IV.32 View of Güler family's apartment in Block 76, renovated by IBA Altbau (team-architect: Heide Moldenhauer), photographed by Esra Akcan, Berlin, 2012.

Figure IV.33 Views of apartments in Block 76/78 and 81 renovated by IBA Altbau (team-architects: Heide Moldenhauer and Cihan Arın), photographed by Esra Akcan, Berlin, 2009–2016.

hoc or sustained solidarities between squatters and immigrants, MacDougall gives a detailed reading of the pamphlets and local newspapers generated by the squatters in which the "foreigners" were treated with "a wide array of emotions ranging from well-meaning paternalism to passive indifference to outright hostility."[132] Some publications mourn Kreuzberg's becoming "a Turkish ghetto rather than a West German district," others complain about the "flood of Turks" as one of the evils threatening the neighborhood, and most references to "we" as the agents of political struggle exclude immigrants.[133] Noncitizens from Turkey were usually reported to have a low participation rate in squatters' rallies, most likely due to their insecure legal status.[134]

The lack of noncitizen participation in matters relating to public areas, the mosque controversy, and the paradox of the political left in Germany failing to develop critical strategies against racism raise several questions about radical democracy and ethics of hospitality. The IBA Altbau team often used the term participatory architecture as a synonym of democracy. Taking the expression from Adolf Arndt's thesis of 1960, "democracy as architect/builder" (*Demokratie als Bauherr*) became a common motto. In a press conference introducing IBA-1984/97 on October 30, 1981, Senator Volker Hassemer asked: "How does one build his city? How does 'democracy as architect/builder' work?"[135] Orlowsky gave a conference speech on citizen participation and identified IBA as the democratization of city building.[136] IBA organized a conference in Martin Gropius Bau on November 21–24, 1984, titled "Democracy as Architect/Builder." Participants included Hämer, Lucius Burckhardt (Basel and Kassel), Hellmut Becker (Max-Planck Institute), Julius Posener (Akademie der Künste), Peter Hall (University of Reading), Nathan Glazer (Harvard University), Michael Lipsky (Massachusetts Institute of Technology), and Peter Grottian (Free University of Berlin).[137] In IBA's *Idee Prozeß Ergebnis* exhibition in 1984, the prominent Berlin historian Julius Posener defined urban renewal not only in terms of repairing the dwellings—or even the streets, squares, Kita, and schools—but also in terms of repairing the democratic behavior so that those who are affected by the renewal are also part of the democratic process, and so that active and mutual education can occur.[138]

However, it is hard to settle on the conclusion that participatory architecture is synonymous with conventional democracy. It is also hard to determine who the legitimate representatives of an urban renewal in a residential district are. Many members of the Neubau team criticized the insistence of the Altbau team on participation, viewing participation as a disabling of architectural expertise and a shortsighted view of future inhabitants. Many opponents of participatory architecture could speculate that the majority of the German population would not have voted for the unique apartment layouts that resulted from Kreuzberg's urban renewal—a criterion they would never uphold for wealthy clients' houses. Many architects who were committed to residents' participation became disillusioned with the process because of its opportunistic manipulation by the policy makers (this will be discussed in stop V). Many members of the Altbau team admit that several problems, especially those related to the limits of noncitizen participation, remained unresolved. Arın says: "We used the term 'democracy as architect/builder' at the time ... but it is more correct to define this term as a movement against the authoritarian urban renewal methods, rather than democracy itself [as a political system]. ... In the context of Germany in general, I think IBA-1984/87 was a chronological marker. There were attempts to include the foreign population in this initiative, with limited success."[139]

Nonetheless, the Altbau team made a step toward radical and plural democracy, however instinctively they might have done so and however unresolved it turned out to be. The conventional definition and boundaries of democracy were under scrutiny in European intellectual circles at the time. In an interview with Hämer for the newspaper TAZ, reporters asked how the democratic process was pursued at IBA, given the challenging number of groups in the "Kreuzberg mix"—including the "petit bourgeoisie, Turks, Alternatives, [and] Autonomous." The Altbau director responded by emphasizing Kreuzberg's tradition of "unprecedented tolerance, and the acceptance of the difference of the other. The urbanity of this borough relies precisely on the differences in its population and building types."[140] This conversation is indicative of the question over democracy in the context of irreducible plurality. Ernesto Laclau and Chantal Mouffe had presented their thesis on radical democracy, most notably in *Hegemony and Socialist Strategy* of 1985, as a response to the crisis of the Left on the one hand, and the positive proliferation of new movements, such as the new feminism, minority movements, and noninstitutionalized ecology movements on the other hand. For a new theorization of the Left as seeking a "free, democratic and egalitarian society," it was necessary to put a stop to the privileging of a certain class or group as the locus of revolutionary transformation, and to acknowledge that the defense of equality in an irreducibly plural world would involve formerly unimaginable struggles. According to Laclau and Mouffe, "The task of the Left therefore cannot be to renounce liberal-democratic ideology, but on the contrary, to deepen and expand it in the direction of a radical and plural democracy. ... It is not the abandonment of the democratic terrain but, on the contrary, the extension of the field of democratic struggles to the whole of civil society and the State."[141] Radical or plural democracy in a century of international immigration and diaspora has to be conceived of as a necessarily open and continuously expanding struggle carried on by and with previously unexpected subjects. In this theory, democratization is a perpetually open, never-ending process: "A project of radical and plural democracy recognizes the impossibility of the complete realization of democracy and the final achievement of the political community. Its aim is to use the symbolic resources of the liberal democratic tradition to struggle for the deepening of the democratic revolution, knowing that it is a never-ending process."[142]

This project of radical democracy must have also necessitated a new ethics of hospitality in contrast to the dominant, Kantian notion of hospitality, in which the foreigner or the noncitizen is seen as an other whom a citizen needs to tolerate out of a sense of duty, but not necessarily be truly hospitable to. In this limited hospitality, the authority and superiority of the host is perpetuated, and the guest (worker) is entitled to have only the requests that are commensurable with the views of the host. In drawing the boundaries beyond which the noncitizens could not speak, it would not be unfair to conclude that IBA Altbau still functioned within the frameworks of limited hospitality. The question then remains: What would another notion of hospitality be like, one that defines the open architecture to come?

1 Aras Ören, *Berlin Üçlemesi* (Istanbul: Remzi Kitabevi, 1980), 82–83 and 214 (translated by Esra Akcan). The Turkish is: Hangi adamlardı, bu biçim / Sokaklar yapmışlar? Bu evleri, / bu birbiri içinden çıkan duvarları, / birbiri üstüne devrik bu damları, / damların altında uykulu pencereleri / yol kenarlarındaki su tulumbalarına bakan? / Kimlerdi onlar, kazmalar küreklerle, / Cetvellerle, bütün bunları yapanlar? / Kendileri için olduğunu bilselerdi / mutlak başka yaparlardı: açınca pencereleri, / dolardı gökyüzü içeri şıngır mıngır. … / Naunyn Sokağına bakan evlerin / öncepheleri, kıçını sana çevirmiş, / sağır transport işçileri gibidir ki / taşıdıkları yükün pek ağırlığına aldırmayan. /…/ Sana neyi anımsatıyor başka / Sıvaları dökülmüş bu cepheler / sırıtan tuğlalar, bu yara izleri? / Kimler dersin, buralarda oturan? / Perişan balkonlarda böyle sardunyalar diken: / Romatizmalı ayaklarını sürüyerek / alışverişe çıkan şu ihtiyarlar mı? / Onlar değil mi haklar istemişlerdir / Devletin kendileri üstündeki / Haklarına karşı, bugünkü şu / Demokrasinin temeline can koyarak? /…/ Bu evlerde şimdi oturan sen değil misin? / Bu arka avlularda küf tutmuş, / Kavga günlerini üstlenen, sürdürecek olan. **2** Aras Ören, *Was will Niyazi in der Naunynstrasse*, trans. Achmed Schmiede and Johannes Schenk (Berlin: Rotbuch Verlag, 1973), and *Die Fremde ist auch ein Haus*, trans. Gisela Kraft (Berlin: Robbuch Verlag, 1980). **3** For a further literary analysis, see Leslie Adelson, *The Turkish Turn in Contemporary German Literature: Toward a New Critical Grammar of Migration* (New York: Palgrave Macmillan, 2005); Azade Seyhan, "From Istanbul to Berlin: Stations on the Road to a Transcultural / Translational Literature," *German Politics and Society* 23, no. 1 (2005): 152–60; Rita Chin, *The Guest Worker Question in Postwar Germany* (Cambridge: Cambridge University Press, 2007). **4** Adelson, *Turkish Turn*, 20; Chin, *The Guest Worker Question in Postwar Germany*, 84. **5** In addition to Hämer's articles and interviews in IBA publications, see Hardt-Waltherr Hämer, "The Center City as a Place to Live," *Urban Design International* 2, no. 6 (1981): 18–20; and "Rénovation urbaine: Pour des relations plus sensibles avec la ville," *Archithèse* 6 (1984): 45–46; "The Other Face of IBA: Careful Renewal in Kreuzberg," *Spazio e società* 8, nos. 31–32 (1985): 79–86; "Es gibt noch viel zu tun! Behutsame Stadterneuerung der IBA," *Deutsche Bauzeitung*, September 1988; Manfred Sack, ed., *Stadt im Kopf: Hardt-Waltherr Hämer* (Berlin: Jovis Verlag GmbH, 2002); "Hardt-Waltherr Hämer Interviewed by Lore Ditzen," *Architectural Review* 176 (September 1984): 28–32. **6** Hardt-Waltherr Hämer, interview by the author, March 24, 2012, Ahrenshoop, in German, 00:04:00–00:07:00. Both audio and video recordings of this interview are in the author's collection. **7** Hardt-Waltherr Hämer, "Stadterneuerung ohne Verdrängung—ein Versuch," *Arch Plus* 29, no. 1 (1976): 2–13; Hardt-Waltherr Hämer and Stefan Krätke, "Urban Renewal without Displacement: Assessing an Experiment in Charlottenburg: The Prelude to IBA's Activities in SO36," trans. Eileen Martin, *AD* 53, nos. 1–2 (1983): 27–30; Manfred Sack, "Der Mensch, der Architekt," in *Stadt im Kopf*, 19–131. **8** Hämer and Krätke, "Urban Renewal without Displacement." **9** Cihan Çelik, interview by the author, July 2, 2012, Berlin, 00:10:47. Both audio and video recordings of this interview are in the author's collection. **10** Ibid., 00:45:45.

11 Aras Ören, *Was will Niyazi in der Naunynstarsse* (Berlin: Rotbuch Verlag, 1973), 59. In German, the selected lines are: Was für ein Vorgang ist das, / daß wir einer auf des anderen Leiche steigen, / um zu bestehen? / Wer weiß, wieviel Leute das / gleiche wollen und doch, / ohne es zu merken, / gräbt einer das Grab des andern. **12** Çelik, interview by the author, 00:12:37. **13** Hämer, interview by the author, 00: 37: 39. **14** Gerald Blomeyer, "Berlin Builds: New Competition Procedure for Rehabilitation Areas"; Klaus Duntze, "Berlin SO36: Die 'Dritte Runde'. Neues von den Strategien für Kreuzberg," *Arch + 40–41* (November 1978): 2–13; Karin Stolley, "Urban Renewal," *Architects' Journal*, October 28, 1981, 867–70. **15** For pre-IBA participatory, self-help, and squatting activities in Kreuzberg, see Carla Elizabeth MacDougall, "Cold War Capital: Contested Urbanity in West Berlin, 1963–1989," PhD diss., Rutgers University, 2011. **16** Der Senator für Bau- und Wohnungswesen, "Berlin," Report. (no date, probably 1978), B 78/014, Landesarchiv. **17** IBA, *First Projects in Careful Urban Renewal*, brochure for *Berlin Building Weeks 1980*, 20, B 78/014, Landesarchiv. **18** "Hardt-Waltherr Hämer, interviewed by Lore Ditzen," 29. **19** The principles were published several times, and in slightly different long and short versions. I have reproduced here the version distributed in English, but I replaced "careful" with "gentle" before urban renewal. See IBA-Altbau, "Twelve Principles," in *International Building Exhibition Berlin 1987: Examples of a New Architecture*, ed. Heinrich Klotz and Josef Paul Kleihues (New York: Rizzoli, 1986), 242–43. **20** Wulf Eichstädt, "Die Grundsätze der behutsamen Stadterneuerung," in *Idee Prozeß Ergebnis: Die Reparatur und Rekonstruktion der Stadt* (Berlin: IBA, 1984), 111–13. For a condensed version of the Twelve Principles, see *Deutsche Bauzeitung* 122, no. 9 (September 1988): 15; Hardt-Waltherr Hämer, "Twelve Principles of Careful Urban Renewal," *Domus* 685 (July–August 1987): 70–71; Manfred Sack, ed., *Stadt im Kopf*, 195. **21** Hardt-Waltherr Hämer, "Die Kunst der Proportionen," in *Idee Prozeß Ergebnis*, 13–19. **22** IBA, *In der Luisenstadt, Studien zur Stadtgeschichte von Berlin-Kreuzberg* (Berlin: IBA, 1983); Dieter Hoffmann-Axthelm, *Baufluchten: Beiträge zur Rekonstruktion der Geschichte Berlin-Kreuzbergs* (Berlin: IBA, Transit Buchverlag, 1987). **23** Karl-Heinz Fiebig, Dieter Hoffmann-Axthelm, and E. Knödler-Bunte, eds., *Kreuzberger Mischung: Die innerstädtische Verflechtung von Architektur, Kultur und Gewerbe* (Berlin: IBA, Verlag Ästhetik und Kommunikation, 1984). **24** Olcay Başeğmez, "Interviews mit türkischen Gewerbetreibenden in Kreuzberg," in *Kreuzberger Mischung*, 186–89; Yalçın Çetin, "Ausländisches Gewerbe in Kreuzberg SO36," in ibid., 181–85. **25** For the squatting culture, see MacDougall, "Cold War Capital." For an explanation of the relationship between radical rock groups and squatting in Kreuzberg, see Timothy Brown, "Music as a Weapon? *Ton Steine Scherben* and the Politics of Rock in Cold War Berlin," *German Studies Review* 32, no. 1 (2009): 1–22. **26** Çelik, interview by the author, 00:25:54– 00:34:01. **27** Archiv IBA, Folder: Kreuzberg SO36. A3 SO/17, Sammlung Baukunst, Akademie der Künste (hereafter AdK); Hämer, "The Other Face of IBA." **28** Archiv IBA, AdK. **29** Paul F. Duwe and Karl Johaentges, "War die IBA iba-flüssig,"

Deutsche Bauzeitung 121, no. 4 (1987): 12–42. Quotation: 18. **30** Der Senator für Bau- und Wohnungswesen, "Berlin: IBA," report (no date, probably 1978), p. 48, B 78/014, Landesarchiv. **31** IBA, "Modernisierungsprozess in Kreuzberg SO36 (Strategiengebiet) 1978–1980. Ausstattungswünsche Mietzahlungsbereitschaft Modernisierungsbetroffenheit" Report. Berlin: IBA, December 1981, p.22, B 81/063, Landesarchiv. The report listed the problems: "This high concentration of foreign population could hardly be counteracted by the exclusionary measures taken up to now, e.g., restriction of migration. ... Essential problems are: (1) Lack of information among foreigners (2) Informational deficiency among Germans (and within the administration as well) about the housing needs and housing desires of the foreign population (3) Lack of dialogue (4) Severe limitations for foreigners in the decision-making process due to their political inequality (5) Extreme undersupply of social support systems (schools, day care centers) (6) The inadequacy of the traditional residential structure (kitchen, living room, small workers' apartments—the reality that part of the housing market is not accessible to foreigners) and the different socio-cultural and family size requirements of the foreign population mostly for larger apartments. Grievances." **32** "Projekte Luisenstadt SO36. September 1981. Arbeitsbericht," report, 1981, A81/061, Landesarchiv. **33** IBA, *First Projects in Careful Urban Renewal*, 28 and 30–31. **34** The archival documents pertaining to Block 81 can be found in Archiv IBA-Alt/Stern (1979–1990), A 57 SK/75–A 58 SK/80, AdK. Details in the oral histories with architects, residents, and tenant advisors that I conducted and are cited in this chapter have been checked against documents in these archives, my observations on site, and publications. **35** Cihan Arın, "Analyse der Wohnverhältnisse ausländischer Arbeiter in der Bundesrepublik Deutschland—mit einer Fallstudie über türkische Arbeiterhaushalte in Berlin-Kreuzberg," PhD diss., Berlin Technical University, 1979, and "Die nationale Identität ist für den Alltag ohne Gebrauchswert," *Frankfurter Rundschau*, September 24, 1983, No. 222, 14. **36** Cihan Arın, ed., *Ausländer im Wohnbereich* (Berlin: IBA, Express Edition, 1983); Cihan Arın, Sigmar Gude, and Hermann Wurtinger, "Verbesserung der Wohnungsversorgung kinderreicher ausländischer Familien," report by ARAS (Arbeitsgemeinschaft Ausländer im Stadtteil) commissioned by IBA. April 1984, A84/088, Landesarchiv. **37** Yabancıların Yabancılar Politikasına İlişkin Görüşleri/Stellungnahme der Ausländer zur Ausländerpolitik," (Berlin: IGI [Initiativkreis Gleichberechtigung Integration], May 1981). Prepared by Cihan Arın, Safter Çınar, Necati Gürbaca, Hakkı Keskin, M. Yaşar Öncü, and M. Niyazi Turgay. The item is in Cihan Arın's and the author's collections. **38** Ibid., 2. **39** Ibid., 24. **40** Kunstamt Kreuzberg, ed., *morgens Deutschland abends Türkei* (Berlin: Verlag Frölich und Kaufmann, 1981). **41** Cihan Arın, Regina Bittner, Onur Suzan Kömürcü, Stephan Lanz, and Erol Yıldız, "Migration und Stadt," in *Project Migration* (Cologne, Germany: DOMIT, 2005), 638–51. **42** Cihan Arın, interview by the author, July 4, 2012, Berlin, in Turkish, 00:00:00–00:05:12. Both audio and video recordings of this interview are in the author's collection. **43** Ibid., 00:23:50. **44** Ibid., 00:46:18.

45 "Bruchbude müßte nicht sein: IBA-Studie Wohnungsnot von Ausländern," *Die Tageszeitung*, November 19, 1985. See also Cihan Arın, "The Housing Market and the Housing Policies for the Migrant Labor Population in West Berlin," in *Urban Housing Segregation of Minorities in Western Europe and United the States*, ed. E. Huttman (Durham, NC: Duke University Press, 1991). **46** Arın 2012 interview by the author, 00:45:02. Arın also claims that the 10 percent quota, already a discriminatory regulation, was used even in more biased ways in the IBA Neubau segment, by paying special attention to placing foreign residents other than Turkish immigrants into the new buildings: "Given the international prestige of housing produced for the IBA Neubau, it was preferred to assign 'Western, civilized' residents to these units" (ibid., 00:56:10–00:56:45). **47** Berlin Senator for Building and Housing, *Berlin: Eine Stadt auf der Suche nach der Zukunft. A City in Search of Its Future* (Berlin: Berlin Press, May 1983), 42. **48** Grün-Alternative und Basisgruppen, *Immigranten-und Asylfragen*, brochure, Berlin, c. 1980. **49** Arın, 2012 interview by the author, 00:25:53–00:27:26. **50** Klaus Meyer-Rogge, "Das Bessere ist des Guten Feind—Bauen in bewohnten Häusern," in *Idee Prozeß Ergebnis: Die Reparatur und Rekonstruktion der Stadt*, 130–33. **51** Hans-Günter Kleff, *Vom Bauern zum Industriearbeiter: Zur kollektiven Lebensgeschichte der Arbeitsmigranten aus der Türkei* (Mainz, Germany: Verlag Manfred Werkmeister, Ingelheim: Manthano Verlag, 1984), 175. **52** Ibid., 181. **53** Hans-Günter Kleff, interview by the author, June 27, 2012, Berlin, in English and Turkish, 00:02:40. Both audio and video recordings of this interview are in the author's collection. **54** Ibid., 00:07:40, 00:22:40–00:25:43, 00:26:10–00:27:35. **55** Cihan Arın, "Analyse der Wohnverhältnisse ausländischer Arbeiter in der Bundesrepublik Deutschland," 224 and 244. **56** Archiv IBA-Alt/Stern (1979–1990). A 57 SK/75–A 58 SK/80, AdK. **57** Benita von Davier, interview by the author, August 2, 2012, Berlin, in German, 00:10:00. Both audio and video recordings of this interview are in the author's collection. **58** Ibid., 00:33:48, 00:21:59. **59** Ibid., 00:27:52. **60** Suzan Nişancı, interview by the author, July 6, 2012, Berlin, in Turkish, 00:13:54, 00:54:00. Both audio and video recordings of this interview are in the author's collection. **61** Ibid., 00:57:01. **62** Ibid., 00:31:18–00:35:36. **63** Ibid., 00:59:04. **64** Ibid., 00:12:12–00:13:54, 00:24:21–00:25:05, 00:29:11. **65** Çelik, interview by the author, 00:02:00–00:04:09. **66** Nişancı, interview by the author, 00:36:00–00:39:30. **67** Martin Domschat, interview by the author, August 6, 2012, Berlin, in German, 00:24:02–00:29:50. Both audio and video recordings of this interview are in the author's collection. **68** Ibid., 00:20:00. **69** Ibid., 00:50:00. **70** Ms. Demir, interview by the author, July 2009, Berlin, in Turkish. An audio recording of this interview is in the author's collection. **71** N.K., conversation with the author, July 2009, Berlin, in Turkish. **72** Arın, 2012 interview by the author, 01:08:00. **73** Çelik, interview by the author, 00:07:00. **74** Kleff, interview by the author, 00:05:30–00:06:21. **75** Arın, 2012 interview by the author, 01:03:00–01:04:00. **76** Tenant (name not disclosed at the tenant's request), conversation with the author, July 2009, Berlin, in Turkish. **77** Nişancı, interview by the author. **78** Ibid,

01:00:00–01:05:54. **79** Cihan Arın, interview by the author, July 2009, Berlin, in Turkish. See also Arın, 2012 interview by the author, 01:05:14. **80** Ipek family, interview by the author, summer 2012, Berlin, in Turkish. An audio recording of this interview is in the author's collection. **81** Kleff, interview by the author, 00:21:00–00:22:00. **82** Arın, 2012 interview by the author, 01:05:30. **83** Hildebrand Machleidt, interview by the author, July 12, 2012, Berlin, in German, 00:31:00–00:34:10. Both audio and video recordings of this interview are in the author's collection. **84** Tuğrul family, interview by the author, May 27, 2012, Berlin, in Turkish, 00:28:36. An audio recording of this interview is in the author's collection. **85** Ibid., 00:27:12. **86** Ibid., 00:33:31. **87** Ibid., 00:07:00–00:10:00. See also Safter Çınar and Leyla Kubat, "Bildung oder Aufbewahrung? Zum Schul- und Ausbildungsschicksal ausländischer Kinder und Jugendlicher," in *Ausländer im Wohnbereich*, 167–82. **88** Tuğrul family, interview by the author, 01:07:12–01:07:58. **89** Heide Moldenhauer, interview by the author, May 28, 2012, Berlin, in English, 02:43:30. Both audio and video recordings of this interview are in the author's collection. **90** Ibid., 00:07:03, 02:25:15. **91** I worked on this collection when it was still in Moldenhauer's personal archive. Since then it has been acquired by Landesarchiv in Berlin. **92** Amy A. Da Ponte, "Candida Höfer's Türken in Deutschland as 'Counterpublicity,'" *Art Journal* 75, no. 4 (2016):16–39. **93** Heide Moldenhauer, "Planungsalltag am Kottbusser Tor," in *Idee Prozeß Ergebnis: Die Reparatur und Rekonstruktion der Stadt* (Berlin: IBA 1984): 134–37. **94** Moldenhauer, May interview by the author, 00:22:13. **95** Moldenhauer, "Planungsalltag am Kottbusser Tor," 134–37. **96** Benita von Davier, interview by the author, August 2, 2102, Berlin, in German. **97** "Frauenprojekte," Archiv IBA. A34 SO/118, AdK. **98** Otur ve Yaşa Report to IBA, 13.4. 1981. Archiv IBA, AdK. "Frauenprojekte," A34 SO/118, AdK. **99** "Elisi Evi. Türkischer Frauen- und Mädchen-Laden, e.V.," IBA Brochure, B92/091, Landesarchiv. **100** Ibid., 1. **101** Moldenhauer, May interview by the author, 02:00:00–02:03:09. **102** Arın, 2012 interview by the author, 01:22:00. **103** Moldenhauer, May interview by the author, 02:40:00. **104** Ibid., 01:06:00–01:15:01. **105** Ibid., 00:32:00. **106** Ibid., 00:40:06–00:42:40. **107** Ibid., 00:43:41. **108** Ibid. and Heide Moldenhauer, interview by the author, May and June, Berlin, 2012, in English (both audio and video recordings of this interview are in the collection of the author). **109** Akbar Behkalam to Hardt-Waltherr Hämer, Letters of 30.3.85, and 2.4.85, Archiv IBA, Block 81, Folder A58, SK/80, AdK. **110** *Mehmet Berlin'de / Mehmet aus Anatolien*, Exhibition September 6–November 9, 1975, Kunstamt Kreuzberg and Berliner Festspiele GmbH (Berlin: Dieter Ruckhaberle, 1975). **111** Çelik, interview by the author, 00:15:00. **112** Moldenhauer, May interview by the author, 02:22:20; Hämer, interview by the author; Kleff, interview by the author, 00:10:24. In Kleff's view, unlike the members of the original squatting movement, the squatters in

the late 1980s approached Berlin opportunistically and turned the movement into a sort of revolutionary tourism (01:14:47). For self-help projects, see Gerald Blomeyer and Barbara Tietze, *Die Andere Bauarbeit* (Stuttgart, Germany: Deutsche Verlags-Anstalt, 1987), 142–55; Uli Hellweg, "Zwischen Ausweg und Irrweg: Selbsthilfe," in *Idee Prozeß Ergebnis*, 178–83. **113** Moldenhauer, May interview by the author, 00:50:00. **114** Güler family, interview by the author, July 2012, Berlin, in Turkish, 00:20:48. Audio recording of this interview is in the author's collection. **115** Ibid., 00:00:00–00:05:40. **116** Ibid., 00:43:51. **117** Ibid., 01:00:46. **118** Ibid. **119** Hämer, interview with the author. **120** This was confirmed during all my interviews with the architects, tenants, and tenant advisors cited above. Also see Wulf Eichstädt and Deniz Göktürk, "All Quiet on the Kreuzberg Front," trans. Tes Howell, in *Germany in Transit: Nation and Migration*, ed. Deniz Göktürk, David Gramling, and Anton Kaes (Berkeley: University of California Press, 2007), 354–56. Original interview with Wulf Eichstädt published in *Die Tageszeitung*, 1 Nov. 1994. **121** Arın, Bittner, Kömürcü, Lanz, and Yıldız, "Migration und Stadt," 641. **122** Arın, 2012 interview by the author, 00:52:41. **123** Ibid., 01:38:14. **124** Archiv IBA, Folder A3 SO/15, AdK. **125** "Fatih-Moschee soll im Juni geräumt werden," *Der Tagesspiegel*, May 9, 1987; "Fatih-Gebetshaus geräumt," *Die Tageszeitung*, November 24, 1987. **126** "Bolle: Pläne für Moschee über neuer Finale sind 'vom Tisch,'" *Der Tagesspiegel*,, August 2, 1987. **127** Wulf Eichstädt, interview by the author, July 5, 2012, Berlin, in German, 01:02:56–01:07:13. An audio recording of this interview is in the author's collection. **128** Kleff, interview by the author, 00:59:21–01:01:12. **129** Yalçın Çetin, interview by the author, September 8, 2012, Berlin, in Turkish, 01:27:53. Both audio and video recordings of this interview are in the author's collection. **130** Arın, 2012 interview by the author 01:33:45–01:37:08; Eichstädt and Göktürk, "All Quiet on the Kreuzberg Front." **131** MacDougall, "Cold War Capital," 170. **132** Ibid., 209. **133** Ibid., 210, 222, and 223. **134** Eichstädt and Göktürk, "All Quiet on the Kreuzberg Front." **135** "Senator Dr. Hassemer zur IBA," *Deutsches Architektenblatt* 12, no. 13, December 1, 1981, 275–76. **136** Werner Orlowsky, "Bürgerbeteiligung," Conference speech, 31.7.1983, B 91/143, Landesarchiv. **137** IBA, "Demokratie als Bauherr," Conference Program. B 84/098, Landesarchiv. **138** Julius Posener, "Stadtreparatur–Weltreparatur," in *Idee Prozeß Ergebnis*, 48–53. **139** Arın, 2012 interview by the author, 00:37:39, 01:45:00–01:45:38. **140** Klaus Hartung and Benedict Mülder, "Da kannst du lange buttern—Es bleibt doch Buttermilch," *Taz*, May 16, 1987. **141** Ernesto Laclau and Chantal Mouffe, *Hegemony and Socialist Strategy: Towards a Radical Democratic Politics* (London: Verso, 1985), 160. **142** Chantal Mouffe, "Democratic Citizenship and the Political Community," in *Dimensions of Radical Democracy: Pluralism, Citizenship, Community*, ed. Chantal Mouffe (London: Verso, 1992): 225–39. Quotation: 238.

STROLL 4

From Kottbusser Tor to Schlesisches Tor

After stopping at Blocks 76 and 78 and Block 81—bordered by Dresdener, Oranien-, Adalbert-, Naunyn-, and Waldemarstrasse—let's continue our stroll in East Kreuzberg, from Luisenstadt to SO36 in IBA's nomenclature. If one took a turn onto Dresdener Strasse after leaving the Kottbusser Tor train station (Figure 4.1), one would immediately notice the big orange Kita building with a wide ramp leading inside from the street (Figure 4.2). This is the former garage in the triangular Block 80 that was turned into a child-care center as part of IBA Altbau. A large percentage of the children in Kreuzberg belonged to immigrant families, and the number of kindergartens there was far below the level specified by German regulations during the 1980s. For this reason, IBA channeled a large portion of its resources for infrastructure buildings to nurseries and primary schools. Of the twenty-four child-care centers (14 nurseries, 10 schools) built in IBA Altbau areas, the center on Dresdener Strasse was probably one of the most noticeable, as it transformed the exposed reinforced concrete exterior of the garage building into a façade with a metal latticework thinly veiling the new brick surface and created a continuous roofscape with the surrounding buildings.[1]

If one continued on Dresdener Strasse to Oranienplatz, stood in the center of the square, and looked left and right, one would recognize the importance of the green belt running north-south all the way to the river at the one end, and the former Berlin Wall at the other, which is filled with sculptures, promenades, and playgrounds (Figure 4.3). This was one of the largest landscaping initiatives undertaken as part of IBA Altbau, in addition to the 320 inner courtyards that were renewed with greenery, pavement, playgrounds, and sports areas. IBA Altbau provided 740 playgrounds in East Kreuzberg, including the many located in this public park.[2] The paved central square of this park is filled with orderly trees and benches along the edges that provide places to rest or wait for one of the many buses whose routes pass this point (Figure 4.4). If one walked east from the square along Oranienstrasse and looked left and right to shops, restaurants, bars, cafes, and outdoor seating areas (Figure 4.5), and looked up to the well-painted façades and renovated window frames decorated with lattice curtains and satellite dishes (Figure 4.6), and if one proceeded to the Adalbertstrasse, the site of the long-standing Hasır restaurant and made a 360-degree turn, scanning both streets from this corner, one would realize what an enormous and socially significant venture IBA Altbau had successfully completed (Figure 4.7). Despite the possibility of walking around its sites, IBA Altbau was a building exhibition that was only partially meant to be seen. Most of the work of participatory architecture and urban renewal with those affected was about the process, which was not necessarily meant to be put on display during IBA's launches in 1984 and 1987. Thus, IBA Altbau was a building exhibition that challenged the hegemony of vision in the culture of architectural exhibitions.

When I reach Block 79 at this corner, I am invited to Yıldırım's apartment, whose entrance is on Naunynstrasse, at the northern side of the block (Figures 4.8 and 4.9). She had come to Germany in 1971 from Bayburt, Turkey, after marrying her husband who had immigrated in 1968. She gave birth to her four children in Germany. The state of the Kreuzberg apartments before the urban renewal had made quite a mark on her memory. "Of course I remember my old apartment," she says. It leaked so much that it was as if "water was pouring off the walls and off the window frames. Our toilet was outside, the apartment was one room and a kitchen. You used to enter the room from the kitchen. There were coal stoves, the windows were broken, it was cold. ... I feel like I'm having a heart attack when I remember it now."[3] Trying to fix the leaks on her own, she went to the Housing Office and turned on the tap to run water to explain her problem, as she spoke no German. The Housing Office gave her insulation material that she applied to the walls herself, but the structural damage must have been too severe to fix with such temporary measures.[4] She therefore appreciates the professional renovation of her apartment done in the 1980s during the urban renewal. Despite the option of moving into a temporary apartment on Oranienstrasse, she chose to stay put during the construction between 1980 and 1984, and she even gave birth to her youngest daughter in the midst of all the repair work being carried on around her. As a parent who did not work outside the home, she used to offer tea to the construction workers. Her son, who overhears and joins our conversation, also remembers the construction process as a child. He says that the worker who renovated the windows spoke Turkish and that as a childish game, he and his brother used to break at night what the workers had constructed during the day—an activity to which the workers responded with maturity.[5] After Yıldırım gave birth to her youngest daughter, she asked to move to a bigger apartment that faced the front, which was fortunately granted, even though she had to complete some significant parts of the renovation herself. She vividly remembers the architect at the time, who did not speak Turkish but could explain the changes in the building somehow using signs and drawings. "He was very engaged with us, he was explaining, trying really hard," Yıldırım says.[6] "I am happy now, thank God. For someone who spends all her time at home, the apartment must be good. In that way, she will be happier," she concludes.[7]

This architect must have been Uwe Böhm from the IBA Altbau team, who was responsible for Block 79. Now a photographer, he began to question the role of the architect as a student at the Technical University of Berlin and while taking part in a citizens' initiative in Klausenerplatz, he tells me during our interview in 2012, in his home office. He lives in one of the apartments that he renovated in Block 79 and to which he moved during IBA (Figure 4.10). He realized the importance of participatory urban renewal back then in a devastated city where "the integration of foreigners had not taken place," and he was therefore happy to work with Hardt-Waltherr Hämer in IBA Altbau.[8] The official numbers indicate that 703 out of 1,287 residents and 313 out of 363 children in Block 79 were noncitizens in 1980.[9] They were tenants with reasonable desires who wanted to live in renovated apartments, he recalls, although he also mentions some differences among the residents: the intellectuals and students wanted loft spaces, a relatively new residential type in Berlin, which meant pulling down many walls in apartments or creating galleries in attics; many people preferred French windows to

Figure 4.5 Shop windows on Oranienstrasse between Oranienplatz and Heinrichplatz and around the Kottbusser Tor area, photographed by Esra Akcan, 2009–2016.

expensive balconies, which is why a passerby would notice an unusual number of French windows in Block 79 (Figure 4.11 a–b); and the Kurdish families usually had modern, while the Turkish families had more conservative tastes, he says.[10] He confirms that few of the noncitizens participated in any of the meetings about the renewal except those that concerned their own apartments, because their anxieties about their jobs and apartments were enough for them to deal with during those difficult times for immigrants.

Leaving Block 79, if one continued on Oranienstrasse, one would reach Heinrichplatz (Figure 4.12), come across Ayşe Erkmen's mural on the walls of a corner building at Heinrichplatz, composed of scripts conjugating the untranslatable Turkish tense with the "miş" suffix (Figure 4.13 a–b). One would also notice the SO36 near Heinrichplatz, a former famous scene for punks that had been closed until 1984 and then was the site of the IBA Altbau exhibit *IBA vor Ort*, where Heide Moldenhauer had her display on women and architecture (see Figure IV.26). With the contribution of Theo Winters from STERN (*Gesellschaft der behutsamen Stadterneuerung mbH*, Society of Gentle Urban Renewal), the successor to IBA Altbau, the art and music space was further renovated and reopened in 1987.[11] If one then walked to Görlitzer Bahnhof at the junction of Oranien-, Manteuffel-, and Skalitzer Strasse, one would continue seeing the IBA renovated Altbau buildings, now home to dense urban life in Berlin (Figure 4.14). If one looked above the elevated railways at the Görlitzer Bahnhof, one would see the dome and four minaret-like towers on the roof of a five-story building in a typical Berlin block—the pop-up mosque whose construction was negotiated after the original request for a mosque was rejected (stop IV) (Figure 4.15). Next, one would reach the Lausitzer Platz on which the brick Emmauskirche (an evangelical church) stands, and whose landscaping was undertaken by IBA Altbau (Figure 4.16). Looking across, one could immediately see the Elişi Evi (house of crafts) on Skalitzer Strasse 50, the intercultural consulting and education association for women and girls that was founded with IBA Altbau's support and that is still in operation (stop IV, Figure 4.17). Continuing along the wall of the Görlitzer Park, one would notice the narrow blocks on the left, composed of many buildings renovated by IBA Altbau (Figure 4.18). If one turned and strolled between these blocks, one would walk along tree-lined cobblestone streets enclosed by stone buildings that have satellite dishes (Figure 4.19). A group that named itself Arbeitsgruppe 58, for instance, prepared a handout on August 7, 1980, for one of these blocks with which they called all the residents to their participatory meeting where they would explain the urban renewal process. They listed questions that residents might want to ask, to make sure that the urban renewal would be to their benefit:

> Must I move out? No!
> Must I buy my apartment? No!
> May I get new neighbors? Yes [there will be empty apartments in the building]!
> May I buy my own business? Yes!
> Will I get help with my financial difficulties? Yes!
> Can I afford this? How much will it cost me? 4.80 DM/qm [4.80 Deutsche marks per square meter].
> What must I pay [initially]? Nothing!

Will I save through [using] self-help? Yes!

Can I control my savings? Yes!

Can you explain with an example? Yes!

Cannot one begin the repair immediately? Yes!

Can a bath and heating be installed? Yes!

Will the back buildings be destroyed? No!

Who will have a say in the modernization? You!

Will I stay in my apartment? Yes![12]

Continuing to the Schlesisches Tor train station, let's stop at Block 121, whose urban design and three buildings were undertaken by Álvaro Siza.

1 *Internationale Bauausstellung Berlin 1987: Projekt-übersicht* (Berlin: IBA, 1987), 254–55; Gernot and Johanne Nalbach, *Berlin Modern Architecture Exhibition Catalogue* (Berlin: STERN, 1989), 150. **2** Hardt-Waltherr Hämer, "Es gibt noch viel zu tun! Behutsame Stadterneuerung der IBA," *Deutsche Bauzeitung* 122, no. 9 (1988): 8–15. **3** Yıldırım, interview by the author, May 27, 2012, Berlin, in Turkish. 01:15:50, 01:23:30. An audio recording of this interview is in the author's collection. **4** Ibid., 01:23:30–01:24:17. **5** Ibid., 01:34:31. **6** Ibid., 01:26:00, 01:36:00. **7** Ibid., 01:39:05. **8** Uwe Böhm, interview by the author, August 3, 2012, Berlin, in German. Both audio and video recordings of this interview are in the author's collection. **9** *Internationale Bauausstellung Berlin 1987*, 230. **10** Böhm interview by the author., 00:29:04. **11** Franz-Michael Rohm, "SO36 vom Aus bedroht," *Volksblatt Berlin*, October 11, 1987. **12** Archiv IBA-Alt/STERN (1979–1990). Kreuzberg 20 36 (Strategien für Kreuzberg)–A3 SO/17, Sammlung Baukunst, Akademie der Künste.

STOP V

A Building with Many Speakers:
Open Architecture as Critical Participation[1]

Autonomy versus Participation?

In the German newspaper *Mittelhessische Anzeigenzeitung*, an anonymous Hüseyin A. listed the following advertisement:

> Apartment wanted: Young Turkish family with four-year-old daughter seeks a three- or four-room apartment. ... Warning: ... We have just one daughter now, but soon we will multiply like locusts. In a few years, we will have several loud, dirty children with bad manners who will raise hell in the building. These little urchins will run around screaming all day, and you won't understand a word they are saying. ... The only time the laundry will not be there [in the Hof] is when we invite our countless relatives and acquaintances to grill [food] with us. By the way, we slaughter our lambs in the bathtub on principle. If we move in, the entryway will smell like garlic and exotic spices. Deafening Turkish Jada music will waft from our open windows all day. At least once a week, the woman of the house will be beaten to the point [where] she needs hospitalization. For this reason, we will be a well-known address for the local police. ... Knifings are normal to us.[2]

This apartment seeker's ironic words are not dissimilar to the spirit of German hip-hop in the late 1990s[3] or of the Kanak Attak immigrant movement, whose members included the prize-winning writer Feridun Zaimoğlu. Embracing the common pejorative attribute *kanak* for Turkish immigrants and turning it into an empowering symbol, Kanak Attak's members expressed cynicism about the "dialogue culture" that had become an overused trope of multiculturalism, and they criticized this supposed conversation for its expectation that Turkish immigrants would simply assimilate into German culture without also expecting Germans to question their "own complicity to subordination."[4] As unidentifiable as he or she might seem, the writer of the advertisement was responding in a similar way to the official and cultural housing discrimination in Germany. Even though this chapter records events and projects that took place before the advertisement was published, the words of "Hüseyin A." provide some context to the Kreuzberg that would soon become home to a culture that had similarities with Kanak Attak.

The building complex analyzed in this stop is also representative in the way it responded to a major divide between IBA Neubau and Altbau that materialized as the polarity between autonomous and participatory architecture. While the IBA Altbau team saw user participation as a synonym of democracy in architecture, the Neubau team diagnosed it as a disabling of architectural expertise and an invitation to mediocrity.

Nonetheless, IBA Neubau had some participatory meetings with citizens under Katerina George's and Günter Schlusche's responsibility. Hille Machleidt, a coordinator of IBA Neubau, complains about the perception of his team as the "bad guys" in the German media (as opposed to their enthusiastic reception in the international press), because of the assumption that they were not democratically oriented or because Josef Paul Kleihues, director of Neubau, was politically on the right.[5] Schlusche remarks that Kleihues had to be much more open to participation after the 1981 crisis (stop I), even though he "instrumentalized participation to gain public support, because he was not really interested in participation actually."[6] Nonetheless, the strong voices in the Neubau team openly disparaged participation at many instances: for example, Kleihues explained his position as a fight against "the denial of artistic needs and the rejection of artistic dimension by pointing to urgent social problems."[7] And in introducing IBA in one of its earliest exhibition catalogs, he said: "Rejecting this claim [of "aesthetic rationality and artistic innovative impulse"] by arguing that the relief of urgent social need is more important is an error of political judgment, although it is admittedly an effective means of political defamation."[8] These comments make it clear that Kleihues did not believe users could make any meaningful contribution to the design process. A cynicism about participation is also apparent in IBA's consultant Vittorio Magnago Lampugnani's statements: "To democratize the process of decision making does not mean that decision making should be transferred to the lowest level. ... The present advocates of participation fear and challenge the division of competences within society, and exhaust themselves in mainly sentimental and useless general pleadings for more democracy, rather than rationally examine the points which the public must share and the points which they must delegate to experts and artists. ... Artistic and intellectual commitments must continue to fight against mediocrity."[9] Douglas Clelland introduced IBA's embrace of the democratic process as fellows: "But in so doing it has had to cope with the mediocrity which seems to be an inevitable concomitant of democratic control. ... For all the mediocrity and compromise, IBA has attempted to discover forms which enhance the status of individual life, ones which foster non-oppressive social cohesion."[10] In another article, he identified the contrast between IBA Neubau and Altbau as the one between a well-composed ballet and mere noise:

> Kleihues wished to stress the role of the artistic dimension in architecture and invited those architects whom he considered to be capable of so performing. The work, embodied in the countless competitions, can be considered a dance—a celebration of movement and space—a type akin to ballet. The artists are dancers at the front of the stage, the lights focused upon their dexterity, the audience and corps enthralled participants. ... In the Altbau department of IBA on the other hand, Hardt-Waltherr Hämer wished to stress the social dimension of architecture. Placing great accent on the participation of the population in his less war-damaged, yet multiply deprived areas to the east of the city, Hämer decided to spread the available funds as widely as possible to rehabilitate the housing stock while building social infrastructure. His chosen architects are unlike those of Kleihues—either survivors of the 1968 generation or architects renowned for their social consciences. The dance there has been more like a post-war mass quick-step or even a discotheque. There are no prima ballerinas, no artists, just noise and enjoyable bustle.[11]

As a result of this reaction against the democratization of architecture, usually with derogatory words, the Neubau team must have invited architects who advocated the autonomy of architecture, even if the implications of this phrase varied for different architects. In addition to Oswald Mathias Ungers (stop III), Kleihues openly said: "We must make the effort to fight for an independent architecture, an autonomy of architecture not against but for people."[12] Kleihues defended IBA Neubau's position as an advocacy for the autonomy of architecture, which he believed was a higher mode of engaging with humanity, but which would involve perpetuating an architectural language that would be accessible only to the insiders: "This is both an indication and an explanation of the greater need felt by architects today to find their way back to a language which can generally be understood. Ultimately—we must be clear about this—this means a convention. A convention which recalls things from far away, goes back to primary ideas, and so also touches on the question of autonomy of architecture (architecture as art)."[13] In his premise that architecture already had a convention and resembled a text in a language that could be read by those who are erudite in that convention, Kleihues was drawing the border between those who would be included and those who would be excluded from "reading" architecture. A theory that started with the assumption that members of a society have a common architectural language and thus the discipline of architecture could be autonomous and still serve the society at large could hardly envision a space for the immigrant, the newcomer, of a future society whose members would not necessarily be similar to those of the present society. Thus, the autonomous architecture that Kleihues defended was a reflection of the ideology that denied the possibility of Germany becoming a country of immigrants. Defending autonomy against participation in this context implied, consciously or not, a nationalist revival that perceived Germany as a land of Germans.

Lampugnani also theorized on architectural autonomy as one of the two main "thought-models" of architecture.[14] In one of his comprehensive articles on a survey of modern architecture, mostly in Europe, he identified typology and functionalism as the two discourses to which all architectural movements of the past three hundred years could be traced. By the typological thought-model, Lampugnani meant the idea of architecture as a "scientific" discipline, responding to the "internal" concerns of the profession with invariable principles. By the functionalist thought-model, he meant the conceptualization of architecture as a practice responding to specific contingent conditions and "external" requirements.[15] While Marc-Antoine Laugier, Jean-Nicolas-Louis Durand, Aldo Rossi, and Carlo Aymonino were the architects of the typological school, according to Lampugnani, Carlo Lodoli, Le Corbusier (in some cases), Louis Sullivan, Frank Lloyd Wright, and Hans Scharoun were the protagonists of the functionalist thought-model. Lampugnani argued that these categories should be porous, stating that the city of the 1980s would neither be typological nor functionalist, but one that would integrate continuity and change simultaneously.[16] Nonetheless, the initial conceptualization of the "internal" and "external" concerns of architecture was premised on some unjustified borders that defined what architecture was and was not. This distinction usually appealed to those who defended the autonomy of architecture and considered attention to form as the only indispensable concern—with other matters seen as temporary and replaceable occupations that might or might not guide design.

Figure V.1 View of Álvaro Siza's building Bonjour Tristesse in Block 121 for IBA-1984/87, photographed by Esra Akcan, Berlin, 2009.

In his publications throughout IBA, Lampugnani continued to contrast the care for social problems and the idealism of architecture: "A pragmatism bowing to the real or—for the most part imagined—'dictates of the present life' would be an irresponsible way to approach the problem, only an attitude of bold idealism is capable of pointing to solutions which represent a constructive reply to the contradictions which are inherent in reality in time and space, and which will thus retain their validity."[17]

In this perceived opposition between autonomy and participation, Álvaro Siza's design for Block 121, which was a new building but employed by the IBA Altbau for its own areas, stands as a good example of a third option.

Álvaro Siza and the Permeable Block

Álvaro Siza's building, commonly known as Bonjour Tristesse, and Block 121, where it is situated, have a peculiar place in the division in IBA (Figure V.1). This was a new building, like those Kleihues was in charge of, but it was constructed in the far corner of East Kreuzberg, next to the Schlesisches Tor train station, and thus was under Hämer's directorship. It was Siza's first built structure outside his native Portugal. Soon after its construction, he would be acknowledged as an accomplished international architect, and win the Pritzker Prize in 1992.[18] Yet during IBA, Siza's foreignness—in particular, his identity as Portuguese—presented a problem for the conservative German media. For example, an article appeared in *Berliner Stimme* supporting the reduction of funding for IBA and criticizing Siza's selection for his alleged inability to understand West Berlin.[19] IBA Altbau opened an invited international architectural competition for Block 121 in 1980 among the offices of Uli Böhme (Berlin), Planungsgruppe Stadtbereich (Aachen), Álvaro Siza (Porto, Portugal), and Volker Theissen (Berlin).[20] After winning this com-

Figure V.2 Views of the interior halls in Álvaro Siza's building Bonjour Tristesse in Block 121 for IBA-1984/87, photographed by Esra Akcan, Berlin, 2009.

petition, Siza designed not only the corner apartment building (Bonjour Tristesse) but also the overall concept of Block 121 and two other buildings in it (a kindergarten and a senior citizens' club). Bonjour Tristesse (1980–84) includes forty-six apartments (seven different types of one- or two-bedroom apartments ranging from sixty-four to eighty-five square meters), ten apartments for the elderly, five shops, and three shops with housing attached (Figure V.2). Peter Brinkert worked with Siza as the contact architect.[21]

Siza had already been invited to Berlin by the International Design Center to brainstorm about a design for a site in South Tiergarten in 1976, and he had previously participated in two other competitions in the East Kreuzberg area. His project for the Görlitzer swimming pool (1979) with a large dome of forty meters in diameter was rejected because the jury found its resemblance to a mosque inappropriate (Figure V.3).[22] Tellingly, Turkish residents' later request to build a mosque near the Görlitzer train station was also rejected, signaling the limits of participation for IBA Altbau—although in general there was enthusiastic advocacy of participation (see stop IV).

Siza's other competition project—at Fraenkelufer (1979), where Inken and Hinrich Baller's building stands today (stroll 5)—was the precursor of his ideas for Block 121 at Schlesisches Tor (Figure V.4). Adding six distinct buildings in the empty spots of the blocks along the canal, without touching the existing structures, Siza suggested an urban renewal strategy that was different from Kleihues's idea of a perimeter block, and one that came out of his own peculiar interpretation of the Berlin block. Noting that Berlin had not been "systematically reconstructed" after the war, unlike many

Figure V.3 Álvaro Siza, Competition project for Görlitzer swimming pool, Berlin, 1979. Model.

other European cities, Siza observed: "Thus the old city–new city duality does not exist in Berlin. We are obliged to slip our projects in between the old and new fragments which never complement each other, which never lend themselves to be reduced into a unity, but which exist as parallel realities."[23] Siza explained that he was very interested in the permeability of the Berlin box (the block), which allowed the public to use the courtyard at least during the day and enabled surprising experiences through the encounters with a church, a school, or a nice garden inside.[24] "When we are on the street, we approach a portal and we find ourselves in an interior court, and then another portal, and we penetrate into another court. In this court, there is a public layout, and if we open another gate, we might find ourselves in a quiet private garden,"[25] Siza observed. In the Fraenkelufer project, the rectangular, triangular, or L-shaped forms of Siza's additions were dictated by their locations, but the additions were always detached and set back from the street, and they often created surprises in the courtyards behind (Figure V.5). Rather than focusing only on the front, Siza proposed to enliven the semipublic life of the back, thus making the Berlin block more permeable. According to Peter Testa, the ideological implications of this operation were quite substantial, given that the courtyards were traditionally associated with servants' quarters, tenements, and small workshops.[26]

Siza followed this urban renewal strategy in Block 121 at Schlesisches Tor, even though this site, having already been heavily built, was not as convenient as many others would have been to express fully the idea of a permeable block (Figure V.6). Bonjour Tristesse and the kindergarten are detached from the adjacent structures on one

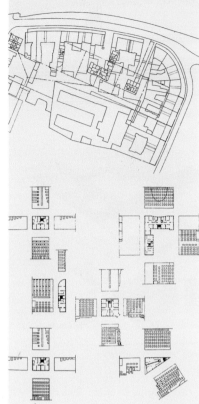

LEFT: Figure V.4 Álvaro Siza, Competition project for Fraenkelufer, Berlin, 1979. Sketch. RIGHT: Figure V.5 Álvaro Siza, Competition project for Fraenkelufer, Berlin, 1979. Site plan and individual buildings.

end—a decision that was highly criticized in the German media as a decadent slit that defied German planning norms.[27] The seniors' club is freestanding and set back, creating a small but lively urban plaza in the front and allowing access to the irregular green space, playgrounds, and sports fields at the back (Figure V.7). (In the competition, the building was slightly tilted, detached, and raised.) The inner Hof of Block 121 is publicly accessible and accommodates multiple connected but independent activities, bringing together neighbors spending time in the smaller niches of gardens, children playing in their kindergarten's garden, teenagers and young adults playing on the basketball court, and seniors meeting in their club (Figure V.8). Following IBA Altbau's principles, none of the existing buildings was demolished, not even the ad hoc line of single-story food vendors at the southeast corner of the block, or the tall U-shaped building with an unbelievably narrow passageway between its wings that is next to Bonjour Tristesse. Interpreting the Berlin block in Kreuzberg, Siza had also noticed the monotonous height of the buildings until there is a sudden disruption by an "explosion of imagination," a "fantastic tension" in the treatment of the corner.[28] Bonjour Tristesse recreates this experience with its round and high corner façade (Figure V.9).

While Kleihues and other architectural theorists behind IBA Neubau subordinated the new buildings to the "gene" of the city (stop I)—namely, the nineteenth-century ground plan with perimeter blocks—Siza's suggestions called for more tension, more

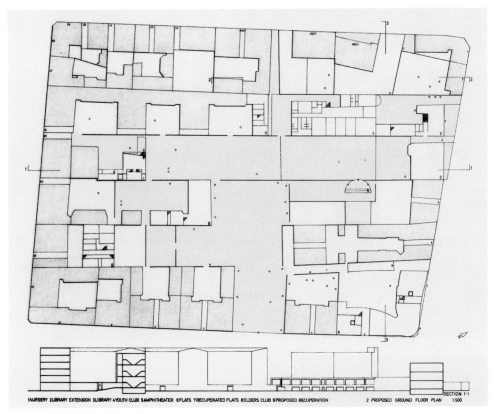

INURSERY 2LIBRARY EXTENSION 3LIBRARY 4YOUTH CLUB 5AMPHITHEATER 6FLATS 7RECUPERATED FLATS 8ELDERS CLUB 9PROPOSED RECUPERATION   2 PROPOSED GROUND FLOOR PLAN   1:500

Figure V.6 Álvaro Siza, Competition Project for Block 121, IBA-1984/87, Berlin, 1980. Site plan.

discontinuity, and more juxtaposition between the existing structures and new ones. Hämer supported the idea of the permeable block as well: according to him, it was another difference between IBA's Neubau and Altbau segments. Unlike the Neubau architects, who prioritized the continuity of the street front, the Altbau team did not mind gaps and disturbances in the perimeter, since this provided more ventilation and greenery in an already congested area. Even the corners of the blocks that had historically remained open could be left unbuilt.[29]

The idea of a permeable and fragmentary block was indeed a welcome architectural corrective to the Altbau areas. Even though Hämer and his team were determined not to destroy any buildings to prevent the displacement of the current residents, it was necessary to increase the ventilation and light in the cramped Hof-spaces of nineteenth-century Berlin, which had become a target of criticism and a motivation for the birth of the modernist housing movement. In his short story "Rear Courtyard," Aras Ören (an immigrant from Turkey) described Kreuzberg in the 1970s as a neighborhood where the sun failed to shine: "You can distinguish Kreuzberg from other parts of the city very easily. First of all, it has more ruins than anywhere else. It has a special color of its own: black and leaden tones overwhelm. It does not have much greenery."[30] Ören writes about a fictional character, a widow named Elfriede Neumann, who has rented the large room of her apartment to immigrants from Turkey and is living squeezed

TOP: Figure V.7 View of the urban square in front of the seniors' club in Álvaro Siza's Block 121 for IBA-1984/87, photographed by Esra Akcan, Berlin, 2012. LEFT: Figure V.8 Views of the Hof-garden in Álvaro Siza's Block 121 for IBA-1984/87, photographed by Esra Akcan, Berlin, 2009, 2012.

Figure V.9 Álvaro Siza, Sketch for Bonjour Tristesse in Block 121, IBA-1984/87, Berlin, c. 1980.

in by the furniture of her entire house, which is now all in her crowded room. She sits in front of her window with a view of the cramped Hof from the early morning hours until evening, waiting to talk to the sun once it enters her line of sight. However, the sun seldom shows up in the Hof-spaces of the working-class areas, because of, he tells Neumann, his contract with the wealthy neighborhoods. She regrets not being able to live in those areas, where she could see the sun in looking out her window into a large Hof. "What are we doing between these walls, in this hole?"[31] she asks herself, demonstrating the challenge faced by the Altbau team in its attempt to turn Kreuzberg into a neighborhood with decent living conditions without destroying any of the buildings that made the courtyards congested.

The small courtyards of working-class neighborhoods in Germany continued to be a topic of immigrant literature. In Emine Sevgi Özdamar's "Courtyard in the Mirror," the reader is presented with fast-moving images that appear one right after another. They are images of the narrator's current and former living spaces, reflected in her mental and physical mirrors in ways that Leslie Adelson has described as the "production of locality … the here and the now," rather than the celebration of "the local as a counterpoint to nation, transnation or postnation."[32] The physical mirror in the narrator's apartment (in Düsseldorf, though the city is never named) reflects the courtyard and the apartments overlooking it, which accumulate images constructing nothing less than a richly textured microcosm of humans, animals, and objects in a city area with memories of both the living and the dead. The narrator realizes that the nun living across the dark courtyard is dead once the nun's lamp stops shining on her mirror, which used to be the first thing she saw in the mornings:

> I now think that the old nun across the courtyard is also dead. When a new dead person comes in, the other dead in the mirror make space for her. Sometimes a bee comes through the window and flies on the mirror among the dead. The dead see it; they also see the steam coming out of the expresso machine on the stove. Or a bird comes in through the open window and flies around the mirror. It takes a shower in the bathtub. I see myself naked on the mirror among the dead. The postman in the courtyard rings a bell. What if he also has a heart disease, like all the other Turkish postmen? Raindrops fall on the balcony and the dead in the mirror. Sometimes hundreds of flies come in and revolve like crazy around the lamp that hangs in front of the mirror.[33]

Even though the Altbau team proved the quality of apartments and urban life could be improved by renovating the existing buildings in East Kreuzberg, it was still necessary to increase the light and air wherever possible on a Hof-by-Hof basis in an area that was known for its cramped courtyards, dark colors, and lack of greenery. Siza's permeable block model was able to do precisely that.

Bonjour Tristesse Housing and Anticipation of the Residents' Voice

Architectural critics often find Siza's forms "silent."[34] Nothing could be further from the truth, when one thinks about the process through which Bonjour Tristesse was produced and inhabited. Siza reinterpreted the terms "contextual" and "regionalist," so often attributed to his buildings, as the "absence of a pre-established language" to emphasize the transformations during the design process.[35] However, it may be that Siza's most remarkable contribution to architecture, at least during the 1970s and 1980s, had to do with his ideas on participation. Before his IBA experience, Siza had worked for the participatory social housing project *Serviço de Apoio Ambulatório Local* (SAAL), which had come out of the revolutionary spirit in Portugal in 1974—an experience that must have caught Hämer's eye and led him to invite Siza to participate in the IBA competitions soon afterward (Figure V.10).[36] During the same period, Siza worked on another participatory project with a majority-Muslim population in the Netherlands (De Punkt and De Komma Social Housing in Schilderswijk-West, 1983–88).[37]

While working on the Bouça (Porto, 1973–77) and São Victor Housing (Porto, 1974–79) for SAAL, Siza elaborated on his ideas on participation, which did not imply surrendering architectural expertise to the demands of "what people want." In interviews and articles, he spoke appreciatively about his frequent dialogues with the future

Figure V.10 Álvaro Siza, Housing for *Serviço de Apoio Ambulatório Local* (SAAL), Porto, Portugal, 1973–77.

Figure V.11 Participatory meeting of IBA-1984/87, Berlin. Álvaro Siza can be seen at the far right.

residents about comfort, space, and color during construction.[38] While these dialogues "enriched the project," the approach of politicians and some technicians was "authoritarian," reducing the role of the architect to that of a "tool for people."[39] Rather than subordinating architectural expertise or giving up entirely on the participatory process, Siza suggested a third option that involved confronting the tensions between architect and inhabitant: "Consequently, to enter the real process of participation meant to accept the conflicts and not to hide them, but on the contrary to elaborate them. These exchanges then became very rich although hard and often difficult. ... For me these participation procedures are above all critical processes for the transformation of thought, not only of the inhabitants' idea of themselves, but also of the concepts of the architect."[40]

In Berlin, Siza attended some of IBA's tenant meetings and explained his projects to the future users (Figure V.11). As Hämer recalled, in a public meeting on Fraenkelufer in the winter of 1979, Siza talked for two hours to the residents, explaining to them Berlin's architectural history from Karl Friedrich Schinkel to Scharoun, as well as his own project's dialogue with the Berlin block. While many would think "the masses" would not understand, Siza knew they did. As Hämer said, "One could rediscover Berlin anew with him."[41] In my interview with Hämer, he commented that he was impressed by the way Siza turned every perceived negative judgment about Berlin's blocks into an inspiring opportunity for new designs.[42] Siza was similarly attentive to safeguarding immigrants' rights during the Kreuzberg project. Rather than blaming economic constraints on Bonjour Tristesse for impairing its architectural quality, as many did in the case of public housing, he welcomed such constraints as a guarantee that his buildings would be inhabited by the lower-income immigrant population that they were intended to serve.[43]

In the Netherlands, the participants seem to have embraced Siza's architectural proposals more than the authorities and professionals did.[44] To respond to the needs of the Muslim residents in this project, Siza worked together with a Turkish sociologist; they communicated with the help of two interpreters who translated from English to Dutch, and Dutch to Turkish. According to Siza, during the process he realized that the conventional organization of council houses in the Netherlands was not appropriate for immigrants who wanted a complete differentiation between the private section of the house and the semiprivate space where men could greet visitors without women

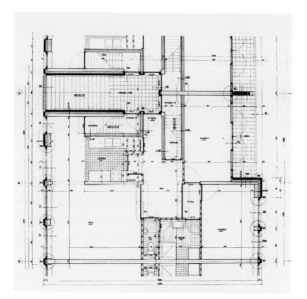

Figure V.12 Álvaro Siza, Housing for Schilderswijk-West,
Netherlands, 1983–88. Plan of the double distribution space.

being seen. While not necessarily encouraging women's separation, Siza proposed a double distribution space at the entrance that could be closed and opened based on the user's preference, which was criticized by other architects as not being functional. During a visit to one of the units after its construction, Siza was happy to discover that the women had turned this second distribution space into an eating area—in his words, "proof that the idea works" (Figure V.12).[45]

Today, Siza finds it unfortunate that participation in public housing is considered a recipe for mediocrity, while dialogue with the client in the construction of a single house is accepted as a usual part of the design process: "I know that many politicians want to take advantage of the civic participation for their own purposes. This can happen. Popular participation in architecture could be even a way to attract very dishonest opportunists. But participation itself is not dishonest, and it seems sad to me that after having shown such enthusiasm toward social subjects in architecture, these may suddenly become something shameful and provincial, which is of no interest to anybody. ... Nevertheless, I still believe that participation is an irreplaceable instrument for a project."[46]

In a handwritten poster put up around the Schlesisches Tor neighborhood, IBA Altbau invited anyone interested to discuss the four competition projects designed for Block 121. "Come and tell us your opinion," the poster said: "Should a day care center be built? Which houses should stay and which ones should be demolished? How should the space inside the block develop? What should happen to the businesses on Schlesische Strasse?" The meeting took place on October 13, 1980, and was attended by fifteen residents, two representatives of IBA (Yalçın Çetin and Thörnig Keller), and three representatives of tenant consulting agencies (including Akdüzün from Otur ve Yaşa). The participants discussed the proposals for the corner building, voiced their concerns about hygiene in the existing school building and the decaying conditions of their own buildings, discussed the placement of the kindergarten in different competition projects, did not reach consensus about the existing food vendors in the southeast corner, and criticized the current organization of the playgrounds inside the block.[47] On November 3 and 4, 1980, two other meetings took place, during which Hämer himself explained the four projects to residents and answered their questions and concerns about the design and construction process. He reassured them that no one would be displaced and that the open areas in the block would be designed through a participatory process. In this meeting, the participants also voted almost unanimously for the building of a kindergarten and a seniors' club. Siza's design was initially criticized by "professional representatives" who often came to the participatory meetings,[48] but it eventually received support from nine participants, a negative reaction from three, and a neutral vote from one.[49]

The Turkish residents participated in the IBA process in matters for which IBA directly sought their approval, such as their own apartments and shops, but they were generally absent from the participatory meetings concerning the public spaces. This seems to be confirmed in the attendance records from the public meetings about the common areas in Block 121, to discuss such topics as the overall design, open areas, school, and kindergarten. Nevertheless, as current renters of the existing Altbau buildings and owners of the businesses on the streets, Turkish immigrants did take part in the renovation process. In Block 121 most of the buildings were renovated by Group 67, and Yalçın Çetin worked on the IBA team as the Turkish correspondent and translator. The process was initiated after winning the approval of the majority of renters in a building; documents were signed ensuring that the tenants would not be displaced; the renovation took place on a unit-by-unit basis to meet the requirements of current inhabitants; and the business owners in the shops and food vendors on the street level filled out questionnaires about the architectural problems in their spaces.[50] Still, the large Turkish families (with up to nine children) presented a challenge in the renovation process because of the small size of the available units.

Çetin worked on the IBA team for areas including Siza's block. After graduating as an economist from Istanbul Technical University, he joined IBA while continuing his education in Berlin. He was especially influential in surveying and preventing the demolition of the pop-up one-story shops in the corner across from the train station (Figure V.13). He vividly remembers the exhaustion that came from being involved in the participatory process for five or six years:

> This is an extremely difficult, time-consuming process, with very little payback. It drains one after a while. One stops believing in the process. I soon decided to move to Muğla [a resort town in southern Turkey]. I believe that urban renewal should always be a participatory process, but I was burned out myself. This is an extremely tough process, but it needs to be done. When the state claims to know best and implements it in a top-down fashion, the result is often full of mistakes. ... After a while, one becomes callous. Talking to hundreds of families, I witnessed very sad Turkish realities.[51]

Figure V.13 Views of the street vendors in Álvaro Siza's Block 121 for IBA-1984/87, photographed by Esra Akcan, Berlin, 2009.

Siza's project went through significant changes during the design process because of the negotiations with the client Schulz KG. According to Nelson Mota, in the four different versions that had to be prepared during the process, Bonjour Tristesse turned from a building originally containing twenty large apartments suitable for the large immigrant families into one with forty-six smaller apartments, lower ceilings, an added floor, and a more monotonous façade than originally planned.[52] Siza commented on the unfortunate changes caused by the economic constraints on the project, not necessarily to look down on buildings with low budgets, but to call for a more informed and realistic approach to public housing.[53]

Siza was not at all idealistic about participation. He criticized the authoritarian politicians who perceived participation as the subordination of architectural expertise to the demands of what they claimed people wanted, and as the reduction of the role of the architect to a tool for people. Despite his frustration, Siza did not give up on the idea of participation and suggested that the tensions between architects and users be confronted, and that the design be a continuous process that came out of these frictions. For example, for each unit of Bonjour Tristesse, Siza designed an unidentified void space accessed from the living room, which was officially approved as a winter garden, but which lent itself to flexible interior use (Figure V.14). This void was a small but effective gesture toward open architecture.

Yüksel Karaçizmeli's Kitchen

Álvaro Siza's design of an unidentified void space in each unit was confirmed as a mode for achieving open architecture in Yüksel Karaçizmeli's apartment. She currently lives in the second-floor corner apartment of Bonjour Tristesse with her husband and their two sons, who both grew up there. We spend time together in the memorable round living room overlooking the intersection—a room she genuinely appreciates, and asks me to thank the architect on her behalf (Figure V.15).

Karaçizmeli came to Germany in 1968 from Adana, Turkey, through the Turkish Labor Placement Office—like millions of other immigrants—and worked for decades in Germany in factories and cleaning services. She still remembers her journey vividly: "We boarded that train, that dark black train in Sirkeci. They had put women in the front and men in the back of the train. We cried all the way. Imagine a twenty-two-year-old woman alone, leaving her country for the first time. Everybody was crying. ... You are alone, you do not know the language. Newcomers lived in Heim at that time. I used to chase dark-haired women on the street to be able to have a few words of daily conversation."[54] She remembers the details of the medical exam equally clearly—a process that took her about ten days. The German doctors examined her whole body at the border in Istanbul, checked to see if she had had an operation or had a serious disease, unhealthy lungs, or bad teeth. Many people could not pass the medical exam and were turned back, she recalls.[55] After her arrival in Germany, she must have read the how-to-behave pamphlets or come across one of the official *Toilettenerlass für Ausländer* (toilet instructions for foreigners). The latter set of instructions, in particular, conveys some of the obscenities that structure the bureaucracies of immigration: "Sit (don't stand) on the toilet seat! ... After purging the bowels, clean the anus carefully with at least two pieces of toilet paper, folded together, until the anus is completely clean. Use the left hand for this."[56]

Receiving this sort of instructions must have been a common experience for newcomers to Germany, since they appear frequently in immigrant literature. In her story "Karagöz in Germany," Özdamar recounts a conversation between a farmer and his donkey on their immigration path. The farmer reads from *A Handbook for Guest Workers Who Are Going to Work Abroad*: "Dear Brother Worker! Toilets in Europe are different than here at home: they are like a chair. Do not stand on top of them, you must sit down on them. For cleanliness, do not use water, leaves, earth or stones, but very fine toilet paper." The donkey makes fun of these guidelines: "Or else someone will lick your arse."[57] It is a historical irony that while such guidelines claimed to teach hygiene to the guest workers, the labor of the same women workers was frequently used for cleaning services in Germany.[58] In another story in the same book, Özdamar tells the tale of a cleaning woman working in a theater, who imagines herself to be Ophelia and converses with the characters of numerous canonical plays of Western literature: "And I'm a water corpse arrived in a green garden. When Ophelia drowned in my country, she came back to Earth in Germany as a cleaning woman. Black hair and white plastic bags, that was enough for her. Nobody noticed that I am the former corpse of a man who wanted to play, who should have played, Hamlet! I am a cleaning woman, so Germany remains clean."[59] Obscene words describing bodily discharges are intermingled with phrases from canonic Western literature in Özdamar's character's mind, bringing the reader face to face with "high civilization" that comes to Germany at the guest worker's expense. It is the economic exploitation of the immigrant woman in employing her as a cleaner that grounds this story in its harsh realities.[60] As surreal as the images in Özdamar's stories are, they are still less brutal in their absurdity than the reality of the immigration handbooks.

In 1979, Karaçizmeli and her husband moved to Berlin for the better work opportunities that the city offered, but had to live in unrenovated old apartments with no bathroom that she still remembers as a challenge.[61] In 1983, they moved to Siza's Bonjour Tristesse, becoming one of the first tenants after construction was completed. Since she had a special immigration status—only a few Turkish immigrants had this status,

Figure V.14 Álvaro Siza, Bonjour Tristesse in Block 121, IBA-1984/87, Berlin, 1980–1984. Plans of early and late versions.

which required passing an interview in German—she was not subject to the ban on entry and settlement that would have prevented them from moving into Kreuzberg at that time.[62] She was pregnant when she looked for an apartment. The housing office showed her many places, some in the center of Kreuzberg, on Adalbertstrasse, and some far away in Moabit, but she preferred to live at this corner as it was close to her work.[63] The Siza building was under construction at the time, and she decided to move in after meeting a representative of the owner, who explained to her the plan of the apartments and let her choose the one she wanted.[64]

She and her husband sent their children to the local school, rather than to one in Turkey—a decision that led many more guest workers to stay permanently in Germany than they originally anticipated.[65] When she discovered that the children were segregated into German and Turkish classes, Karaçizmeli complained, but the principal sent her home, claiming that the German parents had demanded this division. She later regretted not having used her legal right to file a suit. "There are too many Turks," the principal had said rudely. "What do you suggest? Should we tell Germans to make as many kids as Turks?"[66] One of her sons started in one of the best high schools of Berlin, but he soon returned to his school in Kreuzberg after he found it too difficult to be alone in the same class with German children who had parents helping them with English, French, and other subjects.[67] Even though they criticize the moving bans for foreigners that tried to block the formation of immigrant neighborhoods, they admit that mixed urban zones, and consequently schools, would have been better for their children's education.[68]

Figure V.15 View of Karaçizmeli's living room in Álvaro Siza's Bonjour Tristesse in Block 121 for IBA-1984/87, photographed by Esra Akcan, Berlin, 2012.

Over the years, Karaçizmeli had watched through her window as the Berlin Wall was smashed into pieces and the area changed from a relatively silent Turkish peripheral neighborhood into a culturally mixed central location: "Before the wall came down, this was a Turkish neighborhood. The Germans were a minority. Everybody, both the Germans and us, knew each other. When you walked in one direction, there was the wall; in the other direction, the wall again, and the canal across the street. When a stranger came into the neighborhood, we immediately knew he was not from here. My kids used to play on the street—there were almost no cars. The changes were slow after the wall came down, and the first ten years were really beautiful."[69] Since the 2000s, however, this corner has become one of the hippest spots of Berlin, with famous nightclubs and restaurants, and it attracted hundreds of young women and men who "shout and sing loud at 4:00 or 5:00 a.m. in the street, as if there are no neighbors here," Karaçizmeli mentions frequently. When she called the police to complain, the officer she spoke to said there was not much he could do. "This is Kreuzberg," he said, possibly thinking of the famous scene in the movie *Chinatown*.[70]

"I lived here for thirty years, and the policeman thinks he knows Kreuzberg better than me," she comments to me in resentment. Karaçizmeli does not feel like a "foreigner" after forty years of residence in Germany. Originally she never thought she would stay for more than one or two years in Germany, and even passed opportunities that required multiple-year investments, but she has decided to stay permanently.[71] She does not think Germans were necessarily discriminatory against guest workers; and she criticizes those who live in isolation, following traditional Turkish

Figure V.16 View of Karaçizmeli's living room in Álvaro
Siza's Bonjour Tristesse in Block 121 for IBA-1984/87,
photographed by Esra Akcan, Berlin, 2009.

customs.[72] Her husband, instead, criticizes the fact that successful immigrants from
Turkey are not acknowledged enough unless they assimilate on the one hand, and the
dominance of conservatism among the Turks in Germany and in Turkey on the other
hand.[73] Nonetheless, she, her husband, and their children would not like to live anywhere but Kreuzberg. "Do you know why I like it here?" she asks me. "Our grocery
store is Turkish, we can buy fresh fruits and vegetables from a Turkish shop, we can
buy Turkish bread at every hour of the day." "We have no meat problem," her husband,
Mehmet, adds. "We buy it from the Turkish shop, which does not sell pork—there is
no risk of contamination."[74] "I grew up here," their son adds. "All my friends are here,
this is my neighborhood." "When Turkish people leave, Kreuzberg will lose all its character," her husband says—a statement I heard over and over again in my interviews.[75]

Yüksel and Mehmet Karaçizmeli are dreading the day of his retirement, when they will
no longer be able to afford the high rent and will have to move out of their apartment.[76]
"Where else can we find such a bright living room with five windows?" he asks me.[77]
Indeed, the bright, round living room with its many windows is a frequent topic in our
conversation. Even though it was hard in the beginning to cut the carpet in this shape
and place the furniture in a round space, she says: "You can find everywhere a room
like our bedroom, right, but you cannot find anywhere a living room like this. Everybody likes to look out of that window. We used to draw up a chair there, and our kids
loved to watch the street for hours. Now we do the same for our grandchildren" (Figure V.16).[78]

TOP: Figure V.17 View of the *void* space in Karaçizmeli's apartment in Álvaro Siza's Bonjour Tristesse in Block 121 for IBA-1984/87, photographed by Esra Akcan, Berlin, 2012. BOTTOM: Figure V.18 Views of the closed and open kitchen in Karaçizmeli's apartment in Álvaro Siza's Bonjour Tristesse in Block 121 for IBA-1984/87, photographed by Esra Akcan, Berlin, 2012.

Karaçizmeli's family had not participated in the design process of Block 121, but they have inscribed their physical traces on Bonjour Tristesse. As noted above, for each apartment, Siza designed an unidentified void space accessed from the living room, which looks like a winter garden, but lends itself to flexible use (Figure V.17). This void space is one of his crucial architectural contributions in the name of participation, since it prescribes a zone for residents' voice at the stage of architectural design. Many families in the building have used the space for religious practice or as a bedroom for their children. Karaçizmeli turned it into an additional kitchen that can be well ventilated and brought in her own oven, refrigerator and got help from a mechanical engineer that she could find easily through her personal relations in her working place at Siemens.**79** When the owner had explained the apartment plan to her before she moved in, he had not told her about the open kitchen, and when she discovered it, it was too late to move to another apartment. She was shocked because she found the open kitchen inappropriate for Turkish cooking due to the strong smells that would permeate the whole apartment.**80** Therefore, she now has a two-part kitchen: an open section for washing, preparing, storing, and eating food, and another section for cooking, divided from the first part by a glass partition (Figure V.18). Such a reinvention of the space was similar to the transformation processes that took place in Siza's public housing in the Netherlands, and it was enabled by the fact that he had designed a void space in each apartment that can be used as residents choose.

The Seniors, the Children, and the Graffiti Artists

Block 121 contains two more buildings designed by Siza. The kindergarten has white, undecorated surfaces facing the street (Figure V.19), while it creates a sheltered playground at the back amid the gardens and sports areas inside Block 121. Karaçizmeli confirms there has been an understanding over the years that this Hof-garden is reserved for the leisure of the teenagers and children, and they used to go to the Görlitzer Park in their free time, before the park became a dangerous drug scene.**81** The children I meet in the public Hof of the block take me through their secret passageway to this multilevel playground, which has a generous amount of open space (Figure V.20). The seniors' club, in contrast, is situated in such a way that it has a semi-secluded environment with its indoor and outdoor spaces half hidden from sight with landscaping but accessible to anyone interested. The club is a popular meeting place, especially for retired workers (Figure V.21). It is managed by volunteers such as Ms. Rukiye, who has been working here for the past twenty years. After giving me a tour of the big common hall (Figure V.22), smaller meeting rooms, kitchen, and crafts' workshop, she climbs the stairs with me to the roof, which was turned into a vegetable garden in 2015. There an immigrant from Britain employed by the city has planted a lawn, watermelons, tomatoes, and peppers (Figure V.23). Ms. Rukiye invites me to one of the semiannual grills on a Sunday afternoon in September. A single glance at the common hall after I enter the building is enough to let me know that all of the guests are such long-time acquaintances—whether they are sitting silently next to each other or enthusiastically greeting someone at a distant table—that it is easy to identify me as the only stranger in the room. Evidently managing a situation that is familiar enough to her, Ms. Rukiye tells me that I can take photographs freely, and she continues to rush back and forth between the kitchen and the common hall. The space accommodates long dining tables decorated with yellow flowers and napkins of matching colors, and white plastic cups and plates on white tablecloths that create a textured fabric on the surface of the table. The white-yellow color composition is broken by the colorfully dressed neighbors sitting around the tables, some of whom are singing along or dancing to the live music (Figure V.24). Another defining characteristic of the space is the graffiti on the outdoor walls, which can be seen through large windows (Figure V.25).

Siza's building gets its name from the graffiti on top of its round corner façade: "Bonjour Tristesse" (Figure V.26). The inscription, which was discovered when the scaffolding was taken down, looks like the spontaneous and hasty gesture of a dyslexic

Figure V.19 View of Álvaro Siza's kindergarten in Block 121 for IBA-1984/87, photographed by Esra Akcan, Berlin, 2012.

Figure V.20 View from the playground of Álvaro Siza's kindergarten in Block 121 for IBA-1984/87, photographed by Esra Akcan, Berlin, 2012.

hand. It was not indicated in the architect's construction drawings, and multiple stories about its unidentified author add to its enigmatic content. Perhaps it refers to Otto Preminger's movie of 1958, based on Françoise Sagan's novel of the same title. In the movie, Juliette Greco sings "Bonjour Tristesse," while Jean Seberg, who plays practically the same character as her legendary role in Godard's *Breathless*, dances and explains to the audience the reasons for her aloof detachment: "I cannot feel anything he might be interested in, because I am surrounded by a wall, an invisible wall made of memories I cannot lose."[82] Perhaps this is Siza's way of implying that his building near the Berlin Wall would repair the city's urban fabric, but not by forgetting the trauma of World War II or by denying the existence of the wall—a theme that was also present in the IBA projects of Peter Eisenman and Daniel Libeskind (stop VI). Perhaps the graffiti was written by one of the architects who lost the competition to Siza—a common rumor. Perhaps it was a protest against the profit-oriented developer who forced the architect to add another floor to the building. Or perhaps it was the work of one of the arts initiatives that organized workshops during the IBA years near this site.

While "Bonjour Tristesse" has become a beloved graffiti on the building, inspiring many articles and a short film,[83] it has not remained the only one. The Schlesisches Tor neighborhood is famous for its ubiquitous graffiti, to such an extent that householders moving into the area during the recent wave of gentrification are reported to be commissioning cutting-edge graffiti artists to tag their buildings so that "non-artists" will

TOP: Figure V.21 View of Álvaro Siza's seniors' club in Block 121 for IBA-1984/87, photographed by Esra Akcan, Berlin, 2016. BOTTOM: Figure V.22 View of the common hall in Álvaro Siza's seniors' club in Block 121 for IBA-1984/87, photographed by Esra Akcan, Berlin, 2016.

TOP: Figure V.23 Views from street and roof garden of Álvaro Siza's seniors' club in Block 121 for IBA-1984/87, photographed by Esra Akcan, Berlin, 2016. BOTTOM: Figure V.24: View of the semiannual grill in Álvaro Siza's seniors' club in Block 121 for IBA-1984/87, photographed by Esra Akcan, Berlin, 2016.

TOP: Figure V.25 View of Álvaro Siza's seniors' club in Block 121 for IBA-1984/87, photographed by Esra Akcan, Berlin, 2016. BOTTOM: Figure V.26 View of the original graffiti on the façade of Álvaro Siza's Bonjour Tristesse in Block 121 for IBA-1984/87, photographed by Esra Akcan, Berlin, 2009.

Figure V.27 View of the new graffiti on the façade of Álvaro Siza's Bonjour Tristesse in Block 121 for IBA-1984/87, photographed by Esra Akcan, Berlin, 2012.

not. Yet much of the graffiti on Siza's buildings is anonymous and political in nature. In the summer of 2009, I saw the following inscriptions on the walls of Bonjour Tristesse's interior halls: "TGB" (Die Türkische Gemeinde zu Berlin [the Turkish community of Berlin], an activist organization founded in 1983), "Freiheit für Iran" (freedom for Iran), "Fuck you boys," "Support Israel," "Nazis Raus" (Nazis get out), "CuCa Crew ❤," "KTC" (if this was a Turkish acronym, it would refer to the Republic of Turkish Cyprus), "Killer Emine," and "I love you," among many others. Since 2012, an oversized graffiti with large red font inscribing "Bitte Leben" (please live) has dwarfed the original "Bonjour Tristesse." Karaçizmeli remembers the night it must have been implemented with red paint, as she found blood-like stains on her window frames in the morning (Figure V.27).[84]

Graffiti has complemented the façades of Siza's kindergarten and seniors' club as well. In particular, the latter has become a major attraction for graffiti enthusiasts, with no untouched white surfaces remaining today (Figure V.28, also see Figure V.21). The seniors' club's exterior walls are completely covered with graffiti, and the view from the interior is characterized by it. Every time the city repaints the walls white, it takes no more than a couple of weeks for graffiti artists to reclaim them. The process has turned the seniors' club into a temporary exhibition space—never empty, never blank, but filled with periodically changing graffiti. In the spirit of continuing participation, graffiti artists commission themselves as the makers of the constantly changing city surface. Unlike the architectural critics who adore the serenity and silence of Siza's buildings, the city's inhabitants have evidently interpreted his modernist white

Figure V.28 Views of the changing façade of Álvaro Siza's seniors' club in Block 121 for IBA-1984/87, photographed by Esra Akcan, Berlin, c.1984, 2009, 2012 (see Figure V.21 for 2016).

façades as blank surfaces on which to write their own stories. But no need to take a lofty tone; this is to be expected. When there is no effective public sphere in which immigrants can represent themselves, building walls will host the unauthorized voice.

1 Some parts of this chapter were previously published as Esra Akcan, "A Building with Many Speakers: Turkish 'Guest Workers' and Álvaro Siza's *Bonjour Tristesse* Housing for IBA-Berlin," in *The Migrant's Time: Rethinking Art History and Diaspora*, ed. Saloni Mathur (New Haven, CT: Yale University Press, 2011), 91–114. In addition to those parts, this stop includes discussions on the rift between autonomy and participation, and integrates information from my later visits to the site as well as my analysis of additional archival material, new literary works (poems and short stories), and interviews. **2** Hüseyin A., "Miet-gesuche," trans. David Gramling, in *Germany in Transit: Nation and Migration, 1955–2005*, ed. Deniz Göktürk, David Gramling, and Anton Kaes (Berkeley: University of California Press, 2007), 358. **3** Ayhan Kaya, *Sicher in Kreuzberg: Constructing Diasporas: Turkish Hip Hop Youth in Berlin* (Bielefeld, Germany: Transcript Verlag, 2001). **4** For Kanak Attak's manifesto in German, Turkish, and English, see Kanak Attak, untitled item, accessed April 15, 2017, http://www.kanak-attak.de/ka/down/pdf/textos. pdf. See also Feridun Zaimoğlu, *Kanak Sprak: 24 Misstöne vom Rande der Gesellschaft* (Hamburg: Rotbuch, 1995).

5 Hildebrand Machleidt, interview by the author, July 12, 2012, Berlin, in German, 00:27:05–00:31:00, 01:24:30–01:28:19, 02:13:26–02:17:00. Both audio and video recordings of this interview are in the author's collection. **6** Günter Schlusche, interview by the author, November 8, 2016, Berlin, in English, 00:30:26. Both audio and video recordings of this interview are in the author's collection. **7** Josef Paul Kleihues, "Preface," in *Erste Projekte: Internationale Bauausstellung Berlin 1984/87: Die Neubaugebiete—Dokumente Projekte*, vol. 2 (Berlin: Quadriga Verlag, 1981), 8. **8** Josef Paul Kleihues, "Preface," in Ibid., 8–9. **9** "The Facts and the Dreams: *AD* Interview with Lampugnani," trans. Romana Schneider, *AD* 53, nos. 1–2 (1983): 17–19, Quotation: 19. The interview was also published as "L'IBA, est-elle assez radical?" *L'Architecture d'Aujourd'hui* 219, February (1982): xxiii–xxix. **10** Douglas Clelland, "Neubau," in "Berlin: Origins to IBA," ed. Peter Davey, Douglas Clelland, special issue of *Architectural Review* 181, no. 1082 (1987): 22–106. Quotation: 44. **11** Doug Clelland, "Berliner Ensemble," *Building Design* 705, (September 1984): 26–31. Quotation 26–27. **12** Josef Paul Kleihues, "1984 Berlin Exhibition: Architectural Dream or Reality," *Architectural Association Quarterly*, nos. 2–3 (1982): 34–42. Quotation: 42. **13** Josef Paul Kleihues, "Architecture as Desire: Architecture, This Was What I Wanted to Say Needs the Care and Support of Us All," in *Erste Projekte*, 58–71. Quotation: 66. **14** Vittorio Magnago Lampugnani, "Das Ganze und die Teile. Typologie und Funktionalismus in der Architektur des 19. und 20. Jahrhunderts," in *Modelle für eine Stadt*, ed. Vittorio Magnago Lampugnani (Berlin: IBA, 1984), 83–117. **15** Ibid., 83. **16** Ibid., 116–17. **17** Vittorio Magnago Lampugnani, "The Horizon of the Past: South Friedrichstadt: A Potential Model in the Search for New Architectural Values," in *Erste Projekte*, 234. **18** For general information on Siza's architecture, see *Poetic Profession: Lotus Documents* (New York: Rizzoli, 1986); Wilfred Wang and José Paolo dos Santos, eds., *Álvaro Siza, Figures and Configurations: Buildings and Projects 1986–1988* (Boston: Harvard University Graduate School of Design, 1988); Brigitte Fleck, *Álvaro Siza* (Berlin: Birkhäuser, 1992); Álvaro Dos Santos, ed., *Álvaro Siza: Works and Projects* (Barcelona: Gustavo Gili, 1993); Pedro de Llano and Carlos Castanheira, eds., *Álvaro Siza: Works and Projects* (Madrid: Electa, 1995); Kenneth Frampton, *Álvaro Siza: Complete Works* (London: Phaidon, 2000). **19** Leo Dronkers, "Gute Gründe für kurze Leine," *Berliner Stimme*, March 20, 1981. **20** IBA prepared a brochure on the historical development of the area and a comprehensive report on the four competing projects. See IBA, "Zur räumlich-historischen Entwicklung des Blocks 121 (Schlesische Straße): Zwischenbericht September 1980," IBA Brochure. IBA-Neubau Akten, B 80/026, Landesarchiv; IBA, "Stadterneuerung rund ums Schlesische Tor: Entwürfe für die Schlesische Straße 1–8," Berlin: IBA, December 1980. IBA-Neubau Akten, B 80/038, Landesarchiv. For more on the differences among the four competition entries, see Nelson Mota, "Critique: Building Appraisals: Álvaro Siza's Bonjour Tristesse: A Symphony for a Big City," *Journal of Architecture* 19, no. 5 (2014): 779–808. **21** Archiv IBA-ALT/STERN (1979–90) Folder A3 SO/58, Baukunst Sammlung, Akad-

emie der Künste [hereafter AdK]. **22** Fleck, *Álvaro Siza*, 52. **23** Quoted in "Un immeuble d'angle à Berlin: Entretien avec Álvaro Siza," *Architecture, Mouvement, Continuité* 2 (October 1983): 16–21. Quotation: 18. **24** Álvaro Siza, interview with Carsten Krohn, for the *Das ungebaute Berlin* (unbuilt Berlin) exhibition, July 16–August 15, 2010, Café Moskau, Berlin. My source is the video recording of the interview, in the collection of Krohn. **25** "Un immeuble d'angle à Berlin," 20–21. **26** Peter Testa, *The Architecture of Álvaro Siza*, and "Unity of the Discontinuous: Álvaro Siza's Berlin Works," *Assemblage* 2 (February 1987): 47–61. **27** Olaf Schmidt, "Vorschriften und Normen als Determinanten für Architektur," *Der Architekt* 6 (June 1983): 326. **28** Quoted in "Un immeuble d'angle à Berlin," 20. **29** Hardt-Waltherr Hämer, interviewed by Lore Ditzen," *Architectural Review* 176 (September 1984): 28–32. **30** Aras Ören, "Arka Avlu," (1970) in Aras Ören, *Anlatılar 1970–1982* (Berlin: Verlag Hund und Toker, 1991): 11–16. Quotation: 14. **31** Ibid., 16. **32** Leslie Adelson, *The Turkish Turn in Contemporary German Literature* (New York: Palgrave MacMillan, 2005), 43. See also Emine Sevgi Özdamar, *Der Hof im Spiegel: Erzählungen* (Cologne, Germany: Kiepenheuer und Wisch, 2001). For a Turkish translation, see "Emine" Sevgi Özdamar, *Aynadaki Avlu*, trans. Esen Tezel (Istanbul: Yapı Kredi Yayınları, 2012). **33** Özdamar, *Aynadaki Avlu*, 19. **34** For example, see Nicolai Ouroussoff, "Modernist Master's Deceptively Simple World," *New York Times*, August 5, 2007; Emmanuella Vieira, "Éloge du silence et de la simplicité," *Le Devoir*, October 4, 2003. **35** Quoted in "Un immeuble d'angle à Berlin," 33. **36** Yoshio Futagawa, *Studio Talk: Interview with 15 Architects* (Tokyo: A. D. A. Edita, 2002), 200–34. **37** For articles that mention Siza's ideas on participation, see Bernard Huet, "Alvora Siza architetto 1954–79," in *Poetic Profession*, 176–81; Kenneth Frampton, "Poesis and Transformation: The Architecture of Álvaro Siza," in ibid., 10–24, and "Architecture as Critical Transformation: The Work of Álvaro Siza," in *Álvaro Siza: Complete Works*, ed. Kenneth Frampton, 11–65. **38** See, for example, "Un immeuble d'angle à Berlin." **39** Álvaro Siza, "Evora Malagueira," in *Álvaro Siza: Complete Works*, ed. Kenneth Frampton, 160–62; see also 25. **40** Quoted in Frampton, "Architecture as Critical Transformation," 25, and "Poesis and Transformation," 12. **41** Hardt-Waltherr Hämer, foreword to *Álvaro Siza Vieira, Projekte fur Berlin 1978–1984: Ein Skizzenbuch* (Berlin: Aedes, 1985), n. p. **42** Hardt-Waltherr Hämer, interview by the author, March 24, 2012, Ahrenshoop, Germany, in German. Both audio and video recordings of this interview are in the author's collection. **43** "Un immeuble d'angle à Berlin," 21. **44** Siza said: "I could not have defended many of my proposals without the support of the people who participated in these debates—the neighbors of the quarter affected by the project—because there were proposals which the administration, and in some cases even the architects, did not accept due to some preconceptions. If I was able to carry them out, it was thanks to the openness of the people who discussed them without the load of the cultural significance and who were, therefore, more open to reasoning" (quoted in "Fragments of an Experience: Conversations with Pedro de Llano, Carlos Castanheira Francisco

Rei, Santiago Seara," in *Álvaro Siza: Works and Projects*, 34). **45** Quoted in "Getting through Turbulence: Interview with Álvaro Siza by Alejandro Zaera," *Croquis*, nos. 68–69 (1994): 6–31. Quotation: 28. **46** Quoted in "Fragments of an Experience," 34. **47** Minutes of the meeting on October 13, 1980, Archiv IBA, Folder A8 SO/30, AdK. **48** Yalçın Çetin, interview by the author, September 8, 2012, Berlin, in Turkish. Both audio and video recordings of this interview are in the author's collection. **49** Minutes of the meetings on November 3 and 4, 1980, Archiv IBA, Folder A8 SO/30, AdK. **50** Archiv IBA, Folder A15 SO/52–57, AdK. **51** Çetin, interview by the author, Tape 1, 00: 39:16–00:43:09, 01:15:31. **52** Mota, "Critique." **53** Brigitte Fleck, *Álvaro Siza: Architecture Collection* (London: E. and F.N. Spon, 1995), 85. **54** Yüksel Karaçizmeli, interview by the author, July, 2012, Berlin, in Turkish, 00:01:30–00:02:18, 00:09:00–00:1014. Audio recordings of this interview are in the author's collection. The author had held another interview in the summer of 2009. **55** Ibid., 00:03:03–00:04:43. **56** Baden-Württemberg Ministry of Social Services, "Toilet Decree for Foreigners," trans. Tes Howell, in *Germany in Transit*, 341–42. **57** Emine Sevgi Özdamar, *Mother Tongue*, trans. Craig Thomas (Toronto: Coach House Press, 1994), 81. For an analysis of this text, see: Kader Konuk, *Identitäten im Prozeß: Literatur von Autorinnen aus und in der Türkei in deutscher, englischer und türkischer Sprache* (Essen: Verlag Die Blaue Eule, 2001): 83–123. **58** See, for instance, Esra Erdem, "Migrant Women and Economic Justice: A Class Analysis of Anatolian-German Women in Homemaking and Cleaning Services Work on Female Migrant Workers," PhD diss., University of Massachusetts, 2008. **59** Özdamar, *Mother Tongue*, 135 (translation slightly altered). **60** Erdem, "Migrant Women and Economic Justice." **61** Karaçizmeli, interview by the author, 00:14:00–00:16:00. **62** Ibid., 00:23:50–00:26:31. **63** Ibid., 00:18:20–00:23:30. **64** Ibid., 00:29:00–00:31:07. **65** Ibid., 00:26:00–00:27:35. **66** Ibid., 00:42:00–00:43:35. **67** Ibid., 02:47:00–02:49:09. **68** Ibid., 02:38:17–02:40:20. **69** Ibid., 00:51:00–00:52.20. **70** Ibid., 01:05:00–01:06:20. **71** Ibid., 01:35:00–01:38:00. **72** Ibid., 00:30:00–00:32:24, 01:26:31–01:29:45, 01:31:14–01:32:45. **73** Ibid., 01:30:00–01:30:45. **74** Ibid., 01:54:02–01:56:59. **75** Ibid., 01:14:30–01:16:20. **76** Ibid., 00:37:00–00:38:46. **77** Ibid., 01:59:27. **78** Ibid., 01:59:30–02:01:31. **79** Ibid., 00:34:00–00:37:00. **80** Ibid., 00:30:00–00:34:54. **81** Ibid., 00:55:00–01:03:34. **82** Otto Preminger, dir., *Bonjour Tristesse* (Los Angeles, CA: Columbia Pictures, 1958). **83** "Álvaro Siza: 'Bonjour Tristesse' Apartment Building, Berlin," accessed April 15, 2017, http://www.youtube.com/watch?v=noNDkNbV3IA. **84** Karaçizmeli, interview by the author, 01:11:00–01:12:20.

STROLL 5

From Schlesisches Tor to Fraenkelufer

Leaving the senior citizens' club designed by Álvaro Siza in Block 121, let's continue our stroll in the SO36 district of Kreuzberg. If one walked further south on Falckensteinstrasse, one would immediately pass Block 133 on the left, where the legendary Kerngehäuse of the squatter movement was located. Once home to the production of Germany's most famous sewing machines, the Cuvrystrasse factory was owned by the F. W. Müller Company between 1893 and 1977, and after was occupied by a group of young squatters who struggled with the local council to prevent the brown brick buildings from being pulled down (Figure 5.1).[1] During the IBA years, the squatting movement continued to be active, and the IBA team and squatters eventually collaborated on the renovation of the Kerngehäuse through self-help. Wulf Eichstädt, IBA Altbau's coordinator for the SO36 district, identified this initiative as "the pioneer of the movement."[2] Many tenant consultants and members of the Altbau team also credit the squatting movement with protecting the existing buildings from destruction by occupying them, organizing political protests, and appearing in public spaces to gain citizens' support. Carla MacDougall analyzes the complex relationship between squatters and immigrants from Turkey in Kreuzberg during those years, discussing publications and incidents that expose how the squatters ironically maintained the same racialization toward the noncitizens as the conservative politicians and media (stop IV).[3] Nonetheless, in Hans Günter Kleff's words, despite many tensions, "without the squatters, IBA would not have had this much power."[4]

The buildings in this area are now the canvas of Kreuzberg's world-famous graffiti artists (stop V, Figure 5.2) and home to a multicultural population whose members live in buildings renovated by IBA Altbau. One resident, Kadir Ercan, worked as a tenant consultant in the SO36 district during the IBA years, in addition to being responsible for Blocks 90 and 94, as part of the Altbau team. He had arrived in Germany from Turkey in 1979 and decided to stay because of the coup d'état of 1980. The tenant consultants of SO36 were employed by the city, and they mediated between owners, tenants, IBA representatives, and architects. Ercan was skeptical at first that a governmental institution would safeguard tenants' rights—as were the tenants who were so afraid of being evicted that they often said in meetings that they had no complaints about their apartments even when they were speaking in a living room whose ceilings leaked and whose wallpaper was coming off the walls.[5] Tenant consultancy was a new job created during these years specifically for Kreuzberg's urban renewal (stop IV). Ercan recalls how hard it was to explain his career to friends in Turkey or Germany. He soon gained tenants' trust—including those from Turkey, whose language he spoke—and he remembers that the labor-intensive process for renovating one apartment from start to finish took about one and a half years. Rather than using plan drawings, he usually communicated with the tenants in the space in question about their desired changes and room arrangements. As noted above, it was mostly men who represented the family in participatory tenant meetings, and he admits that it took extra effort to hear the requests of noncitizen women—who were usually more concerned about kitchens than their husbands were.[6] Overall, he describes IBA as a near-perfect institution that fulfilled every single tenant request that was technically possible, and Hardt-Waltherr Hämer as an extremely valuable and principled person, whose open mind allowed him to resolve conflicts in long meetings.[7] Ercan believes that urban renewal of this kind was possible only thanks to the social welfare state and citizens who demanded their rights, including tenants and squatters. He admits that the residents who had immigrated from Turkey did not participate as much as other residents, since they were not citizens and the German society did not make them feel like insiders at that time.[8]

If one continued along Falckensteinstrasse (Figure 5.3), crossed the Görlitzer Park (Figure 5.4), and walked all the way to the river, one would reach the blocks along Paul-Lincke-Ufer. Turning right at the canal, one would walk along the four urban blocks intersected by Glogauer, Liegnitzer, Forster, Ohlauer, and Lausitzer Strasse, whose renewal was overseen by Bahri Düleç, an architect on the IBA Altbau team. Having arrived in Germany from Turkey with his parents as a teenager, Düleç joined IBA soon after he graduated as an architect from the Technical University of Berlin in 1980, and he worked for twenty years for IBA's successor, STERN (*Gesellschaft der behutsamen Stadterneuerung mbH*, Society of Gentle Urban Renewal). His diploma project on the analysis of pop-up culturally specific buildings in Berlin and the design of a public bath in the Schlesisches Tor area attracted the attention of Hämer, who invited him to extend his research. As a result, in 1981 Düleç prepared a 132-page report commissioned by IBA.[9] In this report, he wrote an overview of the state polices related to the "integration of foreign employees and their families" (*Eingliederung der ausländischen Arbeitnehmer und ihrer Familien*), especially in Berlin since 1972, and existing buildings used for "social infrastructure" (*Soziale Infrastruktur*)—a broad term used at the time to refer to cultural, educational, leisure, and social networking activities.[10] He gave examples of a few initiatives and buildings of this kind, such as institutions that offered language courses, youth activities, and consultancy in Hamburg, Darmstadt, Frankfurt, and Cologne.[11] He also reported on the Berlin Senate's initiatives related to Turkish- and Kurdish-speaking migrants[12] and the missions and institutional and financial structures of existing nongovernmental organizations in Kreuzberg, including tenant solidarity associations such as Otur ve Yaşa (reside and live), SO36, Dresdener Strasse *Mieterladen* (Dresdener street tenant agency), self-help networks, and political and cultural associations that usually espoused Social Democratic positions such as "Progressive Volkseinheit der Türkei" (progressive national unity of Turkey), "Türkenzentrum" (Turkish centrum), "Verein der Arbeiter-Jugend der Türkei" (association of working youth of Turkey), and "Halkevi e.V." (people's houses).[13] Rather than only blaming noncitizens for failing to integrate, Düleç pointed out the discriminatory practices in Germany and referred to the work of Frantz Fanon—an author often called the "lawyer of the oppressed" during those times.[14] Düleç suggested that the city increases the number of sociocultural institutions for enhancing noncitizens' confidence, which he diagnosed as the major obstacle to their empowerment, just as Fanon did in the colonial city. Düleç proposed that noncitizens be allowed to vote in local elections and that structures such as fountains in urban squares and neighborhood parks in courtyards

Figure 5.2 a–d Graffiti in the SO36 district of Kreuzberg, photographed by Esra Akcan, 2009–2016.

Figure 5.2 e–f Graffiti in the SO36 district of Kreuzberg, photographed by Esra Akcan, 2009–2016.

be built for social gatherings.[15] Years later, he summarized the main thesis of the report as demonstrating the need for governmental regulations to support the growth of culturally specific "infrastructure" buildings for a more sensitive and gentler (*duyarlı*) immigration policy.[16]

In the four urban blocks for which he was responsible, Düleç oversaw the construction of a new kindergarten designed by the London-based architects Robert Maguire and Keith Murray (Figure 5.5), the renovation of a big school building, and participatory renovation on a unit-by-unit basis that involved the meticulous coordination between landlords, tenants, architects, tenant advisors, Senate representatives, developers, and constructors. He identifies the weekly participatory public meetings at the District Committee (*Stadtteilausschuss*) that was established as a result of the "Strategies for Kreuzberg Competition" and continued through the IBA years as one of the major institutional contributions to the participatory process.[17] After long meetings in such hearings, he oversaw the pedestrianization of the Paul-Lincke-Ufer for the length of two blocks along the river, a rare accomplishment given that the rest is open to vehicular transportation, which still functions as one the liveliest public parks (Figure 5.6).[18] Another unique situation that took place in Block 145 was the occupation of two buildings (Forster Strasse 16 and 17) by squatters who included Turkish refugees seeking political asylum (Figure 5.7). Many witnesses confirm that German squatters and noncitizens in Kreuzberg during these years coexisted but had little dialogue. The situation on Forster Strasse was different. Seven families from Turkey squatted in the building in November 1980, an event that was reported in daily newspapers and caused diplomatic tension when the Turkish ambassador called on the residents to stop squatting.[19] Düleç supported the self-help renovation of the squatted units in these buildings. Even though many guest workers did not get involved in self-help projects or participatory meetings about shared and public spaces in other parts of IBA, Düleç mentions that the political refugees and "intellectual" migrants attended the hearings concerning these urban blocks.[20] I talked to a couple of former squatters from Turkey, who confirmed and told me that they had participated in the self-help renovation of the buildings and eventually received asylum with the help of German fellow squatters who collected signatures on petitions supporting their case.[21]

Düleç also presented the IBA experience in Turkey. Invited to Istanbul by the Goethe Institute in 1984, he joined Hämer and Yavuz Üçer for a conference, where he sensed an initial disappointment in the audience, whose members evidently had expected to see extravagant projects and asked utopian questions about the future of cities in the twenty-first century. Hämer, "a down-to-earth man," responded with real-life anecdotes and metaphors, "showing the importance of finding concrete solutions to the concrete problems of the present."[22] When Düleç lectured in Ankara at the invitation of the city's Chamber of Architects, Murat Karayalçın, the head of municipality, attended the lecture to get ideas for his own urban renewal initiative in the Ankara Citadel. Comparing other urban renewal projects around the world to Kreuzberg, Düleç emphasizes the unique conditions of Berlin at the time: it was receiving unprecedented financial support from the rest of West Germany, which allowed IBA to resist the pressures from real estate developers that determine the results in almost any other case. This makes IBA unique, impossible to repeat anywhere else in the world, according to Düleç—not even in Berlin after the wall came down, as he saw when he worked on the urban renewal of Prenzlauer Berg under IBA's successor, STERN.[23]

If one left Düleç's urban blocks and walked to Reichenberger Strasse, one would immediately come across Block 109, where another legendary squatted building, Regenbogenfabrik, is situated at Lausitzerstrasse. The subject of many newspaper articles and photographs, the building received its legal status during IBA years. If one continued walking west on Reichenberger Strasse among the grocery stores and bakeries (Figure 5.8), one would come across a new L-shaped building on the corner of Mariannenstrasse. Designed by Wilhelm Holzbauer and the office of Rave and Rave, this is a typical IBA Neubau building defining a large triangular garden at the back and maintaining the continuity of the street in the front with its brick and stucco façade, carved-in balconies at the corner, stepped-back terraces punctuated with satellite dishes, and rhythmically placed common entrances marked with exterior stairs and surface textures designed using colored bricks (Figure 5.9). Turning left and walking along this building on Mariannenstrasse, one would reach the river again, and the relatively wealthier apartments facing the water (Figure 5.10). One could see at a distance Admiralstrasse 16, another self-help project with twelve apartments developed under IBA Altbau, and memorable for its affordable timber-framed balconies attached onto the reinforced-concrete structure.[24] Finally, one would reach the three separate parts of Hinrich and Inken Baller's building compound. There are two small parts on the street front, facing the river and acting as gates to the peaceful Hof-garden at the back (Figure 5.11 a–c), where the third bigger part is also situated (Figure 5.11 d–e). Elevated above the ground to allow space for entrance gates and garages, and featuring the Ballers' signature angular balconies and roofscape, the building compound has made a mark in Altbau's history as a new building. (Siza had also submitted a design for this site.) Leaving the Ballers' environment, one would complete the loop by returning to the Kottbusser Tor station where our Altbau strolls started.

1 Hannes Kowatsch, Manfred Koym, and Rita Koym, *F. W. Müller's Toy Sewing Machines and the "Kerngehäuse"* (Berlin: Kreuzberg Historical Research Society and Kerngehäuse Craft Center, 2000). 2 Wulf Eichstädt, "Selbstorganisierte Stadterneuerung im Kerngehäuse 1980–2000," ibid., 95–96. 3 Carla Elizabeth MacDougall, "Cold War Capital: Contested Urbanity in West Berlin, 1963–1989," PhD diss., Rutgers University, 2011. 4 Hans Günter Kleff, interview by the author, June 27, 2012, Berlin, in Turkish and English, 01:09:22. Both audio and video recordings of this interview are in the author's collection. 5 Kadir Ercan, interview by the author, August 2, 2012, Berlin, in Turkish, 00:09:41–00:10:17. Both audio and video recordings of this interview are in the author's collection. 6 Ibid., 00:24:18–00:26:19. 7 Ibid., 00:12:12, 00:17:06. 8 Ibid., 00:35:57–00:37:00. 9 Bahri Düleç, "Immigrantenspezifische soziale Infrastruktureinrichtungen in Stadtteilen mit hohem Ausländeranteil," Report prepared for IBA, Berlin, May 1981. IBA B92/092, Landesarchiv. 10 Ibid., 1 and 7. 11 Ibid., 37–93. 12 Ibid., 94–00. 13 Ibid., 101–32. For recent scholarly work on immigrant associations, see Gökçe Yurdakul, *From Guest Workers into Muslims: The Transformation of Turkish Immigrant Associations in Germany* (Newcastle, UK: Cambridge Scholars Publishing, 2009). 14 Düleç, "Immigrantenspezifische soziale Infrastruktenunrichtungen in Stadteilen mit hohem Ausländeranteil," 28–33. See also Bahri Düleç interview by the author, July 5, 2012, Berlin, in Turkish, 01:44:00. Both audio and video recordings of this interview are in the author's collection. 15 Düleç, interview by the author, 00:06:20–00:09:30. 16 Ibid., 00:15:40. 17 Ibid., 00:50:02–00:60:00. 18 Ibid., 00:38:50–00:40:30. 19 "Türkler bir ev işgal ettiler," *Hürriyet D*, November 21, 1980; "Başkonsolos N. Aktan/Yurttaşlarımız ev işgaline katılmasınlar," *Gazete Merhaba*, March 6, 1981; Hans Günter Kleff, *Vom Bauern zum Industriearbeiter: Zur kollektiven Lebensgeschichte der Arbeitsmigranten aus der Türkei* (Mainz, Germany: Verlag Manfred Werkmeister, 1984), 179. 20 Düleç, interview by the author, 00:42:11–00:43:37. 21 At their request, I did not have a recorded interview with them. 22 Düleç, interview by the author, 01:28:00–01:35:01. 23 Ibid., 01:36:30–01:37:52, 01:44:38–01:46:55. 24 Gernot and Johanne Nalbach, *Berlin Modern Architecture: Exhibition Catalogue* (Berlin: STERN, 1989), 137.

Part 3
Open Architecture as Multiplicity

STOP VI

Open History in the Past Subjunctive Tense

The History of Possibility

Historiography in general and architectural historiography in particular concern themselves with the history of actuality. In other words, they seek to explain events as they have actually happened. Unbuilt projects have not changed this rule, despite their ubiquity in history books, since they have usually been discussed for the sake of their actual presence, rather than the absence that they create after being designed. Unbuilt projects are of course part of actuality, as projects, but they also open up a new category that has remained undertheorized. I would like to call this category the history of possibility. This history includes but is not necessarily synonymous with the history of utopia and the history of paper architecture. For the sake of giving each different practice its due attention, let me suggest a distinction between the actual, the possible, and the deliberately impossible in architecture.[1] All projects of deliberate impossibility may one day become possible, and all possible projects may one day become actual. Nevertheless, coming to terms with these diverging histories as identifiable entities would not only let us understand their distinctive features but might also reveal something operating in history as it actually happened.

What are terms of speech to understand the buildable but unbuilt projects, not as projects per se but as unfulfilled capacities or as unfinished, open histories? How can we talk about not only the presence but also the absence they created? Would it matter to suspend our justifiable curiosity about what happened, and instead try to look at what did not happen? And would doing so tell us something we did not know about what actually happened? What are the ways of theorizing possibility in architecture, as a distinct category that is set apart from actuality, how does that theorization inform an open history of architecture, and where would that fit within the larger concept of conjectural history?

The influence of the Hegelian understanding of history may have kept us from wanting to write this open history. The disjunctions and connections between possibility and actuality have been sporadically visited in philosophy, and the concept of possibility in particular has become a topic of modal logic (the branch of logic that deals with modalities such as can, could, may, must, and might). Usually, possibility refers to a capacity, and actuality refers to its fulfillment. If something is possible, it is not (yet) actual; and if it is actual, it is no longer defined as possible. It was Georg Wilhelm Friedrich Hegel in his book *Science of Logic* who defined the relationship between possibility (*Möglichkeit*) and actuality as a logical system that not only implied a theory of history, but also put a strict limit on the set of what is possible.[2] Hegel defines actuality as "reflected absoluteness" (carrying the weight of the Hegelian term "the absolute"), as the "unity of essence and existence,"[3] and thus the "real world" that is moving toward the absolute goal.**4** Conversely, Hegel defines possibility as that which has the capacity to pass over into actuality and will eventually do so. For Hegel, the true nature of possibility is confirmed only by its actualization. In other words, the only way to determine whether a possibility is a true possibility or a vain presumption is the actualized external reality, whether it has already happened or will eventually happen, and that reality is unavoidably consistent and rational. Therefore, the limits of possibility are determined by Hegel's premise of the rationality of the actual. To put this in Slavoj Žižek's words, "The actual is rational. … The Hegelian philosopher's trust in the inherent rationality of the actual means that actuality provides the only testing ground for the reasonableness of the subject's claims."**5** That is, the test of possibility is actuality itself, which makes possibility a much narrower category than it might appear at first sight in the Hegelian system. Actuality, by virtue of its rationality, already infers the true set of possibility.

Necessity (*Notwendigkeit*) and contingency (*Zufälligkeit*) are two concepts (or modalities) that determine whether or not a possibility will pass over to actuality. As common sense tells us, "Something actual is necessary insofar as its contrary is not possible; it is contingent insofar as its contrary is also possible (insofar as things could have turned [out] otherwise)."**6** Contingency implies the dependence on a condition that will determine the absence or presence of an event or phenomenon. While different interpretations exist, contingency has quite a problematic status in the Hegelian system, due to the all-encompassing role of necessity. Hegel says: "What is necessary cannot be otherwise, but what is simply possible can. … Therefore what is really possible can no longer be otherwise; under the particular conditions and circumstances something else cannot follow. Real possibility and necessity are therefore only *seemingly* different; this is an identity which does not have to *become* but is already *presupposed* and lies at their base."**7** Accordingly, real possibility and actuality are intertwined by virtue of necessity, and necessity itself determines what could not have been otherwise. In other words, necessity determines what will always turn into actuality; it determines the process of actuality—i.e., history. Thus, for the Hegelian, necessity determines history. Real possibility is possibility proper, which will sooner or later be actualized; it already possesses a certain actuality; this "not yet" is actually "already there." But mere possibility in the Hegelian sense is the possibility that will not pass over to actuality. Mere possibility, defined as the abstract opposite of actuality, turns out to be nothing but impossibility. In the Hegelian framework, human minds must have difficulty in distinguishing real possibility from mere possibility, an enigma that is resolved with certainty only after real possibility turns into actuality and mere possibility disappears.

According to the theory of history that is implied in this unity between real possibility and actuality, open history is an irrelevant occupation. For a Hegelian, history—or the process of actuality—happens when a possibility is translated into actuality. In that process a new form of things arise, but it is new only to the human eye that a while ago could not recognize the real possibility within the larger set of mere possibilities or vain presumptions. This new actuality, in the Hegelian system, is not a disruption of the former actuality, but simply a better manifestation of its essence. Hegel often calls necessity blind—not because it is not rational, but because its end, or telos, is not visible to the fallible human eye.**8** It follows that, for a Hegelian, writing history does not involve the justification of blind fatalism; but it is nevertheless the understanding of the necessity behind every event. In retrospect, the historian comprehends the necessity of actuality and real possibility. The task of the historian-philosopher is to disclose the chain of events that causes every incident, and to uncover the laws governing the meaningful succession of events. But what, then, is writing history for the non-Hegelian who is suspicious of such a deterministic nature of necessity, and of the rationality of causality? Aren't we trapping ourselves in a Hegelian frame of mind when we are interested only in the history of actuality? One can talk about the possibility of history according to Hegel—which is, as a matter of fact, one of his contributions to the realm of ideas—and one could also reveal the possibility in history that has already or will very soon become actuality, but the idea of a history of possibility is an oxymoron in the Hegelian framework. The history of possibility asks what would have happened if things had turned out otherwise, but such a question is rendered impossible in the Hegelian system by the determinacy of necessity. What, then, is writing history for the author who recognizes that the concept of historical necessity is supported only by an unjustifiable leap of faith in the Hegelian logic? What is writing history for the author who does not think that the historian's task is to uncover the irrefutable and necessary link in the chain of events? What are the topics of the historian who does not define necessity as the only real possibility that will forever and a day turn into actuality? What are the terms for a history of possibility, defined as the history of events that could very well have unfolded otherwise? If it existed, this history of possibility would have been written in the past subjunctive tense.

Rem Koolhaas's Berlin and OMA's Checkpoint Charlie

For stop VI, we return to Checkpoint Charlie (where we had already been at stop II) to discuss IBA's prestigious "Kochstrasse/Friedrichstrasse Competition." Two projects for this competition that were not selected for construction present themselves to be written into a history of possibility (Figure VI.1). Of the twenty-four architects who were invited to submit designs, Rem Koolhaas and his team seemed the least eager to win by following the rules.[9] Koolhaas's competition report reads like a manifesto against the critical reconstruction endorsed by Josef Paul Kleihues:

> Since the recent *rediscovery* of the street as the core element of all urbanism, the simplest *solution* to this complex and ambiguous condition would be to undo the "mistakes" of the fifties and sixties and to build again along the plotlines, as a sign of a regained historical consciousness.
> This approach would restore the Grid, respectfully connect new buildings with the old, and try as much as possible to hide most of the postwar buildings, attempting to make harmless the mistaken ideologies of the past decades.
> But at this juncture, it is important to resist this temptation.[10]

Predictably, the competition jury did not agree. In its evaluation report on Koolhaas's project, the jury declared that it appreciated the "artistic aims, radically pragmatic approach and the quality of the drawings" but rejected the proposal for its failure to "restore the historical state with perimeter building[s] enclosing the blocks and creating the street."[11] This reason for refusal was yet another example of IBA's insistence

Figure VI.1 View of Rem Koolhaas/OMA's (left) and Peter Eisenman's (front right) buildings at Checkpoint Charlie for IBA-1984/87, photographed by Esra Akcan, Berlin, 2016.

on the perimeter block and the street as the so-called gene of the city that had to be reconstructed at all costs.

In fact, Koolhaas had performed an act of subversion that preemptively embraced rejection as a strategy to remain outside the establishment. His project extended well beyond the actual competition site and covered areas that were located in both East and West Berlin. If his project had been actualized, Friedrichstrasse would have turned into a Salon des Refusés all the way from north to south in between the two water canals. In his drawing "From Friedrichstrasse Station to Mehringplatz," the architect collaged previously rejected architectural proposals for East and West Berlin into his design (Figure VI.2). If Koolhaas's competition project had been actualized, Mies van der Rohe's now canonic glass skyscraper on Friedrichstrasse would have been constructed as a reminder that Mies had imagined transparent towers in Berlin long before he actually built them in Chicago. If Koolhaas's competition project had been actualized, Ludwig Hilberseimer's *Großstadt* (big city/metropolis) would have been inserted into Berlin's fabric along Friedrichstrasse as eighteen perfectly parallel rectangular prisms with noncompromisingly identical features. The Gendarmenmarkt would have been reconstructed. This competition drawing was a visual history of possibility itself, imagining Berlin in the past subjunctive sense. It was also a biting comment on IBA's obsession with reconstructing Berlin's nineteenth-century architectural fabric while dismissing its masterful twentieth-century projects. Behind IBA's commitment to criticizing the modernist tabula rasa dictum and respecting history, there was

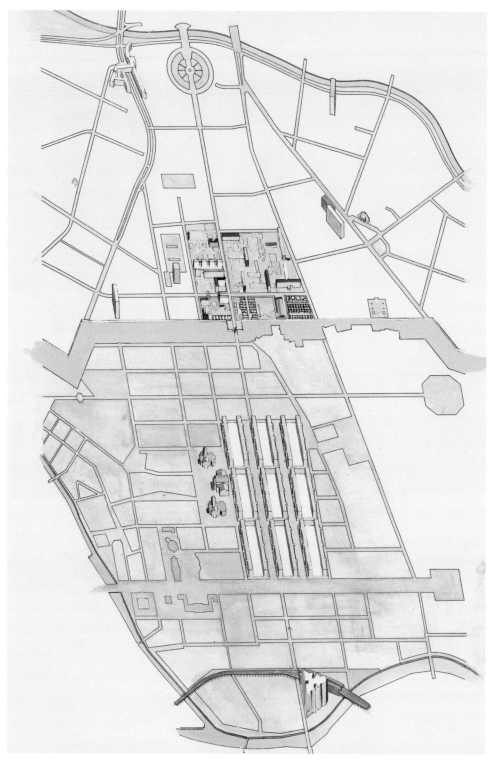

Figure VI.2 Rem Koolhaas, "From Friedrichstrasse Station to Mehringplatz" drawing for "Kochstrasse/Friedrichstrasse Competition," IBA-1984/87, Berlin.

Figure VI.3 Rem Koolhaas and Elia Zenghelis, Project for Roosevelt Island, New York City, 1975.

indeed a contradiction: the recent part of this history was hidden from sight, both conceptually and literally, by constructing new structures in front of postwar buildings to block them from public view.

Inserting unrealized projects into new proposals was a frequent design strategy in Koolhaas's circle at this time. Following his competition project for Roosevelt Island in New York City, a year earlier in 1975 (Figure VI.3), in the new project Koolhaas had proposed making a collage of rejected projects in Manhattan's history, like a visual provocation against the perception of Roosevelt Island as a calm escape from the chaotic metropolis. If this project had been selected, Roosevelt Island would have housed Kazimir Malevich's suprematist Architekton, a harbor that would have accepted the floating structures of Norman Bel Geddes, and a counter United Nations building would have been placed just across the river from the real building in Manhattan. Roosevelt Island would have become a refuge for the abandoned and the rejected projects in architectural history. It would have become a visual history of possibility.

To give another relevant example, of all the projects imagined for Berlin leading up to IBA-1984/87, none was as removed from actuality as "The City in the City: Berlin: A Green Archipelago" of 1977, discussed in stop III in the context of the career of its official author, Oswald Mathias Ungers. Florian Hertweck and Sébastien Marot have recently discovered that Koolhaas contributed to this project more than had been previously acknowledged: he wrote the initial draft of the text, probably in London—a draft that was edited by both him and Ungers during the Cornell summer studios in

Berlin, distributed during the end-of-term student exhibition, and eventually rewritten by Ungers to be presented to the Berlin authorities for the future building exhibition that eventually became IBA- 1984/87.[12] Koolhaas, a former student and employee of Ungers, was joined for the subsequent versions by two teaching assistants at Cornell University, Hans Kollhoff and Arthur Ovaska, and by Peter Riemann (who did the drawings under Ungers's supervision). The project was therefore the result of a rare collaboration and thus exemplifies latent open architecture as a process in which architects welcomed other points of view into their design process (Figure III.8, III.9).

Many of the ideas in the Archipelago project were already present in Koolhaas's version, then titled "Berlin: A Green Archipelago"—most notably the collage of unbuilt structures. As discussed in stop III, this project was based on the false assumption that Berlin was shrinking and did not need any new housing units, which justified the thinning-out process as opposed to urban renewal. In an interview that he gave between the first and second launch of IBA-1984/87 exhibitions, Koolhaas compared urban renewal programs to the futile attempt of trying to keep the brain-dead patient artificially alive.[13] In the draft version of the Archipelago project, he wrote: "Urban repair assumes an inexhaustible demand on each urban location for ever more housing, ever more shops, ever more social facilities. But such assumptions overlook the fact that these areas may be in disrepair exactly because such a pressure does not exist."[14] However, in this quotation Koolhaas overlooks the thousands of applications at the Berlin Housing Office, the guest workers' living conditions, and West Germany's investments in Berlin to keep the population from dropping. For this reason, it is more appropriate to treat this draft as a thought experiment based on the possibility that authorities and residents would abandon Berlin to shrinking (which did not happen).

If Koolhaas's draft version had been fleshed out and actualized, Berlin would have turned into "an archipelago of architecture in a green lagoon of natures." Only the best parts "that deserve to be preserved and reinforced" would have remained, and the rest of the urban fabric would have phased out into nature "so that the history of architecture would [have] coincide[d] with the history of ideas once more."[15] If this draft version had been actualized, a series of social condensers, in the Russian Constructivists' sense, would have been inserted into the islands of architecture to make up for the public functions that might have been lost in the thinning-out process. If history had unfolded according to Koolhaas's version, the unbuilt projects collaged into Berlin would have included the iconic structures of the Russian and German avant-garde. Ivan Leonidov's Moscow Palace of Culture and proposal for the town of Magnitogorsk would have been inserted into Kreuzberg; Mies's rectangular skyscrapers would have been constructed at the end of Müllerstrasse, as edited by Ungers; and Bruno Taut's dome would have been added as a roof over the Olympic Stadium to "correct important omissions" in Berlin's history.[16] Many of these projects would have been stripped of the intellectual and ethico-political ideas that had produced them and which they represented, but they would have been selected for their formal merits. They would have been mixed and matched regardless of their creators' ideology. For instance, the dome designed by Taut, an architect who fled from Germany due to the rise of National Socialism, would have been collaged as a roof over the Olympic Stadium of the Hitler era. Rather than a lack of political commitment, Koolhaas must have thought that this depoliticization would have brought a repoliticization, a new reshuffling of the city parts into separate enclaves of different positions. According to his draft, "the differentiation of the islands should not be only of an architectural nature. Social and political differences should be superimposed on the system of islands, so that the units function also socially as identifiable enclaves."[17]

Berlin Archipelago in Koolhaas's vision would thus have been composed of minicities or social enclaves with multiple ideologies, whose histories would have been in the process of unfolding concurrently. Such coexistence would have been quite similar to that in "The City of the Captive Globe" (1972) drawing, which visualized Koolhaas's argument in *Delirious New York*—a history book with a retroactive manifesto that had started as a thesis at Cornell University (Figure VI.4).[18] Despite his diametrically opposed predictions about the urban density and future growth of the two cities, Koolhaas's Berlin and New York would both have been composed of multiple islands of intellects. The drawings "From Friedrichstrasse Station to Mehringplatz" for Berlin and the "City of the Captive Globe" for New York were both visual histories of possibilities in the making. The latter was a tribute to Manhattan—"the archetype of the metropolitan condition," in Koolhaas's words—filled with skyscrapers on a grid, each devoted to the development of a different theory and mental construction, and each mounting to the sky or collapsing in synchrony with the rise and fall of the philosophical school it lodged. The most fascinating thing about a New York skyscraper, in Koolhaas's view, was that this building type made possible not only the metropolitan density and culture of congestion, but also the coexistence of multiple realities and private activities

Figure VI.4 Rem Koolhaas, "The City of the Captive Globe," 1972.

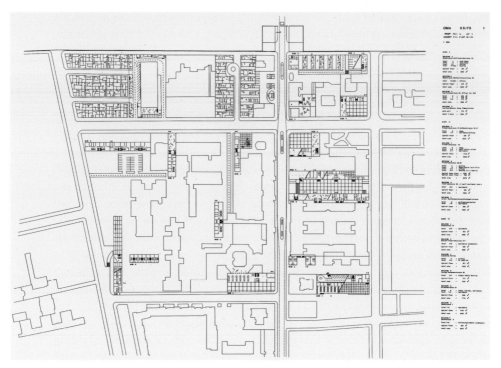

Figure VI.5 Rem Koolhaas, "Kochstrasse/Friedrichstrasse Competition" project for Block 4, IBA-1984/87, Berlin. Plan.

unfolding simultaneously on top of each other, without being burdened by a demand for unity, sameness, or homogeneity. Welcoming all intellectual pursuits, the "City of the Captive Globe" drawing was the visualization of a possible city for an open society.

The collage as a translation of the idea of open society into architecture and urbanism was theorized most comprehensively by Colin Rowe, a professor at Cornell University at the same time as Koolhaas. I find the idea that the personal frictions between the two reflected the much-discussed Cornell faculty's bipolarity between Ungers (with Koolhaas on his side) and Rowe too exaggerated, when their ideas (rather than personal chemistry) are seen from the perspective of history. I will therefore not over-entertain this dispute.[19] Even though their selection of found objects and aesthetic preferences were very different from those of Koolhaas, in their book *Collage City*, Colin Rowe and Fred Koetter had also offered a visualization of the philosopher Karl Popper's idea of open society.[20] Famously making a distinction between the hedgehog and the fox, à la Isaah Berlin—the hedgehog aspiring to find a unitary, totalizing idea, the fox absorbing multiple ideas—Rowe and Koetter offered their theory of an "ideally open and democratic society."[21] The way to achieve this in a city was to collage together what the authors referred to as stimulants: memorable streets, public terraces, composite buildings, urban gardens, and so on. The collage was the medium for the "city of collusive intentions," but as a necessarily decontextualizing and dehistoricizing medium, the collage also stripped all architectural forms of their ideologies and political associations. Any depoliticization is a repoliticization (putting forms in another context with different values and agendas), and Rowe and Koetter embraced irony as

Figure VI.6: Rem Koolhaas, "Kochstrasse/Friedrichstrasse Competition" project for Block 4, IBA-1984/87, Berlin. Axonometric.

a prerequisite of collage. The collage was the medium for enjoying utopian and traditional forms without the "political embarrassment, ... because collage is a method deriving its virtue from its irony, because it seems to be a technique for using things and simultaneously disbelieving them."[22] The collage floated perilously between tactical thinking for the sake of the ethico-political ideal of an open society and cynicism as value-free reactionism.

These differences in the dictionary of architectural references notwithstanding, there was a growing feeling at the end of the 1970s and beginning of the 1980s against unity and totality and in favor of plurality and multiplicity. In other words, inserting previously abandoned and rejected projects into his drawing "From Friedrichstrasse Station to Mehringplatz," submitted to IBA's "Kochstrasse/Friedrichstrasse Competition," was Koolhaas's way of calling for an open society that would secure the coexistence of multiple socialities. To him, this was a vision diametrically opposed to the one that sought unity through the critical reconstruction of the perimeter block.

For the actual area of this competition, Koolhaas suggested different approaches for each of the four blocks in this competition[23]—and none of them was a perimeter block (Figure VI.5, VI.6). For Block 10 (Aldo Rossi's design for this won; see stop 2), Koolhaas offered rectangular, freestanding buildings that were set apart and placed parallel or perpendicular to each other, but he did so not necessarily to create identifiable urban

spaces such as streets or piazzas. This strategy must have been perceived as too similar to the postwar housing schemes that this IBA was determined to put a stop to. For
Blocks 5 and 11 (office of Eisenman and Robertson's design for the former and Reichlin
and Reinhart's design for the latter won), he left the corners empty and fragmented the
block areas—other approaches that the IBA Neubau team clearly disliked.

For Block 4, where he had actually been invited to compete (the design of the office of
Bohigas, Mackay, and Martorell won; see stop II), Koolhaas suggested a low-density,
one- or two-story urban fabric. He justified this choice as a contextual gesture to respond to the height of the Berlin Wall. The wall had already inspired Koolhaas during
his student days at the Architectural Association in London (AA), when he conducted
a field trip in 1971 to design "Berlin Wall as Architecture." Noting the irony in the fact
that the open, free side of Berlin was encircled by the wall like an enclave in East Berlin, Koolhaas made a case for the power of architecture. Remembering it in 1993, he
wrote: "Were not division, enclosure (i.e., imprisonment) and exclusion—which defined the wall's performance and explained its efficiency—the essential strategies of
any architecture? In comparison, the sixties dream of architecture's liberating potential…seemed feeble rhetorical play."[24] While this quotation that implied criticisms of
his teachers at the AA and the architecture of the 1960s might strike the reader as a
contradiction when seen from the perspective of Koolhaas's later ideas, it is nonetheless possible to see in it the hints of the young student's turning into an architect
who would build countless buildings for established clients and states after making
a name for himself as a thinker against authority and against the establishment. In
his competition report for the "Kochstrasse/Friedrichstrasse Competition," Koolhaas
speculated that if the Berlin Wall were pulled down and the city reunified, the section
of the city previously known as West Berlin would be surrounded by a green belt, due
to the fact that the buildings on the green line in East Berlin had already been removed.
The study sketches that cover the area between the wall and Mehringplatz imply that
the urban fabric proposed for Block 4 could be extended to create a long buffer zone
along the wall (Figure VI.7).

If Koolhaas's project had been actualized, the Berlin Wall would have had a suprematist neighbor. The hand-drawn sketches prepared for the competition reveal that the
team members referred to their project for Block 4 as a "Suprematist [Pompei?]," even
though it is hard to determine precisely which aspects of suprematism appealed to the
team at this point.[25] Koolhaas roughly divided the narrow block into five fragments
longitudinally. If this design had been selected and built, the first fragment on the
western end would have been composed of three sets of low-rise high-density buildings that created two new streets running perpendicular to Wilhelmstrasse. Fifty-six
units on same-size plots, some of them being larger units extending to second floors,
would have been placed in a web of courtyards, inner pathways and Lego-like volumes.
Looking at the cut-through axonometric drawing of this ensemble, one feels as if one
has entered a universe of abstract geometric shapes, detached surfaces, and diagonal
vectors (Figure VI.8). Inside, units would have contained freestanding curved or linear surfaces giving directions in space but not encircling rooms, freestanding stairs,
and vertical shafts (Figure VI.9). The study sketches imply that the team designed

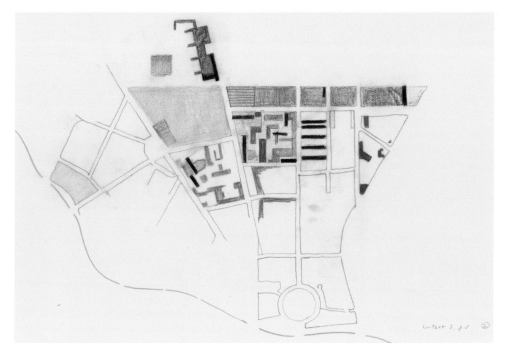

Figure VI.7 Rem Koolhaas, "Kochstrasse/Friedrichstrasse Competition" project for Block 4, IBA-1984/87, Berlin. Study sketch of site plan.

the complex as a composition of color-coded surfaces differentiating between court-yards and interiors, and detached straight and curved lines (Figure VI.10). The second fragment would have been the manual trades center, with a wall-like building terminating the housing on its west and creating an open space on its east. The third fragment would have been composed of the existing higher buildings, turning them into a block within a block. The fourth fragment, close to the eastern end at Checkpoint Charlie, would have provided eighteen houses organized around a new dead-end street and its turnaround, with housing of higher quality built for wealthier residents, because the team "felt that the combination of social housing with such a notorious point could appear to be [a] cynical gesture that would reinforce the negative connotations of both."[26] Finally, the fifth fragment on the Friedrichstrasse end would have provided three booths for customs, US Army, and police officers to accommodate the border-control functions of Checkpoint Charlie (Figure VI.11).

After the jury decided in favor of the design of Bohigas, Mackay, and Martorell, asking the Spanish collective to coordinate the collaboration of six different architects, Koolhaas's Office of Metropolitan Architecture (OMA) was assigned to the Checkpoint Charlie end of the block. In December 1982, the office prepared twelve alternative schemes for the site and a comparison of their plot ratios and the lands that would need to be acquired for each. These schemes used various permutations of a medium-rise building and low-rise booths (referred to as mews in the report), showing them interlocked in numerous ways, flying on pilotis or creating forecourts, standing on the building-line of the street or set-back (Figure VI.12).[27] This exercise was meant to convince the

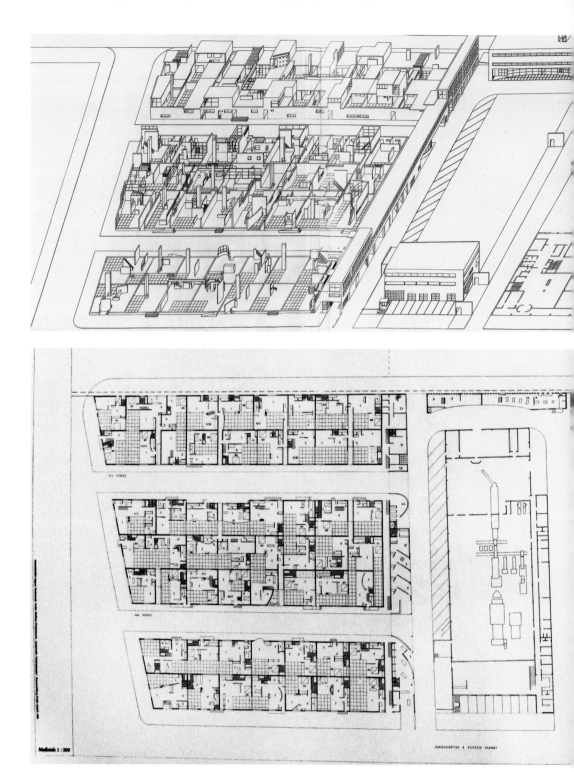

TOP: Figure VI.8 Rem Koolhaas, "Kochstrasse/Friedrichstrasse Competition" project for Block 4, IBA-1984/87, Berlin. Axonometric. BOTTOM: Figure VI.11 Rem Koolhaas, "Kochstrasse/Friedrichstrasse Competition" project for Block 4, IBA-1984/87, Berlin. Plan of Block 4.

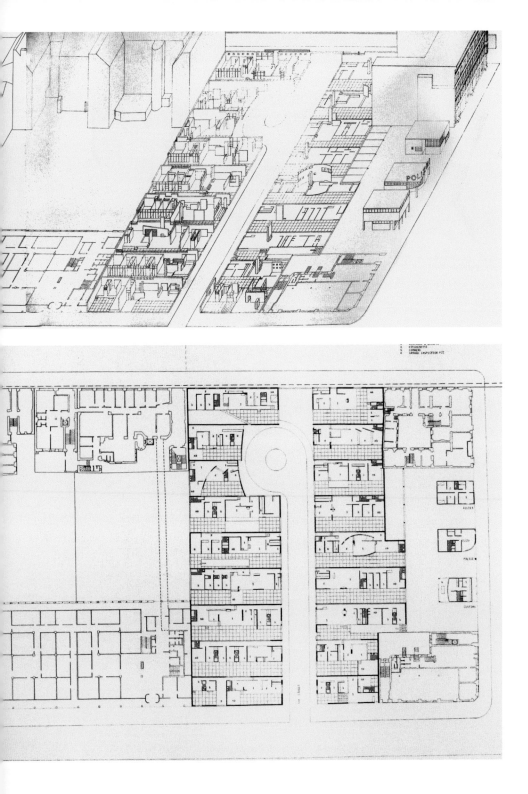

STOP VI   Open History in the Past Subjunctive Tense

311

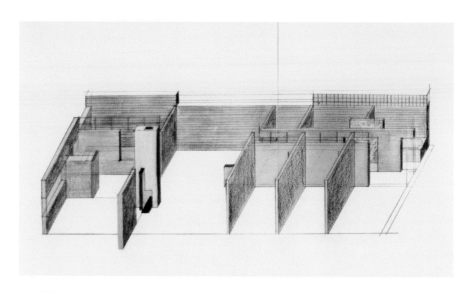

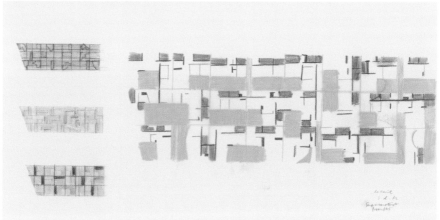

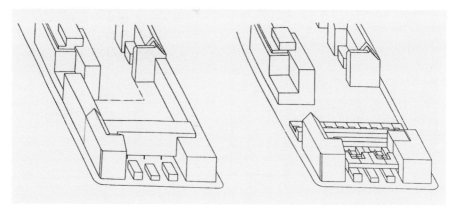

TOP: Figure VI.9 Rem Koolhaas, "Kochstrasse/Friedrichstrasse Competition" project for Block 4, IBA-1984/87, Berlin. Study sketch of a house. CENTRE: Figure VI.10 Rem Koolhaas, "Kochstrasse/Friedrichstrasse Competition" project for Block 4, IBA-1984/87, Berlin. Study sketch of Block 4. BOTTOM: Figure VI.12 OMA, Pages from "Kochstrasse—Friedrichstrasse Study Proposals for Residential Development at Checkpoint Charlie. December 1982," unpublished booklet.

authorities to commission OMA to design a larger site than the infill plot squeezed between two existing buildings along Friedrichstrasse. The report concluded that the schemes "point to the fact that in addition to the above mentioned difficulties, any subdivision of the site is problematic because of the small size of each component. … The extreme tightness of the present boundaries strengthens the view that the entire available land should be studied comprehensively."[28]

Not granted a larger site, OMA (Elia Zenghelis and Matthias Sauerbruch worked on this building) collaborated with Bohigas, Mackay, and Martorell in the design of the eastern part of Block 4, overcoming multiple crises due to the demands of the US forces (see stop II). Architects of the two offices met in London and Berlin and shared design stages.[29] Despite all the frustration, the final building (1987–88) used many early Koolhaasian themes, such as the metropolitan juxtaposition of different transportation systems and programmatic fragments, organized around an elaborate promenade.[30] The explanation report read: "OMA is to establish a retroactive concept based on inherent but latent principles of the urban context. Rather than [a] mere restoration or reinterpretation of the 18th century block, the project set out to the contradictory characteristics of the site in order to invest in the project as a definition of Contemporaneity."[31] The building superimposed different types of housing on top of the border-control functions, as if the horizontally placed fragments of the competition project had been flipped vertically (Figure VI.13). The ground floor, underneath an elevated platform, was still composed of identifiable booths, drew the Allied US forces inside, accommodated their bus turnaround, and provided access to a parking garage and passageway.[32] As noted in stop II, I must have used this passageway to enter the building while it was being updated for new residents in 2012 because of Kreuzberg's gentrification.

On an ordinary day, however, visitors were meant to use a slowly ascending promenade from the discreet common entrance on the left side of the public street façade to an elevated platform at the back, where a pathway along private gardens is situated (Figure VI.14). These are the gardens of the duplex row houses on the lowest housing floor, accessed from the elevated pathway that leads to the outdoor stairway (Figure VI.15), which in turn climbs up to the street in the air facing the public street. The street in the air gives access to interlocking apartments that are on two different floors but entered from only one level for efficient circulation, and an additional gallery overlooks this inner street, which gives access to units on the fifth floor. Finally, stairs to the top floor take one to the outdoor deck, which gives access to smaller units. Climbing up and circling along the periphery of the building by making several L-turns, the promenade meets outdoor and indoor stairways, a pathway on an elevated ground, a street in the air, a gallery, and a deck (Figure VI.16). A tilted cantilevered canopy shelters this deck, but it seems largely oversized for a circulation area of this status. In a possible future, Koolhaas predicted that when border-control functions were no longer needed, the ground floor would be turned into a supermarket (it is now a MacDonald's), but the cantilevered roof would remain as a reminder of the Berlin Wall, and he noted that "at the moment this hovering plane marks the division line between East and West, one of the World's most dramatic transitions within an urban environment" (Figure VI.17).[33]

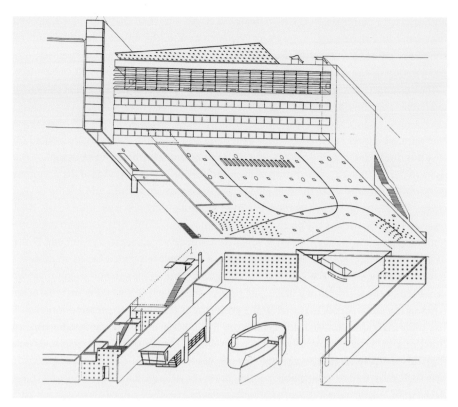

Figure VI.13 OMA, Housing at Checkpoint Charlie, IBA-1984/87, Berlin, 1987. Axonometric.

Aspiring for "contemporaneity," the building raises the question of how contemporary international immigration and the Senate's noncitizen laws played a role in the design process. The building was introduced in a professional magazine as follows: "OMA imagined that a section through the building would represent a section through West Berlin: Allies at the base, followed at the middle levels by larger units to be taken up by Turkish guest workers and their families, with Germans living in small units at the top."**34** Flipping the collage in the vertical direction, the building, in other words, superimposed different nationalities of Berlin: The American soldiers on the ground, the German citizens on the top floors, and the Turkish noncitizens in-between. The collage now distinguished multiple socialities as a matter of national affinities. Making noncitizens visible on an urban façade took a critical stance against the anti-immigration policies of the time, but only by having to stamp their apartments as territories of the stateless.

If Kreuzberg had not been undergoing gentrification around 2012, this building might still have been occupied by the residents I had met earlier: Dagmar Fokken, who had worked at IBA and had lived in the building from the day it was constructed until it was vacated during gentrification, and who walked me through all the secret passageways and her favorite apartments and sent me the newspaper and magazine clippings she had collected about the building; a former East Berliner who had escaped to the West and curiously decided to live in an apartment almost adjacent to the wall; a

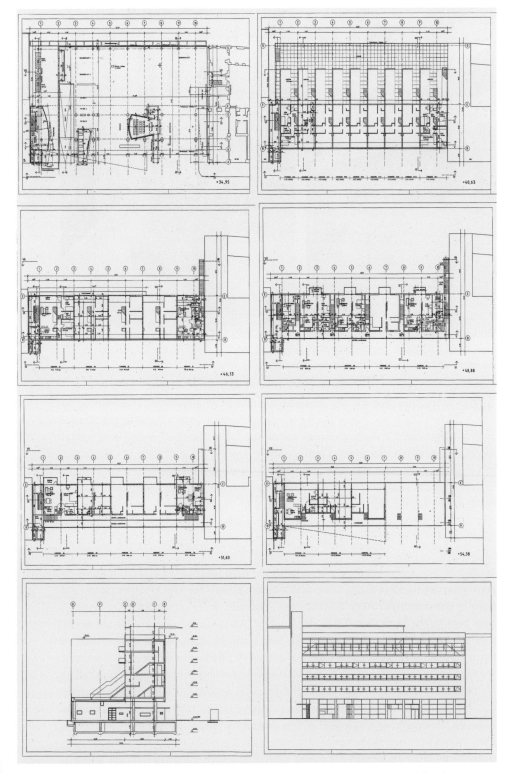

Figure VI.14 OMA, Housing at Checkpoint Charlie, IBA-1984/87, Berlin, 1987. Plans, sections, and elevations.

Figure VI.15 Views of the elevated pathway and gardens of duplex row houses in OMA's Housing at Checkpoint Charlie for IBA-1984/87, photographed by Esra Akcan, Berlin, 2010.

Turkish immigrant who did not speak highly about the unordinary interlocking duplex units because of noise problems; a resident who had made a mural on the interior wall, as I discovered in the apartment vacated due to gentrification; a man with mental health problems who had moved into the apartment for the disabled and who, in Fokken's recollection, often ran naked back and forth along the street in the air. Perhaps unusual tenants were only fitting in a building designed by an architect who was fascinated with skyscrapers because they allowed for the convergence of multiple privacies such as "eating oysters with boxing gloves naked on the 9th floor" (Figure VI.18 and VI.19).[35]

Peter Eisenman and an Avant la Lettre Memorial to the Holocaust

Peter Eisenman and Jaquelin Robertson's design titled "The City of Artificial Excavations"—also submitted to the "Kochstrasse/Friedrichstrasse Competition" for Block 5— soon became the equivalent of a poster child for IBA-1984/87. It was used in announcements for exhibitions and public panels, was included in almost all theme issues of journals, and instantly became a topic of debate by architectural theorists. Eisenman traveled to Germany from New York to make presentations at high-impact architectural conferences such as the Dortmund Conference on April 23–25, 1981, and a conference on German-American relations in urban planning organized by the Aspen Institute in Berlin on September 27–30, 1981. If this project had been selected for construction, there would have been a memorial of superimposed grids on this site, also integrating the three existing and three new mixed-used buildings, a museum, parking, and public gardens (Figure IV.20). Many commentators at the time perceived this project as a

TOP: Figure VI.16 Views of the interior promenade—street in the air, gallery, and deck—in OMA's Housing at Checkpoint Charlie for IBA-1984/87, photographed by Esra Akcan, Berlin, 2010. BOTTOM: Figure VI.17 Views of OMA's Housing at Checkpoint Charlie for IBA-1984/87, photographed by Esra Akcan, Berlin, 2012.

shift in Eisenman's career, despite the similar use of interlocking grids in the House Series that kept him busy from 1968 until the mid-1970s. This shift was described as one from amnesia to memory, from siteless houses to the concerns of the site along the Berlin Wall.[36] Nonetheless, the building was characterized as being, "in the usual Eisenman manner, also a polemic, this time on postmodernist historical reference."[37] On his way to, but not yet totally immersed in, his collaboration with Jacques Derrida and the poststructural turn toward the referential impossibility of architecture, and not yet having published on his search for a nonclassical, and therefore nonrepresentational (autonomous), artificial (arbitrary), and timeless (originless and endless) architecture,[38] Eisenman nonetheless questioned some of the basic constructed values of modernity with this project. There are good indications that the main intellectual source of the project's conceptual basis was the Frankfurt School—a different source than the philosophical and linguistic teachings that are usually associated with Eisenman.

Figure VI.18 Views from an apartment in OMA's Housing at Checkpoint Charlie for IBA-1984/87, photographed by Esra Akcan, Berlin, 2010.

Figure VI.19 An apartment vacated due to gentrification in OMA's Housing at Checkpoint Charlie for IBA-1984/87, photographed by Esra Akcan, Berlin, 2012.

There were at least three versions of the explanation report for "The City of Artificial Excavations." The first seems to have been written for the competition in 1980 (selections from which were used in IBA's *Erste Projekte* catalog); the second is a concise version; and the third is a long, theoretically rigorous one (eventually published in AD), both written in January 1981.[39] All three versions stated the architects' intention to respond to the symbolic location of the site along the Berlin Wall and to "excavate all" of its historical layers. The second and especially the third version further explained the theoretical intentions of the design. According to the third version, "History is not continuous. It is made up of stops and starts, of presences and absences. ... The European city today is a manifestation of such a memory void. As such it presents a crisis not only of history but of architecture itself."[40] Criticizing the "post-modern attitude" that time must be either frozen or reversed—which ends in nostalgia in either case—the report continued:

> The city of Berlin offers a potential alternative to these processes. For it is in itself a record not just of the continuity but of the end of the history of the Enlightenment. In this sense it is a unique object: the locus of a historical void. The wall that runs around and through it already makes it *almost* a museum-city ... it is nothing more nor less than the memory of its own *interrupted* history. The competition site, the intersection of the Friedrichstrasse and the Berlin Wall is the paradigmatic locus of this notion of memory. ... By the middle of this century ~~all of~~ this *chain of* history was rudely ~~interrupted~~ *broken*. In 1945, bombing left Friedrichstadt in ruins. Three buildings remained on ~~the~~ our site, their scarred walls a standing reminder of their beginning and their end ~~of their history~~. Then the imposition of the Berlin Wall in 1961 felled ["crushed" in the shorter version] the Angel of History ~~for good~~ *forever*.[41]

Eisenman's choice of words here is telling. It was not very common at the time in architectural circles to conceive of the present as a culmination of the chain of events starting with the Enlightenment, nor to declare that that period of history had ended with World War II. Eisenman's identification of Berlin as the standing metaphor of the "end of the history of Enlightenment" calls for further exploration. It was indeed the

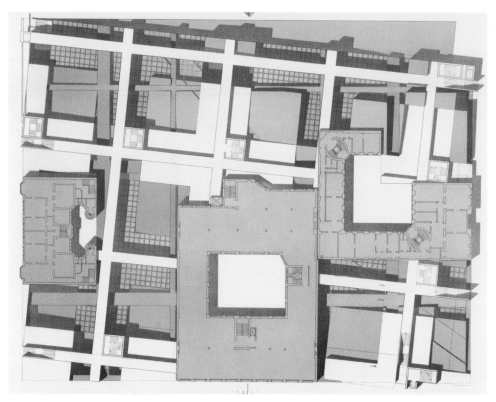

Figure VI.20 Peter Eisenman and Jaquelin Robertson, "The City of Artificial Excavations" project for Block 5 of "Kochstrasse/Friedrichstrasse Competition", IBA-1984/87, Berlin.

Frankfurt School whose members had suggested that this war had cast doubt on the promises and values of the Enlightenment. Writing *Dialectic of Enlightenment* during World War II after being exiled from Germany due to the rise of National Socialism, Theodor Adorno and Max Horkheimer described their work as an attempt to "explain why humanity, instead of entering a truly human state, [was] sinking into a new kind of barbarism."[42] Why was the Enlightenment ending in its own destruction? Eschewing the perception of the Enlightenment as the beholder of reason, freedom, and equality, the authors argued that myth and the Enlightenment, reason and instrumentality, and freedom and triumphalist will to control nature and society were so entangled with each other that the Enlightenment, which had promised emancipation, delivered domination. The last chapter—"Elements of Anti-Semitism," written after the war— "dealt with the reversion of enlightened civilization to barbarism."[43] In "The End of Reason," Horkheimer defined the end of reason as both the intention, or the telos, of the Enlightenment and the manifestation of its failure, thus asking whether there was something inherent in modernity that unavoidably carried humanity toward irrationality and fascism.[44] Moreover, Eisenman's choice of the words "Angel of History," the title of a drawing by Paul Klee, was probably a reference to Walter Benjamin, who had written the words "there is no document of civilization which is not at the same time a document of barbarism" in the essay he penned just before killing himself to avoid being captured by the Gestapo during his attempted escape from the Nazis.[45]

Eisenman's frequent use of the concepts of memory and history might seem less surprising at first sight, given the overwhelming interest in the past among architects of this period and Eisenman's collaboration with Aldo Rossi, the architect of collective memory, whom he invited to give lectures and exhibitions at the Institute for Urban Studies, and whose book's English translation he wrote the introduction for.[46] However, the word "memory" did not have the same connotations in the disciplines of architecture and literary criticism, and Eisenman's interest in memory voids in this project seems more akin to the latter, consciously or intuitively. In *Twilight Memories* and *Present Pasts*, Andreas Huyssen argued that memory had become a cultural preoccupation during the Cold War, largely due to the growing sense that "the major required task of any society today is to take *responsibility for its past.*"[47] Huyssen traced the beginnings of this memory discourse to the 1960s in the United States and Europe—specifically to decolonization, revisionist histories, and civil rights movements. The growing awareness of the Holocaust was another harbinger of critical commemoration. "Human rights activism today," he wrote, "depends very much on the depth and breadth of memory discourses in the public media."[48] The term "void" that Eisenman frequently uses provided an inspiring metaphor for literary critics and philosophers. Even though writing later than Eisenman, Huyssen stressed the cultural implications of voids in the context of the broader history of Berlin's urban space and the debate about memory and countermemory. Karl Scheffler's comment in 1910 that Berlin was "forever to become and never to be" proved to be true for the rest of the twentieth century, marking Berlin, in Huyssen's words, as a city that had been "written, erased and rewritten throughout that violent century."[49] Eisenman made a similar observation about Berlin. The quotation above from the report continues: "The competition site is the symbolic locus of memory. But it is a memory with [an] ambivalent nature: the memory of something that once existed and thrived, but also, its peculiar condition, the embalming of something living in the present. Thus 'Checkpoint Charlie' encapsulates the dual condition of severance and connection, exclusion and inclusion."[50] Memorials to the victims of state brutality and oppression were at the forefront of the public debate about commemoration during the 1980s and 1990s, and Holocaust memorials, in particular—as testimonials to the voids carved into cities by the absence of the Jewish population—were the most instructive.[51] Even though the word "Holocaust" never appeared in Eisenman's reports, and even though the IBA team never saw or discussed this project as a memorial that raised consciousness about the Holocaust,[52] given Eisenman's intellectual sources and the history of Berlin, it is not too unthinkable that if "The City of Artificial Excavations" had been built, it would have been an *avant la lettre* memorial to the Holocaust.

If they had received the commission for the entire site, Eisenman and Robertson would have translated these ideas into physical space in the form of the cut and the void. The design sketches for the competition stage were made out of overlapping grid lines that created cuts in volumes. The person who drew these sketches devoted much attention to designing how the cuts would have materialized in three dimensions, and how the volumes would have cut through and intersected each other (Figure VI.21). A drawing with cut-out parts represented buildings as voids, absences rather than presences (Figure VI.22). Like a scar in memory, the void in this drawing became an index of the

Figure VI.21 Peter Eisenman and Jaquelin Robertson, "Kochstrasse/Friedrichstrasse Competition" project for Block 5, IBA-1984/87, Berlin. Study sketches.

absence of the Jewish population in Berlin, the rupture of Jewish history in the city. In other words, the horrors of World War II culminated in the end of the Enlightenment and materialized in physical space as a void. The void was the index of the annihilation of something that used to exist but did not any longer. The project would have been a memorial to the Berlin Wall, but it would also have meant the questioning of a long history of events that led to the construction of that wall and hence to the void created by World War II.

If they had received the commission for the entire site, Eisenman and Robertson would have refused to reconstruct Berlin's nineteenth-century urban fabric by simply ignoring the traumas of its history. Rather than build an illusion of continuity, the construction on this site would have reminded viewers of the city's disrupted history and taken notice of its gaps in memory. "An archeological earthwork"[53] would have built artificial indexes of the layers of Berlin's history: "Thus the absent wall of the eighteenth century, the foundation walls of the nineteenth century, the remnants of the twentieth century grid as projected upward in the vertical walls of the existing buildings, and finally the Berlin Wall, a monument to the erosion of the unity of the city and the world, form a nexus of wall[s] at different levels which become a composite datum of memory."[54]

While these layers embraced Berlin's memory, one more layer would have been added as an embodiment of antimemory—as an indication of no place in addition to indications of Berlin as a place. The Mercator grid (used almost universally to depict the

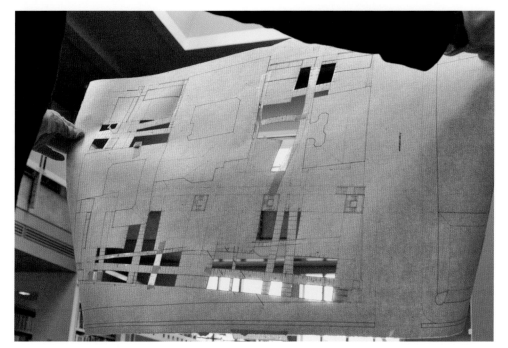

Figure VI.22 Peter Eisenman and Jaquelin Robertson, "Kochstrasse/Friedrichstrasse Competition" project for Block 5, IBA-1984/87, Berlin. Study sketches with cut-outs.

geometry of the globe) would have been superimposed on the city's grid (Figure VI.23): "A universal geometric pattern without history, place or specificity, this grid ties Berlin to the world; it is the most neutral and artificial system of marking."[55] Limestone walls as high as the Berlin Wall would have followed this tilted Mercator grid and would have disrupted the circulation on the ground floor. If it had been built, people would have walked on these walls of the Mercator grid and perceived the layers of Berlin's history as if they were in an archeological excavation.[56] In the "Kochstrasse/Friedrichstrasse Competition," the participants were required to imagine the impact of their projects on the neighboring blocks. Eisenman and Robertson continued to superimpose the city grid and Mercator grid on top of each other on the design of the other three blocks in the site. These blocks would have been encircled with perimeter buildings on the city grid, but another set of urban spaces and buildings would have interrupted this morphology with a series of structures aligned with the Mercator grid (Figure VI.24 and VI.25). In discussing this project, Kurt Forster identified its twofold intention as the acknowledgment of the history of the site and of the fact that Berlin today belongs to the world. The Mercator grid signified that Berlin was both "every place and no place."[57]

In all three versions of the explanation report, Eisenman emphasized the "inaccessibility of the earthwork," which he compared to the ruins of Scottish border castles and the rock garden of the Ryoanu-ji temple in Kyoto:[58] "The imposition of the Mercator Grid first makes inaccessible the foundations of the enlightenment. It also begins to erase their memory. Second it causes the ground plane—upon which has been acted

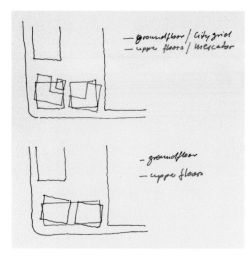

Figure VI.23 Peter Eisenman and Jaquelin Robertson,
"Kochstrasse/Friedrichstrasse Competition" project
for Block 5, IBA-1984/87, Berlin. Study sketch for the
superimposition of city and Mercator grids.

out so much enlightenment history—to become inaccessible—the ground now becomes a witness to that history."[59] What Eisenman calls inaccessibility could well have been the translation of the concept of unrepresentability into physical space. The unrepresentability and unspeakability of the Holocaust, and the impossibility of creating a victim's experience of it, would become one of the central concepts in Holocaust studies in the 1980s and 1990s.[60] Holocaust memorials struggled to get over Adorno's challenge to the writing of non-barbaric poetry after Auschwitz. This challenge was taken into consideration in literary and cinematographic representations of the Holocaust, which refrained from claiming that a victim's actual experience could be represented or re-enacted in a particular medium. The very act of mediation was seen as disrespectful to the victims of the unspeakable violence that took place and as an erroneous belief in the power of representation to re-create what actually happened. Erecting monuments or memorials to Holocaust victims presented its own set of problems: given both the historical and etymological relation between monuments and memory, and the association of monumentality with power, grandeur, prestige, and glory, how could one possibly commemorate the Holocaust with a monumental expression? To follow Adorno and Horkheimer again, if the Holocaust was the major scar on the face of modernity, raising a serious concern about its inherent inability to confront otherness and difference, how could one possibly use conventional monumental practices to represent Holocaust memories?[61] After the 1980s, artists offered to commemorate traumas with countermonumental forms in response to this challenge. To give one example, Jochen and Esther Gerz's "Disappearing Monument against Fascism" in Harburg (1986–91) was a twelve-meter pillar that was gradually lowered as residents of the city signed their names on it to indicate their rebellion against fascism. The complete disappearance of the pillar indicated the symbolic defeat of fascism. If it had been built, "The City of Artificial Excavations" would have become an early example of a countermonument.

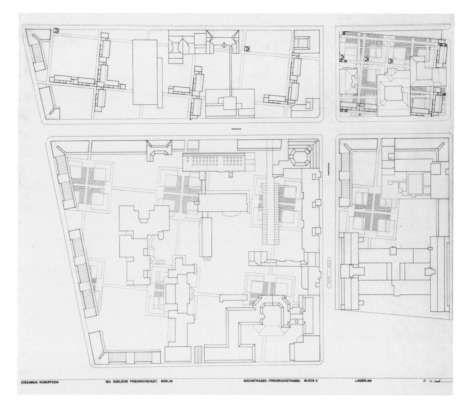

Figure VI.24 Peter Eisenman and Jaquelin Robertson, "Kochstrasse/Friedrichstrasse Competition" project, IBA-1984/87, Berlin. Site plan.

Excited about winning the competition, Eisenman initially saw IBA as a historical landmark. In a letter to Kleihues, he wrote:

> There can be no question that the idea of an international building exhibition is a prodigious undertaking. Merely the organization of sites, the writing of programs[,] the selection of architects and juries has been a work of great value. IBA however is something more than this as was the case of the Weissenhof-siedlung in 1927 which to this day has served as a model for public, low-density, urban housing; the goals of the IBA have a similar aspiration, though the strategy is different. It is this strategy—the reclamation of the inner city, through restoration, in fill and innovation—which seems both unique and challenging.
>
> Far from a display of the latest styles or technology IBA has concentrated on serious, often difficult, programs of work. Thus the results of IBA depend not only on the display of theoretical ideas but the building of buildings.
>
> Should this be accomplished as projected, 1984 will become a seminar [sic] date in architectural history.[62]

In a meeting with Eisenman and Christopher Glaister (Eisenman and Robertson's third partner) on March 16, 1981, however, Kleihues delivered the bad news. Just as the organization had done for all blocks of the "Kochstrasse/Friedrichstrasse Competition,"

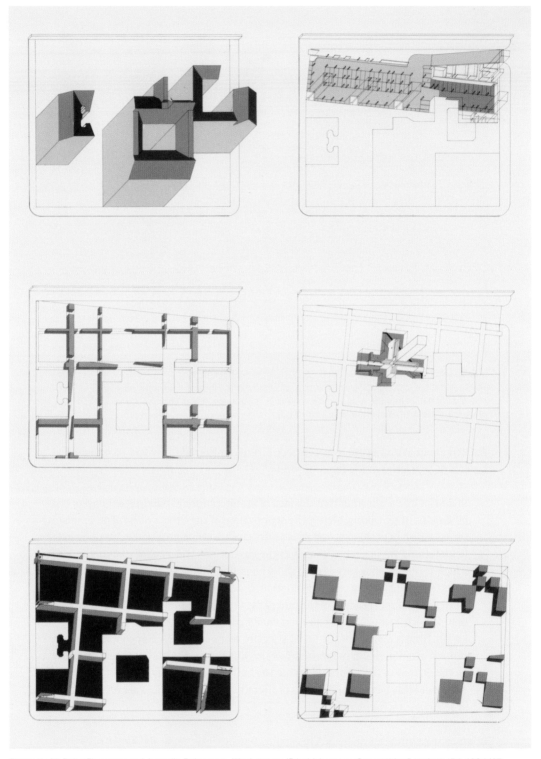

Figure VI.25 Peter Eisenman and Jaquelin Robertson, "Kochstrasse/Friedrichstrasse Competition" project, IBA-1984/87, Berlin. City Layers.

IBA wanted to divide Block 5 and to commission three architects to design three different plots, under Eisenman and Robertson's "overall control of the morphology of the design." In the negotiations during the meeting it was agreed to have two rather than three offices, but "Kleihues stated that there were no funds presently available to IBA to build the museum and garden. He felt that money must be raised privately to fund that part of the project."[63] Over the course of 1981 and 1982, Eisenman wrote several letters to Kleihues and others, trying to convince the authorities to build the memorial or informing them that it would be financially impossible for his office to simply design a smaller building:[64] "What is problematic for us is that we worked very hard both in terms of time and financial resources to produce a result which was worthy of high ideals which you put forward for the IBA. For this, even after winning, we find ourselves in a lesser position than some of the losers and some of the non-participants."[65] Kleihues wrote back about his own efforts to find sponsors.[66]

From these letters, we learn that it was Heinrich Klotz who came to the "courageous defense" of Eisenman's project in the competition jury, and "encouraged [him] to do a 'Peter Eisenman' and ... suggested the idea of 'anti-memory.'"[67] We also understand that Eisenman was skeptical of designing public housing, and preferred to build the memorial.

> It is sad, but I think IBA is one, large competition, exhibition and publication mechanism, but one which has very little heart for the long process of realizing projects. Already we have been turned over to a developer whose only interest is turning the entire site into a giant social housing project. It would be a shame to see this happen.[68]
>
> We could not believe that even with a housing shortage anyone would want to raise their children in the site of barbed wire machine gun emplacements.[69]

In 1985, even Paris was involved. Pierre Vago wrote a letter from the Union Internationale des Architectes, seeking support to build the memorial, but he also sent a note to Eisenman informing him that the requests had gone unanswered. Vago asked: "An action against the Senate of Berlin? From Paris? How much should it cost? How long will it last? And: I cannot imagine that a fair solution is impossible. ... I am so sorry!"[70]

Eventually, Eisenman and Robertson had to align their ideas with IBA's principles in a smaller building with thirty-seven apartments, ten of which were for handicapped people and eleven for the elderly, and in a small museum at the corner of Friedrichstrasse and Kochstrasse in Block 5 (Figure VI.26). The apartments (which ranged in size from one and a half rooms to three and a half rooms, i.e., three rooms and a *Kammer*) contained intentionally ambiguous spaces that could be used as winter gardens or to serve other functions. Hans Kammerer, who had also participated in the competition, designed the building at the corner of Charlotten- and Rudi-Dutschke-Strasse (see stop II.23). IBA served as liaison between Eisenman and Robertson and the developer, GRUNDAG. Dietmar Grötzebach was commissioned as the contact architect who did all the technical and construction drawings, and negotiated in matters relating to licenses and permits. Over the course of 1984 and 1985, Eisenman and Grötzebach communicated with annotated drawings and sketches that were sent back and forth between New York and Berlin (Figure VI.27).[71]

A memorial to its own place in the history of possibility, the built version superimposed the city grid and the Mercator grid as two masses on slightly tilted coordinating lines on top of each other. The façades of the two volumes used different materials and window frames. In fact, the façade of the section that is tilted from the city grid looks much like the site plan of the competition version. This façade has several intersecting grid lines, materialized as stucco surfaces with different colors, and includes conspicuous red crosses that are fragments of a larger grid (Figure VI.28). A domesticated version of the urban garden where residents no longer walked on but between the walls of the Mercator grid was designed in May 1985, but not executed (Figure VI.29). Despite the fact that the project's ambitions were narrowed down to a façade treatment, much like a decorated shed, Eisenman was at pains to differentiate his building from the façadism and nostalgia of postmodernist buildings: "While in one sense our project is a reaction to the failure of modern architecture to understand, enhance, or even conserve the historic centers, the architecture does not adopt the current postmodern attitude where sites and buildings are treated as fetish objects; where fragments of a former urban structure are preserved, the bones are reassembled, the skin and flesh restored or hypothetically recreated, and the new assemblage made to appear as a kind of stuffed animal, embalmed as a form of nostalgia in a so called 'natural' setting."[72]

Figure VI.26 Peter Eisenman and Jaquelin Robertson, Housing at Checkpoint Charlie, IBA-1984/87, photographed by Esra Akcan, Berlin, 2016.

Throughout the whole process from competition to construction, the one point that remained constant in Eisenman's argument was that time was at a standstill. Humanity had never worked through or moved past the trauma of 1945, which was only confirmed by the construction of the Berlin Wall in 1961: "Since 1945 there is both a memory of a time that has been lost forever and an immanence of a time which may be again. This submission deserves recognition because it presents an architecture suspended in this new time as an archeological moment."[73] While calling to come to terms with Berlin's disrupted past, and while constructing the artificial traces of the city's past two hundred years, Eisenman's history stopped at 1961, however, the year when the wall was constructed and when the first labor recruitment contract was signed between Germany and Turkey, after which guest workers started moving into the area. While writing the history of Berlin's traumatic past and erasures, implying that the finale was a consequence of anti-Semitism, Eisenman's historical narrative identified 1961 as the end of history. The present violence occurring in the area was hence not acknowledged in a project that sought to raise consciousness about the many incidents of historical violence on this very site.

In *Cosmopolitan Anxieties*, Ruth Mandel identified the time of Berlin as a chronotope: "continually stretched, pulled between an unbearable memory and contested visions of its future." The city's troubled memories were like "a palimpsest. Whichever layer one looks at, be it the Weimar political polarization and artistic efflorescence, the thirteen

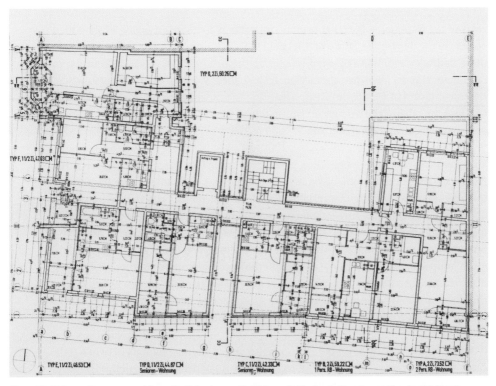

Figure VI.27 Peter Eisenman and Jaquelin Robertson with Dietmar Grötzebach, Housing at Checkpoint Charlie, IBA-1984/87. New York and Berlin, 1984. Second floor plan.

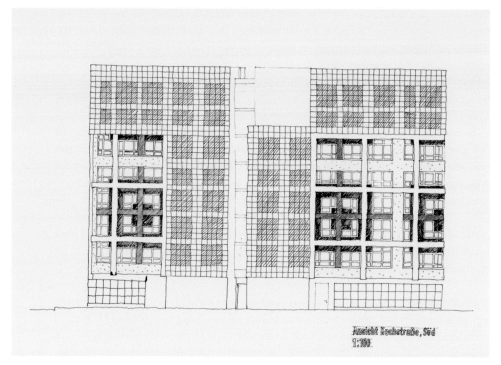

Figure VI.28 Peter Eisenman and Jaquelin Robertson, Housing at Checkpoint Charlie, IBA-1984/87, Berlin. Façade study.

years of the Nationalist Socialist capital, or as the puppet like city-state of the Allied powers in the dangerous games of [the] Cold War, it is ultimately impossible to escape these multiple temporalities when imagining the future."[74] However, in contrast to Eisenman, Mandel identified the racism against guest workers from Turkey as one of the major layers of this palimpsest, deserving the most attention in theorizing Berlin's present, where "the discussion [shifted] from biologically based racism to racism derived from cultural determinism."[75]

Eisenman's reaction against building public housing on this site and his narrative that froze time in 1961 make one question whether he was so intellectually invested in building an *avant la lettre* memorial to the Holocaust on this site that he remained oblivious to the traumas currently being enacted in the area. But these traumas were in plain sight during this time. These were the days when Semra Ertan set herself on fire to protest xenophobia in Germany (on May 26, 1982) and the asylum seeker Cemal Altun jumped out of the window of West Berlin's administrative court to avoid being deported (August 30, 1983). Racialization of guest workers, the Senate's housing laws that discriminated against noncitizens, and immigrants' and the IBA Altbau team's protests against these regulations have already been discussed in this book.

It is not possible to fully cover here the complex and changing relations between Holocaust memory, xenophobia, and the reception of noncitizens in Germany from the 1970s into the 2010s, but recent scholarly work warrants a short summary. The common view during the 1970s, especially in the fields of political science and anthro-

Figure VI.29 Peter Eisenman and Jaquelin Robertson, Park at Checkpoint Charlie, IBA-1984/87, Berlin, 1985.

pology, was that "the Turks are the Jews of today."[76] Mandel and Gökçe Yurdakul and Michael Bodemann have shown how immigrants from Turkey compared racism against them to anti-Semitism, especially after the Neo Nazis' deadly attacks in Mölln (1992) and Solingen (1993), and took the German-Jewish trope as a model for their own cooperative unions, associations, and demands for rights.[77] In literary studies, Huyssen, Leslie Adelson, and Kader Konuk have analyzed Holocaust consciousness and accountability in German-Turkish immigrant literature after Germany's reunification, further complicated by its Armenian counterpart, through the work of authors such as Emine Sevgi Özdamar and Zafer Şenocak whose words best summarize this situation: "In today's Germany, Jews and Germans no longer face one another alone."[78] Michael Rothberg and Yasemin Yıldız have reread Holocaust memory in Germany by taking into account immigrant artists' work, as well as discussions in community organizations.[79] Esra Özyürek has argued that the situation changed in the 2000s, when "the interconnected commitments of European leaders to remember the Holocaust and fight anti-Semitism became one of the grounds for legitimizing racialization of immigrants, and specifically Muslims, by signaling them out as the main contemporary anti-Semites."[80] Matti Bunzl has analyzed the emerging relationship between Islamophobia and anti-Semitism.[81] For our purposes, it might be fitting to quote Michael Brenner in reference to my cautionary remark about idealizing the consciousness against one racism as a guarantee against racism itself or other types of violence toward the other: "It would be mistaken to view the treatment of the Jewish minority in Germany today as representative of the interaction with other religious and ethnic minorities. Fortunately, anti-Semitism is still widely considered a social taboo. However,

Figure VI.30 Peter Eisenman, Memorial to the Murdered Jews of Europe (inaugurated in 2005), photographed by Esra Akcan, Berlin, 2010.

opinions and ordinances against other religious minorities and foreigners are, on the contrary, socially acceptable. There was a time when politicians could express wonderful sentiments about their Jewish fellow citizens and in the same breath warn about the danger of foreign infiltration in Germany."[82]

Not having yet lived through the postunification debates about Holocaust memory and their intersections with postwar migration, Eisenman's *avant la lettre* memorial to Holocaust victims nonetheless is an early indicator of the uneasy triangulation between German, Jewish, and Turkish constructed identities, designed at a time when those on the democratic Left did indeed draw connections between historical and contemporary discriminations against the Jewish and Turkish population, respectively. Turning myself into a resident in Eisenman's IBA building for a while, I decided to respond to this debate with an art installation. "Adding a Layer under the Mercator Grid" picks up history from where it was left in Eisenman's project to include the traumas of the guest workers and refugees from Turkey who were excluded from Eisenman's two-hundred-year history of Berlin's traumas. As a reference to the way winter gardens have been adapted to different uses by IBA residents, the staged photographs of this installation turn a winter garden in Eisenman and Robertson's building—recognizable from its signature square window frames—into a bedroom and reenact six traumatic events that happened to immigrant women from Turkey in Kreuzberg (see Figure III.28). Each story is represented by a staged photograph that freezes one moment before the event and by a quotation from a neighbor or translator under oath working in courts who narrated to me the event in an interview. One of these traumatic stories had taken place in Oswald Mathias Ungers's building (stop III).

In their different ways, both Eisenman's and Koolhaas's teams found IBA's critical reconstruction strategy incapable of responding to contemporaneity. Their competition projects constitute a possible rather than an actual history, yet their ideas soon had important reverberations. Years later Eisenman designed the Memorial to the Murdered Jews of Europe (inaugurated in 2005) (Figure VI.30). Ideas such as the void, a scar, and inaccessibility also found new forms in Daniel Libeskind's Jewish Museum (the design was originally submitted to an IBA competition; the museum opened to the public in 2001).[83] Koolhaas's impact on the profession of architecture in the late twentieth and early twenty-first centuries cannot be overstated. In all their contemporaneity, however, both projects barely came to terms with a contemporary phenomenon that was already visible in Kreuzberg at the time, and that became increasingly constitutive of world cities during globalization. Architecture's conceptual turn to respond to statelessness is long overdue.

---

1 Here it might be useful to remember Robert Harbison, who distinguished the built, the unbuilt, and the unbuildable from each other, even though these categories are undeniably fluid (*The Built, the Unbuilt and the Unbuildable* [Cambridge, MA: MIT Press, 1991]). **2** For Hegel, possibility is defined by a lack of contradiction: "Everything is possible that is not self-contradictory." However, this does not imply the existence of infinite possibilities. Possibility cannot be a boundless category, because such diversity would sooner or later "pass over into opposition" and thus will create a contradiction. Logically speaking, a statement like "everything is possible" is no different from saying "nothing is possible" (Georg Wilhelm Friedrich Hegel, *The Science of Logic*, ed. H. D. Lewis, trans. A. V. Miller (New York: Humanities Press, 1976), 543. **3** Ibid., 541. **4** John Grier Hibben, *Hegel's Logic: An Essay in Interpretation* (New York: Charles Scribner's Sons, 1902), chapter 13. **5** Slavoj Žižek, *Tarrying with the Negative: Kant, Hegel and the Critique of Ideology* (Durham, NC: Duke University Press, 1993), 142. **6** Žižek, *Tarrying with the Negative*, 157. **7** Hegel, *The Science of Logic*, 549. **8** The Encyclopedia of Philosophical Sciences: The Logic, accessed April 6, 2017, https://www.marxists.org/reference/archive/hegel/works/ol/encycind.htm **9** Officially, Rem Koolhaas's name is recorded in IBA reports and publications for the Kochstrasse/Friedrichstrasse Competition. Documents in OMA archives identify the team members as Koolhaas, Stefano de Martino, Herman de Kovel, Richard Perlemutter, Ricardo Simonini, Ron Steiner, and Alex Wall. Model: Batsheva Ronen. "Kochstraße/Friedrichstraße" Manuscript, No. 8003, OMA Archives, Rotterdam. **10** "Kochstraße/Friedrichstraße" Manuscript, No. 8003, p. 3, OMA Archives, Rotterdam. **11** "Preisgerichtsprotokoll. Kochstraße/Friedrichstraße," AP.142.S1.D.63, 142-0089T, Canadian Centre for Architecture, Montreal [hereafter CCA]. **12** Florian Hertweck and Sébastien Marot, eds., *The City in the City: Berlin: A Green Archipelago* (Zurich: Lars Müller Publishers, 2013). In an interview conducted for this book, Koolhaas declares that he must have written and typed the text in London and brought it to Berlin in his suitcase (ibid., 137). **13** "La deuxième chance de l'architecture moderne: Entretien avec Rem Koolhaas," *L'Architecture d'Aujourd'hui* 238 (April 1985): 2–27. **14** Rem Koolhaas, "Berlin: A Green Archipelago," in *The City in the City*, 20. **15** Ibid., 12 and 14. **16** Ibid., 16. **17** Ibid., 18. **18** Rem Koolhaas, *Delirious New York: A Retroactive Manifesto for Manhattan*, 2nd ed. (New York: Monacelli Press, 1994, or. 1978). **19** For several interviews with architects who discuss their memories of these camps and which side they were on, see Hertweck and Marot, *The City in the City*. **20** Colin Rowe and Fred Koetter, *Collage City* (Cambridge, MA: MIT Press, 1978), a selection published in *Architecture Theory since 1968*, ed. Michael Hays (Cambridge, MA: MIT Press, 1998), 92–111; Karl Popper, *Open Society and Its Enemies* (London: Routledge, 1994, or. 1952). **21** Rowe and Koetter, *Collage City*, 97. **22** Ibid., 109. **23** The drawings are located in No. 8003, OMA/AMO Archives, Rotterdam; IBA-Akten, 540 Bl. 1,2,4,8 Landesarchiv. **24** Rem Koolhaas, "Field Trip: A(A) Memoir: Berlin Wall as Architecture," in Rem Koolhaas, *S,M,L,XL* (New York: Monacelli Press, 1995), 226. **25** This school of thought is a muse usually associated with Zaha Hadid, who nonetheless referred to Koolhaas as the first person who realized that her natural inclination toward the work of Malevich was a matter of being at ease with "curved gestures" while working with abstraction. In a recent interview, Hadid said: "I'm absolutely sure the Russians—Malevich, in particular—looked at those scripts [Arabic calligraphy]. His work allowed me to develop abstraction as a heuristic principle to research and invent space. Kandinsky's art also has to do with script. The person who first observed this connection was Rem Koolhaas. He noticed that only the Arab students like me were able to make certain curved gestures. He thought it had to do with calligraphy" (Maria Cristina Didero, untitled review of *Zaha Hadid and Suprematism*, *Domus*, July 27, 2012, accessed April 16, 2017, http://www.domusweb.it/en/reviews/2012/07/27/zaha-hadid-and-suprematism.html). **26** OMA, "Kochstrasse / Friedrich-strasse" Manuscript, unnumbered page. **27** OMA, "Kochstrasse—Friedrichstrasse Study Proposals for Residential Development at Checkpoint Charlie. OMA. 482 1686. December 1982," Unpublished booklet, No.8003, OMA Archives, Rotterdam. **28** Ibid., 1. **29** Matthias Sauerbruch (OMA) to David Mackay, Letter of 17 July 1985; Attachment of OMA Project as it stands on 12 July 1985. IBA, Box: 769-3, Bohigas, Mackay, Martorell Archives. Arxiu COAC, Barcelona; David Mackay, interview by the author, July 9, 2012, Barcelona, in English, Tape 1, 00:36:27. Both audio and video recordings of this interview are in the author's collection. **30** Drawings can be found in No. 8003, OMA Archives, Rotterdam. Also see "Großstadtarchitektur," *Bauwelt* 81, no.15 (April 1990): 754–63. **31** OMA, "Kochstrasse / Friedrichstrasse" Manuscript, "IBA project 207/208 (revised version)" section, unnumbered page. **32** Mackay, interview by the author, Tape 1, 00:45:40–00:46.47. **33** OMA, "Kochstrasse / Friedrichstrasse," 2. **34** Mary Pepchinski, "OMA's Berlin Housing Confronted by Change," *Progressive Architecture* 71, no.13 (December 1990): 17. **35** Koolhaas, *Delirious New York*, 155. **36** Ignacio di Solá-Morales Rubió, "Vom Objekt zur Dispersion: Architettura artificialis," in *Modelle für eine Stadt*, ed. Vittorio Magnago Lampugnani (Berlin: Wolf Jobst Siedler Verlag, 1984), 161–67; Susan Doubilet, "The Divided Self," *Progressive Architecture* 68, no.3 (1987): 81–91. **37** Helene Lipstadt, "Self-Reflection: Eisenman in Berlin," *Progressive Architecture* 9 (September 1981): 38. **38** Peter Eisenman, "The End of the Classical. The End of the Beginning. The End of the End," *Perspecta* 21 (1984): 154–73. **39** Peter Eisenman, "The City of Architectural Excavation." I will cite them as Version 1 (Competition Report) undated, Version 2 "1/12/81", Version 3 "27 January 1981" (with handwritten corrections). DR1991:0018:939, Eisenman Papers, CCA. Selections from the first version were published in *Erste Projekte: Internationale Bauausstellung Berlin 1984/87: Die Neubaugebiete Dokumente Projekte*, vol. 2 (Berlin: Quadriga Verlag, 1981), 284. The third version was published as Peter Eisenman and Jaquelin Robertson, "Koch-/Friedrichstrasse, Block 5," *AD* 53, nos.1–2 (1983): 91–93. **40** Eisenman, Version 3 "27 January 1981," 1. **41** Ibid., 2 and 3. Deletions are differentiated with overstrikes, additions with separate font. **42** Max Horkheimer and Theodor Adorno, *Dialectic of Enlightenment: Philosophical Fragments*, trans. Edmund Jephcott (Stanford, CA: Stanford University Press, 2002, or. 1944), xiv. **43** Ibid., xix. **44** Max Horkheimer, "The End of Reason," in *The Essential Frankfurt School Reader*, ed. Andrew Arato and Eike Gebhardt (New York: Continuum, 1985), 26–48. **45** Walter Benjamin, "Theses on the Philosophy of History," in *Illuminations*, ed. Hannah Arendt, trans. Harry Zohn (New York: Schocken Books, 1968), 256. **46** Peter Eisenman, "The House of the Dead as the City of Survival," in *Aldo Rossi in America: 1976–1979* (New York: Institute for Architecture and Urban Studies, 1979): 4–16. **47** Andreas Huyssen, *Present Pasts: Urban Palimpsests and the Pol-*itics of Memory (Stanford, CA: Stanford University Press, 2003), 94. See also Andreas Huyssen, *Twilight Memories: Marking Time in a Culture of Amnesia* (New York: Routledge, 1995). **48** Huyssen, *Present Pasts*, 95. Also see ibid., 12. **49** Ibid., 51. **50** Eisenman, version 3, 3. **51** James Young, *Texture of Memory: Holocaust Memorials and Meaning* (New Haven, CT: Yale University Press, 1993). **52** Günter Schlusche, interview by the author, November 8, 2016, Berlin, in English, 02:32:00–02:34:45. Both audio and video recordings of this interview are in the author's collection. **53** The term appeared in the competition report but was dropped in the later versions, Eisenman, version 1. **54** Eisenman, version 3, 6. **55** Ibid., 5. **56** Peter Eisenman, "Kochstrasse Housing," *Architectural Review* 181, no.1082 (1987): 60. **57** Kurt Forster, "Eisenman / Robertson's City of Artificial Excavation," *Archetype* 2 (spring 1981), n.p. **58** Eisenman, version 1, 4. **59** Eisenman, version 2, 3. **60** Saul Friedlander, *Probing the Limits of Representation: Nazism and the "Final Solution"* (Cambridge, MA: Harvard University Press, 1992). **61** Huyssen wrote that "the traditional critique of the monument as a burying of a memory and an ossifying of the past has often been voiced against the Holocaust monument as well. ... As a variation on Adorno, who was rightfully wary of the effects of aestheticizing the unspeakable suffering of the victims, it has been claimed that to build a monument to the Holocaust was itself a barbaric proposition. No monument after Auschwitz." (*Twilight Memories*, 258). **62** Peter Eisenman to Josef Paul Kleihues, 17 February 1981. DR1991:0018:938, Eisenman Papers, CCA. **63** Meeting Record. March 16, 1981. DR1991:0018:938, Eisenman Papers, CCA. **64** These letters are in DR1991:0018:938; DR1991:0018:939; DR1991:0018:940, Eisenman Papers. CCA. **65** Eisenman to Kleihues, 27 March 1981. DR1991:0018:939, Eisenman Papers, CCA. Also see 26 January 1982. **66** Kleihues to Eisenman, 07.04.1981, 30.03.1982. DR1991:0018:939, Eisenman Papers, CCA. **67** Peter Eisenman to Heinrich Klotz, 16 April 1981. DR1991:0018:938, Eisenman Papers, CCA. **68** Ibid. **69** Peter Eisenman to Max and Nina Bächer, 28 July 1981. DR1991:0018:939, Eisenman Papers, CCA. **70** Pierre Vago to Peter Eisenman, 30.03.1985. DR1991:0018:940, Eisenman Papers, CCA. **71** These drawings and sketches are in Eisenman Papers, 1991:0018. CCA. **72** Peter Eisenman, Manuscript. Undated. Probably 1988, written for AIA Award application, which the building received. DR1991:0018:940, Eisenman Papers, CCA. Some of this extract is quoted in Andrea Oppenheimer Dean, "Bright Face in a Grim Neighborhood: IBA Social Housing: Eisenman Robertson," *Architecture: The AIA Journal* 77, no.5 (1988): 170–71. **73** Peter Eisenman, Manuscript. Undated. Probably 1988, written for AIA Award application. **74** Ruth Mandel, *Cosmopolitan Anxieties: Turkish Challenges to Citizenship and Belonging in Germany* (Durham, NC: Duke University Press, 2008), 35. **75** Ibid., 90. **76** Leslie Adelson, *The Turkish Turn in Contemporary German Literature: Toward a New Critical Grammar of Migration* (New York: Palgrave Macmillan, 2005), 84–86; Jeffrey Peck, "Turks and Jews: Comparing Minorities after the Holocaust," in *German Cultures / Foreign Cultures: The Politics of Belonging*, ed. Jeffrey Peck, Harry Gray, and Helen Gray

(Washington: American Institute of Contemporary Studies, 1997), 1–6. **77** Mandel, *Cosmopolitan Anxieties*, 109–40; Gökçe Yurdakul and Michael Bodemann, "'We Don't Want to Be the Jews of Tomorrow': Jews and Turks in Germany after 9/11," *German Politics and Society* 24, no. 2 (2006): 44–67. **78** Zafer Şenocak, *Gefährliche Verwandtschaft* (Munich: Babel, 1998), 89. See also Adelson who analyzes Şenocak's work as a strong example of her "touching tales" concept. Adelson, *The Turkish Turn in Contemporary German Literature*, 79–122; Andreas Huyssen, "Diaspora and Nation: Migration into Other Pasts," *New German Critique* 88 (2003): 47–164. For Kader Konuk's analysis of Emine Sevgi Özdamar's *Seltsame Sterne*, and other authors, see: Kader Konuk, "Taking on German and Turkish History: Emine Sevgi Özdamar's *Seltsame Sterne*," *Gegenwartsliteratur*, no. 6 (2007), 232–256. **79** Michael Rothberg and Yasemin Yıldız, "Memory Citizenship: Migrant Archives of Holocaust Remembrance in Contemporary Germany," *Parallax* 17, no. 4 (2011): 32–48. **80** Esra Özyürek, "Export-Import Theory and the Racialization of Anti-Semitism: Turkish- and Arab-Only Prevention Programs in Germany," *Comparative Studies in Society and History* 58, no. 1 (2016): 40–65. Quotation: 41. **81** Matti Bunzl, *Anti-Semitism and Islamophobia: Hatreds Old and New in Europe* (Chicago: Prickly Paradigm Press, 2007). **82** Michael Brenner, "No Place of Honor," trans. by Tes Howell, in *Germany in Transit: Nation and Migration*, ed. Deniz Göktürk, David Gramling, and Anton Kaes (Berkeley: University of California Press, 2007): 216–19. Quotation: 217. **83** Esra Akcan, "Apology and Triumph: Memory Transference, Erasure and a Rereading of the Berlin Jewish Museum," *New German Critique* 110 (summer 2010): 153–79.

STROLL 6

A History of a Possible Kreuzberg

For each new building built in Kreuzberg under the auspices of IBA-1984/87, four or five alternative projects had competed for the same site. An infinite number of possible Kreuzbergs could therefore have existed, if different permutations with these competition projects had been actualized (Figure 6.1). Let's have an imaginary stroll among some of these unbuilt projects, starting from our final location in stroll 5. For the site at the corner of the Fraenkelufer and Admiralstrasse, where Hinrich and Inken Baller's buildings are situated, Álvaro Siza had designed a project that exemplified the permeable block conception much more explicitly than it was possible to do in the Bonjour Tristesse compound (stop V).

Leaving Fraenkelufer, if one passed the postwar housing blocks situated in the gap between the Altbau and Neubau areas, one would have reached the site designated for IBA Neubau's prestigious international open "Living in Friedrichstadt Competition" of 1980. The competition brief had asked the contestants to develop a building and open space concept for 250–300 apartments that would have accommodated 750–1,000 residents (with four-bedroom units making up 15 percent of the total), for the area between Rob Krier's Ritterstrasse compound that was already under construction and the Berlin Museum on the north-south axis, and between Lindenstrasse and Alte Jakobstrasse on the east-west axis. The urban design had to take into consideration the already existing buildings, including the Victoria Insurance Company building and the Berlin Museum, and to suggest a design for the museum's garden. As was the case in all IBA

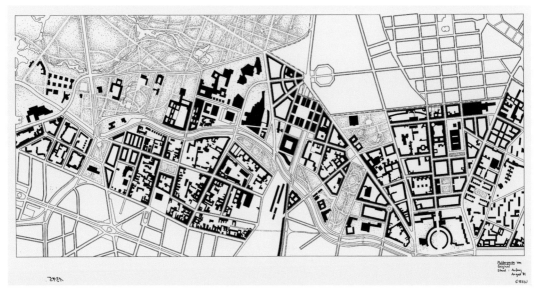

Figure 6.1 IBA Neubau, site plan with competition winning entries as it stands in August 1981.

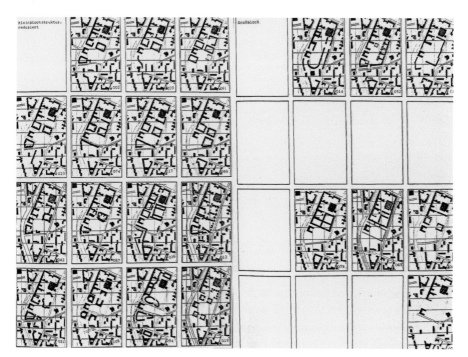

Figure 6.2 Figure ground relations of the entries for "Living in Friedrichstadt Competition," 1980.

competitions, the brief included extensive information on the historical development of the typology and morphology in the area, in this case written by the historians Thomas Biller and Wolfgang Schäche.[1] IBA had received a record number of 101 entries, mostly from German-speaking countries such as Germany, Austria, and Switzerland—which might have been a result of the monolingual competition brief. For the jury, the competition reporters had put the figure-ground relations of the projects into the following categories: "closed small block structure," "reduced small block structure," "open small block structure," "E - W Courtyards," "emphasis on N - S direction," "grand block," "grand form with central figure in museum garden," "open building," and "mixed concepts" (Figure 6.2).[2] The reporters had also summarized each entry's general concept, proposed buildings, street and traffic planning, open space, and design of apartments. Meeting on November 4-6, 1980, after three rounds of discussion and vote, the jury awarded two first prizes—which could not have been more different from each other.[3] If one of the winning designs, the competition project of Hans Kollhoff—an architect based in Berlin, who eventually received the urban design commission with Arthur Ovaska (stroll 1)—had been built, the site would have consisted of three square perimeter blocks in different sizes: the first a closed courtyard building behind the Victoria Insurance Company building; the second composed of two monolithic U-shaped longitudinal buildings and a straight one, which together would have framed the Berlin Museum and the proposed large garden; and the third standing like a pavilion on the southern end (Figure 6.3). Kollhoff had explained his choice as follows: "The theme of a perfect square, chosen for its stabilizing effect on the fabric of the city, becomes the binding element in this particular area and is accordingly varied."[4] If the other winning design—by the team of Gerald Brunner, Franz Rendl, Reinhard Hörl,

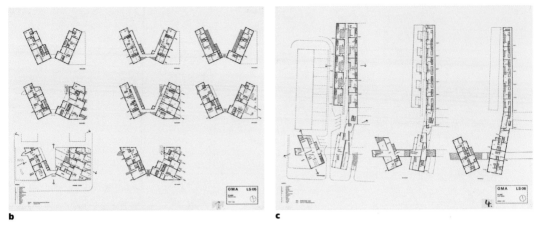

b   c

Figure 6.10 b–e Rem Koolhaas for OMA, "Lützowstrasse Competition" project, Block 647, 1980. **b** plans of middle block; **c** plans of east block; **d** sections; **e** axonometric.

Walter Kirschmayr, and Georg Driendl from Vienna—had been built on this site, there would have been small blocks in the north and, most unusually, a fantasy garden in the south composed of freestanding objects and pavilions that made references to historical architectural elements but by de-familiarizing them. (Figure 6.4). The jury had been skeptical of the freestanding pavilion in Kollhoff's proposal but appreciated the scale of the urban garden and the use of terrace houses; it had found Brunner's proposal joyful, poetic, and ironic, like a "baroque pleasure garden with a mannerist perspective reduction ([eines] barocken Lustgartens mit manieristischer Perspektivverengung)."[5] The low ranking of Rob Krier's proposal (2nd group of purchase) came as a particular surprise, given the architect's involvement in the compounds on the north side of the competition area. If Krier's design had been built, the site would have contained a monumental oval plaza staging the museum, the inner-city types of residences, and reconstructed urban spaces. The jury appreciated these decisions but was skeptical of the building density (stop I, see Figure I.22).[6]

Departing from the "Living in Friedrichstadt Competition" area, one would have walked west along the Besselpark, which was the subject of another competition in 1983, for Block 606. If the kindergarten designed for this site by the Berlin-based Christoph Langhof Architects had been built, three connected pavilions would have arisen on an amorphous platform with a set of minitowers capped by swooping roofs (Figure 6.5). Walking further west, one would have reached the triangular site of the "Wilhelmstrasse Competition" of 1981, including Blocks 9, 19, and 20, bounded by the Berlin Wall, the Hallesches Tor, Wilhelmstrasse, and Stresemannstrasse, for which IBA had invited six mid-career or start-up architects' offices to compete for each of the three blocks.[7] In judging the projects, the jury of established architects paid such special attention to the continuity of the street that the reporters prepared additional comparative diagrams of the designs for this purpose (Figure 6.6). Almost all of the participants complied with the perimeter block mandate. The exceptions were Maurice Culot, whose proposal had an "island in an island" concept and who would have emphasized the buildings as freestanding objects; Douglas Clelland, who would have divided the

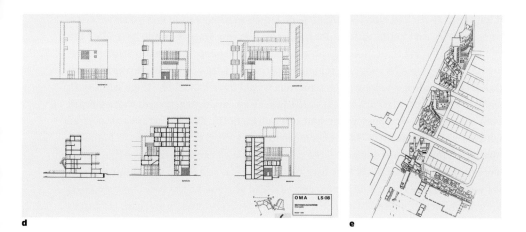

d

e

site into so many small parts that the jury considered it too fragmented; and John Hejduk, whose hedge-enclosed Masque with enigmatic freestanding structures departed the most radically from the competition requirements (stop VII).[8]

Walking north on Wilhelmstrasse to the corner of Kochstrasse, one would have found oneself in the middle of two big IBA competition sites, for which almost 350 possibilities could have materialized. For each project selected as a result of the "Kochstrasse/Friedrichstrasse Competition," whose area covered four blocks, five other proposals were not chosen—which gives the Checkpoint Charlie site about 150 different options. This history of possibility consists of the designs of architects who did not win, including Raimund Abraham, Kollhoff and Ovaska, Rem Koolhaas, Kisho Kurokawa, and Peter Eisenman and Jaquelin Robertson (stops II and VI). Moreover, Bruno Reichlin and Fabio Reinhart's proposal, which won the competition for Block 11, was replaced with another project of the developer's choice. As noted in stop II, according to Günter Schlusche, a coordinator for IBA Neubau, this was a turning point for Josef Paul Kleihues, who then realized that it was insufficient to invite successful architects to execute his visions, because securing the collaboration of developers and policy makers was indispensable. As a consequence, Schlusche thinks that Kleihues admitted the importance of urban planning, rather than focusing exclusively on creating a collection of beautiful buildings.[9] Across the street, on the site where the Martin Gropius Bau stood and the Topography of Terror Museum was built later, IBA organized one of its most symbolically charged international open competitions in 1985, which received 194 entries.[10] The "Prinz-Albrecht-Palais Competition" on the site of the Nazi headquarters and mass murders initially raised public discussions as many hesitated over the possibility of representing the unspeakable horror with an architectural project (see stop VI).[11] The entries for the competition displayed an immense variety of ideas, as if to demonstrate the effects of this hesitation. Some architects proposed Boullée-esque structures with primary forms of sublime magnitude. The site would have contained circular labyrinths if Rafael Moneo's project had been selected, a half-buried cylindrical tower if Jörg Johnen's had been chosen, or a thin, tall cone if Raimund Fein's had won (Figure 6.7 a–c). Other architects used less assertive structures in innovative compositions: John Hejduk's Victims Masque would have filled the site with enigmatic structures like an adventure game (stop VII), Álvaro Siza's project would have provided a convex circular sunken plaza with a tower in the middle, and Giorgio Grassi's low and long brick buildings would have looked like thick walls with small perforations. Kleihues endorsed the latter as a "dialectical project that emerged both from geometrical abstraction and symbolism of the direct meanings associated with the site" (Figure 6.7 d).[12] Other competitors suggested land-art forms: If Raimund Abraham's proposal were selected, the site would have been cut and sliced like a craftwork on topography, if Peter Klimberg, Susanne Krätz, and Georg von Willisen's project were built, the city would have received a grid of stone-firm waves (Figure 6.7 e–f). Many architects proposed turning the area into a well-sculpted formal park with trees and other plants. For example, Jürgen Wenzel and Nikolaus Lang, who won first prize, placed a grid of trees in heavy cast-iron slabs. In Kleihues's words, "these would be a document in 'iron of fear, inhumanity, injustice and despotism' to perpetuate the memory of what already tends all too often to be forgotten or distorted" (Figure 6.7 g).[13]

Crossing the Topography of Terror Museum and Potsdamer Platz and strolling all the way to the Landwehr Canal, one would walk along the half-elliptical Park am Karlsbad, where Richard Meier had designed a project (Figure 6.8). Of all the projects that were envisioned for IBA but remained unbuilt, Meier's housing block must have come closest to realization. The project was not realized because the assigned developer had some disagreements about financial issues. Of the two perimeter blocks that composed Meier's project, the smaller one circled an inner courtyard. Even though Meier did not get to realize this U-shaped block, a building with almost the same mass was eventually built on this site following a design by Jürgen Sawade, Georg Heinrichs, Heinz Hilmer, and Christoph Sattler, at the corner of Potsdamer Strasse and Am Karlsbad. The second block in Meier's scheme would have made a bolder statement. Following the canal's curve, this long, unbroken building would have been hard to miss. Meier lightened the building's bulky effect by dividing it into fragments; giving each its own separate, elevated entrance; and carving out a roof terrace in every fragment— thus producing an unapologetically repetitive scheme, like a high castle wall along the canal. If it had been built, the building's scale would have reminded us of the *Siedlung* (housing estate) projects during the Weimar period. And if it had been built, the residents living on the upper floors along the canal would have enjoyed seeing Hans Scharoun's library and Mies van der Rohe's National Gallery out of their windows, with a glimpse of Alexanderplatz's TV tower at a distance. If things had turned out otherwise, they might even have seen a building selected as a result of one of the Kulturforum competitions, whose saga still continues. Today, with the Berlin Wall no longer there, they would also have been able to see an array of designer buildings, constructed around Potsdamer Platz, including the towers of Renzo Piano and the dome of the Sony Center. If Meier's building had been built, the block along the canal would have contained a park with semiprivate and public zones. Perforated slightly at one edge and totally open to the street at the other, Meier's design would have allowed for more public access to green areas than many other IBA projects. Close to Am Karlsbad, on the other side of the Landwehr canal, one would have seen Mario Botta's

Science Center instead of James Stirling's, had Botta won the competition (stroll 3, Figure 6.9).

Continuing along the canal and turning left onto Lützowstrasse, one would have reached the site of IBA's prestigious "Lützowstrasse Competition" in Block 647, where Vittorio Gregotti's project stands today (stroll 3). Office of Metropolitan Architecture (OMA)'s project for this competition made an equally visible mark in the history of possibility. IBA requested the competition's participants to connect the Landwehr canal and Lützowstrasse by integrating the already designed row houses into their designs.[14] Just like in the "Kochstrasse/Friedrichstrasse Competition," Koolhaas refused to play by the rules, criticizing the tendency to hide postwar structures by building in front of them and filling in the edges of the perimeter blocks. In its report, OMA identified such a restoration attempt as a "conceptual overload and in practical terms absurdly inefficient."[15] In an interview, Koolhaas spoke about it as "a clear indication of the paradox of an ideology which pretends to be contextualist but is completely opposed to the existing context."[16] If OMA's competition project had been built, instead of a perimeter block, the site would have contained eight-story slabs placed in an angle to provide public entrances to the streets of the existing row houses (Figure 6.10 a). Additionally, this solution would have increased the depth of the narrow site and created a series of staggered units of a variety of types, with some duplexes, balconies, terraces, and bridges. Of all the entries, OMA's solution proposed the highest proportion (50 percent) of apartments with four or five rooms without exceeding the predetermined floor area (Figure 6.10 b–d). A building that provided the smallest apartments with the most number of rooms would have been the most appropriate for the big noncitizen families at the time, who could not afford big apartments but still needed more rooms.[17] The jury had problems with the height, traffic noise, building bylaws, and economic feasibility of OMA's design (Figure 6.10 e).[18] If Alison and Peter Smithson's project for the same competition had been selected, IBA would have built a megastructure of sorts, where a street in the air would have connected pavilions providing ramps and stairs. The jury thought there was "a general lack of interlinkage with the surroundings" in this project, and "the effort to draw upon technology ... [was] fraught with problems"[19] (Figure 6.11).

Another unbuilt project envisioned for this area was a kindergarten by Aldo van Eyck. In a drawing, the architect identified himself as the "other Aldo" (as opposed to Aldo Rossi) and said he would take the job if IBA wanted "something 'good', which means something 'reasonable and nothing else,'" using a tone that criticized the organization for excluding his generation (Figure 6.12).[20] In addition, Giorgio Grassi fashioned a project for Lützowplatz that would have provided long and high wall-like buildings (Figure 6.13).[21] Finally, the history of possibility of the Rauchstrasse complex includes ten alternatives to the complex that stands on the site today, on which eight architects collaborated using Rob Krier's urban design.[22]

1 IBA, "Wohnen in der Friedrichstadt. Internationaler städtebaulicher Ideenwettbewerb," Competition Brief of May 1980 (Berlin: IBA 1980), B 80/029, Landesarchiv. **2** "Wohnen in der Friedrichstadt. Vorprüfbericht," IBA report, n. p. B 80/030, Landesarchiv. **3** "Ergebnisprotokoll der Preisgerichtssitzung des internationalen städtebaulichen Ideenwettbewerbs 'Wohnen in der Friedrichstadt,'" IBA report, B 80/029, Landesarchiv. **4** Hans Kollhoff, in *Erste Projekte: Internationale Bauausstellung Berlin 1984/87: Die Neubaugebiete—Dokumente, Projekte*, vol. 2 (Berlin: Quadriga Verlag, 1981), 260. **5** "Ergebnisprotokoll der Preisgerichtssitzung des internationalen städtebaulichen Ideenwettbewerbs 'Wohnen in der Friedrichstadt'," n. p. **6** Ibid. **7** Those invited were the offices of Hausen and Rave, Dietrich von Beulwitz, Jochen Brandi, Maurice Culot, Franz and Hauser, and Tarrago Theilacker-Pons (who won first prize) for Block 9; Graaf and Schweger, Uwe Kiessler, Pier Luigi Nicolin, Rave and Partner (co-winner of the first prize), and Bier, Korn, Zeitler for Block 20; and Helge Bofinger, Douglas Clelland, Halfmann and Zillich, John Hejduk (who won a special prize), Friedrich Kurrent, and Jürgen Sawade for Block 19. The jury was composed of Carlo Aymonino, Werner Düttmann, Klaus Humpert, Kleihues, Jürgen Paul (replacing Anthony Vidler), and Christoph Sattler. See "Internationaler engerer Wettbewerb. Berlin Südliche Friedrichstadt Wilhelmstraße. Bericht der Vorprüfung," IBA Report. 1981. A 81/038, Landesarchiv. **8** Stefan Schroth, "Ergebnisprotokoll der Preisgerichtssitzung des internationalen engeren Wettbewerbs Berlin Südliche Friedrichstadt Wilhelmstraße," IBA Report, B 81/039, Landesarchiv. **9** Günter Schlusche, interview by the author, November 8, 2016, Berlin, in English, 00:14:04–00:15:59; 00:19:39–00:21:20. **10** "Dokumentation: Offener Wettbewerb Berlin, Südliche Friedrichstadt, Gestaltung des Geländes des ehemaligen Prinz-Albrecht-Palais," IBA Report, Berlin, September 1985. **11** Josef Paul Kleihues, "A Non-Place: Competition Designs for the Prinz-Albrecht-Palais in Berlin," *Lotus* 42, no. 2 (April 1984): 101–10. **12** Ibid., 101. **13** Ibid. **14** "Restricted International Competition Lützowstrasse Southern Tiergarten Quarter of Berlin," IBA Competition Brief. Berlin, September 1980, Berlin B 80/19, Landesarchiv; Questions and Answers report (Rückfragenbeantwortung): B 95/019; Jury Meeting Minutes report (Bericht der Vorprüfung), B 81/065, Landesarchiv. **15** "Lützowstrasse," Manuscript, No. 8004, p. 1, OMA Archives, Rotterdam. **16** La deuxième chance de l'architecture moderne. Entretien avec Rem Koolhaas," *L'Architecture d'Aujourd'hui* 238 (April 1985): 2–27. Quotation: 6. **17** "Restricted International Competition Lützowstrasse Southern Tiergarten Quarter of Berlin. Bericht der Vorprüfung," IBA Report, B 81/065, Landesarchiv. **18** "Restricted International Competition Lützowstrasse Southern Tiergarten Quarter of Berlin. Preisgerichtsprotokoll," Berlin, 1981, B 81/034, Landesarchiv. **19** Ibid. **20** Heinrich Klotz and Josef Paul Kleihues, eds., *International Building Exhibition Berlin 1987* (New York: Rizzoli, 1986), 89. **21** "Wettbewerb Lützowplatz Berlin Südlisches Tiergartenviertel," Competition Brief of May 1987, B 87/012, Landesarchiv. **22** *Erste Projekte*, 203–11.

STOP VII

Exit Implies Entries' Lament: Open Architecture in John Hejduk's IBA-1984/87 Immigrant Housing[1]

The Studio for a Painter and Studio for a Musician designed by John Hejduk for IBA-1984/87 in 1982 were elevated houses that had stairs but no gates (Figure VII.1, also see Figure I.7).[2] One could only enter them if one chose to do so permanently during construction. There was no other way but being either perpetually in or perpetually out of the painter's and the musician's house. When their full-scale models were built for the *Idee, Prozeß, Ergebnis* (idea, process, result) exhibition in Berlin in 1984, guests could indeed imagine themselves climbing the stairs of the metal-clad structure of the musician's studio, even if they could not do so physically. They could imagine walking through the door before it was sealed off and then going through the dark cubic space with no windows toward the narrow slit at its end. They could imagine the light that would have entered from that slit, and how that light would have marked a horizon in the dark space, and how that horizon line would have made the corners of the space disappear by virtue of the fact that it extended horizontally on three sides, and how that disappearance would have erased the feel of the space's boundaries, and how that erasure would have made them realize that they were no more sealed inside than anyone outside (Figure VII.2).

Even though Hejduk offered no direct explanations, he left many clues about interpreting these structures. One clue might be a poem in the *Berlin Masque* sketchbook, which was also prepared as part of the architect's competition entry for these projects. "The House of the Suicide" told the story of a resident who loved the work of Paul Cézanne but was frustrated by the fact that his community did not appreciate the painter. He was eventually sealed off behind the welded door, agreeing to his self-imprisonment in a house with no exit or entry.[3] Another line in the same sketchbook might provide another clue: "Exit implies entries' lament."[4] Perhaps the house with no gates did not represent a territory with closed borders, a withdrawal from society, or an elitist exclusiveness, but rather a confident open invitation that trusted the guest to make an unconditional commitment.

Hejduk designed the houses for a painter and a musician as part of his projects for IBA-1984/87. As claustrophobic as it might be to imagine a house with no entrance and exit, it is perhaps more suffocating to discover how common such houses have been for so many women and children living in the neighborhood where Hejduk's IBA projects stand today. For instance, anyone walking east from Hejduk's buildings on Oranienstrasse for a few minutes would have come across the IBA-renovated buildings on Dresdener Strasse. And if they randomly rang the doorbell of one of the apartments,

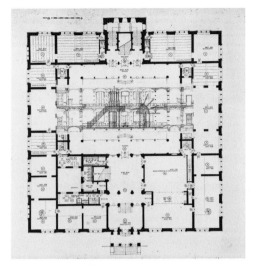

Figure VII.1 John Hejduk, Studio for a Painter and Studio for a Musician, drawn on the floor plan of Martin Gropius Bau for *Idee Prozeß Ergebnis* Exhibition, IBA-1984/87, Berlin.

they could well have met a "Turkish bride" (see stop II for a discussion of this term) who never left her apartment.[5] They could have learned that she had moved to Germany as a young woman with her husband who had found a job as a guest worker, and that she thus became an immigrant in a country whose language she did not speak, and how that migration deprived her of citizenship rights that are the necessary condition of being entitled to human rights in the first place, and how in that deprivation she nonetheless found a way to design a beautiful home of her own in a once decaying but now renovated (by IBA) Berlin apartment where she raised her children and where she spent every hour of every day waiting for a visit from migrant friends, and now a visit from her grandchildren. In what follows, I identify Hejduk's architectural practice as an adventure game, that I interpret as an innovative form of open architecture in which the inhabitant is seen as an actor rather than a spectator who behaves in ways predefined by the author-architect.

John Hejduk and the Architecture of the Adventure Game

Of all the North American architects who participated in IBA-1984/87, none was perhaps as enigmatic and unordinary as John Hejduk. Except for the three projects for IBA, Hejduk did not construct any buildings in the conventional sense during his lifetime (his other famous building, the Wall House, was built posthumously). He was an influential educator (he served as dean of the School of Architecture at Cooper Union, New York, for twenty-five years) and an architect who envisioned in freehand drawings, brightly colored paintings, and laconic poems.

A shift in Hejduk's design practice took place just as he was creating his projects for IBA—a shift that was analyzed in the heyday of structuralist theory as a shift from *langue* to *parole*, from structure to meaning, and from nonrepresentation to narrative.[6]

Figure VII.2 John Hejduk, Studio for a Painter and Studio for a Musician, as exhibited in IBA-1984/87's *Idee Prozeß Ergebnis* Exhibition, photographed by Siegfried Büker, Berlin, 1984.

His earlier work had explored the possible variations of a self-chosen but restricted formal system. The Texas Houses (designed in 1952–62) had operated on the nine-square system and created permutations by shifting the horizontal and vertical variants.[7] The Diamond Houses (1962–67) explored the formal potentials of a system that was generated by placing a diagonal grid in a square plan.[8] Paying homage to Mies van der Rohe, Piet Mondrian, and Andrea Palladio—not for their minimalism but for their disciplined and in-depth formal studies with restrained systems[9]—these house studies were endorsed by Peter Eisenman as exercises within the autonomous sphere of architecture that illustrated the rich scope of formal innovation.[10] Hejduk had later developed the nine-square exercise as an effective pedagogical method. With identical spaces for bedrooms, living rooms, and kitchens, as well as additional bathrooms designed for the sake of symmetry, these houses were viewed as formal exercises of a self-generating system, rather than designs for real people—a situation that would change but would nonetheless partially shape Hejduk's housing designs for IBA.[11]

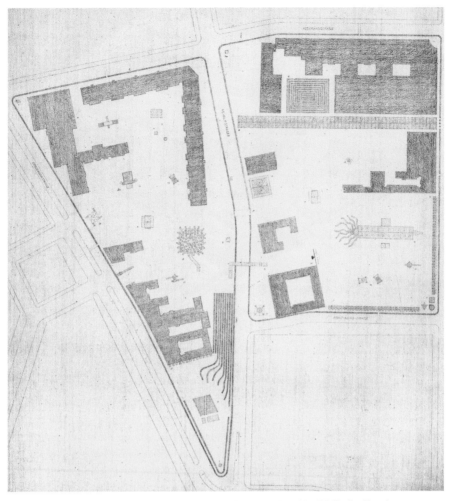

Figure VII.3 John Hejduk, "Wilhelmstrasse Competition" project, IBA-1984/87, Berlin. Site plan.

Hejduk's project for the IBA Neubau's "Wilhelmstrasse Competition" in 1981 involved a shift from these studies. The architect suggested a Berlin Masque, an enigmatic project in which sculpture-like objects and freestanding slender towers were scattered on a site enclosed by a hedge (Figure VII.3).[12] The list of proposed ritualistic structures included reading, pantomime and public theaters; a house for the oldest inhabitant; bell, watch, water, mask, wind, guest, observation, and clock towers; a conciliator's space; a neighborhood physician's unit; a crossover bridge; a lottery kiosk; a book market; and shopping booths (Figure VII.4). If the project had been chosen in the competition and built, the site would have been filled with randomly placed buildings that would have stimulated any imagination in search of metaphors: theaters with tails, façades with eyes, towers like umbrellas, bridges like geometrized caterpillars, kiosks like Medusa heads with bad-hair days, booths like tents, houses like robots on wheels, and so on (Figure VII.5). Seen from above, a hedge would have spelled out "Berlin Masque" in a stylized squarish font.

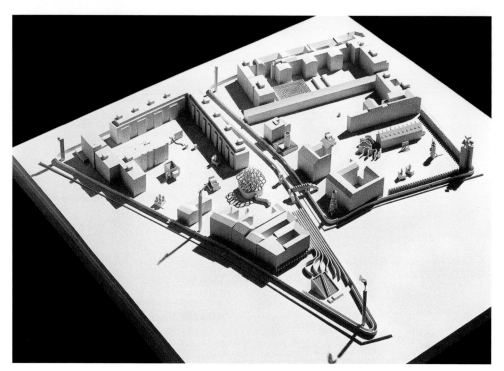

Figure VII.4 John Hejduk, "Wilhelmstrasse Competition" project, IBA-1984/87, Berlin. Site model.

The Berlin Masque sketchbook contained many representations of Hejduk's Wilhelmstrasse project, expressed in poems, stories, sketches of Medusa heads, and drawings of fallen angels.[13] Sketches and texts made separately on different paper were glued onto the delicate yellow pages, as were photographs of existing Berlin buildings (Figure VII.6). Some of the freehand sketches clearly show the initial designs for the Berlin Tower and the Gatehouse projects that were eventually built in the context of IBA-1984/87 (discussed in the next section). The detailed study for Studio for a Painter and Studio for a Musician was added in 1982.

Hejduk also participated in IBA's "Prinz Albrecht Palace Competition" in 1984, on a site that the Nazis used for torture during World War II and where the Topography of Terror Museum stands today (Figure VII.7). Hejduk named this project Victims and proposed to place sixty-seven structures—each with a name, picture, and story—in an area enclosed by a hedge, similar to his "Wilhelmstrasse Competition" entry. These structures would have been placed in the site one after another over a span of sixty years, and the city's residents would have decided their precise location. This must be why Hejduk represented the project with freehand drawings of each structure (Figure VII.8) and worked on one of the ensemble drawings for which the ground plan of each structure was cut out and stitched to the site plan (Figure VII.9). With Victims, Hejduk's form-generating autonomous systems and enigmatic personal muses gained an equally poetic but more accessible political dimension.[14] The mysterious structures were now mobilized to participate in the emerging debate in Germany about Holocaust memorials (see stop VI).

a

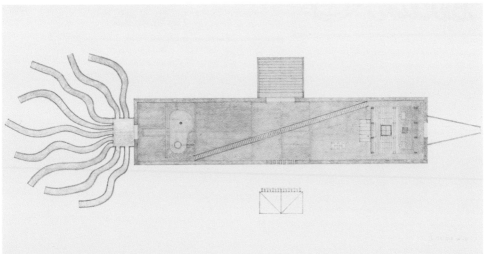

b

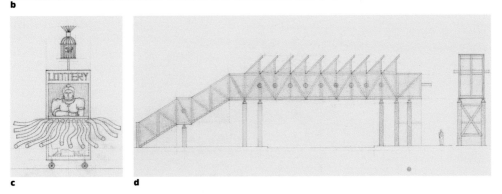

c   d

Figure VII.5 John Hejduk. "Wilhelmstrasse Competition" project, IBA-1984/87, Berlin. **a** Guest towers and shopping booths. **b** Theater masque. **c** Lottery woman. **d** Crossover bridge.

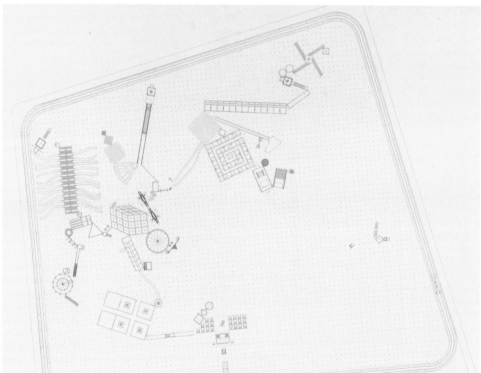

TOP: Figure VII.6 John Hejduk. Page from Berlin Masque sketchbook, c. 1982. Sketch of snake with caption "Berlin" and envelope containing postcards with views of Porta Pia, Rome, and Largo S. Mauro, Solopaca, Italy. BOTTOM: Figure VII.7 John Hejduk, "Prinz Albrecht Palace Competition" project, "Victims," IBA–1984/87, Berlin. Site Plan.

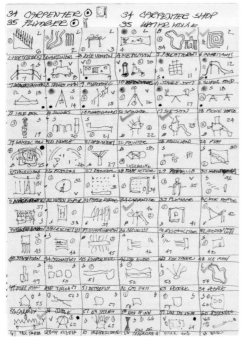

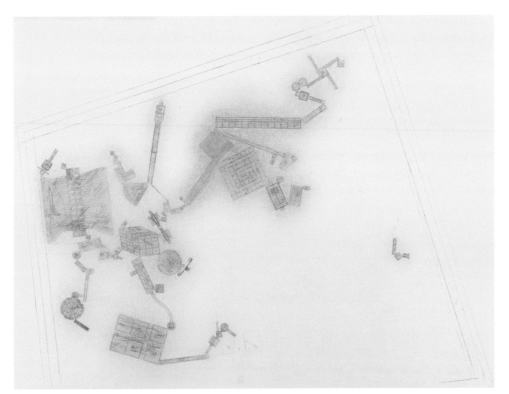

TOP: Figure VII.8 John Hejduk, "Prinz Albrecht Palace Competition" project, "Victims," IBA-1984/87, Berlin. Table of list of characters and study sketches of structures. BOTTOM: Figure VII.9 John Hejduk, "Prinz Albrecht Palace Competition" project, "Victims," IBA-1984/87, Berlin. Site plan with movable parts.

The masque is a theatrical form that emerged in sixteenth-century Europe and flourished in England in particular. Usually having no beginning, end, or fixed plot, a masque could involve singing, dancing, acting, pantomime, and improvisation on an elaborately designed stage. In the vernacular version, players wearing masks would call on the nobles, and spectators could join in the dancing. If Hejduk's Masque had been built in Berlin, guests could have visited the site (or stage), circled the structures in any order they chose, entered the houses, climbed the towers, crossed the bridges, and shopped at booths and kiosks. Reading Hejduk's accompanying texts, the visitor could have joined the dots in multiple directions both within and across writing and physical space. A set of characters allegorized in built structures could have generated an indefinite number of stories in each visitor's imagination.

Hejduk continued to prepare other masques and travelogues until he died in 2000, including several for Venice, Berlin, Lancaster, Hanover, Riga, and Vladivostok (Figure VII.10).[15] For instance, the Lancaster/Hanover Masque (1982–83) would have contained sixty-eight structures—many of which were the same as the ones in Victims—and he wrote stories about these subjects' lives and occupations:

> a widow's house which would involve a moving day each time a woman was
> widowed in the community;
> a rag-and-bone man's wagon pulled by a horse;
> a retired actor with a low voice who performed pantomimes occasionally;
> a Ferris wheel that completed a circle in 24 hours with a timekeeper's place
> attached (and this timekeeper had previously watched another Ferris wheel
> collapse, leaving a dead child in each seat);
> a reaper's house with a private library full of books about the history of reaping;
> a reddleman's place who referred to Thomas Hardy;
> the house of the suicide like the one in the Berlin Masque.[16]

Wim van der Bergh suggested that we might feel like Daedalus's son, Icarus, in Hejduk's Lancaster/Hanover Masque. With utmost childlike curiosity, Icarus welcomed the labyrinth his father had prepared as a playground for discovery instead of seeing it as

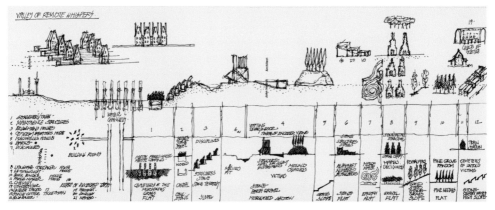

Figure VII.10 John Hejduk, "Valley of Remote Whispers" drawing from "Victims 2," 1993.

352

a prison. He cherished it as a world of myth and magic rather than feeling that it imprisoned him in rationality.[17]

There were also intertextual relations in Hejduk's oeuvre. The buildings and characters moved between different masques: they could appear for the first time in a masque for one city but could be transferred to other masques. Just as actors could embody different characters in multiple plays, so the painter's studio in Berlin was cast as the old farmer's house in the Lancaster / Hanover Masque, and the musician's studio as the widow's house. After a while, in the masques for Russian cities, the structures even had wheels, as if they could travel freely. This inspired the architectural historian and critic Anthony Vidler to name Hejduk's practice "vagabond architecture"—not only because his structures were on wheels, but also because they stood for a nomadic ethic as opposed to institutionalized architecture, not unlike Gilles Deleuze and Felix Guattari's characterization of a nomad space in opposition to the state space. The vagabond was the utmost antidote for the sedentary.[18]

Of the many possible interpretations of Hejduk's work, I would like to entertain the idea of an adventure game as one form of open architecture, an intersubjective play to delineate both a rapport that opens an individual self to a stranger and a happening that evolves over time. One of the critical essays about Hejduk's work published during his lifetime,[19] by Peggy Deamer, termed the architect's oeuvre an autobiography, implying a correspondence between the masques' characters and Hejduk's personal history. An autobiography is different from a diary that may or may not be read by others. The ambiguity of the "I" in an autobiography—which could refer to the author or the narrator or hero—leaves space for curiosity and interpretation.[20] Nonetheless, Hejduk's masques constitute very disjointed and coded autobiographies for anyone who did not know him personally, which is partly why I suggest calling them intersubjective plays that happen in the genre of the adventure game. This necessitates the participation of a second mind, points to the impossibility of a monologue, and confirms the existence of a meaning-construing reader.

The structures in Hejduk's projects are highly personal and enigmatic, impenetrable and uninterpretable with any level of certainty; but they are not the musings of an isolated mind that denies the existence of other minds. Unlike classical stages that put the theatrical play in a separate frame in front of the audience, Hejduk's objects invite audience participation in the theater, just like historical masques. Overall, Hejduk's late oeuvre is like an adventure game in which players wander physically (or virtually with their minds) between the objects—from one masque to another, from one character's life to another—decoding messages, finding a clue at each step and following it to find other clues until stories are revealed and Hejduk's universe makes a bit more sense (even if things may fall into different places for each player). The whole process is like solving a puzzle or an empathic exploration, an adventure game that is predicated on an intersubjective experience.

In an adventure game, players transport themselves into a new world that is free of the memories of the existing world. They have to look around for clues in the environment

Figure VII.11 John Hejduk, Berlin Night, c. 1980s. Watercolors mounted on board. **a** Canal Bridge, End of Night Structure, Security Bureau, Astronomy Observatory, Building Department, Theater Studios and Custom House. **b** Building of Time, Museum of Japanese Armor, End of Night Structure, Museum of Teutonic Armor. **c** Building Department, Clock Tower, the Senate and Council and Jurist Stadia. **d** Ministry of Communications, Record Keeper, Central Archives and Cemetery.

as if they have never been there before, as if they have woken up to a world of which they remember nothing. Unlike what they do in their daily routines, they open every drawer, lift every book, and check every corner; and they collect every possible clue in the hope that it will help solve the mystery of the game. Players are asked to engage with the artifacts of this new artificial universe by leaving behind the symbolic system and know-how of their current daily lives. There is a similar experience in decoding the meanings of Hejduk's intertextual masques (Figure VII.11).

Figure VII.12 John Hejduk, Berlin Night, c. 1980s.
Watercolor mounted on board.

Hejduk's use of the term "masque" to define his work invites us to discuss architecture through the lens of theater and performance studies. The architectural work here is conceived of less as a finished building than as an evolving, performative stage; the architect less as an all-defining author than as a coproducer of a play; and the inhabitant less as a user who is expected to live the life determined by the all-knowing architect than as an active, participating audience member. The hidden meanings and secret codes in Hejduk's masques activate the meaning-construing spectator. This intersubjective experience in the adventure game may involve a one-to-one relationship between the architect and the viewer (just like in interactive art) or relationships among many people to activate a social practice (just like in participatory art). For instance, in Hejduk's IBA project Victims, as noted above, Berlin's inhabitants would have decided the placement of the sixty-seven structures over a sixty-year period. This scenario is somewhat similar to what Umberto Eco identified as "openness" in Luciano Berio's and Karlheinz Stockhausen's musical compositions. Eco likened these compositions to "the components of a construction kit" that the composer hands to the performer, as if he were "unconcerned about the manner of their eventual deployment" (Figure VII.12).[21] During the height of poststructuralist thinking, Eco and Roland Barthes respectively explained "Open Work" (1962) and "Death of the Author" (1968) as historical necessity rather than random choice. Several chronological markers, including the emergence of the modern subject along with the collapse of theological meaning, brought the "sharpening awareness of the concept of the work susceptible to many different interpretations," in Eco's words, and "the birth of the reader at the cost of the death of the author," in Barthes's words.[22]

The concept of the emancipated reader in an open work has inspired scholars to understand the possibility of the visual arts to construct a communal space of collective and political engagement. For example, rereading the history of modern and avant-garde art throughout the twentieth century from the perspective of performance studies, Claire Bishop pointed out that the "desire to activate the audience in participatory art is at the same time the drive to emancipate it from a state of alienation induced by the dominant ideological order—be this consumer capitalism, totalitarian socialism or military dictatorship."[23] Today, the idea of an emancipated spectator in a participatory performance continues to inspire thinkers as a model for an apposite relation between aesthetics and politics. Positing the theater as an "exemplary community form" in *The Emancipated Spectator*, Jacques Rancière wrote of the possibility of realizing a "theatre without spectators" and of challenging the separation between viewing and acting, stage and auditorium, and seeing and doing, so that a spectator is not simply seduced by images but becomes an active participant: "The less the playwright knows what he wants the collective of spectator[s] to do, the more he knows that they should, at any rate, act as a collective, transform their aggregation into community."[24] Whether or not Hejduk intended his masques to embody the intellectual and political potentials I ascribe to them through performance and participatory art theories, his work invites a discussion of the future of open architecture in these terms.

Appropriation as Subordination of the Architect

Hardly any project could have been as far from complying with the requirements in the competition brief as Hejduk's proposal for IBA's "Wilhelmstrasse Competition."[25] The brief for the competition outlined that "the participants are asked particularly to put forward proposals for quality housing suitable for a variety of population groups and diverse requirements."[26] The aim was to increase the number of inhabitants in South Friedrichstadt from 11,000 to 18,000 and to add 500 subsidized apartments on the site (10 percent of which would be for people with disabilities), plus 150 apartments for senior citizens, kindergartens, nurseries, shops, and parking.[27] However, Hejduk's competing project barely provided any public housing or fulfilled the other requirements. The brief listed the need to meet the "requirements of the everyday life of work, school and leisure" and the "dense interpenetration of work, living and leisure."[28] However, Hejduk's project seemed less about work or other everyday activities.

The brief also included a long section written by Thomas Biller and Wolfgang Schäche that gave detailed information about the historical urban development and the construction of landmark buildings in South Friedrichstadt, as well as in the competition area since the 1730s. This report went over the baroque plan by the royal architect Philipp Gerlach and the residential buildings at that time, which typically contained large gardens and four apartments. It described changes in the nineteenth century to accommodate housing for the bourgeoisie, which increased the height of buildings and brought about the construction of side and back wings. The report then stressed that the intense residential and industrial development in the Kaiser era (1871–1918) was "the most decisive period" that determined the "physiognomy" of the area.[29] It pointed out the relative pause in urban growth during the Weimar period (1918–33) and the damage during World War II, and finally criticized postwar traffic planning throughout the 1960s as well as Werner Düttmann's high-rise buildings and mega-blocks as destructive interventions that disrespected the historical fabric (even though the construction of the circular Mehringplatz was reminiscent of the historical lay-out).[30]

All this history guided the competition's basic requirement: "The historical ground plan of the district should be respected and the fragments of the historical buildings which have survived should serve as orientation for the scale."[31] The competitors were instructed to pay particular attention to developments of the Kaiser era: "The character which developed during this period and its architectural expression should be the historical premise to which future plans are oriented."[32] "Our imagination will complete the ground plan," Josef Paul Kleihues noted in his introduction to the "Wilhelmstrasse Competition" report.[33] However, Hejduk's masque was hardly reminiscent of anything in Berlin's urban typology or morphology.

The competition projects of the architects—including Hejduk, Rem Koolhaas, and Eisenman, whose ideas were not compatible with IBA's ideals—were not handled consistently. While Hejduk's Wilhelmstrasse proposal might have been a far cry from IBA values and competition requirements, it was more conceivable that his Victims project could win the "Prinz Albrecht Palace Competition," which had requested a lyrical memorial on a site of Nazi mass murders. However, this project did not win either, and Kleihues explained why—Hejduk's competition project "won the jury's sympathy right from the start, though the enigmatic nature of his sublimated, intellectually complex aesthetic, charged with literary references, appeared obscure to many. ... His work was comprehensible to children, animals and metaphysicians. But it proved difficult to relate to a place charged with guilt."[34] Even though Hedjuk did not win any of the competitions, his projects evidently inspired Kleihues to such an extent that he thereafter looked for a site to build their assimilated versions. Hejduk designed an urban villa in Tegel, and in Kreuzberg both the Berlin Tower housing in Block 11 and the Berlin Gatehouse. The painter's and musician's studios were considered for Block 2 and then for Block 11, although they were never constructed. The Berlin Gatehouse was built in a tiny infill plot on the "Wilhelmstrasse Competition" site. As a result, IBA became the only client to give Hejduk the opportunity to construct buildings in his lifetime, even though these structures were quite different from their original competition versions. Moritz Müller, a graduate of Cooper Union and the contact architect in Berlin, must have helped significantly in meeting the mandatory German housing standards and making sure that the construction was as precise as possible in details.

The Berlin Tower housing at the corner of Charlotten- and Besselstrasse represents a midpoint between the ideas of Kleihues and those of Hejduk. It is not a perimeter block but two parallel five-story buildings with a fourteen-story tower between them, all standing out with bright green metal-clad balconies, awnings, and window frames on a grayish stucco surface (Figure VII.13).[35] The housing complex partly encloses a green area and a playground, which is completely open to public access but nevertheless secluded from the street by its set-back location.

Figure VII.13 View of John Hejduk's Berlin Tower for IBA-1984/87, photographed by Esra Akcan, Berlin, 2011.

The two horizontal wings collectively contain forty-eight apartments with one to three bedrooms. They look similar at first sight, but one of the wings is organized around a glazed gallery loaded on one side with apartments (Figure VII.14), while the other is terraced housing (two apartments per floor share separate building entrances and stairs). Both wings have large balconies overlooking the common green area, which are enlivened with plants, patio furniture, and residents' satellite dishes. The identical side façades of the horizontal buildings along Besselstrasse with inversely sloped pitched roofs create an anthropomorphic metaphor of a face with two eyes, a long nose, and Medusa hair (Figure VII.15). The top-floor apartments have courtyards open to the sky and skylights in the mid-line of the section to account for the height of the reversed roof (Figure VII.16).

Only seven duplexes are located in the narrow high-rise of the Berlin Tower housing, which were originally envisioned as open lofts for artists with service spaces attached as separate small towers. One tower is for the common elevator, another for fire-escape stairs, the third for kitchens, and the fourth for bathrooms and storage—and all four towers are accessible from each loft by crossing separate bridges. This unorthodox ground plan creates an illusion of scale: an extremely slender tower with a minimal footprint (20×20 feet, 9 feet for the service towers) looks like a bigger compound than it actually is. The main tower is textured with rhythmic metal-clad balconies in the form of small cubes with triangular awnings (Figure VII.17). It is one of the few tall buildings in the area, and one of the three built by IBA. The studios for the painter and the musician were intended to be placed in front of this tower, but—as noted above—they were never built.

Figure VII.14 View of the glazed gallery in John Hejduk's Berlin Tower for IBA-1984/87, photographed by Esra Akcan, Berlin, 2009.

Figure VII.15 View of the front façade of the side wing in John Hejduk's Berlin Tower for IBA-1984/87, Berlin, photographed by Esra Akcan, Berlin, 2009.

Finally, the Berlin Gatehouse is located in a narrow infill site of the building block just across the street from the Berlin Tower housing (Figure VII.18). Confirming Hejduk's inclination for self-referential intertextuality, it adopts elements from two of the architect's installations: 13 Watchtowers of Cannaregio in Venice (1979) and Clock/Collapse of Time in Bedford Square, London (1986). The latter, built to commemorate the victims of the Gestapo, was a stick-like installation inscribed with the numbers 1–13 (the number 12 was covered over to indicate that the clock had stopped) falling and rising from a joint and thus alternating between vertical, oblique, and horizontal positions at two-week intervals (Figure VII.19).[36] The whole structure was on wheels. The symmetrical and proportional front façade of the Berlin Gatehouse is composed of two towers on both sides (which were meant to have the numbers 1–12 inscribed on them) and a gravestone-like central mass with a large opening that gives access to the Hof of the typical Berlin perimeter block. An alternative interpretation could be five slender modular towers side by side, rolling up and down.

I have outlined the process from competition to construction and from imagination to realization of only one architect's vision, but similar processes took place for many small and large blocks designed as part of IBA Neubau in West Kreuzberg. An experiment in building collectively, IBA sought to use an integrated and collaborative approach according to which new buildings would not only reconstruct the historical structure but also coalesce. In this coordination, Kleihues, the director of the building

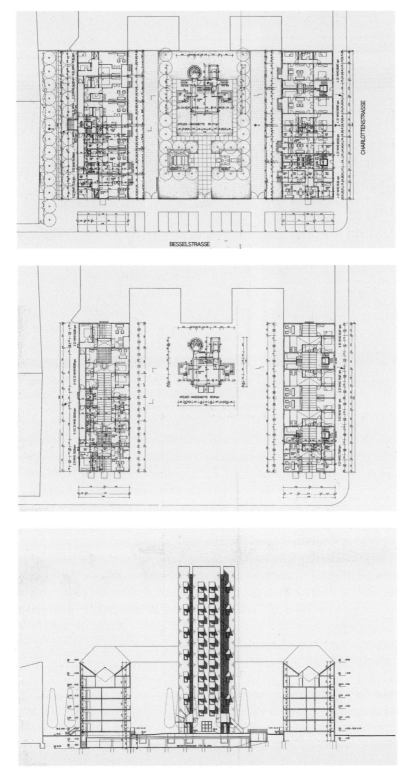

Figure VII.16 John Hejduk, Berlin Tower for IBA-1984/87, Berlin. Plan, section, and elevation.

Figure VII.17 View of the tower in John Hejduk's Berlin Tower for IBA-1984/87, photographed by Esra Akcan, Berlin, 2009.

Figure VII.18 View of John Hejduk's Gatehouse for IBA-1984/87, photographed by Esra Akcan, Berlin, 2011.

exhibition, served sometimes as mediator and at other times as the dictating hand. He served on all of the competition juries and maintained dialogues with the winning architects during the design process. Kleihues defined his role as the enabler of architects: "Unlike other artists the architect is dependent on the support of the world around him, the agreement of those who hold political and financial power, if he is to build at all."[37]

While mediating between the architects and the political authorities, however, IBA-Neubau overbearingly changed designs. Building collectively demanded the subordination of the new buildings into the so-called gene of the city—that is, their assimilation into the nineteenth-century ground plan with perimeter blocks. Architects who refused to comply with this requirement were eliminated in the process despite the quality of their projects or were assimilated into the process only after agreeing to make significant changes. For some architects, the typological design method based on the city's memory made it possible to work hospitably in groups or with collective ideals, which could generate another form of open architecture—but others found that it hindered their individuality.

Yeliz Erçakmak and Noncitizen Rights to Architecture

Once the residents moved in, Hejduk's buildings regained their life as masques. Hejduk presumed that the users of his masques would be willing to enter the circuitous routes of his mind and psyche, and that they would have a great deal of empathy and construe their own stories by putting together the clues in the adventure game that he had prepared. Once Hejduk's projects were occupied—that is, once his authorship phase was complete—the inhabitants took on even more extended roles in shaping their built environment, thereby amplifying the projects' character as open architecture. Out of the infinite number of possible resident appropriations of Hejduk's IBA buildings, let me illustrate one example—one that is unavoidably contingent and partial because it relies on an encounter at an arbitrary time between a random author (in this case, me) and a random resident who happened to live in that building at that particular time.

Having grown up in Dortmund as the daughter of two Turkish migrant teachers, Yeliz Erçakmak now lives in one of the duplexes in Hejduk's Berlin Tower with her husband. She speaks Turkish with a slight German accent, but she pronounces German terms with such precision that I find myself wanting to imitate her as I listen to and transcribe the recordings of our conversation. Working at the Türkische Gemeinde Deutschland (TGD)—one of the biggest and by far the most politically influential civil organizations protecting the rights of Turkish immigrants and noncitizens in Germany—Erçakmak is well aware of the continuing discrimination, although she acknowledges that she has not been subject to it herself. "In general, one could say that there is discrimination," she says. "I do believe that there is a certain level of discrimination in all state buildings, such as kindergartens or public housing. The ad hoc research also adds up to this conclusion. … In Germany, it is common that they would not rent a vacant apartment based on the name of the applicant. This has happened to a friend of mine."[38] We have lengthy conversations about TGD and other civil society organizations in Berlin that work for immigrants' rights and establish anti-discrimination networks.[39]

Figure VII.19 John Hejduk, Drawing reminiscent of Clock/Collapse Of Time from "Victims 2," 1993.

Erçakmak must have adopted the role of mediator already as a child, ever since she was singled out as the only Turkish pupil at school not placed in the "foreigner class." As discussed in stop I, foreigner classes were common practice throughout West Germany in the 1980s to separate citizen and noncitizen (especially Turkish) students, and even university lecturers endorsed this practice. Erçakmak does not know why she was not placed in the foreigner class with the other Turkish students. It could have been her address, she speculates: she lived in a different neighborhood from the children of immigrant parents from Turkey, who came to school on a different bus. Smiling out of a sense of historical distance, she still remembers the fights during breaks in the school day when German and Turkish children threw apples at each other—a memory I expect is vivid in the minds of many children of noncitizen parents who grew up in Europe at the time. As the only Turkish child in the German class, she likened herself to "a ping-pong ball between the two" groups—trying to stop the disputes that could, however, be settled only through the teachers' intervention.[40]

She and her husband were not determined to live in Kreuzberg, belying stereotypical expectations. They chose the neighborhood because of its proximity to their workplaces, but they certainly are not complaining about their choice. "Kreuzberg is a world-famous place. People all around the world make sure to pay a visit when they come to Berlin," she says as further evidence of her appreciation.[41] She had not imagined herself in Hejduk's building either:

> When I saw this building from the outside, I never expected to live here. On the contrary, I told myself that this is an uninhabitable building. It is a bit gray, a bit green; it does not look like a house. I also found it weird that the building is standing in the middle of the site, without a Hof. I did not know that there were small rooms inside the side towers. When I walked along the street, this building always caught my eye; I found it odd. I was curious about the side façade that looks like a smiling face, but I never followed up with my interest. It was rather a coincidence that I moved here, but I am really glad I did.[42]

The changes in the apartment suggest that it is perhaps not the original design itself that Erçakmak likes, but her own version of it. The Erçakmaks use the second floor of the apartment not as Hejduk had intended (as one open space to serve as an artist's studio), but as a divided space with several private rooms. Hejduk's daughter and the architectural students who visited the apartment told her about the architect's original intention, but she still prefers the divided space to an open loft as a more appropriate setup for modern couples.[43] When she explains this, she adopts the role of empowered user who has the last word as long as she occupies the space, which does not necessarily diminish her respect for the architectural community. On the contrary, she empathizes with the groups of 20–30 architectural students who often appear on her doorstep without any warning and expect to be invited in—a request she always grants, even if the apartment is too messy to receive visitors. "Students look at the glasses [camlar]," she tells me. "Glasses?" I ask. "Yes, there are fourteen glass windows in this space, which is very unusual," she explains—a number I had not bothered counting before.[44]

Figure VII.20 View of the balcony in Erçakmak's apartment in John Hejduk's Berlin Tower for IBA-1984/87, photographed by Esra Akcan, Berlin, 2010.

Other curious spaces are the small square balconies with their green metal-clad balustrades and triangular awnings that attract visitors' attention from outside. That the two balconies were rather unusually small, Erçakmak knew before moving in, but she grew to find them functional and quite sufficient. Imagining that the man and woman of the house would each sit on one of the balconies, her husband joked about constructing a bridge by placing a wooden platform in the air between the two balustrades. They now use only one of the balconies for outdoor activities and are amazed that the small space can accommodate not only two chairs and the smallest coffee table on the market, but also their bicycle (Figure VII.20).**45** However, they had to reserve the second balcony for their satellite dish, which barely fits.

Like many other immigrants from Turkey whose apartments are easily identifiable by satellite dishes attached to a balcony or window, the Erçakmaks use their dish to watch Turkish TV channels. After a Turkish immigrant family won its appeal to the German Federal Constitutional Court in 1993 (207 C 171/93), the residents gained legal permission to install satellite dishes as part of their constitutional right to freedom of information. Germany hence started being populated with satellite dishes all around (see Figure VII.24). Visual cacophony according to some people but symbols of demands for freedom of information according to others, the dishes are testimony to the lived forms of IBA buildings. While extending immigrant rights, they simultaneously stamp their houses as territories of the stateless. The satellite dishes scattered all around Hejduk's housing complex, along with other signs of socially imposed

Figure VII.21 Satellite dishes on John Hejduk's Berlin Tower Housing for IBA-1984/87, photographed by Esra Akcan, Berlin, 2009.

absurdity, are more reminiscent of the architect's original masques than the buildings themselves (Figure VII.21). (Coincidentally, Hejduk used satellite dishes in his Subject-Object installation, Figure VII.22).

One of the most idiosyncratic features of Hejduk's main tower is the set of transparent bridges needed to reach the small towers on the sides. Two of these side towers—the ones containing the elevator and the stairs—are for semipublic use, but the other two are accessed from inside the apartments and contain four small rooms for each unit on two floors. The Erçakmaks have a kitchen, bathroom, laundry room, and a reading room in these spaces, each measuring just six square meters (Figure VII.23). Erçakmak smiles tolerantly at the unusual decision to design a transparent bridge leading to the bathroom: it requires undressing and dressing completely in the bathroom, she jokes, and one needs to be constantly on the lookout for people peering into the bathroom door.[46] She appreciates the other three side-tower rooms much more. She can quickly finish the housework in the minimal, efficient kitchen and enjoy the rest of the day, and she feels that the laundry is conveniently detached from the rest of the house. She appreciates how she can cross the bridge to the reading room, and how that act of crossing creates the feeling of leaving the house, and how that detachment allows her to feel outside in another world if she chooses to close the door of the room, or how an open door instead allows her to stay informed about the inside while still being able to read a book,[47] and how that ability to choose to be inside or outside empowers her—in contrast to the voluntary prisoners of Kreuzberg, including the painter and

Figure VII.22 John Hejduk, Subject-Object Installation,
Riga Project. Rosenwald-Wolf Gallery. 1987,
photographed by Hélène Binet.

the musician in Hejduk's masques and the Turkish immigrant who refuses to leave her apartment just a couple of blocks away.

Architecture is by definition open: once inhabited, users appropriate it whether the architect had anticipated or forbidden that, but this is not what defines open architecture. Eco also emphasized this distinction: each artwork is open in the sense that it is interpreted differently in each reception. Indeed, what distinguishes a work of art from a traffic sign, for example, is precisely the number of "different perspectives from which it can be viewed and understood,"[48] precisely the various "resonances and echoes" it can generate in different viewers: "Hence, every reception of a work of art is both an interpretation and a performance of it, because in every reception the work takes on a fresh perspective for itself."[49] However, interpretability does not necessarily distinguish an open work from a closed one. According to Eco, one of the qualities that makes a work open is its intentionally unfinished nature that awaits completion by a performer or audience: "In fact, rather than submit to the 'openness' as an inescapable element of artistic interpretation, he [the artist] subsumes it into a positive aspect of his production, recasting the work so as to expose it to the maximum possible 'opening.'"[50]

In the case of architecture, appropriability—or the fact that a building is almost always appropriated by the inhabitants—does not make something open architecture. Rather, open architecture occurs when an architect embraces or anticipates the quality of openness during the stage of design. For example, participatory architecture (namely, the design that is shaped in part by democratic communal meetings like the ones in IBA Altbau) is one form of open architecture, but not the only one. Part of the reason I have chosen Hejduk's work to exemplify open architecture in this chapter is because he disrupts formulaic categories that would have frozen this discussion in bipolarities such as individual versus collective, aesthetic versus political concerns, complex versus simple communication with the audience, egoistic versus collaborative architects, and top-down versus typological urban planning.[51] Instead, Hejduk's work exemplifies different layers of openness at different stages in its design, construction, and occupation. On the one hand, Hejduk's initial, highly individualized IBA projects are examples of open architecture even if they did not result from collaboration or the reconstruction of collective memory, and they were indeed closed, so to speak, by the proponents of this collaborative typological urban design approach. On the other hand, the active spectators or participant inhabitants recharged the built work with new layers of openness.

Before ending this book, I need to make a last point to clarify why it is important to explore open architecture today. Open architecture is predicated on the welcoming of a distinctly other mind or group of minds into the process of architectural design. It is the translation of a new ethics of hospitality into architecture. For Rancière, the emancipation of the spectator is a way to overcome the impotency determined by the critique of spectacle: "The discourse on the spectacle and the idea that we are all enclosed in the field of the commodity, the spectator, advertising images and so on … generates a kind of anti-democratic discourse and the incapacity of the masses for any political intervention and, on the other hand, it nurtures a discourse on the uselessness of any kind of artistic practice because it says everything depends on the market. … But it's necessary to get out of this discourse, which is a discourse of impotence."[52] Similarly, in the context of an architectural discourse all too willing to boost or condemn the "starchitect" in this spectacle and an architectural determinism too confident of the architect's authority over the lives of users—and moreover in a global practice too content with the fact that a handful of Western professionals design buildings all over the world without paying attention to postcolonial theories or ideas of global art history—open architecture calls for a change in standards. Open architecture can take

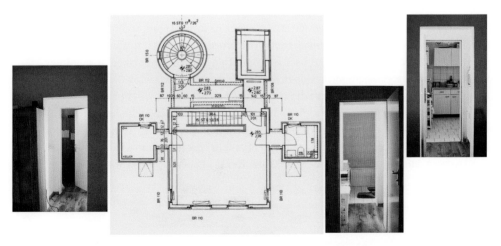

Figure VII.23 Appropriations of side-tower rooms in Erçakmak's apartment in John Hejduk's Berlin Tower for IBA-1984/87, photographed by Esra Akcan, Berlin, 2010.

Figure VII.24 Esra Akcan, "Freedom of Information." Collage on Satellite Dish, Exhibited at Istanbul Design Biennale, 2012.

different forms. Collective urban design, or the collaboration of nonhierarchically positioned architects in a given urban setting, may be one form of open architecture, and so might be participatory design (even though its process remains unresolved), which involves the anticipation of change, user appropriation, and the unfinished or ongoing nature of work. A significant form of open architecture involves viewing the inhabitant as a subject rather than an object who is supposed to behave in ways predefined by the author-architect. Still another difficult but worthy form of open architecture for the global present involves the ultimate welcoming into design of noncitizens: the opening of an individual architect to the stateless, of architectural discourse to the refugee, the diaspora, and the geographical other. Other forms of open architecture might be ...

1 A version of this chapter was previously published as Esra Akcan, "Exit Implies Entries' Lament: Open Architecture in John Hejduk's IBA-1984/87 Immigrant Housing," in *Notes on Critical Architecture: Praxis Reloaded*, ed. Gevork Hartoonian (London: Ashgate, 2015). The text has been revised to focus on the topic of this chapter. **2** "Studio for a Painter and Studio for a Musician," John Hejduk Papers, AP 145.S2.D50, Canadian Centre for Architecture, Montreal [hereafter CCA]. **3** John Hejduk, "The House of the Suicide," in Berlin Masque Sketchbook, DR 1998: 0098:001, John Hejduk Papers, CCA; Hejduk wrote: "Structure: Made of steel panels, / factory painted white enamel. / An eye slit in one elevation. A door in the other. / Roof made of vertical volumetric triangular slivers / Diminishing to a tiny top opening. He / liked to watch the points of light move / along the walls and floor. / The Farm Community in agreement with the / Family sealed up the door by welding" (ibid., n.p.). **4** John Hejduk, "Acropolis," in Hejduk, "Berlin Masque Sketchbook," n.p. ibid. **5** Details about this resident have been withheld at her request. **6** See Michael Hays, ed., *Hejduk's Chronotope* (New York: Princeton Architectural Press, 1996). **7** John Hejduk, "Statement 1964," in *John Hejduk: 7 Houses* (New York: Institute for Architecture and Urban Studies, 1980). **8** John Hejduk, "3 Projects: 1962–66," *AD* 54, nos. 11–12 (1984): 86–88, and "Diamond House Project, House A, 1980," *AD* 55, nos. 3–4 (1985): 66–67. **9** John Hejduk, "Seminar," *Yale School of Architecture Seminar Papers* 2 (1982): 181–224. **10** Peter Eisenman, "In My Father's House Are Many Maisons," in *John Hejduk: 7 Houses*, Also see Manfredo Tafuri, "European Grafitti," trans. Victor Caliandro, *Oppositions* 5 (summer 1976): 35–73. **11** Kenneth Frampton discusses the social production of space in these houses ("Notes from Underground," *Artforum* [April 1972]: 40–47). **12** *Berlin Masque Sketchbook*, DR 1998: 0098:001–057, John Hejduk Papers, CCA. **13** *Berlin Masque Sketchbook*, DR 1998: 0098:001, John Hejduk Papers, CCA. **14** The drawings can be found at AP 145. S2.D55, DR 1998: 0109:001, DR 1998:0109:002:001–037, John Hejduk Papers, CCA; IBA Prinz Albrecht Palace Competition holdings, IBA-Akten, Landesarchiv. See also John Hejduk, *Victims: A Work by John Hejduk* (London: Architectural Association, 1986). **15** See, for instance, John Hejduk, *Lancaster / Hanover Masque* (London: Architectural Association, 1992), *Berlin Night* (Rotterdam: Netherlands Architectural Association, 1993), *Vladivostok: A Work by John Hejduk*, ed. K. Shkapich (New York: Rizzoli, 1989), "Evening in Llano," *A + U* 1 (1991): 127–28, "Oslo Fall Night," in *Columbia Documents of Architecture and Theory* 2 (1993): 7–35; and *Adjusting Foundations*, ed. K. Shkapich (New York: Monacelli, 1995). **16** Hejduk, *Lancaster / Hanover Masque*. **17** Wim van den Bergh, "Icarus' Amazement or the Matrix of Crossed Destinies," in *Lancaster / Hanover Masque*, 81–102. **18** Anthony Vidler, "Vagabond Architecture," Anthony Vidler, *The Architectural Uncanny: Essays in the Modern Unhomely* (Cambridge, MA: MIT Press, 1992), 206–14. **19** See (in chronological order) Alberto Perez-Gomez, "The Renovation of the Body: John Hejduk and the Cultural Relevance of Theoretical Projects," *AA Files* 13 (autumn 1986): 26–29; William Firebrace, "John Hejduk: Lancaster / Hanover Masque," *AA Files* 21 (spring 1991): 78–84; David Shapiro, "An Introduction to John Hejduk's Works: Surgical Architecture," *A + U* 91, no. 1 (1991): 6–7; Hays, ed., *Hejduk's Chronotope*; Jim Williamson and Renata Hejduk, eds., *The Religious Imagination in Modern and Contemporary Architecture* (London: Routledge, 2011). **20** Peggy Deamer, "Me, Myself and I," in

Hejduk's Chronotope, 65–98. **21** Umberto Eco, "The Poetics of the Open Work," in Umberto Eco, *Open Work*, trans. Anna Cancogni (Cambridge, MA: Harvard University Press, 1989; or. 1962), 1–23. **22** Ibid., 11; Roland Barthes, "The Death of the Author," in Roland Barthes, *Image Music Text*, trans. Stephen Heath (New York: Hill and Wang, 1977; or. 1968), 148. **23** Claire Bishop, *Artificial Hells: Participatory Art and the Politics of Spectatorship* (New York: Verso, 2012), 275. **24** Jacques Rancière, *The Emancipated Spectator*, trans. Gregory Elliot (London: Verso, 2009; or. 2008), 16. **25** Hejduk competed for Block 19 (3.29 hectares) in the "Wilhelmstrasse Competition" (which also involved Blocks 9 and 20) against Helge Bofinger (Berlin), Douglas Clelland (London), Jasper Halfmann and Clod Zillich (Berlin), Friedrich Kurrent (Munich), and Jürgen Sawade (Berlin). The jury was composed of Carlo Aymonino, Werner Düttmann, Klaus Humpert, Josef Paul Kleihues, Christoph Sattler, and Anthony Vidler. "Internationaler engerer Wettbewerb. Berlin Südliche Friedrichstadt Wilhelmstraße. Bericht der Vorprüfung," IBA Report. 1981. A 81/038, Landesarchiv. **26** IBA-1984, "Internationaler engerer Wettbewerb: Berlin Südliche Friedrichstadt Wilhelmstraße," Berlin, May 1981. Wilhelmstrasse Competition Brief, 14, Landesarchiv. **27** Ibid., 24, 30, and 46–52. **28** Ibid., 40. **29** Ibid., 94. **30** The competition design for Mehringplatz was by Hans Scharoun (1962), and modifications were made by Werner Düttmann (1968–76). **31** Wilhelmstrasse Competition Brief, 14. **32** Ibid., 94. **33** Wilhelmstrasse Competition Brief, 8. **34** Josef Paul Kleihues, "A Non-Place: Competition Designs for the Prinz Albrecht Palais in Berlin," *Lotus* 42, no. 2 (1984): 101–10. Quotation: 102. **35** The drawings can be found at DR 1998: 0118-120-140; DR 1998: 0118-072-110, DR1998: 0118-09-76, John Hejduk Papers, CCA. **36** Raoul Bunschoten, "oTTEMan, or 'He Is My Relative,'" *AA Files* 13 (autumn 1986): 73–81. **37** Josef Paul Kleihues, "Die Architektur, das wollte ich sagen, bedarf unser aller Pflege," in *Erste Projekte: Internationale Bauausstellung Berlin 1984/87: Die Neubaugebiete—Dokumente, Projekte*, vol. 2 (Berlin: Quadriga Verlag, 1981), 58–71. Quotation: 58. Translation also published as "Architecture, This Was What I Wanted to Say, Needs the Care and Support of All of Us," *AD* 53, nos. 1–2 (1983): 5–9. **38** Yeliz Erçakmak, interview by the author, September 8, 2012, Berlin, in Turkish, 00:02:15–00:30:00, 00:04:00–00:05:26. Audio and video recordings are in the author's collection. **39** Ibid., 00:26:00–00:35:13. **40** Ibid., 00:35:47–00:37:27. **41** Ibid., 00:39:00–00:41:12. **42** Ibid., 00:14:29–00:15:50. **43** Ibid., 00:10:00–00:12:27. **44** Ibid., 00:23:00–00:25:44. **45** Ibid., 00:06:00–00:07:20. **46** Ibid., 00:38:19–00:39:26. **47** Ibid., 00:12:50–00:14:00. **48** Eco, "The Poetics of the Open Work," 3. **49** Ibid., 4. **50** Ibid., 5. **51** For a critique of the contemporary art-critical discussions of participatory art, see Bishop, *Artificial Hells*, 11–40. **52** Jacques Rancière, interviewed by Gabriel Rockhill and Alexi Kukuljevic, "Farewell to Artistic and Political Impotence," in Jacques Rancière, *The Politics of Aesthetics*, ed. and trans. Gabriel Rockhill (London: Bloomsbury, 2004), 77–78.

Appendix

Acknowledgments

The idea of writing this book has been on my mind ever since the days I was working on my doctoral dissertation at Columbia University in New York, which culminated in *Architecture in Translation: Germany, Turkey and the Modern House*. It started as a pilot article on Álvaro Siza and the residents who lived in his building, which I worked on in 2009–10, and published in *Migrant's Time* in 2011, and which made its way in updated form as a chapter here. Very soon, the idea grew into a book-length project.

Many institutions trusted me with this project even when it was in its baby stages and represented in a couple of pages. Without the financial support of these research institutions and universities, it would not have been possible to carry out the on-site and archival research, the writing and the production of this book. These include (in chronological order of their grants): Canadian Centre for Architecture, University of Illinois at Chicago, Clark Art Institute, Forum Transregionale Studien in conjunction with Humboldt University and Wissenschaftskolleg zu Berlin, Department of Architecture at Cornell University, American Academy in Berlin, Graham Foundation, and Cornell Institute for European Studies. Needless to say, I owe thanks to all of the blind reviewers and directors in these grant-giving institutions who must have been confident about the value of this book. I also thank the deans and chairs, Kent Kleinman, Mark Cruvellier, Peter Hales, Lisa Lee, Virginia Miller, and Andrea Simitch at UIC and Cornell University, who were both financially and administratively supportive.

I have many individuals to acknowledge who helped me bring this project to fruition in the archives and on the site. Andreas Matschenz at the Landesarchiv in Berlin; Caroline Dagbert and Alexis Sornin at the Canadian Centre for Architecture in Montreal; and Peter-Klaus Schuster who made the connection with the Akademie der Künste in Berlin. Cihan Arın, Rob Krier, Rem Koolhaas, David Mackay, and Heide Moldenhauer opened their offices' archives to me. Colleagues at Cornell University who participated in IBA-1984/87 and generously shared their memories and work included Arthur Ovaska and Werner Goehner.

This book relies on countless oral histories. In addition to interviewing the residents, the IBA team members, and the tenant advisors, I sent requests for interviews to all of the living architects that are subjects of this book, and integrated those that eventually took place. Among the architects, planners, residents, civil society organizers that I interviewed, I owe special gratitude to Sakine Albayrak, Cihan Çelik, Cihan Arın (who also provided many contacts), Fatma Barış and her family, Uwe Böhm, Yalçın Çetin, Günsel Çetiner, Demir, Martin Domschat, Hartmut Dorgerloh, Bahri Düleç, Wulf Eichstädt, Kadir Ercan, Yeliz Erçakmak, Güler family, Hardt-Waltherr Hämer, Ipek family, Yüksel Karaçizmeli, Karaoğlan family, Hans-Günter Kleff, Rob Krier, Hildebrand Machleidt, David Mackay, Heide Moldenhauer, Suzan Nişancı, N.Y., Yaşar Öncü, Günter Schlusche, A Resident, Tuğrul family, Hatice Uzun, V., Benita von Davier, Yıldırım, and many, many more residents whose ideas shaped this book, but could not be integrated as oral histories due to the eventual outline, or with respect to their own will. How can I thank you enough? I trust that the recorded oral histories that came out of our conversations created some extremely important documents pertaining to this space and time—a very tiny portion of which I could translate into this book.

It would not be an exaggeration to say that I wrote this book in front of several audiences. Between 2010 and 2017, I gave several work-in-progress lectures and conference papers, and benefited from the reception and audience comments. For this reason, I thank scholars who invited me to present lectures on the previous versions of this book, and those in the audience with whom I had conversations afterwards. These include (in chronological order of the invitations) Saloni Mathur at UCLA (who not only published my first article but also invited me twice for presentations); Nezar Al'Sayyad and Mrinalini Rajagopalan for a panel at the Society of Architectural Historians; Michael Ann Holly and Aruna D'Souza at the Clark Art Institute, and my cohort fellows Mary-Kate O'Hare, Stephen Houston, Ivan Gaskell, and Lisa Corrin; Alexandra Kemmerer at the Forum Transregionale Studien in conjunction with Humboldt University and Wissenschaftskolleg zu Berlin, and the graduate students in Berlin who attended my lectures on IBA, including Jette Gindner, Carla MacDougal, Sasha Rossman, and Vanja Sisek; Brian L. McLaren for a panel at College Art Association; Zuhal Ulusoy and Didem Kılıçkıran at Kadir Has University; Irene Sunwoo at Oberlin University; Sarah Herda as the organizer, and Catherine Becker, Bob Bruegmann, Hannah Feldman, and Hannah Higgins in the audience at the Graham Foundation; Stanislaus von Moos at Yale University; Mary McLeod and Rob Wiesenberger at Columbia University; Carsten Ruhl as the organizer, and Kathleen James-Chakraborty, Juliet Koss, Nelson Mota, and Volker M. Welter in the audience at Bauhaus University; Itohan Osayimwese as the organizer, and Anthony Vidler, Courtney Martin, Lisa Young, and Tony Cokes in the audience at Brown University; Kenny Cupers (who was also a co-organizer of my talk at the University of Basel) and Alison Fisher for a panel at SAH; Victoria Beard as the organizer, and Leslie Adelson, Ben Anderson, Thomas Campanella, Jeffrey Chusid, Iftikhar Dadi, Medina Lasansky, Mostafa Minawi, Geoffrey Waite, and Mary Woods in the audience at Cornell University; Avinoam Shalem at Columbia University (even though I decided to lecture on something else shortly before my visit); Peter Christensen at the University of Rochester; Michael Faciejew, Lluís Alexandre Casanovas Blanco, Victoria Bugge Øye, and Spyros Papapetros at Princeton University; Reinhold Martin for a roundtable at SAH; Mary Roberts at the University of Sydney; Berin Gür as the organizer, and Elvan Altan, Cana Bilsel, Ali Cengizkan in the audience at TED University; Bat-Ami Bar On and Paulina Banas at the Institute for Advanced Studies of Binghamton University; Claire Zimmerman and Sharon Haar at the University of Michigan; Irene Cheng, Charles Davis, and Mabel Wilson as the organizers, and Jean-Louis Cohen in the audience at Columbia University; all the staff and my colleagues at the American Academy in Berlin, especially Rebecca Boehling, Timothy Brown, and Mary Ann Doane whose research areas were close to mine and shared their comments; Barış Ülker at the Technical University in Berlin; Peter Lang at the Royal Institute of Art in Stockholm; Andres Lepik at the Technical University of Munich; Kader Konuk at the University of Duisburg-Essen; Sibel Bozdoğan and Eve Blau at Harvard University; Bilgin Ayata at the University of Basel; Jeffrey Kirkwood as the organizer and Nancy Um and Julia Walker in the audience at the University of Binghamton; and many more in the audiences,

Acknowledgments

some of whom I have never met, but their comments made their way into the book in one way or another.

I had many colleagues/friends in my work places who encouraged me with their solidarity when we shared our experiences about the hardships of teaching, administering, and advising, while struggling to give birth to a book, especially Catherine Becker (who also gave extremely insightful comments after reading the Preface), Heather Grossman, and Jonathan Mekinda at the University of Illinois at Chicago, and Annetta Alexandridis, Lily Chi, Iftikhar Dadi, Luben Dimcheff, Mostafa Minawi, Leslie Lok, Philip Lorenz, and Jim Williamson at Cornell University. Needless to say, I have discussed several ideas in this book directly or indirectly in classes, and, for this reason, I would like to acknowledge my doctoral, graduate, and undergraduate students who took my seminars or came to my lectures.

I owe extreme gratitude to Kenneth Frampton and Kader Konuk (with Vanessa Agnew) who generously served as reviewers of the book's final version and layout despite their busy schedules. I hope I have integrated all of their comments in the published version. I would also like to thank Anthony Vidler, who read the final version. I hope my comments will mean as much to my colleagues one day as theirs meant to me just before the book went to printing.

Thanks a million to my research assistants Eda Begüm Birol, who worked on the image adjustments, and Justin Foo, who worked on the Stroll map and collage that has become the Insert page in this book.

I am very indebted to my editor for the publisher, Andreas Müller, who directed the production process intelligently and flawlessly, and Kathleen Bernsdorf and Amelie Solbrig in the production team. My copy editors and proofreaders in English and German, Jeanne Ferris and Michael Wachholz, and indexer Diana Witt were all so rigorous and careful that this book would never have reached its final shape without them. All of the architects who either gave their office documents to publicly accessible institutions or allowed me to publish the drawings in their own archives, as well as residents who allowed me to take photographs of their interior spaces: without your permissions, this book could not have been illustrated.

Needless to say, my greatest gratitude goes to my family Selma and Tuncer Akcan, and close friends for their never-ending support and patience.

Finally, let me dedicate this book to all the Kreuzbergians whose paths crossed for a short or long interval of time in this borough, and who opened their ideas, projects, poems, novels, aspirations, life-stories, and apartments to me.

Illustration Credits

Introduction

Figure Intro 1 Mies van der Rohe, S. R. Crown Hall, Illinois Institute of Technology, Chicago, 1950–56. Ground plan. Mies van der Rohe Archive, gift of the architect. Acc. n.: MR5001.125. Mies van der Rohe/MoMA/Scala

Figure Intro 2 Le Corbusier, Domino system, 1915. Courtesy Le Corbusier

Figure Intro 3 Pierre Chareau, Bernard Bijvoet, and Louis Dalbet, Maison de Verre, Paris, 1928–32. Esra Akcan

Figure Intro 4 Gerrit Rietveld and Truus Schröder, Rietveld-Schröder House, Utrecht, 1924–25. 2017 Artists Rights Society (ARS), New York/ c/o Pictoright Amsterdam

Figure Intro 5 Sedad Eldem, Ağaoğlu House, Istanbul, 1936. Courtesy Sedad Eldem

Figure Intro 6 Sutemi Horiguchi, Okada House, Tokyo 1933. Courtesy Sutemi Horiguchi

Figure Intro 7 Adolf Loos, Müller Villa, Prague, 1928–30. August Sarnitz, *Adolf Loos 1870–1933: Architect, Cultural Critic, Dandy* (Cologne: Taschen, 2003), 74

Figure Intro 8 Kenzō Tange, Tokyo Bay project, 1960. The Kenzō Tange Archive. Gift of Mrs. Takako Tange, 2011

Figure Intro 9 Cedric Price, Fun Palace, 1961–65. Cedric Price Fonds, Canadian Centre for Architecture, Montreal

Figure Intro 10 Superstudio, Continuous Monument, 1969. Adolfo Natalini/Archivio Superstudio 1966–1986 [Adolfo Natalini, Cristiano Toraldo di Francia, Roberto Magris, Gian Piero Frassinelli, Alessandro Magris]

Figure Intro 11 Occupation of the Milan Triennale, 1968. *Casabella,* no. 325: 85

Figure Intro 12 Bernard Tschumi, Parc de la Villette, Paris, 1983. Bernard Tschumi

STOP I: Critical Reconstruction: Open Architecture as Collaboration?

Figure I.1. View from Naunynplatz in Kreuzberg, photographed by Heide Moldenhauer, Berlin, c. 1981. Heide Moldenhauer

Figure I.2. View from Oranienstrasse in Kreuzberg, photographed by Heide Moldenhauer, Berlin, c. 1981. Heide Moldenhauer

Figure I.3 Hasır Restaurant in Kreuzberg at Adalbert- and Oranienstrasse, photographed by Esra Akcan, Berlin, 2014. Esra Akcan

Figure I.4 Initial proposal for the urban renewal sites of Internationale Bauausstellung Berlin 1984, Berlin, 1978. *Bauwelt,* vol. 69, no. 26 (14 July 1978), 1005

Figure I.5 Aerial view of Kreuzberg, photographed by Cihan Arın, Berlin, 11. 2. 1980. Cihan Arın

Figure I.6 IBA-1984/87 (Internationale Bauausstellung Berlin). Directors: Josef Paul Kleihues, Hardt-Waltherr Hämer. Site plan and drawings of buildings on the plate presented at the 17th Triennial of Milan. Drawing by Giovannella Bianchi, Ebe Gianotti, Werner Oechslin, Luca Ortelli. Courtesy: Werner Oechslin, Luca Ortelli

Figure I.7 IBA-1984/87, *Idee Prozeß Ergebnis* (idea process result) Exhibition in Martin Gropius Bau, showing John Hejduk's Studio for a Painter and Studio for a Musician, Berlin, 1984. Unknown photographer, published in Marco de Michelis et al., *La Ricostruzione della Città: Berlino-IBA 1987* (Milan: Electa, 1985), 19

Figure I.8 Cover of *Idee Prozeß Ergebnis* (idea process result). Catalog of the IBA-1984/87 exhibition at the Martin Gropius Bau in 1984. *Idee Prozeß Ergebnis: Die Reparatur und Rekonstruktion der Stadt* (Berlin: IBA 1984), Landesarchiv Berlin

Figure I.9 Model of IBA-1957, Hansaviertel, Berlin, 1957. Published in Karl Otto, ed., *Die Stadt von Morgen* (Berlin: Verlag Gebr. Mann, 1959), 187

Figure I.10 Werner Düttmann, Georg Heinrichs, Hans Christian Müller, Märkisches Viertel, Berlin, 1964–74. Image circulated in IBA publication *Modelle für eine Stadt.* Vittorio Magnago Lampugnani, ed., *Modelle für eine Stadt* (Berlin: IBA, 1984), 35, Landesarchiv Berlin

Figure I.11 Ideal image of Belle-Alliance-Platz (today's Mehringplatz in Kreuzberg), 18th century, reproduced in IBA publication *Modelle für eine Stadt* (creator unknown). Senator für Bau- und Wohnungswesen, *Berlin: Historische Stadtgestalt und Stadterneuerung* (Berlin: Thorman & Goetsch, 1975), 25, Landesarchiv Berlin

Figure I.12 View of Kreuzberg (Mehringplatz and Friedrichstadt) in 1946 after the destruction of World War II, reproduced in IBA publication *Modelle für eine Stadt.* Vittorio Magnago Lampugnani, ed., *Modelle für eine Stadt* (Berlin: IBA, 1984), 32, Landesarchiv Berlin

Figure I.13 Charles Moore, John Ruble, and Buzz Yudell, Tegel Villa Design Guidelines, IBA-1984/87, Berlin. B_Rep_168 (Karten)_Nr_84, Landesarchiv Berlin

Figure I.14 Pages from *Die gemordete Stadt* (1964), written by Wolf Jobst Siedler and Elisabeth Niggemeyer. Wolf Jobst Siedler, Elisabeth Niggemeyer, *Die gemordete Stadt. Abgesang auf Putte und Straße, Platz und Baum* (Berlin: Herbig, 1964)

Figure 1.6a–b Hans Kollhoff and Arthur Ovaska, Tower House in Block 33, photographed by Esra Akcan, Berlin, 2016, 2012. Esra Akcan

Figure 1.7 Horst Hielscher and Georg-Peter Mügge, Study sketches for Block 33, 1982. B_Rep_168 (Karten)_Nr_402, 405, Landesarchiv Berlin

Figure 1.8a–d Franz Claudius Demblin, Horst Hielscher and Georg-Peter Mügge, Jochem Jourdan, Bernhard Müller, and Sven Albrecht, Urban villas in Block 33, photographed by Esra Akcan, Berlin, 2012–2016. Esra Akcan

Figure 1.9a–b Werner Kreis and Ulrich and Peter Schaad, Building in Block 33, photographed by Esra Akcan, Berlin, 2014, 2016. Esra Akcan

Figure 1.10 Hans Kollhoff and Arthur Ovaska, Berlin Museum Garden in Block 33. B_Rep_168(Karten)_Nr_1421_6, 9, Landesarchiv, Berlin

Figure 1.11 Daniel Libeskind, Jewish Museum, photographed by Esra Akcan, Berlin, 2002. Esra Akcan

Figure 1.12 Theodor-Wolff-Park and Block 20 (Ralf Dähne, Helge Dahl, Rosie Grässler), photographed by Esra Akcan, Berlin, 2014. Esra Akcan

Figure 1.13 Rave and Partner, Building in Block 20, photographed by Esra Akcan, Berlin, 2010. Esra Akcan

Figure 1.14 Squatted Thomas-Weißbecker-Haus in Block 20, photographed by Esra Akcan, Berlin, 2010. Esra Akcan

Figure 1.15 Bassenge, Puhan-Schulz, and Partner, Kindergarten in Block 20, photographed by Esra Akcan, Berlin, 2014. Esra Akcan

Figure 1.16 Hansjürg Zeitler, Helmut Bier, and Hans Korn, Building in Block 20, photographed by Esra Akcan, Berlin, 2016. Esra Akcan

Figure 1.17 IBA buildings on Lindenstrasse seen from Block 606 (Gino Valle, Mario Broggi, and Michael Burckhardt), photographed by Esra Akcan, Berlin, 2010. Esra Akcan

Figure 1.18a–b Douglas Clelland, Mario Maedebach and Werner Redeleit, and Joachim Schmidt, Buildings along Friedrichstrasse in Block 606, photographed by Esra Akcan, Berlin, 2016, 2011. Esra Akcan

STOP II: Buildings That Die More than Once: Open Architecture as Collectivity

Figure II.1 Cover of *Casabella*, no. 255, 1961.

Figure II.2 Cover of *Casabella*, no. 288, 1964.

Figure II.3 Aldo Rossi's discussion of Berlin's residential types (Weimar period, IBA-1957 and Stalinallee housing) in *Casabella*, 1964. Eredi Aldo Rossi, courtesy of Fondazione Aldo Rossi

Figure II.4 Aldo Rossi, Cataldo Cemetery in Modena, Italy, 1971. Eredi Aldo Rossi, courtesy of Fondazione Aldo Rossi

Figure II.5 Aldo Rossi with Bruno Reichlin, Fabio Reinhart, and Eraldo Consolascio, "La Città Analoga" (Analogous city) drawing, 1976 Venice Architecture Biennale. Eredi Aldo Rossi, courtesy of Fondazione Aldo Rossi

Figure II.6 A cover page of *Rational Architecture: The Reconstruction of the European City.* Catalog of the exhibition curated by Leon Krier, 1978. Courtesy of Archives d'Architecture Moderne, Brussels.

Figure II.7 Günsel Çetiner, interviewed by Esra Akcan, Berlin, 2012. Esra Akcan

Figure II.8 View from N.Y.'s apartment, photographed by Esra Akcan, Berlin, 2011. Esra Akcan

Figure II.9 "Kochstrasse/Friedrichstrasse Competition," IBA-1984/87, figure-ground relations of the projects submitted to the competition, Berlin, 1981. "Internationaler engerer Wettbewerb Berlin Südliche Friedrichstadt Kochstraße/Friedrichstraße. Bericht der Vorprüfung," Landesarchiv Berlin

Figure II.10 Aldo Rossi, "Kochstrasse/Friedrichstrasse Competition" project, IBA-1984/87, Berlin. Plan. AP142_S1_D63_P9, Aldo Rossi Papers, Canadian Centre for Architecture, Montreal

Figure II.11 Aldo Rossi, "Kochstrasse/Friedrichstrasse Competition" project for Block 10, IBA-1984/87, Berlin. Façades. AP142_S1_D63_P5_1, Aldo Rossi Papers, Canadian Centre for Architecture, Montreal; B_Rep_168 (Karten)_Nr_988_1, Landesarchiv Berlin

Figure II.12 Aldo Rossi, "Kochstrasse/Friedrichstrasse Competition" project for Block 10, IBA-1984/87, Berlin. Façade details. B_Rep_168(Karten)_Nr_1032 and 1034, Landesarchiv, Berlin

Figure II.13 Aldo Rossi, "Kochstrasse/Friedrichstrasse Competition" project, IBA-1984/87, Berlin. Studies of the façade and round column at the corner. AP142_S1_D63_P5, Aldo Rossi Papers, Canadian Centre for Architecture, Montreal; B_Rep_168(Karten)_Nr_1031 and B_Rep_168 (Karten)_Nr_989 Landesarchiv Berlin.

Figure II.14 View of Aldo Rossi's building in Block 10, photographed by Esra Akcan, Berlin, 2010. Esra Akcan

Figure II.15 Raimund Abraham, "Kochstrasse/Friedrichstrasse Competition" project for Block 4, IBA-1984/87, Berlin. Published in: Heinrich Klotz and Josef Paul Kleihues, eds., *International Building Exhibition Berlin 1987* (New York: Rizzoli, 1986), 180, Landesarchiv Berlin.

Figure II.16 Bohigas, Mackay, and Martorell, "Kochstrasse/Friedrichstrasse Competition" project for Block 4, IBA-1984/87, Berlin. Site plan. IBB-644_2012_1, Bohigas/Mackay/Martorell Archives, Arxiu COAC, Barcelona

STROLL 2: From Checkpoint Charlie to Potsdamer Platz

Figure 2.1 Aerial view of towers designed by Grupo 2c (front) and Pietro Derossi (back) in Block 9, photographed by Esra Akcan, Berlin, 2011. Esra Akcan

Figure 2.2 Grupo 2c, Building in Block 9, photographed by Esra Akcan, Berlin, 2014. Esra Akcan

Figure 2.3a–c Pietro Derossi, Building in Block 9, and view of buildings by Grupo 2c, Jochen Brandi and Partner, and Aldo Rossi from this tower, photographed by Esra Akcan, Berlin, 2014, 2010. Esra Akcan

Figure 2.4a–b Self-help Terraces housing in Block 9 (based on idea by Dietrich von Beulwitz), photographed by Esra Akcan, Berlin, 2012. Esra Akcan

Figure 2.5 Romuald Loegler and W. Dobrzański, Proposal for Block 2, 1986. B_Rep_168(Karten)_Nr_1496, 1499, Landesarchiv Berlin

Figure 2.6 Proposal for Block 2, 1986-87. B_Rep_168 (Karten)_Nr_1490, Landesarchiv Berlin

Figure 2.7a–b Myra Warhaftig, Building in Block 2, photographed by Esra Akcan, Berlin, 2012. Esra Akcan

Figure 2.8 Christine Jachmann, Building in Block 2, photographed by Esra Akcan, Berlin, 2012. Esra Akcan

Figure 2.9a–b Zaha Hadid, Myra Warhaftig, Christine Jachmann, Wojciech Obtułowicz and Daniel Karpinski, Block 2, view of Dessauer Strasse, photographed by Esra Akcan, Berlin, 2012. Esra Akcan

Figure 2.10a–c Daniel Karpinski, Romuald Loegler and W. Dobrzański, and Peter Blake, Block 2 with St. Lukas church, view of Bernburger Strasse (sketch of 1986) (a: photographed by Esra Akcan, Berlin, 2014). a: Esra Akcan, b–c: B_Rep_168(Karten)_ Nr_1466, B_Rep_168(Karten)_Nr_1469, Landesarchiv, Berlin

Figure 2.11a–b Zaha Hadid, Proposals for Block 2, 1987. B_Rep_168(Karten)_Nr_415_Bl4, B_Rep_168(Karten)_ Nr_416, _Bl4, Landesarchiv Berlin

Figure 2.12a–g Zaha Hadid, Building in Block 2, photographed by Esra Akcan, Berlin, 2011, 2012, 2014. Esra Akcan

Figure 2.13a–c Rave and Partner; Borck, Boye, and Schaefer; Christoph Langhof; Grötzebach, Plessow, and Ehlers, overseen by Günter Schlusche, landscape architect Hans Loidl, Block 6, photographed by Esra Akcan, Berlin, 2012, 2014. Esra Akcan

Figure 2.14a–d Josef Paul Kleihues, Building in Block 7, photographed by Esra Akcan, Berlin, 2010, 2011. Esra Akcan

Figure 2.15a–b Nalbach and Nalbach; Peter Brinkert; Georg Kohlmaier and Barna von Sartory, Buildings in Block 7, photographed by Esra Akcan, Berlin, 2010. Esra Akcan

STOP III: Opened After Habitation

Figure III.1 June 5, 2012 Memorial in Oswald Mathias Ungers's Block 1 for IBA-1984/87, photographed by Esra Akcan, Berlin, 2012. Esra Akcan

Figure III.2 Aerial view of Oswald Mathias Ungers's building in Block 1 (center) and Zaha Hadid's in Block 2 (bottom left) for IBA-1984/87, photographed by Esra Akcan, Berlin, 2010. Esra Akcan

Figure III.3 Oswald Mathias Ungers, Reconstruction of perimeter block in Charlottenburg, Berlin, 1978. UAA Ungers Archive for Architectural Research

Figure III.4 Oswald Mathias Ungers, Grünzug Süd, Cologne, 1962. UAA Ungers Archive for Architectural Research

Figure III.5 Oswald Mathias Ungers, *MAN transFORMS* exhibition at Cooper Hewitt Museum, New York, 1976. Collaborators: Simon Ungers, László Kiss, and Henry Ferretti. UAA Ungers Archive for Architectural Research

Figure III.6 Pages from Oswald Mathias Ungers's *City Metaphors*, 1982. UAA Ungers Archive for Architectural Research

Figure III.7 Oswald Mathias Ungers with Rem Koolhaas and P. and D. Allison, Project for Tiergarten, Berlin, 1973. UAA Ungers Archive for Architectural Research

Figure III.8 Oswald Mathias Ungers, in collaboration with with Rem Koolhaas, Hans Kollhoff, Arthur Ovaska, and Peter Riemann, Cities within a City/Archipelago Berlin, 1977. Map of Berlin. UAA Ungers Archive for Architectural Research

Figure III.9 Oswald Mathias Ungers, in collaboration with with Rem Koolhaas, Hans Kollhoff, Arthur Ovaska, and Peter Riemann, Cities within a City/Archipelago Berlin, 1977. Remaining city districts. UAA Ungers Archive for Architectural Research

Figure III.10 Model of a study for South Friedrichstadt prepared during Cornell University's Berlin summer studio, 1978. UAA Ungers Archive for Architectural Research

Figure III.11 Oswald Mathias Ungers, Project for Friedrichsvorstadt, Berlin, 1981. Planning of green areas and building. B_Rep_168(Karten)_Nr_1058_2; B_Rep_168(Karten)_Nr_1058_3, Landesarchiv Berlin

Figure III.12 Oswald Mathias Ungers, in collaboration with Bernd Faskel and Hans Müller, Block 1, IBA-1984/87, Berlin, 1982. B_Rep_168(Karten)_ Nr_1059_1; B_Rep_168(Karten)_Nr_1059_2, Landesarchiv Berlin

Figure III.13 Oswald Mathias Ungers in collaboration with Hans Kollhoff and Thomas Will, Housing Complex, Marburg, 1976. UAA Ungers Archive for Architectural Research

Figure III.14 Werner Goehner, "Residential Park at Lützowplatz Competition" project for Block 234, near Lützowplatz, IBA-1984/87, Berlin. Urban villas. Courtesy Werner Goehner

Figure 3.15 a–f Rob Krier (with Aldo Rossi, Brenner and Tonon, Giorgio Grassi, Hans Hollein, Henry Nielebock, and Hermann & Valentiny), Urban design and individual buildings in Block 189 (c, e–f: photographed by Esra Akcan, Berlin, 2012). a: B_Rep_168(Karten)_Nr_901_1, Landesarchiv Berlin, b: B_Rep_168 (Karten)_Nr_141, 145, Landesarchiv Berlin, c: Esra Akcan, d: B_Rep_168(Karten)_Nr_901_5, 6, 8, Landesarchiv Berlin, e–f: Esra Akcan

STOP IV: Gentle Urban Renewal: Participation and Radical Democracy

Figure IV.1 Screen shots from some of the video-interviews carried out by Esra Akcan with the architects, tenant advisors and residents of IBA Altbau, Berlin, 2009–2016. Esra Akcan

Figure IV.2 Hardt-Waltherr Hämer, Ingolstadt Theater, c. 1960. Manfred Sack, ed., *Stadt im Kopf: Hardt-Waltherr Hämer* (Berlin: Jovis Verlag GmbH, 2002); 73, Courtesy Hardt-Waltherr Hämer

Figure IV.3 View of Waldemarstrasse, Kreuzberg, before renovation, photographed by Heide Moldenhauer, Berlin, c. 1980. Heide Moldenhauer

Figure IV.4 View of Block 76/78, renovated by IBA Altbau (team-architect: Heide Moldenhauer), photographed by Esra Akcan, Berlin, 2012. Esra Akcan

Figure IV.5 Views of Block 76, renovated by IBA Altbau (team-architect: Heide Moldenhauer), photographed by Esra Akcan, Berlin, 2012. Esra Akcan

Figure IV.6 Cover of *Kreuzberger Mischung* (Kreuzberg mixture). Catalog of the IBA-1984/87 exhibition at the BEWAG Halle in 1984, curated by Hardt-Waltherr Hämer. Karl-Heinz Fiebig, Dieter Hoffmann-Axthelm, and E. Knödler-Bunte, eds., *Kreuzberger Mischung: Die innerstädtische Verflechtung von Architektur, Kultur und Gewerbe* (Berlin: IBA, Verlag Ästhetik und Kommunikation, 1984), Landesarchiv Berlin

Figure IV.7 Aerial view of Block 81 in Kreuzberg before urban renewal, photographed by Cihan Arın, Berlin, 11. 2. 1980. Cihan Arın

Figure IV.8 Brochures and booklets against the Senate's housing laws and regulations for noncitizens. Cihan Arın

Figure IV.9 Bilingual flyer protesting the ban on entry and settlement, Berlin, c. mid-1970s. Cihan Arın

Figure IV.10 View from a tenant meeting for an IBA Altbau renovation, IBA-1984/87, photographed by Heide Moldenhauer, Berlin, 1980. Heide Moldenhauer

Figure IV.11 View of Block 81, renovated by IBA Altbau (team-architect: Cihan Arın), photographed by Esra Akcan, Berlin, 2011. Esra Akcan

Figure IV.12 Views of the protest against high rents in Kreuzberg, Berlin, July 6, 2012, photographed by Esra Akcan. Esra Akcan

Figure IV.13 View of Kreuzberg renovated by IBA Altbau, photographed by Esra Akcan, Berlin, 2009. Esra Akcan

Figure IV.14 A tenant meeting for an IBA Altbau renovation, IBA-1984/87, photographed by Heide Moldenhauer, Berlin, 1981. Heide Moldenhauer

Figure IV.15 Views of stoves in Altbau buildings in Kreuzberg before renovation, photographed by Heide Moldenhauer, Berlin, 1980–1981. Heide Moldenhauer

Figure IV.16 View of Nişancı family's apartment in Block 81, renovated by IBA Altbau (team-architect: Cihan Arın), photographed by Esra Akcan, Berlin, 2012. Esra Akcan

Figure IV.17 View of an outdoor toilet in an Altbau building in Kreuzberg before renovation, photographed by Heide Moldenhauer, Berlin, 1980. Heide Moldenhauer

Figure IV.18 View of a Hof in Adalbertstrasse in Kreuzberg before renovation, photographed by Heide Moldenhauer, Berlin, 1981. Heide Moldenhauer

Figure IV.19 View of an Altbau apartment in Waldemarstrasse in Kreuzberg before renovation, photographed by Heide Moldenhauer, Berlin, 1981. Heide Moldenhauer

Figure IV.20 View from Cem House in Kreuzberg, photographed by Esra Akcan, Berlin, 2009. Esra Akcan

Figure IV.21 "Blue plan." Urban renewal program of IBA Altbau, Kreuzberg. Berlin, 1981. Courtesy Heide Moldenhauer and IBA Altbau team.

Figure IV.22 Heide Moldenhauer's photographs of residents in Adalbertstrasse, Kreuzberg, Berlin, 1981. Heide Moldenhauer

Figure IV.23 A tenant meeting during IBA Altbau, Kreuzberg, photographed by Heide Moldenhauer, Berlin, c. 1981. Heide Moldenhauer

Figure IV.24 Heide Moldenhauer, Kita (day care center) in Block 78, Kreuzberg, Berlin, when built in 1984, and in 2012. Heide Moldenhauer and Esra Akcan

Figure IV.25 View from a Hof in Block 76, renovated by IBA Altbau (team-architect: Heide Moldenhauer), photographed by Esra Akcan, Berlin, 2012. Esra Akcan

Figure IV.26 Exhibition in SO36, prepared by Heide Moldenhauer, Berlin, 1984. Heide Moldenhauer

Figure IV.27 View of the murals by artist Hanefi Yeter on the corner of Adalbert- and Waldemarstrasse, renovated by IBA Altbau (team-architect: Heide Moldenhauer), photographed by Esra Akcan, Berlin, 2012. Esra Akcan

Figure IV.28 Erased mural on the façade of a building in Dresdener Strasse 10 (attributed to Hanefi Yeter). Public postcard

Figure IV.29 View of the mural on the façade of a stable in a Hof in Block 76, renovated by IBA Altbau (team-architect: Heide Moldenhauer), photographed by Esra Akcan, Berlin, 2012. Esra Akcan

Figure V.9 Álvaro Siza, Sketch for Bonjour Tristesse in Block 121, IBA-1984/87, Berlin, c. 1980. Courtesy Álvaro Siza. Published in Jose Paulo dos Santos, ed., *Alvaro Siza. Works and Projects* (Barcelona: Gustavo Gili, 1993), 101

Figure V.10 Álvaro Siza, Housing for *Serviço de Apoio Ambulatório Local* (SAAL), Porto, Portugal, 1973–77. Courtesy Álvaro Siza. Published in Kenneth Frampton, *Alvaro Siza. Complete Works* (London: Phaidon, 2000), 190; *Alvaro Siza* (Berlin: Birkhäuser, 1992), 153.

Figure V.11 Participatory meeting of IBA-1984/87, Berlin. Álvaro Siza can be seen at the far right. Published in *IBA '84'87 Projektübersicht Stand Oktober '82* (Berlin: IBA, 1982), 11, Landesarchiv, Berlin

Figure V.12: Álvaro Siza, Housing for Schilderswijk-West, Netherlands, 1983–88. Plan of the double distribution space. Courtesy Álvaro Siza. Published in Kenneth Frampton, *Alvaro Siza. Complete Works* (London: Phaidon, 2000), 190; *Alvaro Siza* (Berlin: Birkhäuser, 1992), 249

Figure V.13 Views of the street vendors in Álvaro Siza's Block 121 for IBA-1984/87, photographed by Esra Akcan, Berlin, 2009. Esra Akcan

Figure V.14 Álvaro Siza, Bonjour Tristesse in Block 121, IBA-1984/87, Berlin, 1980–1984. Plans of early and late versions. Courtesy Álvaro Siza. Published in *Idee Prozeß Ergebnis: Die Reparatur und Rekonstruktion der Stadt* (Berlin: IBA 1984), 141

Figure V.15 View of Karaçizmeli's living room in Álvaro Siza's Bonjour Tristesse in Block 121 for IBA-1984/87, photographed by Esra Akcan, Berlin, 2012. Esra Akcan

Figure V.16 View of Karaçizmeli's living room in Álvaro Siza's Bonjour Tristesse in Block 121 for IBA-1984/87, photographed by Esra Akcan, Berlin, 2009. Esra Akcan

Figure V.17 View of the *void* space in Karaçizmeli's apartment in Álvaro Siza's Bonjour Tristesse in Block 121 for IBA-1984/87, photographed by Esra Akcan, Berlin, 2012. Esra Akcan

Figure V.18 Views of the closed and open kitchen in Karaçizmeli's apartment in Álvaro Siza's Bonjour Tristesse in Block 121 for IBA-1984/87, photographed by Esra Akcan, Berlin, 2012 Esra Akcan

Figure V.19 View of Álvaro Siza's kindergarten in Block 121 for IBA-1984/87, photographed by Esra Akcan, Berlin, 2012. Esra Akcan

Figure V.20 View from the playground of Álvaro Siza's kindergarten in Block 121 for IBA-1984/87, photographed by Esra Akcan, Berlin, 2012. Esra Akcan

Figure V.21 View of Álvaro Siza's seniors' club in Block 121 for IBA-1984/87, photographed by Esra Akcan, Berlin, 2016. Esra Akcan

Figure V.22 View of the common hall in Álvaro Siza's seniors' club in Block 121 for IBA-1984/87, photographed by Esra Akcan, Berlin, 2016. Esra Akcan

Figure V.23 Views from street and roof garden of Álvaro Siza's seniors' club in Block 121 for IBA-1984/87, photographed by Esra Akcan, Berlin, 2016. Esra Akcan

Figure V.24 View of the semiannual grill in Álvaro Siza's seniors' club in Block 121 for IBA-1984/87, photographed by Esra Akcan, Berlin, 2016. Esra Akcan

Figure V.25 View of Álvaro Siza's seniors' club in Block 121 for IBA-1984/87, photographed by Esra Akcan, Berlin, 2016. Esra Akcan

Figure V.26 View of the original graffiti on the façade of Álvaro Siza's Bonjour Tristesse in Block 121 for IBA-1984/87, photographed by Esra Akcan, Berlin, 2009. Esra Akcan

Figure V.27 View of the new graffiti on the façade of Álvaro Siza's Bonjour Tristesse in Block 121 for IBA-1984/87, photographed by Esra Akcan, Berlin, 2012. Esra Akcan

Figure V.28 Views of the changing façade of Álvaro Siza's seniors' club in Block 121 for IBA-1984/87, photographed by Esra Akcan, Berlin, c. 1984, 2009, 2012 (see Figure V.21 for 2016). Esra Akcan

STROLL 5: From Schlesisches Tor to Fraenkelufer

Figure 5.1 Squatters of Kerngehäuse at Cuvrystrasse, 1983. Hannes Kowatsch, Manfred Koym, and Rita Koym, *F. W. Müller's Toy Sewing Machines and the "Kerngehäuse"* (Berlin: Kreuzberg Historical Research Society and Kerngehäuse Craft Center, 2000), 103

Figure 5.2 a–f Graffiti in the SO36 district of Kreuzberg, photographed by Esra Akcan, Berlin, 2009–2016. Esra Akcan

Figure 5.3 a–b Falckensteinstrasse between Schlesische Strasse and Görlitzer Park, photographed by Esra Akcan, Berlin, 2016. Esra Akcan

Figure 5.4 a–b Crossing the Görlitzer Park along Falckensteinstrasse, photographed by Esra Akcan, Berlin, 2016. Esra Akcan

Figure 5.5 a–b Robert Maguire and Keith Murray, Kindergarten at Paul-Lincke-Ufer, photographed by Esra Akcan, Berlin, 2012. Esra Akcan

Figure 5.6 a–b Bahri Düleç, Pedestrianization along the Paul-Lincke-Ufer, photographed by Esra Akcan, Berlin, 2012. Esra Akcan

Figure 5.7 Previously squatted Forster Strasse 16 in Block 145, renovated through self-help, photographed by Esra Akcan, Berlin, 2012. Esra Akcan

Figure 5.8 a–d Reichenberger Strasse, photographed by Esra Akcan, Berlin, 2016. Esra Akcan

Figure 5.9 a–e Wilhelm Holzbauer, Rave und Rave, Building at the corner of Reichenberger and Mariannenstrasse, photographed by Esra Akcan, Berlin, 2012, 2016. Esra Akcan

Figure 5.10 Fraenkelufer between Kottbusser Strasse and Böcklerpark, photographed by Esra Akcan, Berlin, 2016. Esra Akcan

Figure 5.11a–e Hinrich and Inken Baller, Building compound along Fraenkelufer, photographed by Esra Akcan, Berlin, 2012, 2016. Esra Akcan

STOP VI: Open History in the Past Subjunctive Tense

Figure VI.1 View of Rem Koolhaas/OMA's (left) and Peter Eisenman's (front right) buildings at Checkpoint Charlie for IBA-1984/87, photographed by Esra Akcan, Berlin, 2016. Esra Akcan

Figure VI.2 Rem Koolhaas, "From Friedrichstrasse Station to Mehringplatz" drawing for "Kochstrasse/Friedrichstrasse Competition," IBA-1984/87, Berlin. Image courtesy of OMA

Figure VI.3 Rem Koolhaas and Elia Zenghelis, Project for Roosevelt Island, New York City, 1975. Image courtesy of OMA

Figure VI.4 Rem Koolhaas and Madelon Vriesendorp, "The City of the Captive Globe," 1972. Rem Koolhaas and Madelon Vriesendorp

Figure VI.5 Rem Koolhaas, "Kochstrasse/Friedrichstrasse Competition" project for Block 4, IBA-1984/87, Berlin. Plan. Image courtesy of OMA

Figure VI.6 Rem Koolhaas, "Kochstrasse/Friedrichstrasse Competition" project for Block 4, IBA-1984/87, Berlin. Axonometric. Image courtesy of OMA

Figure VI.7 Rem Koolhaas, "Kochstrasse/Friedrichstrasse Competition" project for Block 4, IBA-1984/87, Berlin. Study sketch of site plan. Image courtesy of OMA

Figure VI.8 Rem Koolhaas, "Kochstrasse/Friedrichstrasse Competition" project for Block 4, IBA-1984/87, Berlin. Axonometric. Image courtesy of OMA and 540 Bl.1–8, Landesarchiv, Berlin

Figure VI.9 Rem Koolhaas, "Kochstrasse/Friedrichstrasse Competition" project for Block 4, IBA-1984/87, Berlin. Study sketch of a house. Image courtesy of OMA

Figure VI.10 Rem Koolhaas, "Kochstrasse/Friedrichstrasse Competition" project for Block 4, IBA-1984/87, Berlin. Study sketch of Block 4. Image courtesy of OMA

Figure VI.11 Rem Koolhaas, "Kochstrasse/Friedrichstrasse Competition" project for Block 4, IBA-1984/87, Berlin. Plan of Block 4. Image courtesy of OMA

Figure VI.12 OMA, Pages from "Kochstrasse—Friedrichstrasse Study Proposals for Residential Development at Checkpoint Charlie. December 1982," unpublished booklet. Image courtesy of OMA

Figure VI.13 OMA, Housing at Checkpoint Charlie, IBA-1984/87, Berlin, 1987. Axonometric. Image courtesy of OMA

Figure VI.14 OMA, Housing at Checkpoint Charlie, IBA-1984/87, Berlin, 1987. Plans, sections and elevations. B-Rep_168 (Karten)_Nr_1323_2–8; 11–16, Landesarchiv, Berlin; Image courtesy of OMA

Figure VI.15 Views of the elevated pathway and gardens of duplex row houses in OMA's Housing at Checkpoint Charlie for IBA-1984/87, photographed by Esra Akcan, Berlin, 2010. Esra Akcan

Figure VI.16 Views of the interior promenade—street in the air, gallery and deck—in OMA's Housing at Checkpoint Charlie for IBA-1984/87, photographed by Esra Akcan, Berlin, 2010. Esra Akcan

Figure VI.17 Views of OMA's Housing at Checkpoint Charlie for IBA-1984/87, photographed by Esra Akcan, Berlin, 2012. Esra Akcan

Figure VI.18 Views from an apartment in OMA's Housing at Checkpoint Charlie for IBA-1984/87, photographed by Esra Akcan, Berlin, 2010. Esra Akcan

Figure VI.19 An apartment vacated due to gentrification in OMA's Housing at Checkpoint Charlie for IBA-1984/87, photographed by Esra Akcan, Berlin, 2012. Esra Akcan

Figure VI.20 Peter Eisenman and Jaquelin Robertson, "The City of Artificial Excavations" project for Block 5 of "Kochstrasse/Friedrichstrasse Competition", IBA-1984/87, Berlin. DR1991_0018_722, Peter Eisenman Papers, Canadian Centre for Architecture, Montreal

Figure VI.21 Peter Eisenman and Jaquelin Robertson, "Kochstrasse/Friedrichstrasse Competition" project for Block 5, IBA-1984/87, Berlin. Study sketches. DR1991_0018_887, Peter Eisenman Papers, Canadian Centre for Architecture, Montreal

Figure VI.22 Peter Eisenman and Jaquelin Robertson, "Kochstrasse/Friedrichstrasse Competition" project for Block 5, IBA-1984/87, Berlin. Study sketches with cut-outs. DR1981_0018_479, Peter Eisenman Papers, Canadian Centre for Architecture, Montreal

Figure VI.23 Peter Eisenman and Jaquelin Robertson, "Kochstrasse/Friedrichstrasse Competition" project for Block 5, IBA-1984/87, Berlin. Study sketch for the superimposition of city and Mercator grids. DR1991_0018_220, Peter Eisenman Papers, Canadian Centre for Architecture, Montreal

Figure VI.24 Peter Eisenman and Jaquelin Robertson, "Kochstrasse/Friedrichstrasse Competition" project, IBA-1984/87, Berlin. Site plan. DR1991_0018_631, Peter Eisenman Papers, Canadian Centre for Architecture, Montreal

Figure VI.25 Peter Eisenman and Jaquelin Robertson, "Kochstrasse/Friedrichstrasse Competition" project, IBA-1984/87, Berlin. City Layers. DR1991_0018_723, Peter Eisenman Papers, Canadian Centre for Architecture, Montreal

Figure VI.26 Peter Eisenman and Jaquelin Robertson, Housing at Checkpoint Charlie, IBA-1984/87, photographed by Esra Akcan, Berlin. 2016. Esra Akcan

Figure VI.27 Peter Eisenman and Jaquelin Robertson with Dietmar Grötzebach, Housing at Checkpoint Charlie, IBA-1984/87. New York and Berlin, 1984. Second Floor Plan. DR1981_0018_762_791, Peter Eisenman Papers, Canadian Centre for Architecture, Montreal

Figure VI.28 Peter Eisenman and Jaquelin Robertson, Housing at Checkpoint Charlie, IBA-1984/87, Berlin. Façade study. DR1991_0018_925, Peter Eisenman Papers, Canadian Centre for Architecture, Montreal

Figure VI.29 Peter Eisenman and Jaquelin Robertson, Park at Checkpoint Charlie, IBA-1984/87, Berlin, 1985. DR1991_0018_570, Peter Eisenman Papers, Canadian Centre for Architecture, Montreal

Figure VI.30 Peter Eisenman, Memorial to the Murdered Jews of Europe (inaugurated in 2005), photographed by Esra Akcan, Berlin, 2010. Esra Akcan

STROLL 6: A History of a Possible Kreuzberg

Figure 6.1 IBA Neubau, site plan with competition winning entries as it stands in August 1981. B_Rep_168(Karten)_Nr_1394, Landesarchiv Berlin

Figure 6.2 Figure ground relations of the entries for "Living in Friedrichstadt Competition," 1980. Wohnen in der Friedrichstadt. Vorprüfbericht," IBA report, n. p., Landesarchiv Berlin

Figure 6.3 Hans Kollhoff, "Living in Friedrichstadt Competition" project, 1980. Heinrich Klotz and Josef Paul Kleihues, eds., International Building Exhibition Berlin 1987 (New York: Rizzoli, 1986), 201., Landesarchiv, Berlin

Figure 6.4 Gerald Brunner, Franz Rendl, Reinhard Hörl, Walter Kirschmayr, and Georg Driendl, "Living in Friedrichstadt Competition" project, 1980. Heinrich Klotz and Josef Paul Kleihues, eds., International Building Exhibition Berlin 1987 (New York: Rizzoli, 1986), 200, Landesarchiv Berlin

Figure 6.5 Christoph Langhof Architects, Competition project for Besselpark, Block 606, 1983. Heinrich Klotz and Josef Paul Kleihues, eds., International Building Exhibition Berlin 1987 (New York: Rizzoli, 1986), 236–237, Landesarchiv Berlin

Figure 6.6 Comparative diagrams for the continuity of the street prepared during "Wilhelmstrasse Competition," 1981. "Internationaler engerer Wettbewerb. Berlin Südliche Friedrichstadt Wilhelmstraße. Bericht der Vorprüfung," IBA Report. 1981, Landesarchiv Berlin

Figure 6.7 Entries for "Prinz Albrecht Palais Competition", 1985. a: Rafael Moneo; b: Jörg Johnen, Antoine Laroche, Ulrich Wiegmann; c: Raimund Fein Vallendar, Roland Schulz; d: Giorgio Grassi; e: Raimund Abraham; f: Peter Klimberg, Susanne Krätz, Georg von Willisen; g: Jürgen Wenzel and Nikolaus Lang. "Dokumentation: Offener Wettbewerb Berlin, Südliche Friedrichstadt, Gestaltung des Geländes des ehemaligen Prinz-Albrecht-Palais," IBA Report, Berlin, September 1985, p. 143, 127, 91, 69, 121, 103, 63, Landesarchiv Berlin

Figure 6.8 Richard Meier, Project for Am Karlsbad, 1982. Richard Meier

Figure 6.9 a–b Mario Botta, Proposal for Science Center, 1980. B_Rep_168(Karten)_Nr_822_5, B_Rep_168 (Karten)_Nr_825_1, Landesarchiv Berlin

Figure 6.10 a–e Rem Koolhaas for OMA, "Lützowstrasse Competition" project, Block 647, 1980. a: site perspective; b: plans of middle block; c: plans of east block; d: sections; e: axonometric. Image courtesy of OMA

Figure 6.11 Alison and Peter Smithson, "Lützowstrasse Competition" project, Block 647, 1980. Heinrich Klotz and Josef Paul Kleihues, eds., International Building Exhibition Berlin 1987 (New York: Rizzoli, 1986), 84, Landesarchiv Berlin

Figure 6.12 Aldo van Eyck, Kindergarten, Lützowstrasse, 1983. Heinrich Klotz and Josef Paul Kleihues, eds., International Building Exhibition Berlin 1987 (New York: Rizzoli, 1986), 89, Landesarchiv Berlin

Figure 6.13 Giorgio Grassi, Park at Lützowplatz, 1981. Heinrich Klotz and Josef Paul Kleihues, eds., International Building Exhibition Berlin 1987 (New York: Rizzoli, 1986), 64, Landesarchiv Berlin

STOP VII: Exit Implies Entries' Lament:
Open Architecture in John Hejduk's IBA-1984/87 Immigrant Housing

Figure VII.1 John Hejduk, Studio for a Painter and Studio for a Musician, drawn on the floor plan of Martin Gropius Bau for Idee Prozeß Ergebnis Exhibition, IBA-1984/87, Berlin. DR1998_0104_006, John Hejduk Papers, Canadian Centre for Architecture, Montreal

Figure VII.2 John Hejduk, Studio for a Painter and Studio for a Musician, as exhibited in IBA-1984/87's Idee Prozeß Ergebnis Exhibition, photographed by Siegfried Büker, Berlin, 1984. Siegfried Büker

Figure VII.3 John Hejduk, "Wilhemstrasse Competition" project, IBA-1984/87, Berlin. Site plan DR1998_0098_014, John Hejduk Papers, Canadian Centre for Architecture, Montreal

Figure VII.4 John Hejduk, "Wilhemstrasse Competition" project, IBA-1984/87, Berlin. Site model. IBA-1984/87. Published in Domus 627 (April 1982), 24

Figure VII.5 John Hejduk. "Wilhemstrasse Competition" project, IBA-1984/87, Berlin. a: Guest towers and shopping booths. b: Theater masque. c: Lottery woman. d: Cross over bridge. a: DR1998_0098_044; b: DR1998_0098_045, c: DR1998_0098_025, d: DR1998_0098_041, John Hejduk Papers, Canadian Centre for Architecture, Montreal.

About the Author

Esra Akcan is an Associate Professor in the Department of Architecture and the Director of the Institute for European Studies at Cornell University. She completed her architecture degree at the Middle East Technical University in Ankara, and her Ph.D. and postdoctoral degrees at Columbia University in New York. She received awards and fellowships from the Graham Foundation, The American Academy in Berlin, UIC, Transregional Studies Forum with Institute for Advanced Studies in Berlin, Clark Institute, Getty Research Institute, Canadian Centre for Architecture, College Art Association, Mellon Foundation, DAAD and KRESS/ARIT. Akcan's research on modern and contemporary architecture and urbanism foregrounds the intertwined histories of Europe and West Asia. Her book *Architecture in Translation: Germany, Turkey & the Modern House* (Duke University Press Books, 2012) offers a new way to understand the global movement of architecture that extends the notion of translation beyond language to visual fields. Her book *Turkey: Modern Architectures in History* (with Sibel Bozdoğan, Reaktion Books/The University of Chicago Press, 2012) is part of a series that aims at an inclusive survey of modern world architecture and is the first volume in any language to cover the architecture of the entire twentieth century in Turkey. Akcan has authored over a hundred articles in scholarly books and professional journals of multiple languages on critical and postcolonial theory, modern and contemporary architecture in West Asia and its diasporas in Europe, architectural photography, immigration, translation, globalization, and global history. She has also carried her research into visual media in exhibitions. Akcan works and lives in Ithaca and New York City.

Index

394

Captions to the "Map of Stops and Strolls" (Foldout in back cover)

Stroll 1

Figure 1.1c–e: Herman Hertzberger with Inken and Hinrich Baller, Building in Block 30, Berlin, 2009, 2016.

Figure 1.2b–d: Hans Kollhoff and Arthur Ovaska, Urban Design of Block 33, Berlin, 2009, 2014, 2016.

Figure 1.3a–b: Hans Kollhoff and Arthur Ovaska, Long building in Block 33, Berlin, 2014.

Figure 1.4c–d: Arata Isozaki, Building in Block 33, Berlin, 2016.

Figure 1.5a–b: Dieter Frowein and Gerhard Spangenberg, Building in Block 33, Berlin, 2014.

Figure 1.6a–b: Hans Kollhoff and Arthur Ovaska, Tower House in Block 33, Berlin, 2016, 2012.

Figure 1.8a–d: Franz Claudius Demblin, Horst Hielscher and Georg-Peter Mügge, Jochem Jourdan, Bernhard Müller, and Sven Albrecht, Urban villas in Block 33, Berlin, 2012–2016.

Figure 1.9a–b: Werner Kreis and Ulrich and Peter Schaad, Building in Block 33, Berlin, 2014, 2016.

Figure 1.11: Daniel Libeskind, Jewish Museum, Berlin, 2002.

Figure 1.12: Theodor-Wolff-Park and Block 20 (Ralf Dähne, Helge Dahl, Rosie Grässler), Berlin, 2014.

Figure 1.13: Rave and Partner, Building in Block 20, Berlin, 2010.

Figure 1.14: Squatted Thomas-Weißbecker-Haus in Block 20, Berlin, 2010.

Figure 1.15: Bassenge, Puhan-Schulz, and Partner, Kindergarten in Block 20, Berlin, 2014.

Figure 1.16: Hansjürg Zeitler, Helmut Bier, and Hans Korn, Building in Block 20, Berlin, 2016.

Figure 1.17: IBA buildings on Lindenstrasse seen from Block 606 (Gino Valle, Mario Broggi, and Michael Burckhardt), Berlin, 2010.

Figure 1.18a–b: Douglas Clelland, Mario Maedebach and Werner Redeleit, and Joachim Schmidt, Buildings along Friedrichstrasse in Block 606, Berlin, 2016, 2011.

Stroll 2

Figure 2.1: Aerial view of towers designed by Grupo 2c (front) and Pietro Derossi (back) in Block 9, Berlin, 2011.

Figure 2.2: Grupo 2c, Building in Block 9, Berlin, 2014.

Figure 2.3a–c: Pietro Derossi, Building in Block 9, and view of buildings by Grupo 2c, Jochen Brandi and Partner, and Aldo Rossi from this tower, Berlin, 2014, 2010.

Figure 2.4a–b: Self-help Terraces housing in Block 9 (based on idea by Dietrich von Beulwitz), Berlin, 2012.

Figure 2.7a–b: Myra Warhaftig, Building in Block 2, Berlin, 2012.

Figure 2.8: Christine Jachmann, Building in Block 2, Berlin, 2012.

Figure 2.9a–b: Zaha Hadid, Myra Warhaftig, Christine Jachmann, Wojciech Obtułowicz and Daniel Karpinski, Block 2, view of Dessauer Strasse, Berlin, 2012.

Figure 2.10a: Daniel Karpinski, Romuald Loegler and W.Dobrzański, and Peter Blake, Block 2 with St.Lukas church, view of Bernburger Strasse, Berlin, 2014.

Figure 2.12a–g: Zaha Hadid, Building in Block 2, Berlin, 2011, 2012, 2014.

Figure 2.13a–c: Rave and Partner; Borck, Boye, and Schaefer; Christoph Langhof; Grötzebach, Plessow, and Ehlers, overseen by Günter Schlusche, landscape architect Hans Loidl, Block 6, Berlin, 2012, 2014.

Figure 2.14a–d: Josef Paul Kleihues, Building in Block 7, Berlin, 2010, 2011.

Figure 2.15a–b: Nalbach and Nalbach; Peter Brinkert; Georg Kohlmaier and Barna von Sartory, Buildings in Block 7, Berlin, 2010.

Stroll 3

Figure 3.1b: James Stirling and Michael Wilford, Science Center, Berlin, 2016.

Figure 3.2: Brenner and Tonon, Pedestrian bridge over Landwehr canal, Berlin, 2016.

Figure 3.3a–c: Faskel and Nikolic; von Gerkan, Marg and Partner; Pysall, Jensen, and Stahrenberg; Kilpper and Partner, and Schiedhelm, Energy Houses, Block 647, Berlin, 2014.

Figure 3.4a: Zeki Dikenli, Erich Schneider, and Hanno Lagemann, Building in Block 647, Berlin, 2014.

Figure 3.6a–c: Vittorio Gregotti, Building in Block 647, Berlin, 2012, 2014, 2016.

Figure 3.8b: Mario Botta, Building in Block 234, Berlin, 2014.

Figure 3.9a–b: Peter Cook, Building in Block 234, from the street and Hof-garden (with Botta on the right), Berlin, 2014.

Figure 3.10 a–c: Herbert and Siegfried Gergs, Urban design of Block 234, Berlin, 2014, 2016.

Figure 3.11 a–e: Siegfried Gergs, Werner Goehner, and the office of Bartels and Schmidt-Ott, Urban Villas of Block 234, Berlin, 2012, 2016.

Figure 3.12: Klaus Baesler and Bernhard Schmidt, Kindergarten in Block 234, Berlin, 2012.

Figure 3.13 d: Oswald Mathias Ungers, Building at Lützowplatz for Block 220, Berlin, 2012.

Figure 3.14 a–d: Frei Otto (with Torsten Birlem, Jürgen Rohrbach, Manfred Ruprecht, and Ute Schulte-Lehnert, et. al.), Öko Haus Complex in Block 192, Berlin, 2016.

Figure 3.15 c, e–f: Rob Krier (with Aldo Rossi, Brenner and Tonon, Giorgio Grassi, Hans Hollein, Henry Nielebock, and Hermann & Valentiny), Urban design and individual buildings in Block 189, Berlin, 2012.

Stroll 4

Figure 4.1: Exit from Kottbusser Tor station, Berlin, 2012.

Figure 4.2: IBA Altbau, Adaptive reuse of a garage as kindergarten at Dresdener Strasse, Block 80, Berlin, 2016.

Figure 4.3 a–b: The green belt around the Oranienplatz, Berlin, 2016.

Figure 4.4 a–b: Oranienplatz, Berlin, 2014, 2016.

Figure 4.6 a–b: Oranienstrasse between Oranienplatz and Heinrichplatz, Berlin, 2012.

Figure 4.7 a–c: Junction of Oranienstrasse and Adalbert-strasse, Berlin, 2012.

Figure 4.8: Naunynstrasse after renovation, Berlin, 2012.

Figure 4.9: Building in Block 79 (entrance from Naunyn-strasse), Berlin, 2012.

Figure 4.10: Apartment in Block 79 (of IBA Altbau team member Uwe Böhm), Berlin, 2012.

Figure 4.11 a–b: Building in Block 79 (entrance from Naunynstrasse), Berlin, 2012.

Figure 4.12: Heinrichplatz, Berlin, 2014.

Figure 4.13 a–b: Ayşe Erkmen, Mural on Oranien-strasse 18, 1994, Berlin, 2014.

Figure 4.14: Junction of Oranien-, Manteuffel-, and Skalitzer Strasse and Görlitzer Bahnhof, Berlin, 2012.

Figure 4.15: Mosque at Görlitzer Bahnhof, Berlin, 2014.

Figure 4.16: Emmaus Church at Lausitzer Platz, Berlin, 2016.

Figure 4.17: Elişi Evi (house of crafts) on Skalitzer Strasse 50, Berlin, 2012.

Figure 4.18 a–b: Görlitzer Strasse along the wall of the Görlitzer Park, Berlin, 2016.

Figure 4.19 a–b: Görlitzer Strasse and Streets leading to Görlitzer Park, Berlin, 2012, 2016.

Stroll 5

Figure 5.1: Squatters of Kerngehäuse at Cuvrystrasse, 1983.

Figure 5.3 a–b: Falckensteinstrasse between Schlesische Strasse and Görlitzer Park, Berlin, 2016.

Figure 5.4 a–b: Crossing the Görlitzer Park along Falckensteinstrasse, Berlin, 2016.

Figure 5.5 a–b: Robert Maguire and Keith Murray, Kindergarten at Paul-Lincke-Ufer, Berlin, 2012.

Figure 5.6 a–b: Bahri Düleç, Pedestrianization along Paul-Lincke-Ufer, Berlin, 2012.

Figure 5.7: Previously squatted Forster Strasse 16 in Block 145, renovated through self-help, Berlin, 2012.

Figure 5.8 a–d: Reichenberger Strasse, Berlin, 2016.

Figure 5.9 a–e: Wilhelm Holzbauer, Rave und Rave, Building at the corner of Reichenberger and Mariannenstrasse, Berlin, 2012, 2016

Figure 5.10: Fraenkelufer between Kottbusser Strasse and Böcklerpark, Berlin, 2016.

Figure 5.11 a–e: Hinrich and Inken Baller, Building compound along Fraenkelufer, Berlin, 2012, 2016.

Stroll 6

Figure 6.3: Hans Kollhoff, "Living in Friedrichstadt Competition" project, 1980.

Figure 6.4: Gerald Brunner, Franz Rendl, Reinhard Hörl, Walter Kirschmayr, and Georg Driendl, "Living in Friedrichstadt Competition" project, 1980.

Figure 6.5: Christoph Langhof Architects, Competition project for Besselpark, Block 606, 1983.

Figure 6.6: Comparative diagrams for the continuity of the street prepared during "Wilhelmstrasse Competition," 1981.

Figure 6.7: Entries for "Prinz Albrecht Palais Competition," 1985. a: Rafael Moneo; b: Jörg Johnen, Antoine Laroche, Ulrich Wiegmann; c: Raimund Fein Vallen-dar, Roland Schulz; d: Giorgio Grassi; e: Raimund Abraham; f: Peter Klimberg, Susanne Krätz, Georg von Willisen; g: Jürgen Wenzel and Nikolaus Lang.

Figure 6.8: Richard Meier, Project for Am Karlsbad, 1982.

Figure 6.9 a–b: Mario Botta, Proposal for Science Center, 1980.

Figure 6.10 a, e: Rem Koolhaas for OMA, "Lützowstrasse Competition" project, Block 647, 1980. a: site perspective; e: axonometric.

Figure 6.11: Alison and Peter Smithson, "Lützowstrasse Competition" project, Block 647, 1980.

Figure 6.12: Aldo van Eyck, Kindergarten, Lützowstrasse, 1983.

Figure 6.13: Giorgio Grassi, Park at Lützowplatz, 1981.

Graphic design: Jenna Gesse

Layout, typesetting, and production: Kathleen Bernsdorf

Editor for the Publisher: Andreas Müller

Indexer: Diana Witt

This publication is made possible with the support of Graham Foundation and Cornell University

Paper: Hello Fat matt, 115 g/m^2

Printing: Beltz Bad Langensalza GmbH

Library of Congress Control Number: 2018936825

Bibliographic information published by the German National Library

The German National Library lists this publication in the Deutsche Nationalbibliografie;

detailed bibliographic data are available on the Internet at http://dnb.dnb.de.

This publication is also available as an e-book (ISBN PDF 978-3-0356-1377-3)

© 2018 Birkhäuser Verlag GmbH, Basel

P.O. Box 44, 4009 Basel, Switzerland

Part of Walter de Gruyter GmbH, Berlin/Boston

Printed on acid-free paper produced from chlorine-free pulp. TCF ∞

Printed in Germany

ISBN 978-3-0356-1374-2

9 8 7 6 5 4 3 2 1   www.birkhauser.com